GW00673413

BY SAFE HAND

Letters of Sybil & David Eccles

1939–42

For nothing is greater or better than this, when man and wife dwell in the house in harmony, a great grief to their foes, and a joy to their friends, but they know this best themselves.

Homer, *Odyssey*, Book VI, 182–185.
Translation by Maurice Baring

One of the saddest things in life is that we can never be completely known and understood . . . a wife who is one's equal must be the greatest blessing on earth, and I would rather she were my superior in every way than the reverse.

Eugène Delacroix, *Journal* for 9 June 1823.
Translation by Lucy Norton

BY THE SAME AUTHOR

Half-Way to Faith
Life and Politics
On Collecting

BY SAFE HAND

Letters of Sybil & David Eccles 1939–42

THE BODLEY HEAD
LONDON SYDNEY
TORONTO

British Library Cataloguing
in Publication Data
Eccles, David
By safe hand: the letters
of Sybil & David Eccles, 1939–42
I. Title
ISBN: 0–370–30482–9

Printed in Great Britain for
The Bodley Head Ltd
9 Bow Street, London, WC2E 7AL
by Redwood Burn Ltd, Trowbridge
set in Linotron 202 Ehrhardt
by Wyvern Typesetting Ltd, Bristol
First published 1983

CONTENTS

ACKNOWLEDGEMENTS

When the letters were sorted and arranged in chronological order they were typed by Sheena Routledge, the best secretary I ever had, and by St Stephen's Secretariat in the Houses of Parliament. Venetia Pollock told me what to leave out in order to reduce the volume to publishable size. The reader can appreciate how skilful she was. Jill Black gave me invaluable help at all times. Thus the hard work was done by women: it is always so.

PREFACE

In October 1928 Sybil Dawson and I were married by the Archbishop of Canterbury at St Margaret's, Westminster. When the war began we had been in love, day and night, for eleven years. Prosperity had come our way. In London we had moved to Montagu Square and were collecting furniture, pictures and books. We had bought land and a farmhouse at Upper Chute in Wiltshire, and there Sybil was planting trees and making her garden which was to be famous for its annual borders. Life was set fair until early in 1939 when war with Germany seemed certain. We made plans accordingly. Sybil was to take our three children, John who was then eight, Simon five, and Polly nearly three, to Chute; let the land but keep a cow, two pigs and some chickens for the house. I had joined the embryonic Ministry of Economic Warfare as principal adviser on Spain. The letters now published were written between November 1939 and August 1942, during which time I was almost continuously abroad on missions to Spain, Portugal, North Africa and the United States.

Our families had been close neighbours in London. I was born in 1904 in Harley Street, the fourth of five children, a few months before Sybil, the eldest of three sisters, was born round the corner in Wimpole Street. Our fathers were distinguished doctors. Mine practised a severe Presbyterianism which subdued our pleasures. We knew that my mother was unhappy. No one was unhappy in Sybil's home, where religion was not much discussed. Sybil, being good by nature, was not curious to know about God. She looked upon the Church as a social asset which could help to hold society together. By contrast I went on asking myself, 'Does God exist?' without discovering the answer. Except for this difference in attitude to religious speculation there was little to choose in the way we were brought up. We attended day schools until, about the age of thirteen, we went away to boarding schools, where each was exposed to the influence of an exceptionally strong personality. The Headmaster of Winchester, Dr Montagu Rendall, and the Headmistress of St Felix, Southwold, Miss Lucy Silcox, were remarkably alike, extravagant in appearance, dominant in conversation, propagating a passion for art, Italy and the Classics.

Under their influence we acquired many of our common interests. From school Sybil went to the universities of Grenoble and London and I went to Oxford.

My father-in-law, Lord Dawson of Penn, took trouble to educate his daughter in the complexities of human nature, which he understood as well as any man of his generation, so that by the time she married, Sybil had acquired a penetrating and sure judgement. She knew better than I whom one could trust and who would let one down. When I went into politics her view on a colleague or an opponent was swift and reliable. What extraordinary luck to fall in love with a girl with a mind of her own, educated as well as any boy, and with an unerring taste in all things beautiful.

According to the books, our life together broke the rules. Marriage, so Sancho Panza said, was like two people riding a horse, one had to sit behind, and, in the same vein, Lord Hewart, the Lord Chief Justice, a day or two after our engagement stopped me in Knightsbridge and warned me to decide at once which of us was the delicate one. But it was not true of us, either what Sancho Panza said or what Lord Hewart implied. Sybil and I were as equal, and wanted to be as equal, as any man and woman could be. Our tempers were not frayed nor our happiness clouded by exhibitions of superiority. Some things she could do much better than I, and vice versa. I could not mend a fuse and she was useless at arithmetic. These little specialities and weaknesses were of no account. What mattered was her marvellous beauty, the sound of her voice, and the justice and humour of her conversation. If, as the French say, a man is bound to stop loving his girl unless she continually surprises him, then here was the ideal choice, never a dull moment, every day a surprise and a joy.

War attacks such happiness. It splits in half a relationship that has grown closer and closer, laughing together, touching each other, never out of sight or mind. For eleven years we had had no occasion to write letters and now what could we do but plunge into an almost daily correspondence? We each wrote some three hundred letters which when I came home were tied in bundles and forgotten in a little-used cupboard.

Sybil died in 1977. Only then I looked at the papers we had kept from the war. A dozen or more important letters either had never arrived or were lost after arrival. The five or six hundred that survived have been reduced to the scope of this single volume in which are included a few other documents that bear on our correspondence. Having eliminated anything that might give offence, for Sybil and I wrote very frankly about our contemporaries, the rest of the material has been cut by rather more than half. In letters of which only a part is published I decided not to indicate where a passage has been omitted. Drastic treatment, but the pattern of the correspondence is well preserved, being held together by three questions: Why did Franco's Spain remain neutral? How should we have treated France after the Armistice? And what may happen to a marriage when two people who have been so much in love are forced to live apart? The letters should provide some fresh material on the history of the Blockade, some clues to the character of men like Salazar, Franco, Pétain, Weygand and Samuel Hoare, and point up the difference between real love and pot-luck desire.

Re-reading Sybil's letters I wonder if any man could have a more enchanting correspondent. She writes about anything that catches her generous fancy, telling me how she and the children are getting on at Chute and what she hears from our friends working in Whitehall. Her descriptions remind one that the war brought out the best in the English people.

My letters show the extent to which I relied on her to understand the exposed isolation of my position, suspended between the Ministry of Economic Warfare and the Foreign Office—my official rank was Counsellor in the Diplomatic Service. An amateur surrounded by sharp-witted professionals, often I had no clear instructions, and sometimes I was compelled by events to go beyond the instructions I did have, but I never felt alone. I knew that Sybil was at home, encouraging ministers and senior civil servants to believe in me and warning me to be more patient and less difficult with them.

We could talk to each other, the letters flying to and fro uncensored in the diplomatic bag, but we could not live together. The strain began to tell. War shortens everything. Today is desperately real, will there be a tomorrow? You don't know. Take a chance, make love, and if life returns to normal, somehow it will be all right and no one will have been hurt. If there is a special interest in our case it is because of the sort of people we were, proud of our equality and love, and because war, which so often cuts communication between man and wife, offered us exceptional means to tell or withhold the truth from each other.

The letters contain hints that our relations were going to be damaged by the contrast between life in foreign capitals and domestic duties at home. On the journey to Lisbon in January 1942 I took the decision to stop trying to love two people at once; I said goodbye to the girl for whose beauty I had cared so much. Once I had a job in London I was confident all would be well. But the wolfram negotiations dragged on and on. Then came Sybil's letter of 30 May. It was the worst blow, far the worst, I had ever known, but I was ready to fight for her with all I had.

At last on 1 August a telegram arrived in Lisbon asking the Ambassador to release me as soon as possible. I shivered with fright that Sybil and I might find ourselves strangers, or at least no longer in love. One look was enough, and the old enchantment renewed its spell. Then our life changed when in 1943 I was returned to Parliament for the Chippenham Division of Wiltshire. Sybil had a gift for politics and public work. She liked other people and knew how to make them like her. Soon she was in demand as a speaker all over the country, and in the constituency at general elections she pulled in the votes for me.

She was never ill until in 1976 cancer invaded her body. When we had to accept that she was losing the battle she rejoiced at the years we had lived together, insisting that every extra day was worth it. It seems that one can know and love such a girl in new ways when she has gone.

INTRODUCTION
Economic Warfare

Early in 1939 the Foreign Office asked me to transfer from the reserve of officers to the skeleton staff of the Ministry of Economic Warfare (MEW). They wanted someone with experience of conditions in Spain, where Franco and his allies were winning the Civil War. Since 1932 I had been chairman of the British company which had recently built, and was now operating, the Santander-Mediterraneo Railway in northern Spain. Roughly parallel to the Pyrenees, the new line cut across the main railways running like spokes of a wheel with Madrid at the centre. Franco used it to move men and material from Castile to the battlefront in Catalonia. Our main station was Burgos, which was also his military headquarters. I made frequent visits to Spain, learned the language, not well but adequately, and by the end of the Civil War was on reasonable terms with Franco's chief advisers. As a result I was in a position to judge the condition of the Spanish economy and forecast the policy which Franco's ministers were likely to adopt.

MEW, which had taken shape as an offshoot of the Foreign Office, started operations on 2 September 1939. A number of lawyers, bankers and businessmen had been recruited to work with career civil servants in the preparation of measures to restrict trade between Germany and countries likely to be neutral. We studied the experience of the 1914–18 war, and reached the general conclusion that in the event of a second war with Germany an effective blockade should be imposed on all neutrals who could export to the enemy goods of value to his war effort. In total war the goods so classified would cover practically everything from oil and steel to cosmetics for girls in munition factories. Since it would be against our interest for Germany to acquire anything on this enormous contraband list, measures had to be devised to stop neutrals importing these goods, unless their governments gave us reliable guarantees that the imports, and similar goods produced by themselves, were for their own internal consumption. Each neutral had therefore to be rationed and its overseas trade regulated by the issue of navicerts or passports in respect of goods which the British Government was prepared to allow to pass through the Blockade—for example, a ration for oil barely sufficient to keep a neutral's economy going, with no surplus which might find its way to the enemy. The more ready and able a neutral was to do business with Germany the stricter the rationing of its imports which we could try to enforce.

A blockade of this character, designed to control a vast range of goods, had been easier to impose in the First World War when Britain was stronger in relation to the neutrals. In 1939 the Foreign Office and MEW had to decide whether the Allies were in a position to be equally strict with all neutrals. Did we have the naval power to enforce the Blockade? Did we mind if the Blockade drove a neutral into the arms of the Germans? Spain was the most disputed case. What level of imports should be allowed to a country on whose soil only a few months before German and Italian troops had been fighting to secure the victory of the party now in power? My colleagues in MEW assumed that Franco would repay his debt to the Axis powers. They refused to believe that he had enough support among the Spanish people to consolidate his victory without the continuing help of his Nazi and Fascist friends. I knew that neither of these assumptions was well founded. I had been managing a Spanish railway and had seen conditions under the socialist government deteriorate to a point where, about 1935, a rising became inevitable. I had warned my business colleagues that it must come and would be welcomed by a large cross-section of the population. Support for Franco was far greater than reported in the British press. For example, I never had to ask for armed guards at any of the vulnerable points on the three hundred miles of our railway. The surrounding population wanted Franco to win. As the Civil War dragged on I saw for myself how all classes were coming to dislike the Germans and Italians, who took no trouble to conceal the fact that they were using someone else's battles to try out their new weapons. MEW, however, preferred to plan on the assumption that Franco must be so grateful to the Axis powers that within a very short time he would join them in the war against us, and, until that happened, he would be more than willing to export to Germany anything that Hitler wanted.

If this view of Franco's intentions were correct, it called for a blockade of Spain of the maximum severity. Spain should be treated as an enemy from the day war broke out. I thought this would be a mistake and told MEW that I should put a different view to the Foreign Office, since it was the Foreign Office which had asked for me to become MEW's adviser on Spain. Spain was not, I suggested to Sir George Mounsey, the Under-Secretary of State at the Foreign Office, the sort of country our blockaders thought it was. The proverbial Spanish pride would never permit Franco to acknowledge that he owed his victory to foreign powers. Already his generals were talking as though they alone, with no outside help, had won the war. Spaniards had always been like that. Sybil and I used to laugh at their school history books which did not mention the Duke of Wellington and said practically nothing about the British Army in the Peninsular War. In 1939, whichever side they had supported in the Civil War, all Spaniards were sick of bloodshed and would turn against Franco if he led them into another war. As for Franco himself, he cared only for Spain, for the Catholic Church and for shooting rabbits. If one looked at Spain as a whole what did one see? Starving cities with industries at a standstill for want of imported raw materials. Franco would soon learn that Germany could not offer him wheat, oil and cotton whereas the British Commonwealth could. Further, the naval and military experts, who had been consulted by MEW, said that Gibraltar and the entrance to the Mediterranean were vital to us. Did the Foreign Office agree? If so what sense could there be in imposing a blockade on Spain so severe that Franco would be deprived of the most popular reason for remaining neutral, and be in a position to fix the blame on us for the resulting food shortage and unemployment? Even supposing some supplies had been allowed through the Blockade, and then the Germans persuaded Franco to declare war on the Allies, the common people would know where their bread had come from and be on our side, as they were in 1808 when Napoleon invaded Spain. MEW had not been impressed by these arguments, they were against giving any aid to Franco, but the Foreign Office decided that we should look at the Spanish situation on the spot and be prepared to make a more flexible use of the Blockade.

The war began with this fundamental disagreement between MEW and the Foreign Office on how we should treat Spain. The difference might have been reconciled if Hugh Dalton, an intellectual Socialist, had not become Minister of Economic Warfare. Dalton wanted to believe that Franco was in Hitler's pocket, and that these two villains would, sooner rather than later, combine to attack Gibraltar and close the entrance to the Mediterranean. If this was sure to happen then it was right to starve the Spaniards, leaving the Germans to occupy a country in chaos. More sensible views prevailed in Cabinet where Lord Halifax, the Foreign Secretary, was firmly in favour of limited economic aid to Spain. After Halifax departed to become British Ambassador in Washington, Eden, the new Foreign Secretary, would have liked to take a harder line on Spain. The Prime Minister's eye, however, was always on Gibraltar and the entrance to the Mediterranean. He overruled whatever hesitations there were about using economic aid to persuade Franco to remain neutral. This is confirmed by Roger Makins, now Lord Sherfield, who was in charge of Peninsular affairs in the Foreign Office while I was in Spain. He wrote to me recently: 'It was a constant struggle in London to get understanding and support for what you were doing, and we would have had no success without the vision of Winston Churchill.' The War Trade Agreement made with Spain in March 1940 provided Franco with the means to remain on the fence. In a letter to Mussolini dated 31 December 1940 Hitler was to recognise that it was this British policy which kept Spain out of the war. Putting this policy into practice brought me into conflict with my own Department, MEW, as the letters that follow show. Again and again I was saved by the steady support of Roger Makins and William Strang[1] with Churchill in the background.

In Appendix C will be found a list of some of the books, both official histories and personal memoirs, which refer to the events reported in the letters. I have quoted key passages from these books which are relevant to the parts played by Spain, Portugal and French North Africa in the first two years of the war. We were very lucky in our friends, and I like to think the reader will conclude that history is made not only by the great forces that push society this way and that but by individuals, and by how much they trust one another.

1. Under-Secretary at the Foreign Office.

I

The Outbreak of War

November 1939–March 1940

1. The Outbreak of War

The British Delegation arrived in Madrid on 10 November 1939 instructed to recommend the scope of a War Trade Agreement with Spain. The members of the delegation were Edward Playfair, Treasury, Ralph Nowell, Board of Trade, and myself from MEW. Later we were joined by experts from the Bank of England and other financial and shipping interests. In the middle of the negotiations the Treasury withdrew Playfair and replaced him by Hugh Ellis-Rees.

On the Spanish side my opposite number was the Conde de Casa Rojas, an amiable and overworked Spanish nobleman, who favoured the Italians, then also negotiating a commercial treaty. The leading Spanish professionals, whom we learned to respect and like, were Señor D. Vicente Taberna from the Ministry of Commerce and Señor D. Blas Huete from the Ministry of Finance. The Vizconde de Mamblas (now the Duque de Baena), and Señor Pan y Soreluce were invaluable friends in the Ministry of Foreign Affairs. The Minister himself, Colonel Beigbeder, the most anti-German member of the Spanish Cabinet, was personally responsible for persuading Franco to sign an agreement satisfactory to both sides.

On our arrival in Madrid we found HM Embassy in disarray, neither staffed nor organised to cope with war conditions. The delegation were left pretty much to their own devices, although there was a great deal of politics in what we were trying to do and I would have welcomed a member of the Embassy staff at our meetings. The British Ambassador, Sir Maurice Peterson, a caustic and very able man, forfeited the influence he should have had because, as the Spanish Minister of Foreign Affairs remarked, 'Sir Peterson dislikes us on principle.' This was abundantly true; he reminded me of that director of the Tate Gallery of whom it was said that he possessed all the qualities required for the post except that he did not care for pictures.

MEW chafed at the length of the negotiations. They wanted to get on with the war. Why were we giving so much away? Why were we so patient with these pro-German Spaniards? My Department refused to understand the extent to which the Spaniards were exhausted and bankrupt of ideas. Our first meetings showed that

Franco's ministers were undecided on what general principles to run their battered economy. At their request we spent days in discussing the theoretical merits of totalitarian versus liberal systems of trade. Here was an issue that had to be settled before we could make practical proposals for a financial and commercial treaty between Spain and the United Kingdom. With a marvellous contribution from Playfair we won the argument and even persuaded them to devalue the peseta. All this took so much time that if the Foreign Secretary, Lord Halifax, had not supported us, MEW might well have called off the negotiations and imposed the Blockade in the brutal form which they desired. Then what would have happened? Spain would have had little to gain from remaining neutral, and in the opinion of those on the spot the vociferous war party would have persuaded Franco to invite the Germans to cross the Pyrenees and attack Gibraltar.

From the beginning of December 1939 to the end of February 1940 I saw much of Marshal Pétain, then French Ambassador to Spain. I never dreamed that in March he would return to Paris soon to become head of a defeated France and then to make the armistice with the Germans. So it is not surprising that the references to him are scanty, and indeed the only letter wholly devoted to describing him and my relations with the French Embassy never reached Sybil. As a result the reader may have difficulty in understanding how Pétain's confidence in me could have been so important in the Anglo-American negotiations (February 1941) with French North Africa. Why did the Marshal tell General Weygand that he could trust me to secure the approval of the British Government to the agreement which Murphy[1] and I had submitted to the General? To fill this gap in the story I have added the following short account of my dealings with Pétain in Madrid.

When the Civil War ended the relations between Spain and France could not have been worse. The government in Paris, seeing that war with Germany was coming, hastened to mend their fences with their neighbour to the south. They sent as ambassador the best-known soldier in Europe. Franco showed pleasure at Pétain's appointment, but his generals and ministers were not ready to forget that the great majority of Frenchmen had backed the losing side in the Civil War. These recent and bitter feelings made Pétain's mission very difficult.

1. Robert Murphy, American diplomat.

In the autumn of 1939, the French Embassy in Madrid began to negotiate a commercial agreement with the same Spanish officials with whom we were making progress with our War Trade Agreement. The French were getting nowhere. As Christmas approached Pétain lost patience with his delegation and invited me to settle, on behalf of both our countries, the principles on which trade with Spain should be resumed in war conditions. It was in the interest of Britain, an ally of France, that the Spaniards and the French should stop quarrelling. Sir Maurice Peterson and I, without I think referring to London, decided to accept the Marshal's request. The pleasure of the Spaniards at this arrangement was, I suppose, a measure of their dislike of the French. I was rewarded with weekly lunches at the French Embassy, usually alone with the Ambassador, sometimes with one or two of his staff in attendance, never with a woman present.

Everyone was curious to know what the old soldier was like. The Germans put it about that he was getting senile. This was not true. On the main issues of our negotiations he was crystal clear and on the details asked shrewd questions. I went early to discuss the business before lunch. During the meal he liked to talk about the world after the war. What did young Englishmen think they were fighting for? Did I agree that authority must be restored in France, which meant putting an end to the Third Republic with its sordid game of chopping and changing ministers? Did I realise that these crooks swopped places in the cabinet simply to get an extra pension? The corrupt farce had so damaged French morale that the British must not expect the French Army to stand up to the German attack which was coming in the spring.

In these conversations he talked soberly, without emotion, showing no sign of being anxious to get his hand on the power, but he did say that in the First World War he had restored French morale at Verdun, and was probably the only man who could do the same in this war.[2] His simplicity was admirable though I sometimes wished he would change the topic of conversation. He

2. Richard Griffiths in his biography of Pétain (Constable, 1970) quotes a letter from Pétain to General Vauthier, dated 15 January 1940, in which the Marshal says that, as he had done at Verdun in the First World War, he might be able once again to restore the morale of the French Army. Pétain made the same remark to me at lunch at the French Embassy within a few days of writing the letter.

never reminisced like Churchill. He was eighty-four and at that age, if one still thinks penetratingly, it must be on a contracting range of subjects. I was fifty years his junior, fascinated to enjoy his friendship and trust; also, being susceptible to beauty in the human face, I am still moved by the memory of the carriage of his head and the benevolent glance from the clearest of blue eyes. At the end of the war de Gaulle let him be tried and condemned to death. Six years later at the age of ninety-five he died in prison. I thought then, and do now, that he deserved better of his countrymen and of the Allies.

15 November 1939 Chute

My darling David—How is Spain? Is the sun pouring over Madrid lighting up all the dust and shabbiness and is the air as sharp as diamonds?

Have you walked in the Retiro yet, or sat on those wobbly seats with stout matrons who grab their two-year-olds to give them a maternal meal? But perhaps the seats are long since firewood and the war-bred babies raised on a sterner diet. And perhaps there are no longer any boats on that silly little lake or bicycles bowling down the alleyways. But I'm sure there are some lovers, wearing that desperate look of just having been let out for an hour.

I think you are right about our war aims—they're clear enough. But Churchill[1] is the only man who has the courage to voice them. That's why the man and woman in the street like him so much. He makes them feel confident and bellicose. Their hackles bristle at his battle cries.

All the same we don't want to start a 'hate' rampage against the *Hun*. If we do—there'll be no judgement or Christianity left to frame the peace.

All my love—Sybil

1. Winston Churchill had been appointed First Lord of the Admiralty on 3 September 1939. Neville Chamberlain was Prime Minister from May 1937 to May 1940.

16 November 1939 Madrid

Darling Syb—You wouldn't know this hotel [the Ritz]. It is so full that we have to share rooms for the present. That's a pretty rude way to treat an official mission, and my friends were very angry. I sleep with Eddie Playfair from the Treasury. We get on well, so it is all right.

As you come into Madrid you see a great deal of damage, and the University City is a nasty mess, but in the centre there is not much evidence of the war.

We had our first meeting today. It is curious how difficult it is to realise that England is at war and that we must bend all our efforts to winning as soon as possible. If we were not at war we could certainly give some very welcome and very valuable assistance to the reconstruction of this country. As it is it will be more difficult, but we shall manage something.

I think a lot about you and will do so more as the days and probably weeks go by. If you were with us you could make tea and arrange flowers and generally defeat those waves of nakedness that come over men in between bursts of work.

All my love, I wish this was a better letter but I am tired and must change to dine with HE.[1]

—David

1. His Excellency Sir Maurice Peterson, KCMG, HM Ambassador to Spain 1939–40.

16 November 1939 Madrid

My darling Syb—There is a bag going tomorrow, so I can write what I like to you. If you post a letter to me under cover to Gladwyn[1] at the FO and it arrives there on Monday morning it will get here by bag on Thursday.

The situation here is very bad as regards food, much worse than in March,[2] the poor people are starving, eggs 8*d.* each, no meat, no olive oil and some days not enough bread. We ought to be able to make a treaty with people in this condition, but although our first meeting was very cordial one cannot hope to make Spaniards see that their products are not really very important to us or anybody else; and if we can't make them see this we shall not get them to devalue the peseta, and the amount of our purchases in Spain will be very limited.

You can't imagine how funny it feels to go into the Embassy as a member of the staff, and read all the telegrams and hear all the gossip from the inside. Everyone asks after you, really, you have an enormous public in Madrid. You would enjoy it, although the food is so bad and the lifts don't work, and the taxis are scarce, and the coffee is worse than ever. I bought 3 lbs of honey and 2 lbs of cherry jam in St Jean de Luz, and they make my breakfast possible. I reckon I can hold on for three weeks with my little stock. Why didn't I bring a bottle of whisky? What a fool!

Now you are about to have your bath, with some essence, and

you will be in those two rooms I love best, our bedroom and bathroom at Chute. Shutting up Montagu Square[3] has made it lose attraction in my eyes, one tends to dislike a cast-off friend.

Did I tell you I burst open the frame of your photograph and have you on my mantelpiece between the millstones?[4] Gladwyn was very impressed as he saw me in the act of destruction.

There is, in my view, no hope of my being back by the end of the month.

All my love—David

1. Gladwyn Jebb, now Lord Gladwyn, was then a principal assistant secretary acting as Private Secretary to the Permanent Under-Secretary of State at the Foreign Office but he was soon to move to the Ministry of Economic Warfare in order to run Special Operations Executive.
2. When I was last in Burgos.
3. 20 Montagu Square was our London house.
4. Our three children.

21 November 1939 Madrid

My darling Syb—I am staying in this morning as I have a streaming cold and this evening we have a big meeting with the Spanish Goverment at which I shall have much to say.

The more I see of the situation here the less I like it. The poverty, misery and inefficiency are heart-breaking. No administrative competence anywhere, and no leadership. Franco really has failed, and I always heard that if he did fail the only course would be to have the King back. And this is what is happening, a huge reaction in favour of Alfonso; of Alfonso and not of his son because the poor people want to get their friends—800,000—out of prison and they think Alfonso could impose an amnesty much better than his son, and he would stand no nonsense with the Falange[1] but Juan might. Rumours fly, such as that Alfonso is here already, that five persons saw him praying at the tomb of his fathers in the Escorial, that someone else has received orders to brush up the Palace, that he visited Franco by night and is now in La Granja . . .

A sinister side to the picture is that it is pretty certain that Prieto, Negrin[2] and all their gang are encouraging the poor people to demand a monarchy. They say that Franco has failed, that the situation is so bad that any king will fail too, so that the sooner he returns and shows that he too is unable to bring prosperity back the better because, when Franco and Alfonso are both discredited, the Communists will have a chance again.

I do not see how we are going to supply Spain with the raw materials she must have to get her economy going. It would cost £10 million in the next twelve months to make even a start and I can't see how we can buy more than £5 million from Spain which leaves a gap of £5 million and HMG won't make a loan. So where are we?

Peterson is awfully good as Ambassador and very nice to me. I see him every day for an hour and he tells me all that is going on. His wife is *un peu dure*, but efficient and with character.

22 November

Still no letter from you, if I don't get one tomorrow I will telegraph, whatever you do use the bag and send me all interesting letters by it. You can get nothing here, neither news, nor medicines, nor milk nor the simplest things like pens and nibs. So if you read any good articles in *The Times* cut them out and let me have them.

Going into the Ritz restaurant every day—it is crammed full—with our Miss Capper, the Board of Trade typist, is good for my conceit and philosophy, for I am used, so used that it needs our Miss Capper to give me a jolt, to going in proudly with your Eva-Ed[3] self. And I love it when you are in full fig and look so well; but our Miss Capper with the home-made run-ups and bright tight jumpers and the awful shoes, well, that takes me down a peg. She's a nice little girl and has fallen in love with a pansy Frenchman who wears a delicious beard to conceal a weakly pretty face.

All the chambermaids and valets come and coo over the photograph of you and the creatures, '*tan guapa!*' '*que mono!*' and all the rest. When shall I see you all and kiss you? I just feel numb about the prospects, we might break down tomorrow, we might go on for another month. There is a hard core of resistance behind the Spaniards which must be, we think, the ideological sympathies of Suñer[4] and the Falange. It won't bend, it might break.

All my love—David

1. The Fascist Party in Spain.
2. Ministers in the defeated Socialist Republic.
3. Eva Lutyens was Sybil's dressmaker.
4. Serrano Suñer, Franco's brother-in-law, was a notorious pro-Axis minister and head of the Falange.

21 November 1939 Chute

My darling love—Yesterday was gloriously fine and as I now find that my extra petrol expires this week we filled up the car and went out for the afternoon.

The boys were all for the 'aerodrome' so we called first upon the RAF at [Wallop].[1] It couldn't have been a better moment, every manner and description of waspish monster zoomed up and down over our heads and round about us. The boys were in heaven and crept nearer and nearer in spite of all our warning cries. But the authorities were all smiles and no one came to drive them off.

Finally we dragged them away and took a roundabout road to Salisbury, where Michael[2] was quite overcome by the cathedral spire. 'It must be a million feet—don't you think so, Auntie Sybil?'

The extra hour has gone and night falls with a clap—about 5 o'clock. Nannie and I forgot it today and were caught by the dark on the causeway. We staggered down Chantry Lane—the prams bumping and skidding through a soft slush of autumn leaves and the boys skipping with excitement at being out in the dark.

I love you—my dearest David—Sybil

1. Deleted by censor.
2. Michael Bowater, my nephew aged six.

29 November 1939 Madrid

I got your telegram this morning and shall think of you at the wedding[1] tomorrow. Today we have had a grand funeral, José Antonio's (Primo de Rivera) body has passed on its way to the Escorial. Fancy, he is to be buried there among the Catholic Kings, a gay, loud, eloquent young man who founded the Falange and had 6,000 members by 1936. Then he was martyred in prison and made a national hero.

I think I like funerals better than weddings. Nearly all Latins do, and I sympathise. They see that life is so full of broken promises, so utterly futile unless there is something more, that the funeral is the one big gamble, 'to be or not to be', and they love a gamble. This is the final game of Last Across. Is it an unhealthy, a poisonous pleasure that the cortège gives? I don't think so. I see us on the roof of the guard-room at Windsor, watching the funeral procession of George V wind down the hill inside the castle. All earthly guesses over, confronted with the insoluble mystery. I don't see why it should be bad to be thrilled by such a question mark. No wedding could equal it. Not for a man at least, because the fulfilment of his life is not promised by the legitimate hope of children.

I will write again if I can before the bag goes, but will seal this up, as we are sending a packet along today.

All my love, my darling Syb—David

1. Sybil's sister Rosemary Dawson married John Wrightson on 30 November 1939.

4 December 1939 Madrid

My darling Syb—Our discussions are maddeningly slow, and that damned habit of dilatoriness is creeping over everyone. I am now quite well and I think the life and soul of the party, keeping them cheerful and drafting all the memoranda.

There is one thing about the war which is good, and that is the co-operation between France and England. The breakdown of individual sovereignty is the hope of the world. I expect we are working like brothers in many neutral countries. Here I can claim the credit, for with no specific instructions from either of our govts. I have seduced my French colleagues and it is exactly true to say that France and England have now only one policy in regard to commercial relations with Spain, and that this policy itself moulds their political attitude. The head of the French mission[1] is a most charming man, M. du Moulin de Labarthète, who speaks the most exquisite and dramatic French: '*Mon cher Eccles, le moment que je suis entré dans la salle de négotiations je me suis aperçu que vous avez passé par là, et que vous avez laissé les Espagnols "groggés".*' Whatever may come of our negotiations and they are now at their stickiest, this result will be valuable, and I consider that Anglo-French relations will benefit for all time.

The Cresswells[2] took Eddie Playfair and me to the *parador* at Gredos for Sat. night, and Sunday we spent at Salamanca. The air was frosty and metallic, and we all felt very hungry and cheerful. The country between Salamanca and the Portuguese border is new to me and very attractive. Deep clefts between reddish hills and in the clefts flocks of sheep and numbers of black cattle. The abundance of livestock is astonishing and made me realise how disastrously the rest of Spain has been stripped in the Civil War.

We bought two joints, six partridge and honey and eggs, and I thought that food and drink are really the only things worth buying, all the rest is finery. The excitement of hunting for a tit-bit is delicious. We plan to go foraging again next weekend.

Several members of the German Embassy were at Gredos; and a Spanish colonel kept tuning in the wireless to the French and British news, it was enormous fun to watch the Germans concealing their fury, but the good colonel, who had the most charming manners, apologised that he didn't know German and he wanted to hear about Finland.

We have had one of those days of desperate skirmishes trying to persuade individual members of the Spanish delegation to take our view before the big battle is joined tomorrow. If you asked me to bet on the result, that is whether in exchange for a loan the Spaniards will consent to alter the rate of the peseta against the pound, I really should be unable to quote the odds. I find it particularly exciting to be arguing with them about the first principles of economics rather than about this or that commodity. To see the making or the marring of the whole Spanish economy going on under one's eyes, to watch the conflict between the Nazi and the democratic theory of production and finance is a rare experience, and could only come about at this moment when a half-civilised country finds itself in a bankrupt state from which everything has to be built up on new foundations. Everything is possible and nothing is certain. My old friend the Conde de Albiz[3] said to me, '*No se peude decir que esta agua no bebere.*' 'It cannot be said that I shall never drink this water.' That is a

Shakespearian remark. Humanity is capable of anything, folly or virtue. The art of negotiation is to feel for the point at which fixed ideas can be attacked, and if you find a weak spot you never know what size the breach may become.

—David

1. To make a War Trade Agreement with Spain.
2. Michael Cresswell was Second Secretary at the British Embassy in Madrid. His wife Elizabeth was Russian.
3. Legal adviser to the British Embassy.

6 December 1939 Chute

My darling David—I see your point about funerals. They fill the mind and stir the imagination with speculations upon eternity. Now a wedding is quite different. Love forges a link with eternity for all to see. The power to produce children is as grand and insoluble a mystery as ever death is.

I counted the votes for the new committee at the Women's Institute[1] this afternoon—and watched the proceedings from a privileged position beside the stove. There—on the edge of their chairs, upright as pokers, breathing heavily, you have the salt of the earth. With one small bit of their brains they listen to the Treasurer, reporting on a profit of 3*s.* 2½*d.* for teas in October—the *whole* of the rest of them is furiously concentrated on the problem of what they shall give their husband for his supper.

A woman's life boils down to food and boots—boots and food, doesn't it?

The war doesn't look too good. The best one can say is that the Germans must if anything be feeling more uncomfortable about the Russians than we are. Sometimes I have a nightmare and see us six or seven years from now—hungry, miserable and without hope—doggedly fighting on—anyone who comes our way and for no very clear reason. But that's only when I have a nightmare—usually, great optimism prevails at Dean Farm.[2]

All my love—Sybil

1. The Women's Institute at Chute.

2. Dean Farm, our house at Chute, which faces south in a narrow valley that runs down to Ludgershall and beyond to the north edge of Salisbury Plain.

7 December 1939 Madrid

We've done it. The Spanish Government have given in on all the essential points, that is in brief they have realised that their true interest lies in trade with the British Empire and they are prepared to abandon the German theories of a closed economy. You could have heard the old pin drop when their chairman made this statement. I don't know what colour I went, and I didn't dare look at my colleagues. We managed to reply in what I think was the right way, appreciation but very guarded, without a hint of triumph, because I thought it essential to leave them with the impression that they had taken of their own free will a most important and sensible decision. They were visibly moved at our response in this manner. Well, there you are, three weeks' work, 'like a little cat, pushing the stone under water, with little taps, to prevent the mud from rising' as José[1] says.

It will take some weeks to draw up the treaty on the principles that have now been accepted. I am not optimistic that we shall be home for Christmas.

The Prado has been enriched with a number of magnificent pictures taken from monasteries and convents during the Civil War. In particular the new Grecos are superb, much finer than those already there, and much cleaner. It is impossible not to put him enormously high as a disturber of the mind and eye with his extraordinary evocative style. Also I thought the Titians better than ever, the Gloria and the Empress Isabella especially. Reading the life of Carlos V has whetted my appetite for the Titian portraits.

Oh! I wish I knew I was coming home for Christmas. It will be foul here. If only we were sitting opposite each other in the parlour at Chute with the logs burning and a glass of champagne. It's no good getting impatient: His Majesty's Government must come first.

All my love—David

1. José de Aguinaga was chief executive of the Santander-Mediterraneo Railway.

8 December 1939 Madrid

Darling Syb—If the Spaniards would only agree the Economic Warfare clauses of the treaty in advance I don't see why I shouldn't leave the others to work out the machinery for the purely trade part of the treaty. The trouble is they make me a jack of all work, and really I do most of the Board of Trade stuff and all the Foreign Office work as well as my MEW affairs. The Ambassador did not make any of his FO staff a member of the delegation so that I have to represent the FO angle in the negotiations and it may be said to be a permanent interest, and not like MEW, confined to a particular section of the treaty. Someone has to be there to think of how the political aspect comes in, our departmental servants have had ground out of them any pretension that they can look at the affair in the round. It is a bad system, but what else can one suggest? There was an interesting article in *The Times* of 30 November on economic warfare more or less drawing this conclusion.

All my love, sweet, whenever shall I kiss you again?

Love to the creatures—David

10 December 1939 Madrid

My darling Syb—I have just had a letter from you dated 21 November about your trip to the aerodrome (the name was cut out by the censor) with the boys. They must have loved it, and Salisbury Cathedral as well. How I would love to be there this evening for the service! And your description of scrambling down Chantry Lane in the dark was very good, a heart-ache for me. Limmer and Haybourne and the smell of the wet leaves, it all seems so out of reach. Not just because I am in Madrid, but because the war is so foul and before we win will cause so much suffering.

I find myself more pessimistic about the length of the war than most people here but more optimistic about the chances of a real peace when it is over. I don't see how a short war could give the grounds for a real peace, and God knows one doesn't want a minute more of it than is necessary, but you can't heal a vast wound in a fortnight, and our moral disease is so deep; I mean

Europe's moral disease, let alone Russia's and Japan's and all other barbarians'.

And again there is something else to be feared and that is the exhaustion of a long war, such as you can see all round you here, men incapable of concentration, nervy, unusually pig-headed . . . all the disabilities of convalescence shared by the people at large and working upon each other. I saw for instance half a dozen lorries stacked with black coffins, standing on end, going, I heard later, to the public ditch to remove the corpses to some more decent place, and two women walking in the opposite direction to me, seeing the lorries, burst into sobs, no one took any notice, they just went on in floods.

Playfair goes back on Monday, as foreshadowed, and I remain on guard. Will you send to Playfair at the Treasury, Whitehall, letters for me which he will bring back with him.

Later

People are getting pretty bored in Madrid: no golf courses, tennis courts, no horses to ride, no Club Alpinas yet rebuilt on the Sierra, no Parque del Oeste, only a dusty and overcrowded Retiro. In the old days you will remember that the Corps Diplomatique made quite a good show of enjoying their life in Madrid. Now they all hate it, except a couple of Americans who have fallen for the dukes and duchesses.

Your typical civil servant is a terrifying product, almost, even so early as the age of thirty, a mass-produced article. Very intelligent, very suspicious of human nature *per se*, perfect son-of-the-vicar, the vicar's manners, wears a burberry, a black hat turned down all round, a sensible scarf and smokes a pipe. Their salaries are small in comparison with the power they wield, their prospects are secure, their pension adequate to a flat in Bath or a small house at Dorking. They know more about the form of their own subject than it is possible to believe, I mean how it was done in 1890, 1910, in the last war and now, how to draft clauses provided the subject is given them to draft, and in one quality they excel all human beings, they have a devastating power of seeing the flaws in other people's arguments. You will say, 'How good for David!', and so it is, I am learning a lot, but not I hope so much that I shall catch their lack of faith in everything human and divine. Living with them you see that they are really obstacles, bulwarks, barbed wire entanglements, anything obstructive to the wicked ideas of the outside world. They are quite right in thinking that the public, MPs and ministers usually produce half-baked schemes that contain either an element of folly or of dishonesty and that their function is to protect the public against themselves. Their minds are fertile, extraordinarily so, both in thinking out objections to policy they don't like, and in thinking out the proper form in which to express policy that has been agreed by the competent authority.

This mission here has been very interesting to Playfair and Nowell because we came without any definite instructions. Mounsey[1] told me before I started that he had sat on any idea of instructions, steadily maintaining that you could not plan a battle without a map of the country, and telling me that he relied upon my past knowledge of Spain to find the formula which my colleagues, being civil servants, would know how to put into verbal form in accord with past treaties. And so precisely it has happened. The few preconceived ideas we did have between us have all gone by the board and a much simpler, and I think more workable plan, has been evolved by trial and error. Now I am certain that career civil servants couldn't have done this by themselves, any more than I could put into correct form a forty-page treaty. They couldn't do it because they could not divest their minds of all the dusty precedents about Spain, and all that they had imagined Spaniards to be like (i.e. fierce, disreputable and also unworldly). In general I don't think much can be done about the Civil Service except frequent contacts with the outside world, and some change in the traditional roles. Punch and Judy must always act Punch and Judy, banging each other about and so on. If you dressed two marionettes differently you wouldn't expect them to act Punch and Judy. The Civil Service versus the Business Man has got into this legendary type of behaviour, and they must try to change their disguise a bit and then their behaviour will change. The creation of MEW with its mixed FO and City personnel was a stroke of genius; but, and this is what I have only come to realise since I was here, we, the City boys, could not have worked amicably if we had been drafted into the Board of Trade and probably not if it had been the Treasury; with the FO all was well, because snobbishly we admired them anyway and there was no traditional antipathy.

In point of practice, MEW work is really nearer the Treasury and the Board of Trade than the FO; only my section of MEW is genuine FO stuff; and as the war goes on the MEW contacts with the other departments will multiply, and if we should continue at it a year or more I think you will have a hundred people or so, drawn from MEW and the career service who will not be content to see England governed as it has been, and who will be capable of a new technique. The half-way house between the free brigandage of capitalism, and the paralytic centralisation of socialists is being built in this way. We shall see.

Later
We have worked all day on drafting clauses of the Agreement to be taken to London for approval, the more I see of them the more my heart sinks at the prospect of the time necessary to get them agreed in London and then here. Unless the Spaniards are so exhausted that they collapse they will argue every line in a forty-page document. What a nightmare in view!

Do tell me how you are, I want to know how you feel and if you're getting fatter or thinner, and whether you are rheumaticky or collywobbly or anything the matter. I don't know why, I just want to be sure about you. Supposing we were going to walk up to Limmer and look down over the fields at the farm, wouldn't it be heavenly?

Love to the chaps and Polly and to you, my sweetest Syb
—David

1. Sir George Mounsey, KCMG, CB, OBE, Under-Secretary of State at the Foreign Office.

11 December 1939 — 32 Wimpole Street[1]

My darling David—I came up to London this morning to attempt some Christmas shopping and have been at it all day. Nannie went away for last weekend and Nannie Bowater and I had a grand time with the Quartet. Early breakfast, lessons, potting, putting to sleep, lunch, carving the chicken, a walk—shove, shove, up to the farm and round—tea, games, squabbles, threats, bathing, a pirate story—and so to bed and the long day is over.

It's taken the war to turn me into a mother—and often I

wonder if peace were declared tomorrow whether I should turn again to conventional, social, London life like a pony with its nose to a well-known stable.

13 December
At Manheim's I discovered a heart-breaking little Whieldon figure,[2] and send it to you in the bag to remind you of Chute—and perhaps of me as well—sitting beside the fire and piling on another log. ('Don't put on another—I'm going to bed.') I always know before I reach out for one that you're going to say that!

You can stand him on your hotel mantelpiece and he'll make you dream of English farmyards and the scent of earth newly turned by the plough.

Did you ever see such an innocent foolish face?

The children send a waistcoat against the Castilian winds. I don't suppose you'll wear it—but it really wouldn't take much room and could be well concealed. And it might be cosy on a foraging expedition.

It's no good crying out *ad nauseam* that we are fighting this war for principles which we believe make life tolerable if, at the first opportunity, we resort to the same methods as the Germans. If we do that, the affair becomes a low-down dog-fight in no time. You know, one of the depressing features is that practically *no one* seems to have the faintest notions on what lines the war *should* proceed or what our aims *vis-à-vis* Germany and the rest of the world should be. If we had peace tomorrow I don't believe we should have the foggiest idea how to set wisely about it. It would almost be an embarrassment—like a diamond tiara in a working-class home.

I must go to bed.

14 December
How I shall miss you at Christmas—but never mind, I'm really more than a little proud of the reason for my widowhood and that saves the situation and spares me my tears.

I love you, my darling, and think of you more and more as the long weeks go by—I find one gets quite used to this life but won't it be perfect to be really happy again?

I know we shall—Sybil

1. Sybil's family home in London. Lord Dawson had his consulting rooms there.
2. Staffordshire pottery figure of about 1760.

15 December 1939 Madrid

Here begins the last piece for the last bag for Christmas. It is bitterly cold here, grey and hard skies. 'Key-cold' Shakespeare called the King's corpse in *Richard III*, and when we were in the old cathedral in Salamanca a fortnight ago I put my hand on a bunch of enormous silver keys that our verger had left in the door of the cloister, they were so cold they hurt.

The central heating has partially broken down, and the new boiler is supposed to be starting up on Monday. We can only sit in our circular crimson den in overcoats and gloves. Jolly, isn't it? You would have chilblains in no time.

The newspapers make one vomit about the naval action at Montevideo.[1] All but one say that our cruisers had heavier guns than the pocket battleship. The shattering part is, this sort of thing is believed if it is repeated enough. The Germans pay heavy weekly subsidies to the Spanish press for lying in their favour. A friend of José's [de Aguinaga] who is on a Sunday paper has already touched £3,000 since August. We cannot enter this competition. I have been repeatedly asked my opinion on the point at home and here. I see nothing against giving free copy and photographs, or a lunch and dinner, but regular cash subsidies are the agents of the devil. The French agree because they think them a waste of sweet francs, but I hope we take a higher line, and if we do ever get a substantial propaganda fund we must spend it on positive propaganda and not on stopping someone else or lying about ourselves. I told HE the other day that the whole matter turns on whether you think human nature capable of improvement, and whether there is in human nature a fundamental desire to be good rather than bad, to know the truth rather than to be deceived. I answer these questions 'Yes', and it follows that it is not only immoral, but in the long run useless, to try to gain sympathy in neutral countries by lying. The trouble is the short run. People can be corrupted, in fact unless they continually try to find the truth and to do good works they always are corrupted. The Spanish people are exhausted and more than usually corruptible, their standards have been lowered by the Civil War, and altho' there are probably more unselfish patriots about than there were before the war there is a more general moral weakness. 'After the trenches let's make some easy money'; it isn't hard to see how it happens.

Somebody must work for the longer run, and keep alive the tradition of truth being more valuable than lies are exciting, because to those in misery the conflict is not between one kind of knowledge and another but between knowledge and emotion, between a strict diet and a dose of morphia. Trudging to and from the Embassy I wonder over these things, and generally come to the same conclusion, that our way of civilisation can only succeed if the people who run it show much more skill and imagination than they do today.

You have a tree decorated; and the parcels tied with white paper and red ribbon; and the table a pattern of silver and snow; and their stockings to fill? How I wish I were there, perhaps not helping very enthusiastically but greatly appreciating the result. What can I give Polly, supposing I have time and money enough to buy something in Paris? And you too? Really I am bankrupt of ideas in this sterile town.

All my love. I miss you and love you more every day—David

1. The pursuit of the German pocket battleship *Graf Spee*.

17 December 1939 Madrid

My darling Syb—I worked all the morning on a note for the Ambassador about the position of the Franco-Spanish negotiations, which look like breaking down tomorrow. France and Spain hate each other with a venom. No one really gets on with French ministers, though individually the French are the most attractive of people. In this case, and contrary to the advice of the French mission here, the French Government is blackmailing the Spaniards with such shameless brutality that we simply must intervene, and after lunch Peterson drafted a long telegram to Halifax asking him to do so. I hope that great and good man will send for Corbin[1] and give him a sound lecture.

To amuse you I enclose a copy of my notes for Peterson's

despatch to the Secretary of State on 'Access to Raw Materials', which I wrote about last bag. It will be interesting to see what HE makes of it in his despatch. My Board of Trade colleague thinks my ideas dangerously revolutionary, says it is politically impossible and would involve a totally unjustified increase in work in London. To which I reply, 'What other plan have you?' These civil servants have no faith in a better world; and as St Augustine said, you must first believe and then understand. They wish to know, to understand just how it is to be done before they will believe it is possible; and that, in exact detail, is beyond the power of man.

Later
Our enemies here and in other neutral states are making great play with the notion that, if Germany is defeated, Communism will sweep through Europe. Like Charles II they say, 'You will never kill me to make James King,' and they make some impression with this propaganda.

18 December
'Ha! ha! The *Graf Spee* has disappeared.' I said this to Major Campbell, the representative of the Iron Ore Control of UK in the hotel passage, this morning, and round the corner came a square boot-brush of a German. My! What a look he gave us. Rejoicing at our enemy's discomfort was quite common in the Old Testament, but I suppose we are trying to abide by the New. The Germans have sent their No. 1 trade negotiator here, Dr Wolthat, because they heard we weren't doing too badly. It's a nice little compliment and adds to the fun.

Later
I met Juan Mata today, he was a Catalan businessman who became Franco's chief representative in London throughout the Civil War. Now he's back in business, and says he doesn't like it, he had got used to seeing all the telegrams and following the workings of his government, and now he sees nothing but a contract note and a 'I beg to acknowledge yours of the 15th'. It is a grim warning, and I can well see how one could be restless for the hurly-burly of state affairs.

The non-confidential bag is just in with a box of twenty-five cigars for me ex my stock at Dunhill's. However did they come? I am enchanted, and if it was you who told Dunhill to send them you are a very clever and sweet Syb. I feel so gay tonight I pine to see you, and perhaps even chase you round the room as we used to do at Upper Montagu Street.[2]

All my love—David

1. French Ambassador in London.
2. No. 8 Upper Montagu Street, our first house.

18 December 1939 Chute

My darling David—Your letter dated December 10 has just arrived.

Call to Playfair just come through. Tremendously superior man answers me—with unbelievably cultured voice. So bored he can hardly be bothered to go on living and utterly unhelpful.

'No, Mr Playfair was not in the office.' Sweetly I explained who I was and the reason I was ringing up. No good. Superior man incapable of unbending. 'No—he didn't know when Mr P would be in the office.' 'No—he didn't even know when Mr P would be returning to Spain. Hadn't the faintest idea.' At this point I felt he might fade out on me altogether—so hastily offering my telephone no. which he said he couldn't hear (liar) I rang off.

So I shall send this letter by the 3.30 to the Treasury and hope that Mr Playfair's colleague lets him have it. How right you are about civil servants—they are like flies shut up in a very luxurious bottle. And though full of intelligence are even fuller of themselves and the station in life to which it has pleased God to call them.

But when I drove up to the FO yesterday to offer my humble packets for the bag I felt I understood how they came to be like that. One passes beneath the great archway and between the pillars of the colonnade, each stage of one's progress towards the seat of the mighty is calculated to impress—but also to smother and to crush. One's gaze travels over the imposing façade—from innumerable windows green-shaded lamps send out a faint but steady beam—here a grey figure hurries past, there a head is bent in terrific concentration upon some unknown task.

Like bees in a hive those servants of democracy swarm about

their myriad labours. Housed in magnificence—shackled with gilded chains—and their natural energies and aspirations harnessed and enslaved to the traditions of a thousand yesterdays.

Soon they succumb to the conqueror and put on the garments of convention. But their superiority has in it a touch of wistfulness, as though they are conscious of their isolation from the struggles and endeavours of the flesh and blood—the greedy, ambitious, eager world. From which they are for ever shut away behind their sculptured walls—their polished mahogany doors—guarded jealously by a horde of messengers and doorkeepers whose chief task is to frown upon and strangle any stray impertinence or tiresome innovations. People like you—and others in MEW—will do a world of good, but I do feel our government fabric is too vast, it overwhelms the individual and saps his invention and his courage. I am very well—neither plump—nor scraggy. A beautiful colour, no rheumatics or collies. In fact—an alluring lovely wife with not a soul on earth to lure.

I must fly—or miss the post—I love you—Sybil

19 December 1939 Madrid

I dined last night as the guest of the Falange, six of their leading young editors and propagandists. We sat down at 10.30 and got up at 1.30, my head in a whirl and my stomach in revolt. They are wild as hawks, and treated me first to an interminable harangue on the relative difficulty of writing in prose or verse. I made up my *mot* about ten minutes before I was able to get it out, and finally said I was a railwayman and therefore knew that it was easier to drive a train on the rails (poetry) than to drive a car across the plain. This seemed to be about the right note, and we continued in the most extravagant vein till midnight, when I borrowed Lothian's[1] American speech, and told them that as neutrals they had a solemn obligation to think out what sort of Europe we should make after the war. We should be tired and in a bad temper, although victorious, and we should pay attention to the serious proposals of a country like Spain which had itself passed through the experiences of fire. Catsmilk! How they lapped it up! We then had an hour's talk that couldn't be called valuable from the statesman's point of view but what a glimpse of Spanish psychology!

Most of them thought that recurrent wars are inevitable, some of them that they are necessary to perpetuate the heroic virtues or even virtue itself, all of them had a different theory, and they soon forgot I was present. In their most combative exchanges I succeeded in asking if the Christian hope of peace and goodwill was, in their opinion as staunch Catholics, merely an aspiration without any value in reality. This rather upset them, and they talked about crusades and the necessity to fight for the Christian tradition. But not, I said, as an end in itself, surely as a means to peace some day? No, they said, life is always a struggle, and though we can approximate a little to the Christian ideal, there is no peace except in death. You can see perhaps a faint thread of Augustinian philosophy in their ideas.

All my love and how I wish I were there to see you all unpack your parcels. Give Poll an extra kiss.

—David

1. The Marquess of Lothian was British Ambassador to the United States in Washington until December 1940.

20 December 1939 — 32 Wimpole Street

Of course you're right—propaganda must not lie, cajole, bribe or threaten too outrageously—but in a modern world it *must* propagand. And we simply don't pay enough attention to this fact. Squeamishly—distastefully, we attempt a few pamphlets—which for sheer weight of wordiness are guaranteed to split anyone's skull open. The press attempts some cumbersome and smug assurances of Britain's will to live.

But there's no punch anywhere. No bounce and conviction. Of all things propaganda needs punch. And we can do it if we try. For look at Winston and listen to him, and read him with thankfulness. He comes of generations of wealth, success and superiority. 'If any man wants any truck with us let him come and ask for it.' There's something in it. Propaganda is a trifle low. But it's sickening when letters arrive from overseas full of anxious sympathy born of listening to the efficient falsehoods of the Hun.

I have one good story for you. Wilhelmina[1] in answer to Hitler's ultimatum: '*Touchez à mes pays bas et je vous inonde!*' Rather nice.

I love you and miss you more and more too.

—Sybil

1. Queen of the Netherlands.

21 December 1939 Madrid

My darling Syb—How exciting that you have sent me a present in the non-confidential bag. It is due to arrive on Christmas Day. All the Embassy have their tongues out, and now I can add mine in anticipation. I can't send you anything as our bag is only mail.

I have bought the Petersons a really lovely glass jug, enormous, rather like the one I gave Victor, if you remember it. This one is Spanish and about a hundred years old, very fine shape and pond-colour. The Petersons have been so kind to me that I wanted to find them something attractive.

The Ambassador wrote a covering despatch to my note on 'Access to Raw Materials' in which he asked Halifax to give it his personal attention. He couldn't have asked more.

We make very good progress towards the purchase of all our iron-ore requirements from Spain for 1940, but are very anxious about shipping. The Spaniards won't, probably can't, give us any programme of their tonnage needs for each month next year. It is an example of the chaotic state in which they try to carry on their administration.

Cobian[1] dined with me last night. He is completely down; broken-hearted to have watched the spirit of self-sacrifice in his sons and their friends gradually die away in the present months of failure and disappointment. It is a tragedy indeed. I remember how in Burgos last March I was overwhelmed by the enthusiasm and fire of the young Spaniards; and now? All is spent, and turned to bitterness.

After a revolution you must have a great leader to turn the habit of destruction into the work of construction. Here they are all sick children and wild theorists. If they can't save themselves, who can, can we? Certainly not in the long run. What we are doing now is to stem, if we can, the drift to chaos caused by privation and maladministration. To put the country to rights you would need a £50 million loan from UK, France, and USA, and a panel of experts to see that the money was well spent. That is impossible. All we can do is to try to insure against chaos for the next twelve months. The Germans are intriguing against Franco now, because they know that a collapse of this government would throw the whole country into anarchy, as there is no possible alternative. The restoration of the monarchy has been made more difficult by the great deterioration of the economic position in recent weeks.

Later
Your letter by bag arrived just this minute. Darling, I never meant to worry you about not catching the bag. MEW missed it last week. The fact is I get all worked up waiting for your letter all the six days, and then when once there was a flop I was *aplati*. You don't know how much I look forward to your letters, perhaps I don't tell you enough how much I love you and want you and miss you every day and night. There it is anyway.

I am overwhelmed with work and that tiresome drafting of clauses, lawyers can like it, I hate it.

All my love—David

1. Legal adviser to the Santander-Mediterraneo Railway.

Christmas Day | Madrid

Darling Syb—There is a 'safe hand' going back this afternoon and I have ¼ hour to write to you. I simply love the Whieldon figure, it is very good quality and I almost wondered if it was one of Voyez's first models. The big eyes and lips are so characteristic, you remember our *white* haymaker which is a self-portrait of Voyez.

Last night the Petersons gave a buffet supper (marvellous food most beautifully done) to the forty-five employees of HMG in Madrid. We had games and competitions afterwards, in which I failed badly in those requiring physical skill but won the only one where ingenuity had the greater say. Prize a box of peppermints.

I have just been to church and heard a most depressing sermon from a Gibraltar chaplain. Apparently he considers Christianity as an occasional, very rare, solace in a miserable world. A sort of outing to be looked forward to once a year. Very peculiar, I thought.

I have a constant idea that there is a sort of ferment going on at home, in the FO, in MEW, at Brooks's, etc. where the new Europe is being talked out. Of course, it may be just impatience at being here and not there; and the Ambassador says that to be here and not there has great advantages from the creative point of view. Who knows? I want very much to make a speech here to the British colony, if and when we sign the treaty, explaining to them that it is a new kind of instrument designed to share the world's goods.

The relevant clauses are going to be excellent material for the future if they are handled right and given the proper publicity.

All my love, sweet Syb, it is queer to be away from you at Christmas.

Kiss the creatures—David

28 December 1939 Madrid

My darling Syb—The serial letter has not come up to standard this week as work has been overlaid with a round of parties, now finished I'm glad to say. Each member of the Embassy gave one in turn, and we ate and drank more and more with the same people. My tummy quite gave out, and last night I retired to bed at 11 and didn't wake up till 10.30 this morning. The rain and snow have gone and this morning all is sparkling blue, nice and symbolic for my return to normal life.

Our naval attaché returned from London with his small boy just before Christmas, bringing a message, or rather instruction, for me from Winston to prepare a memorandum on how to buy the fifty-five German ships in Spanish harbours. This has been a devil of a job, both because it is extremely difficult in itself, and, as the recommendations made will be considered by the War Cabinet, I must try not to make mistakes. I am pleased to think that Winston was willing to ask me personally to do this, because it must mean that the Cabinet take a favourable view of our effort here. If the shipping position is really bad why don't we start rationing at home? I can't understand it.

Later
As I left the lift just now I saw hobbling along the passage a very, very old man obviously trying to walk only on the narrow strip of dark carpet that borders the flowery centre. I tiptoed after him until suddenly he realised I was behind him, and gave a grunt of annoyance and tottered into the middle of the passage. Boys will be boys.

Our Miss Capper's mother has baked in Norwood a most delicious plum cake and sent it out by the non-confidential bag, we have had a slice each, certainly not more than one at a time, and exceedingly good it was, especially as Thursday is one-course day and our lunch was filthy. We reckon it will last three to four days, but she is young and healthy and will I fear fall to a nibble or so in her bedroom. The Spanish Government has sent me a large crate, as big as a doz. of wine, of muscatels, there must be thirty or forty big bunches and they are rapidly being eaten by visitors and ourselves.

No more time or paper, I love you very much, and am always thinking how lovely it will be to kiss you again. What a peculiar place the world is to be so easily delicious and so easily disastrous.

All my love—David

31 December 1939 Madrid

My darling Syb—We are just back from Guadalupe and I have an hour to write before my change for dinner. After a scramble at the chancery all the morning and a quick lunch we got away at 3 p.m. and reached Oropesa just as the light was failing. Heavy rain all the time. You remember the road from Oropesa is very hilly and not too good, 95 km to the monastery. After we had gone about half-way we stopped in a village, pitch dark in a thick cloud as bad as a London fog, and asked if it was any better further on. 'Far from it,' said a flat-faced oaf, 'a car has already had to turn back, you can't get over the pass.' 'How far?' '40 km to Guadalupe.' We didn't know what to do, and suddenly I said to Douglas Howard,[1] 'This is the question we'll be asking ourselves about going on with the war: to Guadalupe we go.' And after doing about five miles in forty minutes it cleared round a bend and we sailed into the monastery at eight, just in time for dinner with our legs in the *brasiero*.

This morning we woke up in very good spirits, altho' 'the village cock . . . hath twice done salutation to the morn', not twice as Shakespeare says, but a hundred times or more. We went to High Mass at nine, the celebrant being the monk who had dined at our table. It was the most charming service and scene you ever saw. To the left of the altar they had made a Nativity out of every home-made toy imaginable. The stable with the cow and ass in one corner in front, and winding away behind farms and houses, animals, and dancing boys, milkmaids, people in summer dress, some in furs chasing wolves, all cunningly lit with candles helped out by one tin-pot spotlight. All through Mass the village boys—hardly any girls—crowded against the railing in front of their Bethlehem, no one minded, and I think they're right not to mind because the boys become accustomed to find happiness in church, and the Mass is above contamination by such whispered chuckling and nudging. The organ is famous—I don't think you and I heard it—and the organist too. He played such lively, rollicking tunes that we both said, 'This is the Ballet in heaven.' We talked to him afterwards and he gave us one of his poems, the refrain of which told us that when he plays in the church alone, he has to stop for tears, he loves his organ and his Guadalupe so much. No tears today, all gaiety. At the end of the Mass the priest took the Baby—a wax doll, with his legs crossed up in the air, lying in a basket of flowers—and there was a rush to kneel on the chancel step. With a hanky to wipe the toes, the priest held the Baby to each person in turn to kiss, talking and laughing as he went along the row. The news that the kissing was on must have leaked out of church, for bunches of children came dashing in to get a place, and it went on for ten minutes.

The Catholic Church has a grand way of dividing life into the best—the Mother and the Child—and the worst—the Crucifixion, or how man can treat man. To me it is the ultimate analysis. The absence of the Virgin from our Church is one of the inestimable losses that men make when their minds ripen to a point where they are strong enough to recognise something as only symbolically true—which they had believed real—and so to put it away as superstition. You believe in God because you are afraid of him, and you are an Old Testament savage. You are no longer afraid of him, and you don't believe in him, and you are a nineteenth-century intellectual. You are not afraid of him but you love him, and you may find peace. I think that is the argument of the modern Catholic Church.

This sequence of ignorance-experience-wisdom is obviously one of the great rhythms of the world. We all have a shot at it. When you say that it has taken a war to make you know your children, or make them part of you again, it is the same thing. The primitive mother could not escape from them to a life of other pursuits, the well-to-do modern mother has been able to lead a 'fuller' life, and now you find that you don't know if you'll ever go back to the ways of 1931–8. My idea has always been how lucky women are to have made for them by their children a life so wise and lovely. I do not at all mean that you should do nothing but be a nursery-maid, but that what you do otherwise will have its real value on how it shapes you as a nursery-maid. That again is why I want family allowances, because the unit of society is the stable at Bethlehem. That is its abiding symbol.

This rhythm is there for men too. I suppose ambition and the love of money are the false and middle stages in a man's life. As a child he knows neither, as a boy he begins to be sick for both, as a man they may mean everything, and then if he looks closer he may be able to reject them in favour of a quiet and unselfish life. I am very afraid of money. It is so easy to think too much of it, especially if you have my talents at the game of winning it. This war has broken clean with markets and profits and cheques for this and that. I have used my cheque-book once since November to get some cash to come here . . . I must dash to my bath, the clock seems to have turned the hour in five minutes. I hope you aren't bored with all these speculations, I have no other confessor, as you know, and I don't want any other; so long as you will listen, I shall go on with my paper burble as a tit for your tatter while we eat our dinner . . .

Later

NB In your next letter please conceal one packet of ten new Gillette blades.

New Year's Day 1940

I went to bed at five this morning, and the rest of the party I was at say they kept on at it till 7 a.m. Really, what idiots men and women are to overload their stomachs, ruin their tempers, eyes and perhaps morals, all for the lack of a little self-control. What did we do? Well, it began with a dinner to ten by the Cresswells, much drink all round, the Empire broadcast at twelve, a bottle of champagne to every couple, and kissing to beat the band. Elizabeth Cresswell is Russian, where I suppose the cold teaches them that warm embraces are the only ones worth while. Then we went rather unsteadily to a dance given by some British-American club; bad band who were shot out, and then an Englishman played the piano like Charlie Coons or Kuntz, incredibly well. Again more drink and kissing, and a certain amount of irritability, either thro' too much drink or too little kissing, I don't know which; two men in blood, had to be removed, horrid sight. I made a number of feeble attempts to go but was sprung upon by, I must say, the only attractive ladies there; and ended up asleep in an armchair with a v. pretty lill' thing, also asleep. This morning gunpowder caps aren't in it, I smell like a salvo of 12-inch guns, and as battered as the *Graf Spee*. Our Miss Capper may or may not still be the little innocent she was. Nowell and I have grave doubts as she got entangled with a coal merchant.

Later

Pale and weary I went slowly and very carefully along the Castellana to tea with the Petersons this afternoon. Just the three of us, and HE in a very bad temper with the Spaniards on account of Franco's immense speech last night. Roughly what Franco said was, 'The country is in an awful mess, it isn't my fault, you fellows were willing to die in the trenches now tuck up your sleeves and do some work; but know this, I won't have any return to the old liberal capitalist ideas, I want a revolution in Spain and anyone who gets in my way, especially if he is rich or a Monarchist, will get a kick in the pants. As for the world war there is no adequate reason for carrying it on since it is playing straight into the hands of Stalin, and a country once conquered, like Poland, is not a proper reason for other powers to continue the fight.' This last idea made Peterson mad, what the hell did Franco think about Belgium in the last war? Once conquered never to rise again? It really is a monstrous and cynical argument, borrowed from the Germans, and quite regardless of all the wretched Catholics in Poland. I think it will cost Franco much prestige. And after all, I said to Peterson, the Finns have shown us that the Russian menace is not so stupendous, why don't you tell the Minister of

Foreign Affairs that we aren't prepared to hear so much in future about the difficulty of stopping Stalin conquering new countries? No, the Spaniard today is just where Charles V was in 1540, as I pointed out to Mounsey, he is so obsessed with the Bolshevik danger that he is willing to compromise with every other evil to have his hands free for Russia—in 1540 it was for Turkey.

4 January

I have worked all day at Contraband Control stuff. The Admiral at Gibraltar is a good fellow but red tape strangles our efforts to get boats released quickly. On the whole I think neutrals don't make as much fuss as one might expect. When we are at war and the British Navy is going strong that period of decadence you so often and so loudly deplore is swallowed in the old tradition of respect and awe. It is comforting to see.

Touching wood with my left hand I feel I can say that the Spaniards have now accepted all the basic conditions of our proposals and it only remains to argue about the language in which they are expressed. I anticipate a lot of trouble over this, as the text is very complicated and has been drafted by a bunch of lawyers, and they will not like in London to agree to any modifications. However, the Ambassador thinks a fortnight from next Monday should be sufficient.

5 January

That wretched Playfair isn't coming to Madrid at all. He's got caught up in some Turkish negotiations. Of course he says it is very flattering to me to be left with the baby, but I think that HMG are wrong in not insisting that someone who began a negotiation, and began well, should finish the job.

It has rained for a week with only one day of sunshine. They all go about looking wet and bedraggled, you can see the effect of having bought no umbrellas for three years.

Later

Sir Horace Wilson[2] got a filthy letter from a man I don't know saying I must be using my connections with the Santander-Mediterraneo railway to feather my own nest. I am glad to say that Horace wrote back a real stinker, and the Treasury have sent by Eddie Playfair's hand formal condolences. Aren't some people cads?

Last night in bed I pined for you and consoled myself with wild promises of what we would do and say when we meet.

All my love—David

1. First Secretary at the British Embassy.
2. Permanent Head of the Civil Service 1939–42 and the chief industrial adviser to the government 1930–9. Also unofficial chief adviser to Neville Chamberlain on foreign affairs 1937–40.

6 January 1940 Madrid

My sweet Syb—The bag only arrived at midday yesterday, bringing the text of the treaty, and we had to read it thro' and digest it in a few hours before handing it to the Spanish Government at six.

My own special part—the War Trade clauses asking Spain to prohibit in certain ways her exports to Germany and elsewhere—were not at all well drafted, and on such bullying lines, that, with Peterson's approval, I refused to present them. After sleeping on the whole question I decided there was nothing for it but to telegraph home that I could not be responsible for the outcome of the negotiations unless I were allowed to redraft the War Trade clauses in the light of my own idea of what the Spaniards should be asked to stomach. Peterson sent his own piece to Halifax saying he fully supported the views in my telegram. So now we shall see.

MEW look on these War Trade agreements with too general an eye. They do not pay enough attention to the peculiar economic and psychological condition of each neutral. Their one idea is to stop supplies going to Germany, and so every time HMG do anything to help a neutral, MEW insist that in return the neutral must prohibit the export of certain key commodities. This seems to me as primitive as pretending there is nothing worth asking a woman to do except go to bed with you. Each neutral should be considered as a separate case, and the fundamental questions to be answered are, 'In what ways is this country helping the enemy?' and 'How can we best use our bargaining power, at the moment of making a War Trade treaty, to stop what is actually going on contrary to the British interest?'

It is time I described for you the Petersons. The Ambassador is the son of a schoolmaster from the Shetlands who became the head of McGill University in Canada. Principal Peterson glares at you from the mantelpiece of his son's study, with an immense and whiskered head, his eyes angry enough to frighten every bogy, wood-nymph and superstition out of the world, incapable of breeding anything but a fierce son. And Maurice is no exception. He too has a huge head, and his features (save for one blue eye which is walled or stuck unswivelling in his face) are magnificent, his body large and too fat. He has a bad temper, and is outrageously sardonic. Extremely intelligent and, coming from the professional middle class, he is not bred to bear inactivity with grace, or even without some loss of judgement. Therefore not a good diplomat unless the post means continuous and difficult work. His place is in the FO, stirring them all up with his bourgeois ferocity and brains. He loathes the Spaniards.

Angel Peterson—in heaven or earth could there be a more lovely name?—is as tall as I am, beautifully made with broad shoulders and a slim behind, stooping slightly, with a trick of hugging her arms in front of her so that she is poised like a statue in a narrow niche, looking down, unseeing, on the tourists. Her hair black and straight, a curved and large mouth, handsome in the big way he is, nothing ravishing and nothing wrong. She dresses like the wife of a Scottish laird, beret and tweeds and a burberry, good but uninspiring evening dresses. I cannot help liking her very much, but without that agreeable extra sense that one day she might possibly ask me to do something for her. She is devoted to her two—it may be three—sons, and I imagine does most of her own shopping without being very particular what she buys.

They both like bridge, but are bored by parties. At home she sews and he reads. They are not rich and have no desire to be.

The Spaniards only like failures, or people with very exceptional charm of manner, so these two do not and will not get on here. It is a great pity, and I see no very pleasant years for them in Madrid. They are vastly interesting to me, and I sense that he feels in my direction for another man who is thrusting as he, the Shetlander's son, must have thrust to become our youngest ambassador. Seen against their background there is some element of tragedy in their position of representatives of His Britannic Majesty.

8 January
I found Angel Peterson this morning flushed and muddy playing ball with her eldest up against the garage doors in the Embassy courtyard. It reminded me of what Dr Johnson is said to have said about the Bishop playing ball in Berkeley Square. 'There's no harm in it, but he hoped the little boys would throw stones at him if he did'—or something like it. There's certainly no harm in what the Ambassadress was doing, but only the night before some duchess said to me, 'Do you know, your Lady Peterson always gets up at 11.30 and says she must go home because she has to take the boys to the Lycée at half past eight in the morning—and in a filthy old mackintosh too'—actually the respectable burberry. There you are, you must choose between your happiness and your position.
This is being taken home by a safe hand.

All my love—David

10 January 1940 Chute

My darling David—The wireless has made me a present of Tosca, William Tell, and a Mozart quartet in succession. With the result that I'm now in a sentimental swoon and practically incapable of thought. I'm knitting (*knitting* mark you) a beautiful white wool jacket for the boiled eggs—to keep them warm for breakfast. Beside me on the floor are eight exquisite products of our Rhode Island Virgins, on a plate. Now and then they have to be fitted. For the wrapper to do its work it must be just so.
Harris[1] is keen on marriage for our pullets—and I must say I think it's pretty disappointing for them to go on laying those promising but sterile eggs—so we may buy a lusty cockerel and put up the banns. Feeding stuffs are the problem. At the moment these are very short.
I'm glad our monk is still at Guadalupe—our encounter with him is something I'll always remember. I love too your speculations on religion though I'm not much of a hand here at tossing the ball back. Though in my heart I *know* we should try to love and understand God more than we do—yet I don't personally have a great impulse or longing to do so. Touch wood—if it weren't crazy to say it I'd confess to not feeling I need him much (yet)

though if disaster overtook me I'd cling like a drowning sailor. It's shockingly instinctive and there you are shaking your head and muttering that all this comes of being a woman and a mother.

Oh! Your New Year's Eve sounds terrifying—but I'd joyfully be transformed into a drunken and pretty lill' thing if it meant I could tuck up in an armchair with you. I'm beginning to dislike my lonely bed.

11 January
I'm perched uncomfortably in the dining-room, for the boys are playing soldiers, with the table pushed against the wall and John flatteringly insisting that I would have my uses as C-in-C. The day is brilliantly fine and crystal clear with almost Spanish brilliance. The ferrets are nosing about in their box in the barn and this afternoon the boys and I go out with Harris.

Later
The ferreting went splendidly. The sun shone down from a sky of summer blue—not a cloud. We got off early and well wrapped up. But lord it was cold—I had to hide Simon under my burberry—even then he froze to such an extent that at four o'clock he had an attack of giggles that ended in sobs—so we ran home over the molehills and recovered under the administration of a huge slice of hot buttered toast. John stuck it out with no gloves on—really, that boy is centrally heated. He's quite good at the ferrets now and puts them down the holes very neatly.

Darling David—I do so long for you to come home—I lie awake often and think how lovely it will be when you creep into my bed again—I love you with all my heart.

—Sybil

1. Our gardener.

11 January 1940 Madrid

My darling love—As you know, what is happening in these days is a desperate race to arm our distant friends before the storm breaks. The way to arm the Spaniards is to get our agreement through, and I reckon we have two or three weeks' grace left to do it. Dear my love, how I wish you were here with your wise counsel and sweet self to sustain our spirits and judgement. I am actually playing the game better than I have ever done before, but with only half my clubs, if you were here what a display we would be able to give.

Someone sent me a sheaf of oranges on their boughs. I don't eat them, they look so well, but every day the servants take one, and all I can think is that they believe me to be like those silly moorhens who never notice their nest is robbed so long as one egg is left.

Did I tell you I went to Toledo? I think I did. As you say, my memory is bad for everything but cigars. The cathedral was very sunny and gay, in one chapel, unusually shut, there was a service to a Madonna on a silver altar, eight or ten steps of shimmering metal, winking in the candlelight. The chapel organ was small and tinkly, just right for the silvery scene. Bunches of white carnations and one gold and jewelled chalice, better taste than one finds in most Spanish churches. The serving boys wore dirty red under short lace surplices and the priest all in white and gold brocade. Rather precious and perfect, and so divinely different from 'the common muck of the world'.

12 January

Telegrams in last night from FO giving HE and self full powers to do what we think best in the matter of War Trade guarantees, so that's one more fence got over, and in a most cordial and appreciative manner, no signs of fuss or disagreement. It is a pity that more great firms do not trust their representatives on the spot as HMG does theirs. I should like to see a telegram from Eric Bowater,[1] 'I have read and appreciated your arguments and am prepared to leave to your discretion all points raised in paras . . . I would prefer to give way in the following order . . . but do not insist . . .' That is the sort of thing to make the troops loyal and hard-working. And so this afternoon *tout le monde à bataille.*

All my love, darling Syb—David

1. Chairman of Bowater Ltd.

12 January 1940 Madrid

My darling Syb—I did not tell you—and I do now because I like to think you like to know—that the FO slipped a neat little clause into the treaty giving us power, at a later date, to do what I suggested in my 'Access to Raw Materials' paper.[1] I suppose there was some discussion between departments, and the FO said, 'Well, there isn't time to thrash it out now, but let us take powers to think about it at leisure.' I'm quite sure the Spaniards won't know what is up, but that doesn't matter, and when I get home I can find out how best to put the idea into practice. HMG have not sent the Embassy or me any comments on the paper other than the clause itself, which is the best sort of answer.

All my love—David

1. Power to use part of the sterling credit to pay for goods produced anywhere in the sterling area.

13 January 1940 Madrid

My darling Syb—Another piece about the Petersons. I met Angel last night at a cocktail party, her long body hunched up in a chair, 'stiff all over from a ride with the boys', her big hands reddish from the cold, her lips and nails unblushing, frightening away one old man after another as they tried to make themselves agreeable. 'Maurice,' she told me, 'is in a bad temper, he refuses to come out. His fire won't keep alight and this morning he burnt his latest *Times* trying to make it go; what can I do with this awful coal we get in Madrid?' 'Have you any bellows?' say I, who had heard the envoy's curses as his newspaper went up in flames. 'No, I can't find any in Madrid.' So today I went early to the Rastro in search of '*fuelles*'—pretty name—and drew a complete blank, but a lounger who heard me asking for the tenth time murmured something about there being an old gypsy who lived in the Cava Baja near the church of San Isidrio, and who used to make bellows. Off I went to the church, and in a very few minutes tracked down the old hag, black and round as a cauldron, and sure enough, she is a bellows maker, makes three pair a week, and had two on hand, 10 pts. each, so I bought them both, and gave one to the Petersons and one to the Cresswells. The news is now all round Madrid—at least in the *cuerpo diplomatico*—that that charming young Englishman knows where to buy bellows. I must now choose between the chic and the fatigue of being the only person who has the hag's address, or abandon both, and live a quiet life.

15 January

Something bad is in the air today. A pestilential depression has descended on everybody, the Embassy, the Delegation, the Diplomatic Corps, the Spanish FO. One realises that we have only been half at war for four months, that the real thing may be very different, when food is scarce at home, when we see and hear of destruction, read casualty lists, lose friends and hope . . . all these things may come. I felt them coming suddenly in that mist on the way to Guadalupe, but why their shadow should so quickly and so darkly fall on us today I can't tell. As far as our negotiations are concerned it is true, and it was to be expected, that as we draw nearer to signing we are attacked with greater and greater fury by the Germans. Their propaganda of lies and insults is the measure of our possible success. I am not abashed. My friends are a bit down, and naturally I catch their mood to some extent, but if the Spaniards—and it won't be the Spaniards as such but only Franco and one or two others at the top—are persuaded by the Germans to refuse our terms, it will be they who lose and who must come back to us later; we should suffer a blow to our immediate hopes and pride, but in the long run we should lose, as a country, very little. I am not going to succumb to 'the hunger of the imagination that preys on life'.

Diplomacy teaches you that the relations between men and women, and between states, must be expressed in concrete terms, in pacts and treaties and laws, and that these undertakings, to be binding, must be based on a common morality. Aspirations never bound anybody to anybody. People must work through institutions. Chute must have its Parish Council, and should have its playing fields. The villagers must have a means of learning each other's needs and how to fulfil them. The good life does not happen by itself: faith without works won't last. Someone must take the chair, someone write the minutes, someone collect the funds and someone spend them. So with our life in England, with which we are so desperately disappointed, since after 1918 comes

1939, we must overhaul our institutions and our moral background. One acts on the other.

Here we are still in trouble with these damned Germans who keep on saying and printing lies about our intentions, when I pass the German Embassy I feel murderous; very wrong, very unchristian. Next week things will be clearer.

Matters aren't improved by a horrid tendency to gloat at home over a treaty 'as good as signed'. Would you believe it, even Sir John Simon[1] wrote out a few lines of highly complimentary stuff! And it isn't signed, and there's going to be a lot of trouble before it is.

And lordie! How cold it is! The fountains are all frozen up, which is said to be very rare, and the ground is so hard you stub your toe on the mud print of last week's walk. We can't use our sitting-room any more: no heating at all.

I'm having the greatest fun with Marshal Pétain.[2] I love and admire the Marshal very much, but I don't think I like Pétain very well; still, it's the baton that makes the man.

Dear Syb, it is monstrous to say that going away from you makes me love you more, but I haven't been so happy thinking about you, ever before. In my cold bed, I wake up and squeak with loneliness.

I'll write again tomorrow if I can.

All my love—David

1. Chancellor of the Exchequer 1937–40.
2. I wish I had reported something of these interviews. A week later, see letter of 22nd, I became a firm friend as well as an admirer.

20 January 1940 — Madrid

My darling Syb—'I have nothing to say—which is the best reason in the world for writing; for one must have a great regard for anybody one writes to, when one begins a letter neither on ceremony nor on business' (Horace Walpole, 1774). I have no 'piece' in mind to recite to you, but I begin a letter because I like to chat to my love, and I have found in the half-hours so spent the greatest pleasure in Madrid. I expect something will turn up. Turn up indeed, your cake turned up today in that capacious, but not confidential bag, which makes of every Monday a possible birthday, and every diplomat a baby. The first slices of the cake were heaven, and Mrs Capper is at least equalled.

Oh! I know something else to tell you. How queer it was, I feel strange about it still. Dining last night with a grass widow, two girls aged about twenty, and three chaps, we started at 10.30, after drinking too much—except me who so dislikes feeling fuddled—and retired at 12.30 to the gramophone and more drinks. Suddenly I knew I didn't like any of them—the girls were the New Year's Eve set, I hadn't seen them since—and as they didn't seem to be noticing me I put out my hand to the bookcase next to my chair, and pulled down a volume of letters from 'Lord Oxford to a Woman Friend'. I knew who the woman was, Hilda Harrison, because, when at Oxford, I used to go to her house on Boar's Hill as well as to the Asquiths at Sutton Scotney. The book opened somewhere in the year 1923, and there in page after page were descriptions of the Oxford life I remember, of Anthony Asquith[1] and his friends, of Elizabeth and Antoine,[2] of Eddie Marsh[3] and the Bonham-Carters,[4] Garsington,[5] Julian Morrell and Rachel MacCarthy[6] . . . Madrid faded completely, and I went back again to hot days in New College garden, or walking briskly with Sligger[7] round Magdalen on a winter's evening, entertaining with Antony Hornby in Broad Street, but chiefly I remembered, like the chorus in a song, that sense of uneasy loneliness which I felt so often as I turned into Holywell to go home to my digs. I must have *seemed* very happy at Oxford, to Mother, to my friends, perhaps to myself; having a talent for turning aside from unpleasant things I think I disguised what was going on in myself. Only last night I knew without fear of contradiction that what will remain largest in my memory of Oxford is that uneasy loneliness . . . would I be glad if someone knocked on my door and came in, or wouldn't I? Did I or didn't I care for my friends, did they or didn't they care for me? Sitting in my Madrid armchair I was dreaming of these emotional difficulties, when I was quite properly hit with a cushion. It was past 1.30 a.m. and I refused to go to a night club, I just couldn't after my hour at Oxford; one of the girls cried a bit, drink I think, but I have stayed here too long and am bothered now by the number of them who have 'a fixation' (this is the word the one of nineteen used to me) for your loving and quite single-hearted husband.

Sunday 21 January
During the night the snow has piled up again, deeper than ever. This time the trams are defeated, and only an occasional car with chains ventures along the Castellana. My radiators are stone cold and I am muffled up like a Finn; but the coffee is hot and the paper has speeches by Winston and by Halifax that cheer the heart. They will do much good here, and it is noteworthy that both are printed almost in full. The only thing the Germans have managed to do is to get a big black headline, 'Churchill and Halifax say Germany is stronger than the Allies', no one minds that one very much. The Ambassador attributes part of the change in the press, which is not a big change, to our negotiations; I think Finland is more important.

22 January
At lunch with the Wyndham Torrs[8] today were the Duke of Alba, the Pétains (Peterson says the Marshal has married the same woman twice), the Duchess of Santoña, the Condesa de la Maza, and myself. After a fidgety start we had a grand party. Alba gave us a chance by being stupidly aggressive—it is his pop-pop way of speaking rather than what he says—about the danger to private property which must result from paying the cost of the war. The Condesa and I leapt at him, hand-in-hand, brandishing the plain fact that the issue is so fundamental, so overwhelming that a thousand pounds this way or that makes no difference. What is the issue? said the Marshal; and then we were off, an hour and a quarter without a check. Perhaps what the 84-year-old Marshal said was the most interesting, his experience and his age giving to it an authority that your dukes and duchesses cannot peep at. Pétain's line was that we must make a simple peace plan now, he did not agree with the French Government when they put a damper on the War Aims controversy in England, altho' he thought the controversy itself was conducted by a pack of idiotic intellectuals (ha! ha! piped D. Eccles). Soldiers, he said, won't stay in trenches for ever, they must know what is coming afterwards, and equally important, neutrals must decide one way or the other, because the war is so obviously economic ('*Ce jeune homme ici représente le blocus anglais, il me donne plus de confiance que tous les généraux que je connais*'—blush from the *jeune homme*). So let us make posters and placards of our peace plan, not saying definitely how we shall treat Germany, that will depend on how

the war is won, but how we will treat our friends and how we will treat each other. If we can give a promise, that will carry conviction, to put our own house in order, the soldiers will die gladly, the neutrals will join us, and the enemy will collapse.

By this time Alba and the Duchess were silenced, as aristocrats of their age have no idea how to treat large numbers of people decently, and therefore no contribution to make to any peace plan. The conversation was continued between the Marshal, the Condesa (more or less our generation) and myself.

We asked Pétain for the '*grandes lignes*' of the peace plan. He said quite simply that that was our job—the Condesa's and mine—he was too old, but he would offer one or two observations. First he quoted George Washington's speech on his retirement from public life to be a country gentleman at Mount Vernon. It seems he said, 'The main supports of political prosperity are morality and religion . . . and morality cannot exist without religion.' The first thing, said Pétain, is to recognise that man did not, never could make the world, or deserve the world by his own labour on it. The world is given to man, in trust for the whole human race past, present and to be born. Absolute property (shiver from Alba) cannot exist, nor can absolute equality. Article 1 on the placard would be a restatement of the existence of God as the Creator of the world, and of the brotherhood of man implied in a Heavenly Father. Other articles would outline practical machinery for putting into effect the Christian doctrine: free trade, mobility of labour, access to raw materials, one armed force for the whole bloc, etc. The sort of plan we talked of is not so important as the idea of having a plan, and one restricted to how we intend to treat each other and our friends. It was extremely interesting, and the Marshal and I parted with a warm embrace.

24 January

I have missed a day in your Madrid diary. Yesterday at six we had our first full meeting with the Spaniards since we submitted the text to them three weeks ago. Since then we have been arguing in sub-committees in a rather unsatisfactory manner. However, all went well yesterday—we got out at five to ten—and I have agreed with them all the War Trade clauses which might have given trouble. We are therefore left with a number of details and differences of small importance on the financial side. How long these will take to agree I don't know, I should think a fortnight, as the Spaniards—who only have one team of negotiators—are carrying on discussions with two other countries at the same time. The whole business is quite mediaeval and reminds me of the life of Charles V I was reading at Ruthin, where it was common for an embassy to leave the Netherlands for Madrid in one April and return the next, or even after two years. The Germans may make some last-minute troubles for us but I do not think that, once the War Trade clauses have been agreed as they have, there is any other ground so favourable for kicking up a fuss.

—David

1. Film director.
2. Prince and Princess Bibesco.
3. Sir Edward Marsh, private secretary to Winston Churchill 1917–22 and 1924–9.
4. Lady Violet and Sir Maurice Bonham-Carter.
5. The house of Philip and Lady Ottoline Morrell.
6. Daughter of Sir Desmond MacCarthy, later married to Lord David Cecil.
7. F. F. Urquhart, Dean of Balliol.
8. Brigadier W. W. T. Torr, CMG, DSO, MC, was British Military Attaché in Madrid.

22 January 1940 Chute

My darling David—It must be the approaching shadow of great events[1] that gives us a new edge to the perceptions and sharpens the sight. I take a keener pleasure than ever yet in the common things of the countryside. A trick of light above a frost-bound field—a mute and miserable bird on its twig. And I store up all the children's nonsense as so much priceless treasure.

'Do you think, Mummie, if I caught Hitler that they'd make me an officer?'

'The Air Force couldn't have a fight above the clouds, could they, Mom? There wouldn't be room. It's full of dead people.'

I'm sure I've a lot in common just now with the murderer

eating his final breakfast. His tongue curling with relish round the last bursting sausage, while the hangman waits outside.

All my love, darling David—Sybil

1. i.e. the end of the 'phoney' war.

27 January 1940 Madrid

My darling love—What you say about going back to the City after the war is much on my mind. I ought not to be tempted into day-dreaming about circumstances I can't guess at. By fits and starts I am ambitious, and am not without 'the illness that should attend it', but when the fit comes I realise I behave more like a good minister than a good civil servant. I say to myself the FO might be an exception, but this might be due, how much I can't tell, to admiration for the present Secretary of State;[1] I don't think I could work for Eden,[2] but without insulting Frank Phillips[3] it is safe to predict that I would rather work for Halifax in any capacity than go back to the CM.[4] All the chaps in the Embassy here cheerfully declare they would follow me if I started any movement; poor dears, it's so boring in Madrid I expect they would follow as far as Paris, or even Dover.

I love you for saying you'll be in it too, and I know it is true, we shall not desert each other, we have survived our tenth year. For two people to begin with such happiness is sometimes an obstacle to the realisation of themselves outside their home; it may develop into a positive barrier against ambition and success; when it does, the world's well lost, and we shouldn't blame such fortunate creatures for stepping aside from public life. Any example of happiness is precious, and infectious, it cleanses the air of fouler stuff.

29 January
Do you remember El Greco's huge martyrdom of San Mauricio? It was in the picture gallery at the Escorial, where it had been intended for the church, but Felipe II wouldn't have so many bare legs in such a place. Now it's in the Prado, clean and shining like a stained-glass window. I love it more than any picture I know. San Mauricio, a Roman commander, persuaded his whole legion to

accept martyrdom rather than renounce the faith. Philip, I suppose, wanted a picture of hundreds of mangled, but decently clothed, soldiers, El Greco painted, not the moment of death itself, but S. Mauricio and his officers speaking together just after they had taken their decision. Very near them in the sky are angels with the palms and laurels they are going to win; further off, in false perspective, you see the same officers with their men, shrunk and secondary, some being killed, others doing ordinary things. The effect is to exalt and isolate this group of life-size figures, who are at peace with the idea of death. Their faces and gestures have a beauty, gentleness and love that reconciles me to all the evil in the world. Death is over them and they are happy.

El Greco has quite put out of my head all the other painters in the Prado.

All my love—David

1. Lord Halifax, Foreign Secretary 1939–40.
2. Resigned as Foreign Secretary, 1938; Secretary of State for Dominion Affairs, September 1939; War Office, May 1940.
3. Chairman of Central Mining and Investment Corporation in which I worked before the war.
4. Central Mining.

31 January 1940 Chute

My darling love—The last few days have been sad ones for our lovely Chute. On Saturday night it froze again with dreadful suddenness and rained at the same time. We awoke on Sunday morning to a world in icicles. I have never seen anything like it. Every blade of grass, each twig and bracken stem was entombed in ice. We all exclaimed upon the beauty of the scene and in the excitements and anxieties that followed quite failed to realise the sinister and evil power of all this wizardry. For at ten o'clock Mrs Stainton[1] appeared in floods of tears to say that during the night her baby who had been ill for some days became desperately bad (he had pneumonia) and the doctor had been and said that oxygen was vital and at once. Could I do anything? We gave her cups of tea and some comfort and after a struggle with the chains I set out over glassy roads to Andover. All telephones broken. I threw myself on the mercy of the Matron at the Andover Hospital who is a superb woman — and she and Packer between them produced the equipment and with their advice dinning in our amateurish ears we set out on the journey home.

The baby looked and sounded dreadfully bad — but Mrs Austen[2] was on duty and a tower of strength and between us we gave it a first dose of oxygen. In the afternoon Daddy[3] struggled up the icebound hill like a saint and gave some kind advice to bolster up the mother and help out the doctor who couldn't get back that day.

So with one thing and another we failed to notice our drooping trees under their icy burden. By tea time the branches had begun to snap. And on it went all night long. I lay in bed with my fingers in my ears and couldn't sleep a wink. Oh, David, you can't imagine how dreadful it was to hear!

So still the night was. Uncanny, evil and quiet. And every few moments another bough would crack like a pistol shot and go crashing to the ground. All night it froze and rained alternately, piling up the ice, wrapping it round and round — and in the grey morning all was desolation — boughs everywhere — trees drooping and maimed. I just burst into tears and wept like a lunatic. It seemed so destructive, brutal and wanton. Somehow it just got me — and I behaved with shameful weakness. Chute has made up for so much and even it was not to escape destruction.

Mummie was an angel and full of consolation and Simon made me a whole fleet of paper boats 'Because you are sad'. But I couldn't stop thinking of you and Monday was just no good, I couldn't lift my head up.

Mercifully the baby was better and needed attention, so that helped a bit. By this time the whole countryside was encased in ice and impassable. Yesterday the same. No sign of thaw and Mummie, Grandnan and I watched the snow-laden sky all day terrified lest it would fall and with its additional weight complete the wreck. But it didn't. Today the thaw set in and after skidding to Andover through incredible wreckage of boughs, snow drifts and telephone wires — the ice was loose enough for Harris,[4] Hawkins[5] and I to go round the small trees shaking it off. These are not hurt. The baby is better again. And now that we can get to work on reconstruction our spirits are higher. Harris cried as well as I!

1. Wife of the man who kept the pub at the top of the hill leading down to Dean Farm.
2. Our invaluable cook.
3. Lord Dawson of Penn.
4. and 5. Our gardeners.

1 February 1940 — Madrid

I lunched with the Petersons, the Pétains and General Muñoz Grande who is minister without portfolio, and now that Suñer is in half-disgrace he has more influence with Franco than anyone else. A man about forty-five, very dark and hatchety, with great character and no nonsense about him, lived much in Morocco, a brilliant soldier: I was much impressed, and thought him far the ablest leader of the New Spain I have met. We had a long talk on the need to keep people on the land, rural housing, travelling cinemas, buses, midwives, and altogether I got the idea that he could and would do much for Spain. My Spanish is just equal to this sort of conversation, but not with facility.

All my love, I pine to see you, talk to you.

—David

3 February 1940 — 32 Wimpole Street

My darling love—That uneasy loneliness which makes the young suffer a great deal—the memory of its pangs washed over me in a huge wave as I read your letter. We may be poor—we'll certainly be older by the time this war is over—but we'll be together and at any rate one can never again be tortured by the obscure miseries—the incomprehensible melancholy of youth.

I love you—Sybil

4 February 1940 — Madrid

Darling Syb—If only I could have you here for a week, a day even, I have given so much lately to other people, so much of my good spirits, that I pine to be refreshed and to draw from you comfort and cheer just as at night I draw sleep from your precious self.

The El Greco rooms in the Prado are like the treasure chamber of some cathedral, suddenly as you come to the door a flood of jewelled light breaks on the dingy old Velasquez, Italians, and Coellos. You know how when you are motoring in Spain you can cross a dusty grey plain, climb a little pass and round the corner all is light and colour. Just this sort of breath-catching joy comes from the first glimpse—long before you can distinguish particular pictures—you have of the two El Greco rooms. I reject all Somerset Maugham's nonsense in *Don Fernando* about Greco. And when you see such beauty, such exquisite work of man, doesn't it give one hope, that after wars and more wars, sieges of three years, air-raids, Bolshevism and God knows what horrors, still there are lovely things and still we can hope for more artists who will live to make more lovely things? Our temporary difficulties are nothing to their achievements.

5–6 February

Again we have made progress with the negotiations and I begin almost boldly to say that Friday week will see the Ambassador's pen in action. He continues to be furious with MEW on my account, I hope he takes action. He said to me, 'Why don't they see we are in a life and death struggle, everything they care for is at stake, and the damn fools want to employ worn-out diplomats for the sake of preserving the hierarchy.'

Wilfred Greene,[1] Francis Rodd[2] and Eddie Playfair are in Rome carrying on similar negotiations with Italy. Eddie writes to me by air mail saying he has pulled the Master of the Rolls's leg, and Francis's, by telling them that if I could be spared from Madrid the Rome Agreement would be through in a week or two. They must be having great fun together.

François de Seynes[3] dined with me and three of the girl friends last night, we had an excellent dinner after two cocktail parties, but what astonished me was that they (Spanish haw-haw girls) didn't like him. There may be some pretty deep antipathy between the Spanish and the French. I find François very agreeable, as always. I'm appallingly snob in my dining friends now, but Madrid is too small to draw back, no one seems to have an intellectual or professional acquaintance, and I much prefer the aristocracy to the business classes. I long to turn my back on the lot of them and dine *à deux* with you for a month, with the legitimate hope of going to bed afterwards. Here it becomes really tiresome how many offers of bed one gets in the most casual way, morals have suffered very much during the Civil War.

7 February
My chronicle seems to have broken down this week, so have my clothes, etc. All at once I notice my shoes want mending, I have gone thro' the seat of one of my pyjamas, some holes appear in socks and hankies, I'm dreadfully bored with my suits, my old black hat is truly my old hat, no more decent toothpaste, or lanoline or hair stuff . . . Everything points to my return. I must get this agreement signed, make a speech about it to the colony, which HE has promised them I will, and off I shall go.

I lunched today with the Fontanars,[4] they are the most attractive married couple I have yet met in Madrid. He is about forty, very English and a thoroughly sound and intelligent man. The Condesa is perhaps twenty-eight, the daughter of Urquijo the banker, and as pretty and lively as say Rose Hinch[5] (Isabel is really much prettier!). They are the one thoroughly happy married pair I know, and are famous for it; they both love books and pictures, and all things agreeable, and only talk politics at intervals and then with a detachment and good taste rare in Spain. He pretends to do some work for an insurance company, but I don't think it is very serious. They have two Grecos and a Goya, the Grecos not very good, one too early and the other too woolly, looks as tho' he did it quickly to make a bit of cash. On the other hand the Goya is most interesting as it is the first serious portrait he is known to have done, and although he has taken too much trouble the talent he shows is prodigious. They also have a lovely library, a small boy about four, and altogether I can promise you'll like them very much, if we are ever here on a visit and can do a little lunching and dining.

All my love—David

1. Master of the Rolls.
2. Lord Rennell.
3. A great friend of ours who married the daughter of the Swedish Ambassador in London.

4. Conde and Condesa de Fontanar, leading Spanish Royalists.
5. Viscountess Hinchingbrooke.

6 February 1940 Chute

My darling love—Lettie Benson[1] spent one afternoon with us. She is a scrawny, lively creature and Ruby Lindsay's[2] oldest friend. They call each other by affectionate, abusive and girlish names. 'Hi, Scum,' and so on. If they hadn't both of them a good deal of intelligence and charm—it would be pretty tiresome. I find these highly-born creatures very interesting to study. It seems to me they are full of wit and intelligence—but very little wisdom. They sparkle without judgement—and are the natural prey of quacks and charlatans. They exhibit a taste for the bizarre and the eccentric and will be off down the wind after any new sensation. In a way they are childish in spite of their ease and sophistication. They don't possess the hard-headed common sense of the middle classes who have known the struggle.

But there is one altogether admirable quality. They are indestructibly gallant. Nothing dismays them, they rarely complain, they *never* whine. When life has taken a bad turn they ignore it. They rarely discuss their troubles and if they are unhappy they merely gossip and laugh in brisker tempo. I admire them very much for this—it's a grand characteristic. It's in such moments that one sees on what bold lines their class is built.

I'm reading Elizabeth Bibesco's new novel.[3] It's odd when in life she is such a bore that her books should still be so enchanting.

Darling David, I do love you—Sybil

1. Lady Lettice Benson.
2. A friend of the Asquiths and a great gardener.
3. *The Romantic.*

14 February 1940 Chute

I'm quite all right—but just sometimes solitude turns into loneliness and then I have a disastrous premonition that the last green years are going to waste away.

What will you look like when I see you again? Funny, isn't it—we've never been three months apart. Are you fat or thin? Older or younger? I have an idea you may have changed. Perhaps I have too.

Anyway I know I'll leap internally for joy—get it signed, my sweet, get it signed.

I love you—Sybil

10 February 1940 Madrid

Darling Syb—I keep thinking of you at Chute and all the trees, perhaps it won't be so bad when the leaves come, and you know in other countries they cut back big trees much more rigorously, and then they grow again. I'm glad to feel how much you love Chute. If anything ever happened to either of us the other would always love Chute still more because of what it had meant to both.

Yesterday Pepe Mamblas took me to lunch with the Duke and Duchess of Sueca, to see their Goya which he said was the best portrait Goya ever did. The picture is a dream. A life-sized portrait of the Condesa de Chinchon, quite young, in a white satin ball dress edged with blue, sitting facing you on a small chair against a dark background, nothing else in the big canvas. Her hair is fair and fuzzy, in it blue ribbons and green feathers. The face is thin and exquisitely painted, and everything else, hair, hands, dress, chair, etc. slightly impressionistic and rendered in the same harmony of understatement. The effect is as though you met at a real ball. You would naturally look first at her face, and there it is, a simple sort of beauty quite perfect to see and you would be fascinated, at any rate for a moment or two, and when you came to look at her arms and dress and where she was sitting, your eyes would be a little dim from the radiance of the face and you would see all these extras a trifle mistily, and of course you wouldn't see the background at all, because you couldn't take your eyes off the lady. It seemed to me that Goya had meant to put all that in his picture, if he had not had some such notion I don't know why the world is unanimous in calling it a masterpiece. (Sueca was offered £60,000 for her.) Everything except the face is carelessly painted, but it must be deliberate or the result would not be so overwhelming. It is a vision of that 'first sight' when we are said to fall in love.

So many Spaniards have told me that after three years away from their houses in Madrid, not knowing if they would ever find any of their lovely things again, when they came back and little by little 'recuperated' now a bit of furniture, now a picture, a carpet, a few books, they seldom felt intense joy to see these things again; nearly always they are surprised at their own indifference. They want, they say, either new things or nothing at all. There is some profound emotion behind this attitude, some aftermath of tragedy that Shakespeare would have seized in a line. (When the maid asks Desdemona what on earth she feels like after listening to Othello's terrifying outburst, what does Desdemona say, is she upset? 'No, faith, half-asleep.') Of course all these people here are still convalescent from the Civil War, they are not yet re-arranging their gutted houses, but I think they speak the truth when they say that their possessions have lost some of their value for always. Take note of this curious fact, and see if it does not happen to us after our war.

Sunday

I am writing shakily on my bed, as I have to dine and dance with the Greek Minister and his wife tonight, and have been all day at La Granja, so a little rest comes in well between the two. The sky was blue, the sun quite warm, the gardens empty, birds singing, water bubbling in the gulleys—a most pleasing scene and we had a lovely walk right up beyond the lake to the edge of the woods where the mountain with its snow begins. Lunch at our old friend the Europeo, fried eggs and veal cutlets, and an excellent red wine which I warmed in front of the stove to the great amusement of a party of officers.

Monday

The Greek party was vast, stifling and boring. I left at two, among the first. I danced a little with the Sueca, and Carmen Ybes, and one or two diplomatic ladies, and then had a turn with the young lady who is causing me so much trouble, pleaded work and went to bed. The consequence is I am in great form today with my nose on the trail of a real whale of an idea about stopping German trade here. Our Miss Capper is now typing out my memorandum and I shall go along to Peterson in half an hour.

Tomorrow is our great day, we are meeting the Spaniards 11–2 and 6–9, we ought to break the back of their opposition in six hours. My chaps are nervous. We have been given too many instructions, but I contemplate doing some Nelson blind-eye stuff if things go too slowly. After the way MEW want to treat me I have no more respect for them and I shall try to finish off the treaty as I think it can best be done. My belief in knowing where HMG's interests lie is strong enough to overcome qualms about London. Peterson's approval is all that is necessary, and he will play up.

Wednesday
We had a terrific day yesterday and again this morning. I can't say we have agreed on all points but we are a lot nearer, and I really think the Spaniards are getting sick of arguing. It is a great thing to outlast a Spaniard in argument. There is some obstacle in the background that keeps holding us up. Peterson says it is German influence. I think it is partly that, but more the effects of the Civil War, both *our* attitudes during the war—the Duchess of Atholl[1] and the Dean of Canterbury[2]—and *their* weariness after the struggle. In some ways I think we have been too ambitious in the scope of our treaty, but if it comes off, well and good. The expense of good humour and optimism required to keep the whole thing going and within the bounds of possible achievement has been terrific. I find I have lost weight and grown grey hairs, signs, I suppose, of the conflict. Nowell and Ellis-Rees,[3] my two colleagues, did very well this morning, maintaining HMG's most awful instructions with a charm and firmness they had never shown previously. I wish I could have lunched with them afterwards to congratulate them in earnest, but I had to dash off to meet some Spanish Foreign Office people—the Gladwyns of Madrid—and to listen to a long and rambling conversation on the war and the Spring offensive. For the moment I can't take these things in, but I did manage to have a crack or two at German cynicism, which is the feature of Germany's attitude to them in the Civil War that now causes most heart-burning. One wants them to get out of their heads that some countries are their friends, others their enemies, for ever and for aye. History books don't show constancy of friendship between nations but constancy of self-interest. There is no other principle. And our self-interest now is the preservation of a Christian Europe. If

some country, who helped us in a past and temporary emergency, now plays false to this Europe we all long for, that country must cease to be our friend. It is the only line of conduct open to honest men; and nations must be honest as well as men. I must go to the Embassy and report progress to HE.

15 February
Gladwyn wrote to me at great length. Says Halifax enjoys my letters. That is really good news. They seem calm in the FO but prepared for something disagreeable. I long to be home. We are having another struggle tonight, I will write to you about it in the morning.

Friday
Well, it didn't go off so badly. Although they refused our final offer, their refusal was half hearted, and when I got really worked up (my friends said I looked as if I would eat them) the Spaniards said they would refer to ministers and I'm sure they'll give in. Tomorrow we shall know. I'll send you a wire saying all is over.

My darling love, I do so want you. Just to hold you once again. I know I shall rave with fury at all the delays on the journey. You *must* come up to London to meet me. In the best possible circumstances I can leave here next weekend. Peterson has been told he can hold me as long as he wants, but I'll get round him.

Love to Polly and Simo', my dearest Syb—David

1. 'The Red Duchess.'
2. 'The Red Dean.'
3. Treasury representative replacing Edward Playfair on our mission.

20 February 1940 — Chute

My dearest love—Harris, Hawkins and I have spent some hours on the apple tree which is going to be a real teaser to bolster up. We shall have a great struggle before giving in—and we may pull it off.

I've been reading *The Bridge of San Luis Rey*.[1] How lovely it is—it loses nothing by the years. It may be a frail work but it houses a magnificent conception. Do you remember Madre

Maria del Pilar: ' "Even now," she thought, "almost no one remembers Esteban and Pepita, but myself. Camila alone remembers her Uncle Pio and her son . . . But soon we shall all die and all memory of those five will have left the earth, and we ourselves shall be loved for a while and forgotten. But the love will have been enough; all those impulses of love return to the love that made them. Even memory is not necessary for love. There is a land of the living and a land of the dead, and the bridge is love, the only survival, the only meaning." ' There's comfort in it.

The Americans are a joke—aren't they? They're so mortally afraid of being involved that they hardly dare clap when they feel like clapping nor hiss when they're so inclined and the result is a kind of muted 'Hear hear' with an anxious look round to see if too many people are listening.

Rather like you, my sweet, when I kiss you in the street!

1. By Thornton Wilder. I gave Sybil this book before we were engaged.

19 February 1940 Madrid

My darling Syb—We have had an exciting weekend. On Saturday morning we met the Spanish negotiators for what we had hoped would be the last full meeting. Not at all: they counter-proposed on our final offer in such a way that there was no possibility of our accepting. We had then to estimate whether they were really prepared to break off negotiations on this one outstanding point or whether it was another bluff. They said they were ready to break. Our troops went and had tea with Peterson in the afternoon and we decided (1) to report home the Spanish counter-offer (2) to make it clear to HMG that we thought it unacceptable (3) to make use of an appointment that Peterson already had to see the Minister of Foreign Affairs on Monday morning, to tell the Spanish Government that we were prepared to break on their counter-offer.

My chaps were terribly depressed on Saturday evening, partly the result of such long negotiations and partly because they (I included) rather doubted if Peterson would have time to put the complex points about the financial clause at issue in such a way that the Minister of Foreign Affairs would understand, and could afterwards withdraw [his opposition]. I admit I went up to bed pretty gloomy. On the mat inside my door was an invitation from the Duchess of Tetuan to a drink next day at 7.30.

Now Blanquita Tetuan is the MFA's[1] housekeeper. He lives in the Palacio Viana, a magnificent house near the Royal Palace, and she, a widow, has a couple of rooms on the third floor. I thought that heaven was on our side, so in the morning I rang her up and said that our negotiations had gone sour and could she arrange for me to have a talk to the MFA that evening. She would do her best. When I returned from lunching near Toledo there was a message to say that Beigbeder would see me at eight sharp in his private apartments.

With some difficulty I found him in a library on the ground floor, where he lives in three rooms quite cut off from the rest of the Palace, which only begins to be lived in at the first floor. His study is lined with bookcases to the ceiling, unfortunately with glass fronts, filled with a past Duke of Rivas's collection of eighteenth-century bindings: very fine. He adores Morocco, and all over the room were Arab clothes in incredible stuffs and colours. He began by making me put on a velvet robe and look at myself in a long glass in his bedroom. I didn't fancy charades in the place of commerical treaties but it was a necessary preliminary. His bed is beautiful, high and nearly square, covered with a purple damask shot with silver, and a velvet back, it had either been used for the birth or the loves of a king, I didn't quite gather which.

He thought we should want a drink while we talked, but no one answered the bell. 'This is typical of the Spanish administration, we must get it for ourselves.' On hands and knees we searched the cupboards to find the bottle and some biscuits.

He began by talking of war psychology. He knew well what it meant to the nerves of a people to be fighting a war. The French, during their recent negotiations here, had shown frequent signs of irritability. He had calmed them and an agreement would be signed. For three months he had heard of nothing but good temper on our part, progress slow but always progress. Now for the first time he learns of a deadlock, frayed tempers, etc. He would intervene personally and all should be settled in a few days.

I got in my first word after ten to fifteen minutes of this sort of stuff. I said that I was glad he realised that calm or irritable we were the representatives of a nation at war. I thought that his negotiators did not always reckon with this circumstance. What had they told him would be the results of a breakdown in our negotiations? With charming frankness he said he had heard that this would mean no loan for Spain, but otherwise trade would go on very much as usual, buying a little, selling a little, and no tiresome obligations for Spain to begin to repay her pre-war debts. Sadly and slowly I began to disillusion him; in war the exports of the United Kingdon and of the British Empire were subject to control by licence and supplies were inadequate to the demand, and with no agreement Spain could not hope to obtain the share of these essential raw materials that she needed. It was obvious HMG had to ration buyers in existing circumstances, and where in the queue of purchasers would Spain be if we returned to London empty-handed? He was very impressed. Did I really think there was need to hurry the conclusion of the treaty? Certainly, prices were rising and stocks falling.

He then asked what was the particular obstacle to our agreement, and I think he was just nicely prepared to listen to a technical argument. The obstacle is their unwillingness to make adequate provision in the treaty for the transfer to the UK of current financial payments such as insurance premiums, royalties, patents, interest, dividends, personal expenses of UK subjects in Spain, etc. I asked him to consider the history of the UK, how in a narrow and damp island we had come to support a population of over forty millions, simply by exporting our financial services as well as our goods. We could only live by continuing this system of being the world's financial centre. Therefore when we offered Spain, for the first time in our history, the unique advantage of spending 45 per cent of the proceeds of her sales to the UK on goods grown or produced outside the UK in the sterling area, it was obvious that the remaining 55 per cent must be so used as to satisfy the business and banking community in England that the whole arrangement was just and reasonable. He said that he had always looked on the UK as a fat cow that would give much milk if properly handled. I said that I had aspirations to be a farmer and could heartily agree with the second half of his observation.

We then discussed in detail the objections raised by the Spaniards to the methods proposed by us for making these financial transfers. He mentioned their dislike of setting up a precedent which other countries having financial claims on Spain would try to copy. 'But,' I said, 'they are not fat cows.' He easily agreed that it was not possible for us to admit comparison with Switzerland or Belgium. The sense of personal honour for once worked in our favour. In the end he promised to give instructions to the Spanish Delegation to withdraw their proposal and to agree to ours. 'Mind you,' he shouted at me as I crossed the courtyard, 'I am going to treat you as a special case, not because I love you, but because the British Empire is rich.' 'And I prefer,' I replied echoing round the patio, 'my own merits to your imagination, our friendship will be more lasting.' And with that I went upstairs to thank Blanquita for arranging everything so happily.

The next day Peterson went to see him and he more or less repeated the assurances he had given me. He made one half reservation which I'm sorry to say Peterson didn't kill there and then. We thought we had coached HE in all the points, but there is always just one that is forgotten. However, the verdict of my friends in the Ministry of Foreign Affairs who talked to Beigbeder after Peterson's visit is that all will be well. We are now waiting to be called to a meeting. So far (Tuesday 7 p.m.) no sign.

Today 20th February is the first hot day of spring. I seized the chance to go to the Escorial for lunch. The sun was so warm we could only stroll about and sit on stone benches, glowing with heat, that a week ago were covered with snow.

Did I tell you that the Madrid police have just begun to insist that you cross the road only at the lights, and only when the lights are green? How the Madrileños hate discipline! They gather on opposite kerbs in two angry teams ready to spring at each other when the whistle goes. They always played with the traffic like matadors with bulls, seeing how near they could get without accident, and irritating the drivers into bellows and roars on their hooters. Spaniards have a special taste for the pure risk and the pointless noise. Every street gives examples. Now they have to submit to discipline or a fine of two pesetas, and I notice that the new game is to hang about until the policeman is engaged writing in his book the receipt for one of these fines, this is the exquisite moment, then with a smile fit for heaven, they dash across the red lights and escape in triumph.

Cities are made for men, for whole crowds of men and there they must submit to all sorts of restrictions on their liberty for the sake of each other. They must not go against the lights, or pour slops out of the window, or shout themselves hoarse, or sit down in the road, or pick the flowers in the park, or swim in the lake, or climb the trees . . . The more advanced the civilisation the greater the restrictions. Progress then consists in a gradual loss of liberty. The country is different. The country is made for *a man*, not for men. A man can do in the country what he likes, subject to God's restrictions, the wind and the weather, the seasons and the soil. I do not see how any true man can hesitate about the choice.

Thursday

We are hung up again waiting for the Spaniards to give way on yet another point. Truly this is a trial of patience and good temper. Peterson has lost both his completely, and is off to Gibraltar in such a rage that his servants cower and his staff communicate with him by notes. The Board of Trade has recalled Nowell who departs on Sunday. I begin to feel lonelier than ever, and to wonder how long I can keep it going without some final disaster. Everyone says (Yencken[2] an exception), 'Why don't you give in?' But I won't. Half the trouble is the German influence, and the other half is the Spaniards' state of inefficiency and convalescence, which by patience can be improved. It must be wrong to walk out of the House of Commons just because one never gets a chance to do any good. It must be wrong to abandon this stage, and I won't do it. I do still think the Spaniards want the treaty and will sign, but I am at the point where I must say, 'Lord, I believe, help thou my unbelief.'

We had two hours with the Spaniards this morning and again failed to reach an agreement. That one mistake of Peterson's last Monday has thrown everything into the melting-pot again. Still my teeth are fast in the dog's throat and I won't unloose till he squeaks.

Give my love to Polly and Simo', and kiss them both.

All my love, sweet—David

1. The Minister of Foreign Affairs, Colonel Beigbeder.
2. Counsellor at the British Embassy in Madrid.

25 February 1940 — Madrid

My darling Syb — On Saturday morning I sent the enclosed letter to the Vizconde de Mamblas[1] who has been acting as go-between for me and the MFA since last Sunday's meeting. I hope you'll approve, I know it is a risk to start bullying, yet I see no way out of our impasse except courteous pressure. And as I believe what I say in the letter to Mamblas I hope it doesn't sound false or priggish.

After an early lunch Ellis-Rees and I left for Valladolid. The English College is a very old Catholic foundation. Titus Oates was a student there, but left in debt and bad odour. Walsingham had spies among the students, and well he might, for it was there the plot was hatched to poison Queen Elizabeth's saddle. The outside of the building is a poor brick affair, but inside it is agreeable without being out of the way. The Rector, Monsignor Edwin Henson, made us very comfortable and I had a sitting-room (smelly with stale wax and upholstery) with an egg-briquette fire. Henson about seventy, past his prime, got very nearly drunk at dinner — the local wine is delicious — talks more about the estate and rents and crops and money than about God or his work as Rector. He has a passion for roses, and showed us, pruned to within a few inches of the soil, over 200 varieties. 'There,' he said, 'is a huge heap of rose cuttings, they shall be burnt tomorrow or the people round will come and steal them and then they'll have as fine roses as I have.' Very Christian, I thought.

Talking of the difficulty of running a kitchen in a Spanish monastery, the Rector said, 'Either you must reconcile yourself to women servants or you must look out for one-legged sailors; because men always get drunk, and you want to have something to take away to teach them a lesson and to keep them on the premises!'

I went to High Mass this morning sung in plainsong by twenty-five students, and the Rector and three professors. The church is round (hexagonal rather), with chapels off at six sides, the main chapel being the chancel. It is a very pleasing effect as the choir stalls face each other. Every Sunday one of the students has to preach for ten minutes. The boy this morning was very impressive and attacked his sermon with a will, he comes from Wigan and is twenty-four. They start at nineteen and stay six years doing theology and philosophy and are then ordained priest. They have to be nominated by some English bishop to get in, and when they've finished the bishop gives them a job. All the teaching is done in Latin, and I gather they speak it like English. Father Holland and Father Hardwick, who assist the Rector, are first-rate and we had long talks last night and this afternoon after lunch.

I enjoyed very much my excursion into the heart of the Catholic faith but I am no nearer adopting it (you will be relieved to hear). The fascination is their understanding of human nature.

All my love—David

1. Member of the Spanish Ministry of Foreign Affairs.

Letter to the Vizconde de Mamblas at the Spanish Ministry of Foreign Affairs

24 February 1940 Madrid

Dear Pepe—Monsignor Henson has asked me to stay the night at the English College in Valladolid. I am just off and expect to be back for dinner tomorrow.

If you approve, I wish you would tell the MFA from me that I am really unhappy at the prospect of difficulties in our negotiations gradually forcing both governments to behave badly towards each other. The first signs are already visible.

I set great value on good manners and sweet reason at any time, but at this moment every tiny proof that Great Powers can behave to each other like friends, without raising their voices, is enormously precious. A big effort should be made to preserve the spirit of give and take, which has so far informed our discussions. From our side I can promise you that I keep this duty steadily in view, but it would not be honest to hold out hopes that His Majesty's Government would agree to a proposal, which all of us here know to be unacceptable in principle and unworkable in practice.

Yours ever—David

[To this the MFA replied on 25 February, 'Tell Eccles I agree, but he must try to be as patient as I am.']

29 February 1940 Chute

My dearest love—How I wish I were with you. You would still have to battle through the interviews and conferences unaided—but there would be a burble to come back to in the evening and the ever-present problem of my unpunctuality would chase heavier burdens into exile. But in spite of every rebuff—of course you mustn't give in or give way. Victory is waiting round the corner. When they seem most obstinate they may be nearest to breaking point. In London there is confidence in your success—an enormous appreciation of the difficulties. One of the most difficult problems must be how to strike a line between patience and authority. If they once get 'used to you' then we might just as well take away the pillow. No wonder, my sweet, that you are thin and grey-haired—I ache to number myself among the victims to your elderly charm.

But I'd sooner remain a widow than that you should come home one hour too soon—for I positively know you will triumph in the end. I went to London last week as you know—and saw quite a lot of people.

Tonight in the bath we were discussing an historic personage of great interest to Simon in his lessons.

'Is he dead?' enquires Polly.

'Oh yes,' I reply.

'Who shot him, then?'!!!

Poor sweets, they're nurtured on blood and thunder.

Darling, I'm for my lonely bed—with Simon snoring on one side and Polly calling out on the other. They talk often of you—but I think of you and hold you in my heart night and day.

—Sybil

28 February 1940 Madrid

My darling Syb—Do you know that altho' my day begins here about 9.30 a.m., when I get out of bed, and goes on till 9.30 p.m. when I dine, I hardly have read 200 pages of ordinary books since we arrived? There is always something official to read or write, some interview, some conferences among ourselves or some meeting with the Spaniards. It is true I usually take from two to five for lunch, but the meal lasts two hours here and then I go for my walk in the Retiro. You can see what spare time I do find goes into letters to you and odd jobs like having my hair cut.

Yesterday I had to refer to the file on 'Enemy Exports' and I saw that in three months I had written a dozen or more minutes, and I think my style has altered. It is more severe and less embroidered. The sentences are shorter and the sense more exactly given. I hope it is so, as I should be very pleased to have a reputation for 'minuting'. I can imitate the Halifax despatch style quite fluently, e.g. the letter to Mamblas I sent you by Nowell on Monday. That is all right for grand occasions (I blushed when I called Spain a 'Great Power' in that letter, but you know how they love flattery), the difficult style is the everyday style in which you want to record shortly your view on what someone else has said. This style must be dispassionate. You must only think of the beauty of the words after you have fixed the meaning of what you want to say. The artist must wait till the informant is fully satisfied. As *you* would know well this requires discipline on my part, but with continual self-reminders I think I am making progress in the right direction. Of course great civil servants combine truth with beauty, the classic example is the Balfour Note,[1] which sparkles like a diamond cut to a perfect shape. Every entrant to Whitehall should learn it by heart.

English is a resilient and living language. It is very hard to write dully in English. You can write wildly or clumsily or loosely or unintelligently but you can't kill English words, like you can French words. I mean that French words are like chestnuts and can be arranged as *marrons glacés*, but English words won't be frozen, they are always alive and tugging in a sentence, one against the other, like dancers in a ballet. I am actually conscious of this 'live' quality in our language.

You can see behind all this another sign of that fundamental idea that is slowly growing in my thoughts, that life is organic, that it can't be split up into so many men, so many women, so many votes, so many pounds, so many civil servants and so many amateurs. That the precious quality is to be found in the relations between men and women, and between mankind and its material wealth, and, I begin to add, between man and God. Therefore I can't say if this view of language comes to me of its own, or if I have imposed it on language in response to a general principle which I wish to see extended and proved over as wide a field as possible.

Thursday 29

I feel better because there are at last some signs of a thaw. My letter to Mamblas was the turning point. Peterson is in Gibraltar. It is perhaps a good thing.

Yesterday I lunched with the Fontanars and am going to a concert with them this evening. To be with a happy marriage is so rare and so refreshing that I wish I saw them every day. They showed me a letter from Alfonso XIII about the burial of José Antonio Primo de Rivera in the Escorial, 'This is one more slap in the face for me but this time at least I share it with Felipe II.' The Spanish Government have behaved foolishly about José Antonio. Whatever talents he had or didn't have he is a symbol of the generous youth of Spain which believed in a new Spain and died for the belief. Some monument somewhere would have been appropriate and might have served to perpetuate the ideas he stood for; but to bury him with the Catholic Kings was the one sure way of mixing up what he had given Spain with an older tradition and a stronger history than his. The risk is real that his burial there will work against the survival of his reputation, even to the point that one day the Royal Family will again be in power and will eject his bones from their mausoleum. The Falange have been foolish and I am sorry because in Spain anything is valuable that helps to foster and to preserve the will to put the country before the individual. José Antonio's memory had a big part to play in this national service. It is compromised in El Escorial.

I had a man from our Ministry of Information to dine last night, and he said on leaving, 'Good night, my dear, bless you.' Spain makes one very anti-pansy. I hate 'em.

All my love—David

1. On the founding of a national home for the Jews in Palestine.

3 March 1940 Madrid

My darling Syb—Did we ever go to Lupiana and Brihuega together? I have an idea that it was with Arthur Byne[1] that I went before. Past Guadalajara you turn right, and on the edge of the tableland you find the monastery of Lupiana brooding over the valley and village far below. In the fifteenth century three courtiers decided they could not go on bowing and scraping any more so they retired here to found a religious community. The result is perfect, and how enviable! The courtyard ranks among the finest in Spain, with its three tiers of cloisters, each different, and carved in warm orange stone that goes to perfection with the blue of heaven and the green of the box hedges. The church which was large has now no roof, and the owners—in 1848 it became a private house—have put a lily pond in the nave and a fountain in the chancel. You can still see big patches of polychrome on the walls, and today the bees were humming in and out of the myrtles and magnolias that line the pool. Outside is a terrace garden alight with almond and fruit blossom and almost too noisy with birds. Mamblas and I sat on a stone bench, and had to hit our heads to remember that somewhere there is a war and that men no longer have the time or the heart to build and to retire to such a place.

Afterwards we motored along the valley, following the red, brown and orange willows to the edge of another plateau, from where we could see for miles and miles olive trees and spring corn and part-coloured flocks browsing on last year's stubble. The spirit responds to the vastness of the Castilian landscape. Details become unimportant, manners improve. The niggling Nonconformist conscience could not flourish here, or the landlord feel himself a different being from the peasant. No wonder Spanish country people are so courteous for in that tremendous frame of sky and earth differences between one tiny man and another disappear. The wretched slum tenant and the Park Lane householder are forced to think for themselves as living in two worlds without a bridge.

Monday

I must now begin some account of the final and furious stages of our negotiations. On Saturday morning the Spaniards again put off an interview with my Treasury colleague, who had a point of vital importance to settle; and I received no answer to my new formula about using insuring claims to meet financial transfers. I went down to the Ministry and made a row. The MFA saw me, because, I think, I frightened his secretaries so much that they forced me into his room. He was as agreeable and helpful as ever, he pulled Casa Rojas (the head of the Spanish Delegation) out of a conference with the Swiss and told him not to go back till he had settled my complaints. They produced unofficially a new formula which is more favourable to us than the old one, and fixed an interview for the Treasury man. I am quite certain that if the MFA were not firmly decided that the treaty must be signed his underlings would drag on the discussions till we all lost our tempers and went home. Whether this result would be due to sheer laziness, inefficiency and ignorance on their part, or to anti-British influence in the background, we shall never know. I incline to the former and the Embassy to the latter explanation.

During the weekend it became clear that the MFA was likely to get pushed out very soon and Serrano Suñer take his place. This unpleasant piece of news greeted Peterson on his return from his southern trip, which he had loathed and during which he had heard all sorts of complaints from British subjects against the Nationalist régime. He lost his temper all ends up: said he would insist on my breaking off negotiations as he wasn't going to sign any treaty if Serrano Suñer were the MFA. We ought to 'put the screw on' in every possible way, what earthly good was it trying to be accommodating to a set of . . . ? To make things worse I had laid on his table a memorandum and a draft telegram concerning Franco-Spanish trade. Marshal Pétain had sent one of his men to consult me on the French Government's wish to denounce, after only eight weeks of life, the Franco-Spanish Commercial Agreement owing to a number of petty difficulties, the blame for which was about fifty/fifty. I advised very strongly against denunciation of a treaty that neither side had yet made a serious attempt to carry out, and for a number of other reasons. Peterson roared at me, 'If I send this telegram advising against denunciation of the French agreement I can't advise breaking off our own negotiations.' I said that this was so, and I stood by my advice to the French, if he didn't approve he must tell the Marshal himself. He said he would think it over. That afternoon he sent my telegram and another from himself saying that whoever was MFA we ought to carry on our negotiations. We had had a very nasty morning.

Tuesday

Monday evening the Spaniards communicated officially to us their new formula for the financial transfers, and it will be accepted at home; so the great difficulty is solved. There remained the subsidiary question of some £1 million bills outstanding in the hands of British banks. On this we deadlocked completely, and with a bad conscience on our side since neither Ellis-Rees nor I think the pretensions of the London banks are just. Finally we persuaded the banks' representative to agree to telling London that we did not recommend pressing the Spaniards any further for special treatment for these bank creditors. Incidentally the idea of favouring international bankers against ordinary creditors has a bad political flavour, since all new totalitarian states rave about the 'hegemony of the Jewish moneylender'. Not very easy to get this across Mr Montagu Norman,[2] but it is a factor. Anyway if London agrees to abandon the banks, we shall be finished.

All my love, I'll soon be kissing you—David

1. American antique dealer who was Randolph Hearst's agent in Spain.
2. Governor of the Bank of England.

7 March 1940 | 32 Wimpole Street

Walton and Virginia[1] dined at 32 on Tuesday and he told me that the chant of your praises mounts higher every day and the murmurs often reach his ears. 'Don't urge him to come home too soon, Sybil, he has just got to pull this thing off.' As if I don't cry out for the laurel leaves as loudly as anyone else. It's sad that they failed in Rome. Walt thinks this will have had a psychological effect on the Spaniards—and indirectly perhaps make things harder for you.

I think of you, hope for you and love you, what fun we shall have even if you are only here a month or so—it's quite a long time to love in. There is a general revolt among wives and London will be lived in again by the summer. And life once more shall resume some kind of normality, friends will meet and talk and dine and take the war and Hitler's threats in their daily stride.

I wonder if I shall be shy when I see you—or astonished that this gaunt, distinguished, grey-haired, ravishing diplomat should be my husband.

I kiss you—Sybil

1. Mr and Mrs Butterworth: he was an American diplomat who helped us throughout the war.

10 March 1940 Madrid

My darling love—My last letter to you went in Friday's bag, and the next morning came the telegram from London accepting our proposals for solving the last difficulty in the way of signing the treaty. I rushed off to the Ministry to tell them (as you say) 'all is over, take away the pillow', and of course, though delighted, they had to put up half a dozen silly little changes they had thought of in other parts of the text. By two o'clock everything was in order, and I asked how soon could their documents be ready for signature? Monday evening, or Tuesday morning at the latest? Casa Rojas started to shilly and shally about the shortage of skilled typists in the Treaty Department, and I knew there must be a huge rat just coming out of his hole.

Out he popped in confused and embarrassed language. Confidentially, Casa Rojas must tell me, as a friend, that the Italian Ambassador had returned to the charge on Friday and offered the Spaniards truly astonishing concessions if they would sign his agreement before ours. Such is the price that totalitarian states pay for their prestige. The MFA had told the Ambassador, Casa Rojas assured me, that he could only think of Spain's interest, which was clearly to put into operation the British treaty as soon as possible, but if the Italians could finish off their text, incorporating these concessions, in a couple of days, he would sign them first. I told Casa Rojas, who had the cheek to ask me not to mention all this to Peterson, that the Italian *démarche* was public property, and that, once our documents were ready for signature, to hold up completion would raise issues outside the competence of a Trade Delegation, and I must ask for instructions. However, I wished to be assured that in the normal way they could sign on Tuesday. He was shaken, and admitted this was so, and we parted coldly.

As an aside I must tell you about the peculiar physical reaction which I suffer when HMG's prestige or interests are ever limited, or in the same breath compared with those of another state. Three times in our negotiations this has happened to me. The first was when, in answer to the Spaniards' request for a larger loan than we are offering, Nowell insisted that 'in present circumstances the UK *is not in a position* to find more money than the amount suggested'. The second was when the Spaniards asked us to modify some important point in our demands 'because it would serve as a damaging precedent for their negotiations with Switzerland, Holland, etc.'. The third was on Saturday when Casa Rojas indicated that we should have to wait for the Italians. On each occasion the same sort of thing happened to me as to people who hate blood and are suddenly confronted with a bad street accident. It has nothing to do with preconceived ideas or outraged principles, the reaction is purely physical. I feel faint, and liquid inside from the waist down. It must be that the national tradition, the sediment of our history, acquires the force of instinct, and, when in danger, the power of moving the bowels. You can ask the Viscount[1] for a diagnosis.

To go back: Peterson didn't receive the news as badly as I had feared. He suggested very sensibly that we should tell the Spanish Government that, while we were not competing in any races to sign treaties, we could not be kept hanging about indefinitely. He proposes to see the MFA tomorrow, and to fix a time limit—a day or two beyond Tuesday. So there you have the stop press news at midnight on Sunday.

Monday

In the mud again. The MFA refused to give Peterson a date this morning, saying that Franco wanted the Italian agreement first. We are going to try tomorrow to get a definite answer. I wish I could tell you more but there is no time.

My troops are very depressed but I shall rally them in the morning.

All my love, sweet, I have to hold myself in hand to prevent a breakdown in temper.

Soon it will be over—David

1. My father-in-law, Lord Dawson of Penn.

13 March 1940 Chute

My darling love—In a way I don't want to write to you—I like to think you are almost on your way home—yet if I don't it will be tempting providence and you won't come.

Withers's man has been chain harrowing Bauks Hill and I can see him at it still—driving his red tractor over the ant heaps and across the down. It is spring at last—rain and shine—storm and wind. The daffodils are popping through—birds wake one in the morning once again and sound half surprised at recovering their voices—the herbaceous borders are breaking and every bush is in bud. The trees have lost their harsh black winter outline and are softened by a pinkish haze, flung over them like a veil. It's very exciting living through a country winter and watching the long drama unfold. A new experience for this cockney at any rate. I've never felt before such a sharp appreciation of spring. What heaven it is when the sun first makes patterns on the carpet and shows up the bashes in the paint—and one can rush out into the garden upon any impulse without first wrapping up like Captain Scott.

Friday 15

A glorious morning with a sharp frost that is melting fast. I've just been out to see Harris and my hand is so cold it won't send the pen straight. In the early morning it's lovely to watch the sun creep across Bauks Hill and start climbing up on our side—it lights up all the hillocks and leaves the hollows in shadow and the white frost lingers there all morning.

All my love, dear sweet—S.

14 March 1940 Madrid

Darling Syb—Since I wrote to you on Monday we have been faced with one stupid little objection to signing after another, nothing of the slightest importance, just delaying tactics of a disgusting and dishonourable kind. I quite expect HMG to lose their temper any day now and telegraph recalling the Delegation.

The peace in Finland, and the Italian agreement with Germany for the supply of coal, have injured our prestige, so that it is against an increasingly difficult background that we have to go on pressing the Spaniards to sign. The Finnish business is very bad. It shows that material prosperity, which was the only goal of modern Sweden, and I suppose of Norway, unfits a nation for upholding the true principle of conduct in the world as it is today. We used to say, 'Look at the Scandinavians, how well they have arranged their lives, the standard of living is high, poverty and extreme wealth are absent, they are at peace with all the world.' But when the storm comes, what can they do? Where now is the excellence of their social system? They thought they could preserve their wealth and comfort without being prepared to lose their lives for their principles. A melancholy tale, but not without hope if the lesson is well learned.

Our relations with Italy illustrate Mussolini's implacable hatred against the democracies who put on sanctions. He will never forget. He says to himself, 'There is an odd chance the morale of the Allies will crack, if I threaten to go in with Germany. I want a patched-up peace that will preserve the totalitarian system, if Adolf [Hitler] goes down, so may I, and anything rather than that.' Since our War Trade negotiations with Italy have failed, the Italians will feel the pinch badly, as they can't get the raw materials they want except from the British Empire. Then the Italian press will explain the bad economic situation by blaming England. You see a nasty campaign is about to begin. The Spaniards cannot fail to be influenced by all this. If only we could have finished our treaty a fortnight ago.

The bag came in at 11.15 and I seized your letter and went down to the Ministry for what was likely to be a very difficult session. They kept me waiting (for once I was glad) so that when I was summoned I was on top of my form after being with you for twenty minutes. And it went well. I can't make out if they are determined to stick to the time limit they have given the Italians, or will try another series of delays to give them more time. It is certain the Italian negotiations have made almost no progress in the last two days. Anyway, the Spaniards have at last consented to begin making their parchment copy of the treaty, and this morning they didn't make any fresh objections to the text. I gave them an eloquent description of the poverty in the provinces as contrasted with the luxury of holding up in Madrid so advantageous a treaty. The whole government are getting worried at the stagnation in trade, and feeling that they must do something, even if it is signing with us against the wishes of Italy. That is my impression. Peterson says I'm all wrong, that it is just another trick to throw dust in my eyes.

I'm glad you hear that they realise at home what a struggle it is. They never say anything agreeable in their letters from MEW or the Board of Trade, but that is civil service tradition.

Eddie Playfair writes me a full description of the Rome negotiations. I don't think the outlook is as bleak as one would gather from the papers. P. Loraine[1] must be a very good ambassador and a horrible man. When shall we get someone who is both a good ambassador and a man of charm?

I must have over-stressed my grey hairs! I pulled a lot out and they don't seem to be growing again, so you won't get a shock. If you are shy I shall just kiss you till you give up.

All my love. I will write again before the bag goes if I have a second.

—David

1. Sir Percy Loraine, HM Ambassador to Italy.

17 March 1940 — Last letter from Madrid

My darling love—On Saturday morning they gave in, and we sign tomorrow at 6 p.m. The submission of our treaty to Friday's cabinet wasn't anything more than the official excuse for a week's delay, which Franco and Suñer forced on Beigbeder to please Italy. Ministers must have approved the principles of the agreement long ago. As far as I could find out the Italians are not ready to sign anything, so prestige-hunting has proved a failure, for they will find it hard to withdraw big concessions once offered. Totalitarian prestige costs too much, and may be ruinous, like a collection of orchids, which have got a man a reputation and which he hesitates to put down in bad times for fear of injuring his credit; and then one fine day the bailiffs come and seize not only the orchids but every stick of furniture he has. The end of totalitarian régimes may come like that.

Reading through the exquisite top copy of the treaty last night, and making allowances for parents' blindness to their children's faults, I know that it is something 'picked from the ruin and chaff of the times'. The Spaniards themselves don't understand how they came to agree to an instrument which is opposed in thought and word to the pro-totalitarian and anti-democratic policy which they officially pursue. The answer is what they pursue with their heads they hate in their hearts. Beigbeder's remark, 'I make an exception of you, not because we love you, but because the British Empire is our best market,' was only an excuse to himself, it wasn't true, and he has since said so, though not to me. Nothing that Spain does is done simply from the angle of 'man can live by bread alone'. The admixture of spiritual elements may not always be happy, sometimes it is fanatic, cruel and contrary to what is right, but a mixture it always is; and in our treaty as much as anywhere else.

I wonder if anywhere in the British press or in Parliament anything will be written or said that touches the heart of the business. It won't matter much if it isn't . Institutions make ideas by being worked, however curiously they may be designed. Individuals do things, but neither the camera nor the biographer tells you what they were really like. Only an occasional artist, once in a lifetime.

This is the end of the Madrid chronicle. Writing to you has been the gold thread in the wild pattern of four months. I have all your letters, and one evening in the dim distance, we will read them dovetailed with mine and we shall be surprised at the picture of the wood, which for so many weeks has been lost among the trees. There has never been a day in which I have not thought of you and loved you, and I long to be with you now, more than at any time since we first met. In a few days we shall be together; if I can finish up here, and the Embassy in Paris will squeeze me into the 'bag' aeroplane, on Friday I shall reach London. For a day or two I must stay in London to deal with some urgent points in connection with the coming into force of the treaty on 1st April. After that I shall ask for a few days' leave. Don't forget to give me the van number as I want to try for some extra petrol.

Your telegram has just come. It does seem queer to be packing up here. We've just found there is no silk ribbon to be had in Madrid for binding up the treaty and sealing the ends. However, one of the typists has some red, white and blue left over from Christmas, and we've done it with this: I shan't show it to Peterson till it is too late for him to complain. It looks a bit flashy.

It will be heaven to see you, and I'm sure I can manage a little leave. We could spend a few days away from Chute if you'd prefer. Will you stay in London for Easter? Anyhow, I'll see you, kiss you and love you on Friday and we can talk about plans. See that Mabel gets some ice, and we'll have a bottle from No. 20, middle on left as you go in. Or if you think we should dine at 32,[1] don't let us offend them by refusing.

All my love, darling Syb—David

1. With Lord and Lady Dawson.

II

Portugal, Spain and the Fall of France

April–November 1940

2. Portugal, Spain and the Fall of France

The Agreement with Spain signed and in operation, I had hoped to stay in London working with MEW, but we had not reckoned with the situation in Portugal. The Madrid Embassy had been strengthened and was in good order. Nothing similar had been done to put the Lisbon Embassy on a war footing. The small staff, squeezed into dreary rooms in the Ambassador's residence, could not be expected, without considerable reinforcements, to secure from the Portuguese the detailed co-operation which we looked for from our ancient ally. At the request of the Foreign Office and the Treasury I was sent on 30 April to take charge of the commercial side of the Embassy and to persuade the Portuguese Government to assist our war effort in a variety of ways.

The Embassy agreed that the chancery must be removed to a building where it could be organised to deal with HMG's business in wartime. We were lucky. The Bank of Portugal put me on to a palace suitable in every way for our new offices. The Ambassador himself was a more delicate problem. Sir Walford Selby had many delightful qualities, but he did not possess the stamina to be head of a mission in such trying conditions. In quieter times he had got on well with Portuguese officials but he lacked the self-confidence and the lucidity to impress the only man who counted—Doctor Salazar, the head of the Portuguese Government. As soon as Selby was satisfied that I was capable of holding my own, he left to me almost all the business that required direct contact with the Prime Minister and his staff.

Salazar, so beautiful to look at, so fascinating to talk to, was then at the height of his powers, immensely popular, but saddened by the shadow of the war, which lay across his cherished plans for the reconstruction of his country. An academic by profession, without much experience of the rough and tumble of public life, his vast knowledge of the world came from books. Like Maynard Keynes, he added to the mastery of his special subjects the magic of clear, persuasive language in which with rare felicity he expressed whatever he had to say or write. An expert in public finance, his real love was for the history and traditions of Europe. His religion meant so much to him that he judged and spoke of all big subjects in the context of his faith. Almost in one breath he would talk to me of coal-freights and Christianity, I was back at Oxford having a tutorial, and what trouble he took to persuade me that economic policy must be treated as subsidiary to the moral framework within which the citizen can work for the good of his country and the salvation of his soul. Later I discovered that he had a prejudice which was to influence the course of the war. He did not much like the Americans. They had, he said, got their values wrong. Everywhere older and poorer societies were copying the manners of the New World without realising that they were cutting the roots of their own civilisations. HMG had not reckoned with these views. The British Embassy expected that when it looked certain the United States was coming into the war, victory for the Allies would seem inevitable and Portugal would give us more help. It did not happen. In matters relating to the Blockade Salazar interpreted his neutrality more strictly than when the United Kingdom was alone. I chided him about this and he replied, 'You think like I do. You have a sense of the world as a whole, but the Americans have only a continental outlook. They will dominate the Peace Conference. Europe will become a satellite of their economy and without knowing what they are doing they will open the door to Communism.' I said it need not be so bad, and anyway we, the allies of Portugal, could not win without the Americans. He was not satisfied.

Before France fell Salazar had begun to send for me on any matter which concerned Anglo-Portuguese relations. We talked in French in his room at Sao Bento high above the city and the great river below. He expected me to be ready for whatever he had on his mind. Many topics had nothing to do with finance or the Blockade; I remember an evening when the list had been settled of the Portuguese decorations to be given to HRH the Duke of Kent and his suite, who were coming in June 1940 to the eight-hundredth anniversary of the foundation of Portugal. Salazar said, 'What about yourself? Would you like a decoration?' 'No, thank you.' He rose and moved to the window. 'Look down there at the homes of my people. I have their respect. Perhaps also their love. That is the only decoration worth having.' At these interviews, however long the agenda, he had no one with him to take a note, but he forgot nothing, and long afterwards he would quote the exact words we had used. I recorded what he said about the business in hand, and wish the rest had also been written down but there was no time for that.

The Salazar I knew was by any standard a great man, from whom I learned many scraps of wisdom that became treasures in my memory. I accept that he stayed in office far too long. Our powers decline and we become the tool of others. On my last visit, years after the war, I found him unhappy and a prey to fears. It was said that he allowed the secret police to do things we all regretted. But, in the early days of the war, when defenceless neutrals were easily persuaded that the defeat of Britain must follow the collapse of France, he never concealed his hope that we would win, and he took risks on the assumption that someday, somehow, we would.

France fell and panic swept half the population of Lisbon. Waves of demoralised refugees, often beside themselves with grief, besieged the British Embassy. At different times I was offered in return for any sort of passage to America a bundle of bank-notes, gorgeous jewellery and a Rolls-Royce. The Portuguese community—it was understandable—were badly shaken by German propaganda and the stories told by the refugees. However, when news of the Battle of Britain began to come through, we were able little by little to restore confidence in the ability of the United Kingdom to hold out. In the midst of all the rumours the arrival of Sir Ronald Campbell to take the place of Sir Walford Selby greatly strengthened the British Embassy. Campbell, who had been Ambassador in Paris, was just our man, courteous to everybody, rich in experience, dispassionate in his judgement, unruffled in a crisis, assuring us, with a touch of the best Foreign Office cynicism, that nothing was ever as serious as we thought it was. One day, for example, when things had gone very wrong and we expected an explosion, he broke off the meeting and rang for the chef to tell him there was just time to make a better apple charlotte for lunch, 'You know, the brown stuff on top must crunch and taste burnt.' We all loved him.

Reading my letters, memory suggests that I did not give Sybil an adequate account of the squalid behaviour that demoralised Lisbon when France fell. War is like a bull-fight. In the arena, playing a real game with death, men make jokes and rush about apparently as cool as cucumbers, but on the benches above, watching, holding their breath, the spectators are turned to jelly with excitement and fear at second-hand. In neutral Lisbon we were spectators. The hysteria of the refugees, the sobs of despair, how different they were from the spirit in England where Sybil was sharing the rationing and the air raids with friends and strangers, all in good heart. The demented atmosphere in Portugal played into the hands of the Germans. It seemed that the best personal reply an Englishman could make was a show of exuberant confidence in our ultimate victory. Lisbon society was small, any diplomat with a position of some consequence, and my relations with Salazar ensured that, was watched to see how he reacted to the news of the war. I took the prettiest women to the best restaurants and I attended or gave a party almost every night. The Ambassador preferred to stay indoors. The Portuguese were delighted. I got into scrapes. For example, one morning, having met a dark beauty on a deserted beach, I invited her to lunch, afterwards to discover she was not French, as I thought, but the daughter of a German military attaché. Salazar was informed about this incident and much more. He had heard, he said, that I was enjoying the society of Lisbon. He had a suggestion to make. If I were thinking of giving a ball he would have put at my disposal a rose-tinted palace not far from the city. He seemed perfectly serious, indeed he was never anything else. But what a gesture at a time when Britain's fortunes were at their lowest! He approved our confidence in ourselves. The Germans could not compete in light-heartedness and, although some members of the British colony were shocked, the social bravado paid off. Should I have told Sybil more about these goings-on? It would have been better if I had, but I felt guilty at the contrast between her kitchen at Chute and my frivolities in Lisbon, and afraid, very afraid, she would be upset and find her life even more dull.

While I was in Lisbon I met for the first time Sir Samuel and Lady Maud Hoare. What sort of man was the Right Honourable Sir Samuel Hoare, GCSI, GBE, CMG, who as British Ambassador to Spain figures so largely in the Letters? Can one explain the difference between his published account of Franco's policy and the facts as witnessed by members of his staff? We owe it to the many Spaniards who helped us in the war to answer this question.

Hoare thought that a well-connected and superbly intelligent man like himself had a duty to tell inferior mortals what to do. His contempt for the lower classes was matched by his admiration for authority, which led him to take a kinder view of Mussolini than his predecessor at the Foreign Office, Anthony Eden, had done. He made the notorious 'Hoare-Laval pact' which earned him a place among the 'Guilty Men'. These were a list of public men held responsible by a large section of British opinion for appeasing the dictators and failing to re-arm Britain in the 1930s. Hoare came to the Embassy in Madrid handicapped by the label of a 'Guilty Man'. However, his mission was a success and he lived down his bad reputation.

Sir Samuel and Lady Maud Hoare, on their way to take up his post in Madrid, suitably dressed for a garden party at Buckingham Palace, arrived in Lisbon on 30 May 1940, and stayed two nights in the Embassy. I was living in the house and was present at the talks which Hoare had with Sir Walford Selby. Hoare opened the conversation by assuring us that only with reluctance and under extreme pressure from Churchill and the King, had he accepted the post of Ambassador to Spain. He could only spare a month or two as he was going to be appointed Viceroy of India.[1] He was confident that in this short time he could obtain from Franco a firm guarantee that Spain would remain neutral for the duration of the war. Selby, instead of being exasperated by his self-assurance, was struck dumb, and only just managed to ask me to describe the situation which Hoare would find in Spain. I told him that in the cities the people were near starvation and that we heard from good sources that Hitler's efforts to persuade Franco to come into the war against us might be on the point of succeeding. Hoare turned pale, cried out that he had been deceived, said his mission was useless and he would go back to London in the morning. This was the first of many times when I was to see him panic. Selby and I rallied him as best we could, but when he reached Madrid he kept his private aircraft waiting ready to take him home and he had to be persuaded to unpack.

He was a man of parts. His staff soon came to admire his knowledge of the world, his social gifts, and his talent for administration, but they never got over the bouts of physical and moral cowardice. A bat circled the ceiling of his study. He flung himself under the sofa calling out for me to kill it with his tennis racquet. On another occasion when rumours reached him that German troops were about to cross the Pyrenees he invented an offer of a place in the War Cabinet which it was his duty at once to go home and consider. We knew that this story was pure fantasy but we saw how much he needed the pretence of going back into government

1. Sir Samuel Hoare had been Lord Privy Seal with a seat in the War Cabinet until 3 April 1940, when he became Secretary of State for Air.

as a tranquilliser for his nerves. Another instance: my letter of 6 January 1941 tells how he went to pieces during the wrangle over compensation for our nationals in Tangier. It was pitiable to see such cowardice in a potentially great man.

No Allied or neutral ambassador saw Franco and his ministers as often as Hoare. In these interviews he used the prestige of his distinguished career with the greatest skill, at the same time pretending he knew nothing about diplomacy. The Spaniards, who love drama, were loud in praise of acting of such high order. Having had an unrivalled experience of the strengths and weaknesses of public men his account of Franco's character and policy during the Second World War should be the most valuable we have. It certainly would be if his well-written book, *Ambassador with a Special Mission* (Collins 1946), did not lead to a conclusion which can only be explained by his ungovernable desire to secure the applause of posterity.

Torn between conflicting opinions about Franco's attitude to the war he settled for the wrong one. Did Franco from the first to the last wish to see Germany win? Was he always hoping to find the right moment to bring Spain into the war on Germany's side? Was neutrality forced upon him by Allied pressures he could not resist? Hoare very much wanted to believe that this was the truth, for then he could take to himself the credit for keeping Spain out of the war. The Embassy staff knew that this version of Franco's intentions was false. In this we had the support of Salazar. We told Hoare that British policy could be firmly based on the assumption that Franco genuinely wished to remain neutral. Without this assumption we should have got the jitters and we could not have justified to ministers in London the continuation of our economic aid to Spain. Our view proved to be correct but it did not square with Franco's public statements. These were outrageously pro-Axis. They frightened Hoare and infuriated the House of Commons, but we stuck to our advice that they should not be taken too seriously. First because Franco was waiting to see who was going to win the war and in the meantime was obliged to string the dictators along, letting them believe he really did intend sooner or later to invite the German Army to enter Spain and attack Gibraltar. He did not mean what he said, and was telling a different story to Salazar. He judged shrewdly that Hitler would not risk an opposed entry into Spain. The popular resistance to Napoleon's armies was a warning which no one was allowed to forget. Secondly Franco had to placate the pro-German party within his own ranks until he could reduce the power of Serrano Suñer, his brother-in-law, who led the chorus of support for Hitler and Mussolini. This explanation of Franco's double-talk did not suit Hoare. He saw himself as the hero who alone stopped Franco from doing what was nearest to his heart.

After the war it became known that Hoare was writing a book based on the assertion that Franco always wanted the Germans to win and remained neutral against his will. This caused resentment among our best friends who had done so much for the Allied cause. When I told Hoare that his version was not correct, he lost his temper, and pointed to an appendix in which he was including messages that passed towards the end of 1940 between Hitler, Mussolini and Franco. In these documents, captured in Berlin, Franco flatters the dictators, hopes for their victory, and says he will join them at a suitable moment. The British Embassy knew at the time that some such messages were being exchanged, but all of us, Arthur Yencken the Minister, the Service attachés and I, told Hoare that Franco was an old fox, playing for time, and playing successfully. Hoare tried not to believe us. He half wanted to telegraph to London that the game was up. I consulted Salazar. He gave similar advice to that which we were giving Hoare. We now know from another document captured after the war that Hitler was coming to the same conclusion about Franco's real intentions, for on 31 December 1940 he writes to Mussolini that Franco had let them down, preferring to take economic aid from the Allies to keeping his promise to join them in an attack on Gibraltar, which had been planned for February 1941. Did Hoare know of this letter? I cannot say. Churchill printed it in his *History of the Second World War* (Cassell 1948–54). It goes far to confirm that Franco wanted to remain neutral and that our economic aid gave him the means to do so.

In his book Hoare is unfair to Portugal, a country of which he spoke as some Australians speak of New Zealand. Salazar and the British Embassy in Lisbon were essential partners in the campaign to keep Spain neutral. In this campaign, the single most effective action, the one that gave Franco the most powerful and easily understood reason for not entering the war, was the Tripartite Agreement of July 1940, under which Britain financed the purchase by Spain of Portuguese colonial products and allowed the shipments through the Blockade. Hoare knew very well the importance of this agreement but he refers to it so briefly that it must be deliberate. The boost given to Spanish imports was a turning point in the history of the Peninsula, but he had had no part in opening the door to trade with Portugal. The original idea came to me in Lisbon, I then cleared it with the Departments at home, and in Lisbon the text was negotiated by Salazar, the Spanish Ambassador to Portugal, who was Franco's brother, and myself. After the signing, Nicolas Franco took a copy of the agreement to Madrid.

To balance his vanity, his jealousy and fits of nerves, Hoare had high qualities of immense value to the state. He was a dedicated patriot and a devoted monarchist. His talent for administration was such that officials who had worked for him rated him the best administrator they had ever served. I owe him a great deal. He taught me how to organise able civil servants, each with his own job knowing what is expected of him, and not only feeling part of a common enterprise but having access to all the information necessary to see his job in relation to the work of others. He showed me how to plan a conversation according to the character and influence of the person to be interviewed. He made a note of the points he was going to raise, jotting down key phrases, and if he was not satisfied or agreed with Yencken or me that he should add this or take out that, he would throw away what he had prepared and start again. What a joy it was to watch him infiltrate the hierarchy of the Catholic Church! What a textbook he could have written on how to persuade a Spanish cardinal that you and His Eminence think alike! And what of Lady Maud? She was impeccably correct, more like a business partner than a wife. The unkind said that, having no children, she devoted herself to the luggage. She did much more than that. Sam knew how much he depended on her, and if, as she said, he had always been a prey to panic, he could not have had so long and distinguished a career without her constant and wise support. Hoare was an example of the exceptionally able man whose faults almost outweigh his virtues, but not quite. He deserves qualified praise in the history books.

30 April 1940 Lisbon

My darling Syb—Standing on the asphalt—a *Vogue* cover in your new suit with raised hand—I *did* so wish (in that great empty aeroplane) you could jump in and come too. I have loved our interlude between two embassies, our intermission. In Madrid with all the troop of the delegation I did not miss you half as much as I will here. This is a beautiful house in its way, lovely big rooms; Lady Selby is in England; HE[1] has one suite and I another. I feel immensely overhoused after Motcomb Street[2] and even Chute.

In my bedroom the covers are a sensible plain blue, the furniture rosewood, mosquito-wire outside the windows, the harbour straight below. A great many hoots and sirens all the time, but I shall get used to that.

Lisbon at first sight—the streets and wall-gardens—seems more like Italy—Naples or Sicily—than anything I've seen in Spain. Flowers everywhere. Oranges and reds predominate, but as I look closer I expect I shall find every sort. Oh! I'm going to miss the tulips at Chute. It plunges me in gloom.

—David

1. His Excellency Sir Walford Selby, KCMG, CB, CVO, His Majesty's Ambassador to Portugal 1937–41.
2. We had rented a small house at 17 Motcomb Street from Jim Byam-Shaw early in the war.

2 May 1940 Chute

My darling love—All day I hopped about like a cat on hot bricks—seeing that silvery albatross dodging wildly through the clouds and across the heavens with a fleet of Messerschmitts in furious pursuit. What an ass your wife is over aeroplanes.

Today the boys and I took sandwiches and set out on an enormous bike ride. We went by the causeway to Tidcombe and from thence by way of the Grafton Road to Wexcombe—over the Plain to Ludgershall and so home. Fourteen or fifteen miles in all! They rode beautifully and never faltered, and Simon wouldn't even admit to being tired when we reached Chute. Very stout for under six. There was one glorious moment when as we crossed a small railway bridge a train roared underneath—and the party exchanged frantic and cordial wavings with the stoker and the guard.

Darling—I wonder how it goes and how your first days are shaping. John said to me today, 'I expect Daddy is seeing the government by now.' 'No, I don't think so,' says I. 'He will feel his feet during the first week or two before taking any plunges.' To which our creature astutely replied, 'Yes, I bet he's going round all the Embassy finding out what each one can tell him before he tries anything else.'!

I do love you so, my sweet, and I have never been happier than during our five weeks. It was perfection to be together after that long lonely winter—such happiness makes a bagatelle of wars and one can live on its memory for months of separation. I hope—darling David—that you're as happy as I am.

All my love—Sybil

5–9 May 1940 Lisbon

My darling Syb—Lisbon is the most adorable place. The combination of blue skies and sea, the colours and the gardens, have gone straight to my heart. I wish the Embassy wasn't sunk in a slum where dogs bark and cocks crow almost all night. The hollow sounds of metal from the docks, and the sirens, are romantic enough to be agreeable, but the background noises are altogether unwanted.

It needed a European war, and a very peculiar turn in that war, to bring me to this life of luxury. The Ambassador and I eat nearly all our meals *à deux*. We breakfast on the terrace in an embrace of flowers, the orange juice the best in the world. A superb chef sends exquisite lunches and dinners to be eaten with the finest silver and linen under the gaze of George V and Queen Mary. It's a fraudulent life.

I should love you to be here in times of peace. There's not a shadow of doubt Lisbon would enchant you, much more I think than Madrid or any coastal place in Spain we know. But now it is as well you are not here. There is a murmur of gravity about the conduct of the war that is gathering to a roar, and Portugal cannot be deaf. Norway was like the first stroke on a funeral bell, I don't know how anyone could have registered the event with joy. You know what I thought. I am learning much from spending a week or two with the Duke of Wellington.[1] The shapes and size of cannon may change in a hundred years, but not the men behind them, nor the broad lines of European strategy, nor the need for leadership. At Vimeiro Wellington was thirty-nine, at Torres Vedras forty-one. He argued with HMG as skilfully as he fought with Masséna. That is fundamental. The agent abroad has always two opponents and must face both ways. He cannot possibly do this unless he is free from paralysing instructions and is big enough to substitute his personal faith and plans for the misfits cobbled up at home.[2] Altho' he has no instructions imposed on him he must understand the government at home, and very carefully consider their probable reactions to his policy, because in the last event he cannot win. HE doesn't quite grasp this, yes, I think he does, but there is a streak of silliness in him that clouds good thinking.

Lady Selby arrived by air yesterday in a nice grey flannel suit and a somewhat latticed jumper that showed a sensible bodice behind; a hat like the boys wear and a zip bag of portmanteau size in what looks like leatherette. The salt of the earth, down with Chamberlain and the old gang, bring Labour into the government, our generation have made a 'bloody' [*sic*] mess. The very type for a tight corner, if you twig my meaning. HE giggles at her, experience has doubtless taught him his place.

9 May

I saw Salazar yesterday and was immensely impressed, nothing I had heard could have equalled the dignity, good sense and charm of the best-looking dictator in Europe.

Last night I dined with François and Margareta[3] and had lots of fun. The French are windier than we are. As the news is so much better from the Spanish frontier, and Salazar has deported the leaders of the Quisling bunch, things are easier, and we shall have a little time to work out a satisfactory plan. A week ago it was most unpleasant.

As a bit of political news I should tell you how surprising it is to find the British colony here mad keen on a change of government at home. I thought they would be old-stagers.

Darling Syb, how I would love to kiss you. You don't know how much I love you. When is your photograph coming?

All my love—David

1. The Embassy has a fine bust of the Duke and a good set of his despatches from the Peninsula.
2. There is no reference here to my instructions for Portugal. I wrote them myself.
3. François and Margareta de Seynes.

8 May 1940 Chute

My darling love—God! The Prime Minister's[1] speech was frightful. Smug—self-satisfied—school-masterish, absolutely no fire, nor assurance that efforts will be redoubled to prosecute the war with energy, courage and imagination. And when he had the cheek to preach at us, that we 'do not yet realise the extent or the imminence of the threat which is impending against us' I dare swear half England longed with your wife to administer a sound kick in the pants to that self-righteous and ineffective gent who calls himself our leader. His vanity and mental rigidity give a misleading appearance of strength in times of peace—but today we need dynamic force to oppose the Germans. He simply *will* not do.

Roger Keyes's[2] speech has made a tremendous impression. That's the kind of man who appeals to one. Somebody who is ready to take a risk when the prize to be won is worth it. He's in the tradition of the worthiest and bravest of our race. To hell with these quaking old men. There is general criticism of the government in the press today—even Auntie[3] raises her voice against the Prime Minister.

Today has been divine—not a cloud and the sun has improved the tulips a lot—though they're nothing approaching the perfection of last year. We packed up the picnic basket and I pushed it in the pram, with Polly perched on top—through Collingbourne to the big black yew. There's a lovely stretch of grass fringed with scrub and silver birches just behind the yew— and after racing about for half an hour the pair consented at last to sit down and eat a gigantic tea of cucumber sandwiches, lettuce, bread and butter, honey, cake, chocolate biscuits and fruit jelly!! Then we plodded home rather heavily over Bauks Hill. But even with that tea inside, they insisted upon rolling down the banks of that grass dyke until their apoplectic cheeks made me call pax and enforce it. It was a lovely afternoon and we're all three sunburnt and ready for bed.

1. Neville Chamberlain was Prime Minister until 12 May 1940.
2. Admiral Sir Roger Keyes, MP, had made a devastating attack in the House of Commons upon the naval conduct of Narvik and on the naval general staff.
3. *The Times*.

[I returned to London on 17 May 1940 to obtain approval for abandoning the idea of an orthodox War Trade Agreement. Instead I was to offer the Portuguese Government the commercial agreement which is outlined in my memorandum to Dr Salazar on 22 May. The Germans attacked France on 10 May. By the 21st, when the aircraft taking me back to Lisbon had to land at Bordeaux, all French roads leading south were choked with refugees.]

24 May 1940 — Chute

My darling love—Last night there was a big ARP[1] practice at Ludgershall and Nan and I turned up with the vans. Too funny it was for words. Such squabbles about who did turn up at the 'Rendy Voos' and who didn't. Who gave orders when he shouldn't and who didn't when he should. How disgraceful it was when the fire brigade overshot the mark.

But they're a worthy lot on the whole and determined to do their duty—so if and when the Huns arrive they'll be up and about the business.

Your four days in London came as a tonic to our friends and to me. Rose Elliot[2] who I saw again on Wednesday told me that Bill had been full of grateful praise for your high spirits and confidence and so was Walton [Butterworth] as you know. Oh—it's impossible, darling, that we should lose this war when we've got as much and more spirit than those brutes on the other side.

Yesterday in Ludgershall there were a number of men from tank units and the RAF just home for a week's rest after being in the fighting ever since the invasion of Holland and Belgium. Though they were only ordinary men—their accounts were interesting. They say the *mêlée* on the other side is incredible. Like a furious mediaeval battle with tanks instead of horses. They describe extraordinary things. A unit of tanks proceeding down a road in preparation to join another unit meet instead some Germans careering along in the opposite direction—after a set-to they turn themselves to the right-about to rejoin their own friends—when not at all—there are some more Germans waiting for them. Off they lollop, this time prepared for Germans and nothing else and find themselves firing away at some French units instead.

Apparently we are fighting half the time behind the enemy lines, if lines they can be called. These chaps at Ludgershall never clapped eyes on any large masses of German infantry and remain perfectly calm about the motorised units, which to the amateur seem so alarming, conclusive and swift. They say, 'Of course the fellows advance—they haven't any choice half the time, because we're behind them.' It's all very peculiar and hard to understand, isn't it? But obviously a bright idea on the Germans' part. What a silly letter this is—but it's hard to marshal one's thoughts and attain any coherence.

My darling, I love you—take great care of yourself and come home safely to me.

—Sybil

1. Air Raid Precautions.
2. Wife of Air-Marshal Sir William Elliot.

26 May 1940 Lisbon

My darling Syb—Selby and I had one and three-quarter hours with Salazar on Saturday. He welcomed my proposals and is going to put them to the Spanish Government immediately. The opening of the interview was comic. You know how Selby twitters and repeats the same idea (generally quite a good one) about six times. Evidently Salazar has had enough of this. He settled down to read his memoranda and notes while Selby launched into a carefully rehearsed piece about the advantages of Iberian neutrality. This went on for ten minutes and by chance, just as he drew his first breath, Salazar had finished his notes. The Great Man looked straight at me, and said, 'I want to begin by discussing certain essential requirements of Portugal in the next eight months.' He never looked at Selby or made one reference to anything in his pretty speech. Cruel, but salutary, and we made progress thereafter.

Salazar's character reminds me of Shakespeare's last plays. He seems to have solved the difficulty of living on the two planes of the ideal and the material. He is Prospero on the island at one minute, and Prospero the administrator of government at the next. You must play a sort of Ariel's part, jumping from coal-freights to Christianity, and from the Rights of Property to the purchase of salt-cod. I like the acrobatics very much, for here is the first man I have met who really convinces me that he is equally genuine on both planes. Victorian hypocrisy in nineteenth-century England made a disgusting smudge of the two worlds.

You remember I said the invasion of France would rouse neutrals from their panic, I tried this out on Salazar and he responded beautifully. I don't think Italy will come in. If we win while she is still blackmailing and howling against us I am afraid it will be many years before we can forgive the Italian Government such filthy conduct.

I kiss you, my sweet Syb—David

Mr Eccles's Note to Dr Salazar outlining an Anglo-Spanish-Portuguese Agreement on Trade dated May 22 1940

Most Secret

1. The maintenance of neutrality in the Iberian Peninsula has been, from the outbreak of the war, an interest vital both to Portugal and to the United Kingdom. On this point His Majesty's Government have from the first made their attitude perfectly clear, and have always recognised that the personal influence of the head of the Portuguese Government is the strongest factor making for peace in the Peninsula. They do not hesitate, therefore, to ask Dr Salazar to undertake the difficult and delicate task

of securing from Spain certain practical assurances concerning her intention and ability to remain neutral.

2. Believing that the key to the Spanish situation is to be found in consolidating the régime of General Franco, and that the chief danger to this régime comes from economic distress, exploited by foreign agents, His Majesty's Government are prepared to make available at Spanish ports, before the end of June, one hundred thousand tons of wheat. The precise sources from which this wheat will come have yet to be worked out but the bulk will probably be secured by diverting cargoes from the United Kingdom or other nearby destinations. Payment for this wheat may be made through the Anglo-Spanish Clearing. The French Government will co-operate in finding the quantity of wheat required.

3. His Majesty's Government are ready to assist Spain to buy Portuguese Colonial products, subject to a guarantee of non-re-export, by agreeing that payment for them should be made through the Sterling Area account of the Anglo-Spanish Clearing. This account has at present a large balance in favour of Spain, representing the unspent portion of the loan recently made by the United Kingdom to Spain. If further finance is required it will be sympathetically considered when the amounts involved are known.

The list of the Colonial products to be acquired shall be agreed by the three governments, and it is hoped that all the goods can be transported to Spain in Portuguese ships.

4. His Majesty's Government desire that the sums received for Portuguese Colonial products, paid for through the Anglo-Spanish Clearing, shall not be converted into another currency, but spent within the Sterling Area.

5. The essential requirements of Portugal, of which a provisional list was drawn up by Count Tovar,[1] have been sympathetically studied in London, and certain assurances can be given.

6. Before communicating these proposals to the Spanish Government His Majesty's Government wish to discuss with the Portuguese Government the nature of the assurances which should be asked from Spain. HM Ambassador and Mr Eccles will refer to this question tomorrow. In the meantime they hope Dr

Salazar will consider what steps he can ask General Franco to take to consolidate his position.

7. Dr Salazar will note that the proposals contained in this memorandum require considerable elaboration in detail, but it is hoped that the general outline is sufficiently clear to enable him to estimate the plan as a whole.

22 May 1940

1. Salazar's principal adviser on economic affairs.

31 May 1940 Chute

Sykes is head of our Local Defence Volunteers and has nearly sixty men. They work on two-hourly shifts during the night time in posses of three. His area stretches along the causeway from Tidcombe to Conholt. He seems pretty efficient and the patrols started last night. I've lent him your field glasses and bicycle. He didn't want guns or rifles. Apparently the chief task is one of accurate observation and prompt information. The military in fact beg them not to shoot off at the enemy for this is a privilege they wish reserved for themselves. So when sighting anything odd and suspicious the patrol leap cannily on to bicycles and make for the nearest telephone (an emergency box is being installed on the causeway) and in thirty minutes we are promised some lorries stuffed with battle suits. All our signposts have gone. Not one is left on any country road. The towns still keep theirs. Everything from signposts to aeroplane production is moving with unusual swiftness. This is satisfactory and at the same time madly irritating for it demonstrates so clearly that if we care to be efficient we can be so. But not before thousands of brave men's lives have been sacrificed and the country fallen into grave danger.

A little while ago it would have taken three months to remove the signposts—now it has taken three days. I hope and pray that from this war we shall rise new men and women, poor, hardworking and god-fearing with the country unified through every class, as it has never been yet. There was a great attendance at church last Sunday. I went to St Mary's for evensong and it was full. The service was ordered, so mercifully Mr Freer wasn't left to his own resources. The Archbishop's[1] message wasn't very good—too roundabout and verbose—but I don't think anyone minded much. The instinct for prayer was there all right. We ended with three verses of *God Save the King*—rendered wheezily but with great spirit by Mrs Freer.

Darling love, I think of you and love you always. We've had such happy years and never has there been a luckier woman—we've got memories enough to lighten the darkest days. Take care how you come home. The children send their love and I kiss you, my sweet.

—Sybil

1. Cosmo Gordon Lang, Archbishop of Canterbury.

29–30 May 1940 Lisbon

My darling Syb—Sam Hoare's aeroplane brought me a letter, or it may have come by courier, from you enclosing your cutting about the old dug-out. His appointment really is wicked. More about him later when I've dined alone with him and Lady Maud. I loved getting your letter. Altho' the news gets worse and worse my spirits are not at all clouded, I know that (always provided the French don't give in) we'll be all right. I wish I was at home to cheer the chaps on. Lisbon needed a tonic, and how it has worked! The change is electric, the Portuguese Government are doing all we ask, the press is wildly pro-British, the German club has been raided, and the worst of them expelled or jugged for having arms. All this happened because I persuaded Salazar we have not lost faith in ourselves. Ridiculous old fogies in the British colony were staring miserably at the departing prestige of the United Kingdom like a lot of children gaping at their balloons floating away, and a broken string dangling from their fingers. Not doing a damn thing. Out of what Roger [Makins] calls 'David's usual effervescence' has come quite a bit.

Lady Selby and I are frightfully naïve to Sam and Maud [Hoare]. If only their names weren't those of the polar bears at the zoo. It makes me think of our Sunday morning trips, clasping bags of old veg. dashing from cage to cage. I remember looking at you in your mink coat, standing in the polar bear pulpit with the chaps, and wondering suddenly how it all came about, you and the chaps and the coat and the half-crown for the keeper. I had a moment of wild speculation and then the last piece of fish was thrown, and we began to clamber away to other parts.

Lady Maud has one big gambit: 'Oh, *really*, Mr X, I am *so* interested to hear you say that, because when Sir Samuel and I were—etc., etc.' Sam says everything three times, 'Yes, yes, yes', 'Quite quite quite', not thoughtfully, but mechanically, like St Vitus's dance. He's a miserable creature, and all my stored anger turns to pity. The silly little lies about how he was pressed against his will to take on the job, not just by the Secretary of State but by everybody you can imagine . . . how tired he is after the unceasing work of the War Cabinet, day and night, night and day, wrestling with these vast and awful problems . . . Madrid he first thought would be a holiday, now I've cured him of that, and he is wondering how short a time he can decently stay . . . other work may be forced upon him. Dorothy Selby says that every time she sits down to a meal with him she has to say to herself, 'God forgive him for being one of the men who have brought my son to be fighting in Belgium, or dead, at this moment.' Walford [Selby] says that the continued self-confidence of a man who has begotten so much that is disastrous and abhorred is a miracle of heavenly grace, and we should be grateful for the capacity of self-deception to which man can attain.

Moi, je l'écoute. And when a man has a bad conscience—which in fact Sam has—and he has been in the War Cabinet for months, you can learn a lot by judicious questions. I am mastering the technique of HMG as quickly as I can, and have sucked Walford's fertile memory dry of the history and organisation of the FO. Sam is being subjected to the same pumping *re* the Cabinet. I shall soon be ready to pop in through the breach that is visibly widening in the old hierarchy.

All my love, my darling Syb—David

Letter to
William Strang, CMG, *Under Secretary, Foreign Office*

1 June 1940 Lisbon

My dear Strang—You ought to know that something extraordinary and unforgettable is happening here. Salazar has made up his mind that whether we are victorious or defeated Portugal shall stand by England. All show of neutrality has been dropped. The more difficult the Allied position becomes the more resolutely he supports our cause.

He has come to this decision—naked to enter a blizzard—because he is a good man with the courage to pursue what he knows is right. This quality in his character is transparent in his writings. I drew attention to it in my April memorandum. In the last few weeks he must have withdrawn into himself, meditated on the meaning of the invasion of the Low Countries, and taken his decision.

He has certainly been helped by his faith in the Secretary of State.[1] I can feel the emotion in his short, careful references to 'a common attitude to God and man', 'those who believe in Christianity must surely be victorious'.

In the past few days he has shown me, by a variety of kindnesses and attentions, exactly what he thinks, and with a superb taste, which seems to say, 'I am making this decision for England, I want you to realise its full meaning, but no heroics please, what it is right to do, it is right to do quietly.'

Yours sincerely—David Eccles

1. Lord Halifax.

5 June 1940 Lisbon

My darling love—We all think that morale in England must be very high as a result of the Dunkirk operation, and that the croakers must have disappeared. The Portuguese are delighted with our withdrawal and see in it all the virtues that won the Peninsular War. I've written home to say that if the Portuguese aren't afraid of Italy why the hell should we be? Only a firm refusal to go on placating one super-bluffer will stop the nonsense. Oh! I should like to have a go at him and beat him up. Gerry Villiers[1] always said I was the most bellicose man in MEW and I always hotly denied it, but perhaps he was right.

You remember I asked Walton [Butterworth] to get President Roosevelt to do certain things in connection with my mission? Well, he's got double what I asked. Isn't it splendid? I sent him a telegram of thanks today. Also I asked Roger [Makins] to let him know how things are going here. You might tactfully find out, if you see either of them, if he has done so. If not, tell whichever one you do see to get into touch with the other.

The Times has done us (4 June) very well on the Portuguese celebrations,[2] all the papers here reproduce the leader. How much good those things do! We are still the dispensers of flattery and approval, whose kind words are greatly prized. That means we have a responsibility to judge rightly, and must come all the greater cropper when we judge wrongly, as most of the press did about the Spanish Civil War. However, there is no disputing that the Portuguese renaissance under Salazar is a fact, and a very remarkable fact. The last paragraph of *The Times* leader was excellent. I would be disposed to take very seriously any advice Salazar gave on how to plan the new Europe.

All my love, dear sweet Syb—David

1. Foreign Office official seconded to MEW.
2. On the occasion of the eight-hundredth anniversary of the founding of the Portuguese state.

6 June 1940 Chute

My darling and only love—The last ten days have been full of anxiety and excitement. As I told you Rosie[1] had to bear day after day with no news. Then at dinner last Friday came a telegram, 'Landed at Folkestone, in colossal form!!'. . . . We flopped with joy, relief and spent nerves and pulled ourselves together again with a bottle of Scotch holiday champagne. At 1 a.m. the following morning the telephone pealed and thinking it could only mean one thing[2]—I sprang from bed reaching for the old tin hat. Not at all—who should it be the other end but John.

At Folkestone that evening the men had been hurled into trains as they landed and packed off anywhere. John lay in his, soggy with sleep for several hours. Then with a jolt they stopped and a country voice cried liltingly, 'All change,' so out they tumbled—weary, footsore, half asleep. Collecting himself and his chaps on the deserted platform John went off to enquire where they were. 'Ludgershall,' came the truly surprising reply. 'Ludgershall?' echoed our astonished brother-in-law, sleep banished in an instant—and before you could say Jack Robinson or anything like it he was over the road and into the call box. The odd bits of his Division were camped hurriedly at Tidworth which presents the most cosmopolitan scene: Belgian soldiers rub shoulders with French sailors—marines and British Expeditionary Force jostle on the roads; the Frenchmen got down to it quickly and have collared all the prettiest girls. On Saturday John was given two nights off and spent them here. Mummie here too. He had lost everything except the very dirty battle suit he was wearing. Nothing left, beyond a looted revolver. He hadn't had more than two hours' sleep at a time for a fortnight and hadn't had his clothes off for a week. His feet were blistered, his eyes were red—but he was as lively as a cricket. Rosie iodined his feet and washed his hair—I dressed him up in your clothes while Nannie washed his! Marion put her best foot forward and we entertained the returning hero in as noble a way as possible! Oh—David, what times they have been through!

Orders—counter-orders—orders—counter-orders—issued by a bewildered High Command—brave but out-classed and outwitted by a dazzling new technique that moved from phase to phase with lightning swiftness before they could hope to fathom its intricacies. John couldn't speak too highly of our men. For a fortnight they had retreated—never given a chance to make a stand or show their worth. What could be more depressing and demoralising? Yet their morale and their discipline never wavered. The final march to Dunkirk in the sand dunes and under shell fire was horrible and mighty hard on the feet! John met Peter[3] in Dunkirk but he was shipped off first and looking back the last thing he saw was old Pete marshalling his men on the mole. Pete didn't get off till Monday and was lucky to get away as late as that. Men who can arrive home cracking jokes after such an adventure—beards bristling on their chins, reeking of sweat and motor oil—can't be beaten by Germans.

—Sybil

1. Sybil's sister Rosemary Wrightson whose husband John had been in France with the BEF.
2. i.e. a call to turn out with the Home Guard to meet a threat of invasion.
3. Peter Wrightson, his brother.

9 June 1940 Lisbon

My darling Syb—We live in a terrific whirl but on this front we are more than holding our own, as far as I can judge. The Mediterranean is a curious place and a tremor in Ankara sends a ripple all the way to Gibraltar and vice versa. I saw Salazar again on Friday and found him as attractive and helpful as ever. Now I am deep in conversations with Nicolas Franco, the Spanish Ambassador here; it is very useful that he is the Generalissimo's brother and that he can, and does, often ring him up. Lisbon is therefore the ideal venue for these negotiations.

I have had a big tiff with the Treasury and won hands down, which pleases little Selby very much, as he has always regarded them with deep suspicion.

Go up to London and encourage our friends. I can feel through their letters that they want a tonic. Open up the champagne that is in the lavatory at No. 17 and make champagne cocktails.

All my love—David

11 June 1940 Chute

My darling love—Alas, my darling, we have all been wrong, or perhaps we were just hoping against hope, since it seemed impossible that Italy[1] should forsake her traditional friends simply because pique had in 1935 thrown her into the Teutonic embrace. I still feel in my bones that were one in Italy now the people would still be friendly and sad and possibly horribly frightened of the pit into which they will without a doubt be flung by their German friends. What a defeat it is for the Catholic Faith. Mussolini is stronger than God. The Almighty is at a discount. But He will take a big revenge. I must admit to feeling dreadfully depressed about it. That lovely country—those simple people who are ready to deny their faith, scorn their Pope and spurn their friends and take instead a dark plunge into barbarism. I suppose Hitler has a half-nelson on the Duce and this combined with Musso's personal hatred of the English and his desire to share the spoils of victory (what a hope, poor mutt) has done the trick. But it's like the Ice-er Creamers to wait until the French are fighting for their lives on another front—before declaring themselves. I think we shall find that the leopard hasn't greatly changed.

Today *The Times* was a bit gloomy on the increased difficulty of Spain remaining neutral owing to the intervention of Italy—Italian officers in Franco's army—Italian agitators everywhere. What do you say?

My darling, goodnight, I do love you so.

—Sybil

1. Mussolini declared war on Britain on 10 June 1940.

16 June 1940 Lisbon

My darling love—Tomorrow I shall have a letter from you, after fourteen days' fast. I'm no camel in this respect, and hate so long a gap. If it happens again I shall telegraph just to have your love and name on a type-strip.

The immorality of Mussolini's act (I can't bring myself to write 'Italy's') blinds me. There must be a curse on us. Something like the flood will drown the world all but a handful. Nature perhaps is correcting in a violent way an immense failure on humanity's part to adjust its moral behaviour to its scientific discoveries. 'I showed you how to make an aeroplane to help you get about the world, and you use it for destruction; very well, you must disappear and someone else will come who will use it to creative ends.'

In September and October I was dismayed in an atmosphere of adventure, not feeling well as you remember, but as the Spanish negotiations went on, and finally were successful, and when at home again I found no difficulty in laying hold of and working out our Portuguese policy, then I began to have confidence in a world that had confidence in me. *You* had a better spirit from the beginning, and are always my comfort and joy. I know sometimes I get cross with you. I wish I never did. These are moments when I am a little mad, by mad I mean a little undisciplined in my head; inside which my thoughts go on marches and counter-marches enough to fill history books. And occasionally these mechanised troops, having been foraging a good part of the night, are out of hand in the morning. Sometimes I am a little mad.

Noel Coward[1] and Madeleine Carroll[2] came to lunch. He smells too sweet and snobs too often, and pushes his chair back and eats cross-legged, but I like him immensely. His heart is in the right place, he would say 'my inside heart'. *Cavalcade* in action, the retreat to Dunkirk, heroes and heroines, the whole world dressed up for tragedy, and his dream life becomes our real life—Madeleine is a very fine woman in build and appearance and talks very sensibly but doesn't attract me; I prefer Sylvie Oliveira[3] who has come here with her parents en route for Brazil. I must get out before Wally Windsor[4] and all her friends arrive. I should not be able to behave well to them, and I long to be at home.

I saw the Spanish Ambassador this morning on his return from Madrid. He told me that Spain would remain neutral, and that it was largely due to our proposals; that they had better manners than Mussolini and would not raise the question of Gibraltar at this time; that the Italian army is rotten and no one knows anything about their navy. Very encouraging, I thought.

All my love, my dearest Syb, I do so love you and wish to hold you again.

—David

1. Playwright and actor.
2. Actress and film star.
3. Daughter of Sr Regis de Oliveira, Brazilian Ambassador in London.
4. We knew that the Duke and Duchess of Windsor would shortly arrive in Lisbon.

18 June 1940 Chute

My darling love—Your letters tumble in and make encouraging reading. I'm so glad to know you're in such good spirits. Here we are quite undismayed and Churchill[1] provides the right tonic for all. His speech[2] last night was very good—first class—I wonder if you listened. I wasn't perfectly certain if the thickening of the voice could be put down to emotion or whether there had been just that one extra brandy at dinner. Anyway I like to believe it was emotion.

As to the Frogs—well, one is heartily sorry for them—the vicious speed and shattering blows of this war have dismayed and broken them. But how awful for them to have to submit now to the insults which Hitler will put upon them. It makes one more than ever determined that such a catastrophe shall never happen here. And it won't. Even the Germans can't ride tanks across the Channel—and as Winston remarked, 'We have a fleet which some people overlook.' One worries about the French navy. Will we seize it? Or if its surrender is made a condition of the Armistice can we blow it up? In just this infinitesimal corner of England one finds the older people a bit shaken and downcast. The very young—our Dorothy for instance—are quite untouched—ten minutes after the surrender of France they are whistling at the kitchen sink—the middlings scratch their heads but are quite determined to get on with it and are ready to believe Churchill when he says we can pull victory out of the melting-pot if we work and pray hard enough. The Secret Session should now be useful. For there are undoubtedly several directions in which things could be speeded up. Mobilisation of man- and woman-power chief of all. Here the machinery definitely rattles and groans and could do with an oiling. But this will come. Anyway have no fears for us.

We are even exhilarated by being on our own. No one left to desert us—no more failing friends to support.

I love you—Sybil

1. Prime Minister since 10 May 1940.
2. The 'finest hour' speech.

17–18 June 1940 Lisbon

My most dear Syb—I want to see you. If only for a few minutes, and if only for another and a longer goodbye. I do not know how we shall prosecute the war to victory, I think it rather an idle question, but we shall find a way, and find it suddenly. Do you remember our journey—Douglas Howard's and mine—to Guadalupe last January? Look up my letter, and you will see that we were caught in an impenetrable fog and that all counsel, local and our own, was for staying where we were. But I wouldn't do it; a few kilometres and we came into starlight and a clear road to our objective. Now we are in this fog in the war, and round the corner is the starlight.

For twenty-four hours I have tried to find adequate reason for telegraphing to the FO to announce my return. It would be so much easier to be resisting the enemy at home; and I should see you, which I so desperately desire. But there is no adequate reason. Selby and the Portuguese Government, and even Sam Hoare in Madrid, all insist that I should stay in the Peninsula.

So long as the Peninsula remains neutral there is much to do which I can do perhaps better than the rest of them. Though the chance is faint there is still a hope that we can keep Spain out of the war. I have begun to shape the arguments that must be used once France is completely crushed and occupied. Pétain's defeatism is a sad blow. I got a whiff of it on 3 May, when I read a telegram he had sent to Paris on 23 April *re* the Spanish situation. As soon as he became Vice-President of France I knew things were bad. He's a soldier, and he says to himself, 'Militarywise we can't win in France; give in and save as many troops as I can; a professional game has been played and lost.' He has no sense of the stake in civilisation. He has no connection with reality when he uses the phrase 'an honourable peace' with the Germans. The Germans can't make a 'soldier's peace' an honourable peace, this is the language of ancient history. He is eighty-four, and very lovable. I forgive him, but not France, who should have bred younger and stouter leaders.

Later

We have been to call on the French Legation again. In the courtyard, in the hall, on the stairs and in the rooms are men and women sobbing. Blinded with crying they are stabbing at hessian with bodkins in an endeavour to pack up, what I couldn't quite make out, but it looked like Red Cross things for refugees. One woman fainted, apparently on seeing me. A mother and boy of fifteen leant up against a statue howling and gasping. A man of fifty tried to write a letter, but his hand shook so he gave it up. I'm not sure if you can realise what war is like till you see people in this state. I don't suppose our people would do this, not our country-folk. These were all bourgeois. I was dreadfully sorry. I wanted more than ever to come home and share whatever similar trials are in store for us, but even the French Minister, his beard matted with weeping, begged me to stay. It is moving to be appreciated.

19 June
The Treasury have just sent me a telegram telling me to do all sorts of things with the Bank of Portugal—negotiations which will take two or three weeks at least. This puts an end to my hopes of getting back. Oh, my darling dear, I do hope and pray you will be all right! I know your heart is very stout. You will stay with the children, won't you? I want you all together at Chute, and I shall trust in God to keep you all safe.

All my love, now and always—David

22 June 1940 Lisbon

My darling Syb—In one of your letters, which have been coming all higgledy-piggledy by rail, sea and air, but the more the better—you ask about my negotiations. According to the rules I am not supposed to write about such things when bags are so uncertain. However, here goes, in pencil because I have a bad 'Lisbon' throat, a small temperature, and am in bed for half a day.

On 30 April I came here to make a War Trade Agreement, the draft for which I had in my pocket. Our demands were stiff because London thought the ancient ally should play up. On arrival I found Lisbon in a panic, in danger of a fifth-column *coup d'état*. A disturbing element was a widely-held belief that the British, on grounds of general dislike of dictators, were against Salazar's régime; another was the social unrest occasioned by the economic repercussions of the war; a third the hostile attitude and pan-Iberian ambitions of the extremists in Spain.

I came home to report with the following propositions as the basis of a new policy:

(a) in the middle of a European war Portugal is unarmed
(b) the maintenance of Dr Salazar's régime is in the interests of HMG
(c) his régime is threatened from without by Spain, and from within by economic distress
(d) the neutrality of Spain depends largely on Italy's attitude to the war, and the ability of the Germans to exploit Spain's economic difficulties.

I therefore proposed to leave on one side the making of a War Trade Agreement with Portugal until we could strengthen Dr Salazar's position and make a fresh attempt to secure the neutrality of Spain. I put forward a scheme designed to do both at the same time. We were to ask Dr Salazar to convey this offer to the Spanish Government:

(a) 100,000 tons of wheat to be diverted to Spanish ports before the end of June
(b) Spain to have the right to buy the products of the Portugal colonies and to pay for them out of the sterling proceeds of her own exports to the United Kingdom
(c) additional credit facilities to those we gave in our Madrid agreement, if the Spaniards required them

At the same time Salazar was to ask the Spanish Government for certain assurances regarding their neutrality, and anti fifth-column measures.

This scheme, which commended itself to Lord Halifax, had some secondary objects:

(a) to build up Dr Salazar's own position in Portugal, chiefly through saving his colonial markets
(b) to give him a vicarious lesson in anti fifth-column tactics
(c) to show the Spaniards that the Anglo-Portuguese Alliance was alive
(d) to use someone to make the offer of economic assistance who might possibly be able to secure political assurances at the same time. This I knew *we* could not do.

Dr Salazar did not disguise his satisfaction at these proposals, which he communicated to the Spanish Government without delay. The Spaniards called a special cabinet to discuss the scheme, and conveyed their acceptance, both to Dr Salazar and to me, through their Ambassador in Lisbon, with every show of gratitude. The Ambassador here is, as you know, Franco's brother. I began at once to discuss with him the commercial and financial details.

During these discussions Sam Hoare passed through Lisbon, obviously keen to get credit for improving Anglo-Spanish relations, but, on a wink from Roger [Makins], I let him see there was nothing doing. Dr Salazar refused to see him.

Italy then came into the war and all our work was in danger of collapsing. Salazar and Franco had some swift exchanges with a view to making a joint declaration of neutrality. To this at first the Spaniards agreed (it would have been an unbelievable triumph for our policy) but at the very last moment they yielded to Axis pressure and declared themselves non-belligerent. What did that mean? Everyone wanted to know, and to my surprise and pleasure I was the first to be told. The Spanish Ambassador sent for me as soon as he had received the explanation from Madrid. Nicolas Franco asserted that they meant nothing more by non-belligerent than they had previously meant by neutral, the new phrase was used to please the Axis and the extreme *Falangistas* who were looking for an excuse to throw over the government. General Franco was as firmly determined as ever not to have a shot fired on Spanish soil. We did some skating round the Rock of Gibraltar.

All this shows clearly enough how weak Franco's government is. That was and is our great danger. The Quislings could so easily turn Franco out and set up a puppet Axis government.

So much for the past. I am now working on a new scheme to allow for the disastrous change in the situation which a German-occupied France will mean. The failure of the French army—which in one of your letters you very kindly said was fighting heroically, I wish it had—leaves us with an entirely new strategic problem in the Mediterranean. Later I will tell you what I have in mind.

I must have been dreaming or dozing because I see by the clock I have been writing to you nearly two hours. I think of Chute a great deal, and pray for you every night. We shall live through strange times before our victory is in our hands. I don't feel any regrets for the past that embitter my hopes for the future. You know that you either have or have not a pain in your middle, there are no two ways about it, and I haven't a pain in my middle about the future. I examine my conscience, and say, 'Can we lose?' and the answer comes back like an echo, 'No, we can't.' That is all you need to know.

All my love, my dearest Syb, and please kiss the children.

—David

25 June 1940 Chute

My very dear love—I can only speak for this one small village—but here the spirit is excellent and courage and determination are high. Young Mrs King is a testimony of the Chute mood. Standing at her garden gate, arms akimbo, she says to me: 'What I say is, give us all a gun. Why shouldn't the women shoot too—I'd like to learn to shoot, I would.' Her eyes flash and one feels in advance quite a pang of sympathy for the hungry parachutist who is unlucky enough to knock at the Kings' front door.

Since last week I have had offers from Harriet Phipps[1] (do you remember High Price?) and Billy Biggs[2]—also a long cable from Peter;[3] all offering a home and everything else to our children for the duration. When the first cable arrived I was tremendously touched—but quite unmoved by it. Then things got worse—the two other cables came and the insidious forces of propaganda began to make themselves felt. Mummie came down and discussed the problem, which was a great help for in airing our views I came to this conclusion:

That I probably shouldn't let the children go without me. I ought to go with them for if I didn't, who knows when I should see them, if ever, again; that I simply couldn't face leaving England at the moment. Whether this is selfish and not in the best interests of the children I simply do not know. But in my bones I feel that Refugee-itis isn't the spirit which will win the war. Though one can't apply that term to young children who certainly ought to be saved as much as possible. But I couldn't face letting them go alone and if I go with them it means turning my back on England and you in the biggest crisis of our history. Poor children are being emigrated without their mothers. If rich children go with theirs—it means that the educated women who might possibly encourage and help their poorer sisters, clear out—simply because their money enables them to buy a passage. I can't feel this is right. One secondary aspect of the problem is that as one can't take any money to the USA it means living on charity once one gets there. Perhaps for several years. Here is an opportunity to practise what you have so consistently taught—that property and power are only justified if they be used wisely and well and their duties and obligations observed with loyalty. Isn't it the duty of our class to be calm and stay at home? Write to me your views on this complicated matter.

All my love, my dearest dear—Sybil

1. Mrs Howard Phipps of Westbury, Long Island, USA.
2. An American banker.
3. My brother.

25 June 1940 Lisbon

My darling love—Your hands must be very brown from working in the garden, and your hair a bit fuzzy, and your eyes a deeper colour. I don't doubt our two youngest are very happy, and John too: I wish I could be the fourth in your nursery. Our life has been as near perfect as our wildest guesses might have made it. I don't recollect we were ever jealous of anybody else. It is a tremendous test to pass unscathed. If I looked at one or two girls it was always to realise where my heart lay. And I don't know that a man uninterested in women in general could be very satisfactory to one woman in particular.

I have learned a great deal about the collapse of France, I do not think it wise to put it into this letter, but I have made some notes, and I will one day tell you the sickening story of treachery, weakness and shame. You will have difficulty in believing your ears, but, sad to say, it is true. Are we quite sure we have no similar canker at the heart of our public life? I pray so, but we must be vigilant. I distrust the Duke of Windsor; he and his Duchess are coming here to stay next week. I shall watch him at breakfast, lunch and dinner with a critical eye. Tomorrow we meet the Duke of Kent at 10 a.m. and afterwards I'm going to try and find Reynaud[1] who is suppposed to be here in hiding. (The French Legation say that he is accused of taking money from HMG and fears for his life; I said that was impossible as HMG had, most regrettably, not been in the habit of spending money on strategic objects; this raised the only smile of the week.) Anyway I am charged to persuade the little man to fly to England and join General de Gaulle. No one knows where he is, so I'm going to turn sleuth for a change. I assure you life is a pure fantasy, and half the things I say and do might as well be dreams, and my arm is (metaphorically) blue with self-pinching to persuade myself that it is not all a joke or a crime.

The effect on the character will be severe, but I can't judge from the middle of the stage what the result is likely to be. I am now so accustomed to going ahead of my instructions and to forcing policy on HMG that I have constantly to remind myself that there are still rules to be observed. In this I am greatly assisted by the Duke of Wellington, for on reading his despatches, or a part of them, from the Peninsula, I was astonished to see that, although he ordered every single detail of the campaign, he never failed to report every single detail, with the greatest courtesy and precision, to the proper authority in Whitehall. A very salutary example.

On the other hand what could be more encouraging than this from Lord Nelson, writing about his unauthorised pursuit of Napoleon to Egypt: 'The only objection I can fancy to be stated is, "You should not have gone such a long voyage without more certain information of the enemy's destination": my answer is ready—who was I to get it from? The Government of Naples and Sicily either knew not, or chose to keep me in ignorance. Was I to wait patiently till I heard certain accounts? If Egypt was their object, before I could hear of them they would have been in India. To do nothing I felt was disgraceful; therefore I made use of my understanding, and by it I ought to stand or fall.'

That's the stuff for you. What a pair, Wellington and Nelson! Why the hell don't we breed them now? I asked Selby this question at dinner and he said, 'Because modern women think too much about their own bloody [*sic*] lives and too little of their children's and their country's.' I said, 'Well, what about modern men?' 'Nearly all buggers,' he said, 'or if they aren't that, they're weakened by the rise of women to financial and social equality; take it from me, young man, the sexes enjoy a joint dignity and strength, and if you add to the woman's you detract from the man's.' We should think over this philosophy, it represents, I daresay, the real marrow of the Victorian age. Pretty bad-tasting to you and me; but what of the results of our way?

I wish you goodnight; I wish I were kissing the top of your head as you sat, most annoying in your chair, skimming some novel when I wanted to go upstairs. Then I should plead for you to come too, and leave defeated with a huge sigh.

All my love, sweet—David

1. Paul Reynaud was French Minister of Finance until he succeeded Daladier as Prime Minister of France on 21 March 1940.

28 June 1940 Chute

My darling love—I hope you find little Reynaud, he at any rate had more than marrow in his bones. I still have faith in the French people—the countrymen and women, and don't pass the harsh judgement on the army that you do. The BEF bring home a different story of courage and endurance. Some were weak-kneed perhaps and this was usually the fault of their equipment or their generals—others were as brave as can be.

After all, if it hadn't been for Abrial and his French marines at Dunkirk, combined with the superb British resistance at Calais and the French at Boulogne, we shouldn't now be rejoicing in 350,000 men safely bestowed about the fields and woods and downs of England. Every soldier who played a part in these scenes would agree with this so don't be too hard on the Frogs. The canker, as you call it, is to be found (I'm sure) in their public and municipal life—I pray like you that it doesn't fester here unobserved. Somehow I don't think so. The English have led lazy, self-indulgent lives of late—and have forgotten God and country. But they can still be aroused quickly and easily to such a ferocious display of energy and patriotism that one can't lose faith in them. Oh! no—we're all right—but I just wonder whether it will be beyond our powers to carve out a new world from the ruins. You're right, my sweet, I'm brown and horny and all my nails are broken!—but the garden looks lovely, even though the grass is burnt to a cinder, the lilies are out and in the evening light they shine like stars among the deepened blue of the delphiniums. I look at them and sigh as I shut the garden door and go in to my bath—what a waste that this should be our most brilliant summer for many years. It would have been so perfect to have shared it with you and heard at weekends our friends' voices across the lawns. But we've got a sterner task so goodbye to wistful thoughts. One day you will be home and we shall be together again.

I love you always, darling David—Sybil

3 July 1940 Chute

I met at Nan's the other day a woman who has spent all her life in France and the stories she had to tell of corruption and treachery were quite amazing. She assured us that anyone living in the country couldn't help but be aware of the rot that's been spreading everywhere during the last ten years. Communism had seeped through every chink in the national organisation—the generals in the French army were infected by it. Cash was the password anywhere. Pollution, treachery and a fatal inertia had overcome the robust France we once had known. She was really interesting if a bit depressing.

The van is now to be used as a maternity ambulance while waiting for air-raid work! I'm booked to carry Mrs Fox to Melksham Hospital when she's taken with her sixth in a few days' time. It being her sixth we shall probably collect the baby on the way!

All my love—Sybil

4 July 1940 Lisbon

Dearest Angel—Did I tell you about the Duke of Kent[1] and his family? He really adores them, is afraid of his wife and idolises his son. The Duchess wants more children but he won't agree as he says it may not be possible for him to feed them. 'I'm a nuisance to everybody, I can't do a job suitable to my rank, and I can't do a little job beneath it; all I can do well is talk to people and take an interest in their work.' 'My wife doesn't want the children to know there is a war; I try to tell my son about it and he won't believe me, what can I do to convince him?' He wants very much to settle down to a self-respecting job, he isn't stupid, but he isn't thoughtful, he's a touch brilliant.

I had lunch with the Windsors today. I wouldn't give ten shillings for Wallis, she is a poor creature. He adores her and is in fine health. He has accepted a job[2] under great pressure from HE and your affectionate DE, you'll see about it in the papers. A very cunning solution. It means some recognition at last for her. He's pretty fifth-column, but that's for you only. I'm dining with them on Saturday and will give you more titbits thereafter.

It's frightfully hot, and I am sticky all day until my tepid bath. I don't mind the heat and think I am working well and at a satisfactory speed. Certainly the history of the Peninsula in 1940 can't be written without knowledge of these peculiar negotiations.

All my love and when oh! when shall it be real and not on paper?

—David

1. The Duke of Kent led the delegation from the United Kingdom to the celebrations of the eight-hundredth anniversary of the foundation of Portugal.
2. Governor-General of the Bahamas.

5 July 1940 Chute

My darling love—there is a pause—a barely perceptible pause in the day's operations—lunch is over, the afternoon walk has not yet begun. So here is a short letter after my long one of yesterday.

We had a shower this morning and all rushed out to look at it. So novel a phenomenon it was. Harris has sunstroke—I must force a honey-bee upon him. He is really quite bad and has taken to his bed—so Hawkins and I are busier than ever. Your hedge has been beautifully clipped and trimmed and looks quite plump and imposing though the thin bit in front of the house annoys me whenever I look at it—why was I such a fool as to stick to that silly little thorn tree so long? Your lawns, alas! are far from beautiful. They are both quite brown and it's useless to struggle with the plantains for the ground is like iron. We should only leave dusty brown patches everywhere and probably fail to uproot properly. Harris is in favour of waiting for a wet spell.

The new kitchen garden is doing nicely and we have a big crop of peas and early potatoes. I manage to send a small hamper to

Father each week and occasionally some to 32 Wimpole Street. Tortoiseshell butterflies are everywhere. They flutter through the windows and die terrible deaths against the panes. We are doing our duty with scrap iron, wastepaper and bones. The Village Dump—in a corner of Mustey's field—is now an imposing sight. Mrs Austen has been appointed Jam-Maker-in-Chief and organiser of the Chute WI Jam-Making Centre. This is a brilliant national scheme for pooling all surplus fruit which the individual cannot turn into jam from lack of sugar. This fruit is pooled and used for jam-making at local centres who are entitled to apply for sugar on a community basis. The jam to be sold at cost price when finished. Rather a cunning idea. This afternoon I go to see Withers on ploughing matters—then on to the Vicarage to fetch myself some honey from the Vicar's hives. Home—tea and an excursion with Simon after rabbits!

All my love, my dearest dear—Sybil

8 July 1940 — Lisbon

My darling Syb—Yesterday after lunch (Sunday) I went with Sylvia Oliveira for a long drive and we ended up at 6.30 on the lines of Torres Vedras and walked along the ridge for a mile or so. I like to live over our military history. The country on both sides is beautiful. Fields of maize and vineyards and patches of pine trees. The houses white with browny-red tiles, rather like the tiles on Dean Farm, perhaps a little greyer. The evening was cool as there had been a storm the night before and I imagined how pleasant such a landscape must have seemed in the dreams of the Portuguese sailors as they discovered the world in the fifteenth century. Any man, after a hard life, would be glad to come to rest in such a place.

I saw the Windsors again. Really, I don't like them. They have no charm for me, and I dislike her quite a lot; a battered warhorse in a halo hat, it is most unattractive.

I am homesick again. It comes in spasms, and I can't tell why. The interviews with the representatives of the Pétain government[1] sickened me inside and made me nervous—just a little nervous—about our own civilian population. It will be a narrow squeak. Another ten years of complacency and drift and we too might have collapsed. Now France may go Nazi out of disgust. I feel it in my bones. The French Constitution is hopeless, it must be reformed, and I hope de Gaulle has the sense to say so, but it must be reformed by Frenchmen and not by Germans. I have seen one or two letters from unoccupied France—one very good from Marseilles—assuming the war is over and that we shall all be the better for a dose of German efficiency and strength thro' joy. You have to pinch yourself to be sure you are reading genuine stuff, and it shows no sign of being written under pressure. Madame Reynaud said the same sort of thing to a man I know only ten days ago.

All my love, dearest Syb—David

1. MM. Chastenet and Bressey called on me with messages from the Vichy government. The letter describing this interview was lost. Some four letters during this period never reached Sybil.

11–12 July 1940 Lisbon

My darling love—Are our letters like a couple of people talking at once, not listening to each other? Do I pay enough attention to what you write? You may think I am more interested in what happens here than in you and in Chute. It is not so. When, without warning, I think suddenly of home, it is you who come nine times out of ten on to the screen. The children turn up occasionally, but very seldom in front of you. As I love them very much, this is a proof that I love you much more.

I am fretting now because I can see no end to my mission in the Peninsula. Yesterday Lord Halifax sent a long telegram to Sam Hoare, which was repeated to Lisbon, beginning 'Following a suggestion from Mr Eccles, HMG have decided on a new economic policy towards Spain and Portugal, the main features of which are . . . after communicating in principle this policy to the Spanish Government I consider the detailed discussions could best be undertaken by enlarging Mr Eccles's negotiations in Lisbon.' Well, what can I do? I can't father the child and refuse to bring it up. You see I am caught in the projects of my imagination, I cabled the Secretary of State to say that all the Spanish negotiations must be held in Madrid, as we cannot continue indefinitely under Salazar's umbrella. There are some intimate things which can only be discussed between Spain and the UK direct. Sam Hoare immediately picks this up and says, 'I agree, Mr Eccles should come to Madrid at once!' Here I am, the Treasury's sole representative, in the middle of a most tricky financial negotiation between Portugal and the UK and I can't be in two places at once. I am flying to Madrid tomorrow, Saturday, and returning here Monday.

The tragedy is—at least it is my personal tragedy—that HMG now consider me the Iberian wizard, and nothing else. But it's all wrong. I can just speak Spanish and can't make myself understood in Portuguese. The advice I give on Peninsular affairs, which has so impressed them at home, is the result of 95 per cent of deductions from, and reflections upon, sound general principles and 5 per cent local knowledge. These principles will apply on broader fields, *at home* I mean, and I hate to be reduced to the size of an expert. The man who would give me good advice is George Lloyd,[1] is there any chance you could see him?

Oh! they are silly about Pétain and France at home! Can't they see that the French Revolution, the doctrines of the Encyclopaedists and Rousseau expired the day that the Armistice was signed? Back to the Bourbons is the cry! No nonsense about Third Empires or upstart Buonopartes. Right back to Louis XIV they will go; and if well led will become a great danger to the interests of His Britannic Majesty. Remember I say this on 12 July 1940. It is an intolerable stupidity to imagine that the French people will be content to attribute their immense disaster to anything but an equally immense cause: and to what cause? Why, to the failure of the French Revolution. It's as obvious as the sun in the sky.

Why can't we have a weekend together? What heaven it would be, you would pour out all the gossip and I should have an idle hour drinking it in and looking at you, and then we could walk round the garden and take a little but not too much notice of the children, and have dinner *à deux* and go to bed. Oh! hell, what a life.

All my love—David

1. Lord Lloyd, formerly High Commissioner for Egypt and the Sudan, was appointed Secretary of State for the Colonies, 12 May 1940. He had always given me much encouragement.

14 July 1940 Chute

My dearest love—Yesterday Mrs Fox was delivered of her sixth amid the fleas and filth of Mrs Moore's cottage at Lower Chute. The midwife didn't dare remove her in the midst of her toils—since we might have had the baby on the Plain and in the black-out. So we took her off instead later in the day. Poor thing—not much fun for her—but she bore up very nicely being bumped down the stairs and heaved into the van on my beautiful green stretcher to the accompaniment of old Mrs Fox's idiotic remarks: 'Well, she's over the worst of it now—ain't yer, Gertie?' Groan from Mrs F being bumped over the top of the spare wheel. 'Fancy—our sixth and the biggest one we've had.' Stony look from me.

Then came lacrimose farewells from Old Grannie, the dirtiest of the lot, and we were off. The midwife in her car behind—Mrs Eccles driving the van with the infant rolled in shawls on the seat beside her and in terror lest the patient all alone in the back should roll off her stretcher. However at Ludgershall the nurse parked her car and joined us—though I still kept the baby, which was a vision of beauty—pale pink, nice and sound with yellow fluff. I felt I'd like to rush home and start in straight away. The midwife was very chatty, trained at the London [Hospital], an admirer of Sir Bertrand [Dawson] and Lord Knutsford. Chatter chatter.

'You just close your eyes, Mrs Fox, and have a little sleep.'

As if a little sleep were to be had for the closing. We had a special permit to cross the Plain (most of it is closed) and as we slowed down before the sentries they caught sight of the prostrate Mrs Fox and waved us by—standing on tiptoes as we passed to heave a manly sigh over Wiltshire's latest Potential Mother. Upavon was passed—we bowled through Devizes. 'I 'ad ter fight 'arder for 'er than fer the lot of them,' said Mrs Fox. 'A little sleep, Mrs Fox,' crooned the midwife. And so to Melksham and the Cottage Hospital where the postman helped us heave the stretcher into a ward that looked like an air-raid shelter. It was all over and we bustled home munching lardy cakes and telling tales.

I do love you—Sybil

17 July 1940 Chute

My dearest love—No—I don't think our letters are like a couple of people talking to each other without listening. Considering their erratic departures on a journey no longer without hazard I think they link up with each other remarkably well. There is at the moment only one missing link. I have never had your views on sea-evacuation[1] (another of our glorious contemporary additions to the English Dictionary). I expect you wrote them to me and they died a glorious death en route—and I know what form they take for you sent them to Mummie. Still I should love to read them for myself. Because I know they are very exhilarating and stout-hearted.

God! How glad I am now that I turned the project down with firmness. The cat-calls and the reproaches that are now flying about inside and outside the Mother of Parliaments make one shudder. Ho-ho screech the Labour Members. So now that the children of the rich have got safely away the children of the poor are to be abandoned. Of course, it's a distortion of the facts. All the same I feel it's pretty poor that ministers who spend evenings on the BBC exhorting the public to endurance and courage should at the same time be scuttling their children out of the country. And there are others in high places who've been jostling and stumbling to get out. It's pretty sickening—and just about the best argument for doing away with the gentry that could possibly be presented to any full-blooded socialist.

Darling D, I've read your letter of 12 July again. What exactly do you mean by the France of Louis XIV and the Splendours of Versailles? I suppose a despot? i.e. a Fascist, a Nazi on the German model?—The result (a) of domination and fear (b) of disgust at the rotten and poisonous condition to which ill-directed democracy has brought France? We all think this is what is actually going to happen in France. But you must think a great deal more—since you are dissatisfied with our conclusions and find them inadequate. Send me some more meat. I still entertain some hopes for democracy. But to succeed it must become a positive and dynamic force—and it must be shorn of all its hampering bureaucratic trimmings that make it just about as capable of running a race with Hitlerism as a baby in long clothes.

But don't let's have the iron hand of compulsion—there's

something particularly grand about an association of free men. But I admit that to do any good against authoritarian régimes they must be animated by the same ideals to an extraordinary degree. In war this comes from a sense of common danger—in peace it is certainly more difficult to achieve. Perhaps a revival of Christianity and faith in England as the leader of Europe would provide the motive power.

We've certainly got to put our ideas in order well in time—for only we, *I hope*, are going to run Europe when this business is over.

Oh, dear!—I'm as lonely for you as you are for me. It's cruel—but I love the letters in which you cry out a little against our separated lives. But I have long been schooling myself to hear that you've got to stay in the Peninsula and so it doesn't surprise me to know it now for certain. It is wonderful to think how they value you—though I know your fear of being pigeon-holed as a specialist. And it would be an idiotic waste to abandon you for ever to Spain and Portugal, though at the moment we all realise how vitally important it is to keep the Peninsula sweet. What *would* happen to the Mediterranean if your mission (and dear Sam's) failed? It's a horrid thought. So one has a certain sympathy with the powers that be for wanting to keep you where you are for the moment. I would make a huge effort to see Lloyd if you wanted me to. Tell me to do it again in your next letter. Then I shall know that you really mean it and that it's not a suggestion thrown out in a moment of uncertainty. I want to be sure—sometimes one can make a mistake about such things. I'm certain I could get half an hour out of him. And what an excitement to be in London again!—I haven't been for two months. Not since the day you left. Sometimes, in spite of rural joys, I know myself to be a Cockney at heart.

Darling David—I love you so very much—Sybil

18 July

Mummie reports that the Duke of Kent came and spoke to her the other day and said he knew you and that you were a *very* bright fellow indeed—that he loved talking to you even if your conversation was too clever for him (rather sweet that!) and that you couldn't possibly be spared from the Peninsula as you were dealing so ably with a situation fraught with difficulties and very important to our cause. I've bridled quite a lot at hearing this.

My love to you

1. i.e. sending children by sea to America for the duration of the war.

17 July 1940 Lisbon

My darling Syb—Madrid was a wild success. I had a tremendous welcome. Things are going well there and our efforts have made some impression. I'm hoping to go back again soon. Sam has done well altho' physically he is very frightened but it is an impediment like a stutter and doesn't matter as much as I had thought it would.

I hate evacuation of children. It is quite contrary to that building of society on the family which I think essential. We are all one and should stick together. The children must experience the rough with the smooth or they will not love and understand their country. Canadian-fed brats won't be the same. No, no, evacuation is a mild form of suicide, and only to be pardoned in those suffering from pain or loss of mental balance. And you said you would go too. That, of course, finishes it. I could not possibly do without you, and won't contemplate it.

I am horribly stuck in the Peninsula, but the work is of importance. I'm mad you didn't get all my commentary on Pétain because I wrote a really valuable account, knowing him as I do, and having such a chance. Gladwyn and Roger both write rather gloomily that they fear the slide to the left in foreign politics, it wouldn't matter much in home politics, but abroad it is disastrous to ally ourselves with the dregs of Fronts Populaires.

Your description of the midwifery in the van was first rate. Oh! I wish I was there! Instead I am being seduced by the Windsors who have made a dead set at me, and by heaven when they turn their united charm on, it is hard to resist. She is incredible, she changes so when dressed up, her figure exquisite, in a black evening tight top to a pear-green skirt with magnificent jewels. And he has a confiding manner of talking that is dangerous to a degree. Anyway I dine twice a week. They are the arch-beachcombers of the world. Wallis is a very vulgar woman in gesture, she sticks her beautifully scented face within two inches and just asks to be kissed, only of course you don't do it. It is so deceitful to take advantage of the fact you can't smack her.

Ring up Roger [Makins] and ask if he ever got a memorandum about MM. Chastenet and Bressey, I must know for certain.[1]

All my love, my sweetest dear—David

1. This important document about Pétain's representatives never reached its destination. Nor did two or three letters to Sybil in which I wrote about Pétain.

21 July 1940 Chute

My darling dear—The borders are a dream, I wish you could see them. We ended on Friday with a tea-party for three Australian officers who turned up full of politeness and party manners which rapidly disappeared under the influence of drop scones and honey! By the third cup of tea they were coming across a treat and one of them announced: 'Do you know, Mrs Eccles, we weren't a bit keen on this tea-party idea. This morning we had a sweep on your age and it came out as eighty-eight.'

At this another chimed in: 'Yes, and when you turned up to fetch us in your van, old Bill here came to haul me out and said, "Take a stiff pull at yourself, old man—she's arrived and she's about sixty-seven" '!!

This sort of badinage went on through an enormous tea during which they ate us out of sugar and home. Then in the middle of everything John [Wrightson] turned up with a fellow officer from Tidworth—which couldn't have been bettered. For the ideal Empire building is to bring soldier and soldier together. John was wonderful with them and the conversation flowed. In the middle of it the largest guest of all—a Major Bursden, six-foot-seven—leaned across to me and enquired, 'Do you think I might see all the house before I go? I'm very fond of houses and it would remind me of ours at home.' Rather sweet.

So over the house we went and as we wandered through the rooms he told me about his wife and three small sons and we sympathised with each other. At parting they all asked if they might come again—so Rosie and I hope that we've done the Empire a good turn.

All my love, my darling David—Sybil

Simon (who is Australian-mad—to John's lieutenant): 'Are you an Australian?' *J's lieutenant*: 'No, I'm a Scotsman.' *Simon* (very disappointed): 'Oh! I see, just an *ordinary* soldier.'

Huge joy of all three Australians!

Begun 20 July 1940 Lisbon

Darling dear Syb—It's 3 p.m. and frightfully hot. I am in my shirtsleeves and feel like taking off my trousers. At five I have to see Salazar and tell him all about Madrid. On the days when I am going to see him I always feel gay. Our Peninsular policy—the economic side—works well. We have removed all doubt about the vitality of the Anglo-Portuguese Alliance; given sufficient support to Franco to build him up to a point where he could resist the first German ultimatum delivered the day their troops reached Hendaye. The knowledge in Spain that we are solidly behind Portugal has helped much. I came here just in time.

Now the battle is transferred to London. Hugh Dalton, that renegade Etonian, has laid hold of MEW and aspires shortly to be Foreign Secretary. He hates dictatorships on principle; Franco in public and in particular, and Salazar in private and half-heartedly. Therefore seeing that the Peninsula has now open communications with Germany and must be regarded as an adjacent neutral, he would like to teach the dictators a lesson by starving them out with a ferocious system of rationing. Nothing could make the entry of Spain into the war on Germany's side more certain. Dalton has his knife into Maurice Ingram[1] and Phil Nichols[2] as the authors of our policy which failed over Italy. He should blame Percy Loraine and Francis Rodd. I always thought and often said appeasement would fail; because Mussolini wanted to join in against us, he never stopped saying so, whereas Franco wants to be neutral, and Salazar would like to fight with us if he had any arms. This is a fundamental difference making appeasement in the case of Italy a bad bet and in the case of Spain a good one. I have written a paper for Dalton trying to put this across, and now await the answer. If he cuts up rough on ideological grounds I have arranged with Selby and Hoare to come home for a few days and argue our case with the Cabinet.

We all read Hitler's speech with scorn first and love for our families afterwards. We do not forget you in this topsy-turvy war where I am comparatively safe and you in danger. I think very often and lovingly of all of you, and am glad the children are not older. Their insouciance must be a great help.

Later

Salazar really is a wonder: so quiet, so efficient, so romantic and, I can't help adding, so extraordinarily fond of me. Make no mistake in what way. He lives in seclusion with an old housekeeper, and a small girl (I believe aged seven) whom he has adopted. No one has ever detected a sexual impulse in him, either to right or left. Therefore his affection may be considered pure. We had a long talk about Spain, and the probable duration of the war, which he puts at two to three years. I wonder if he is right. Before I leave I shall do something I have never done before, and that is ask him for a photograph.

His outstanding gift is his capacity to see every problem in the round, he knows how it has arisen, what is its importance in the general picture of Portuguese policy, how it will develop if various alternatives occur, who are the men handling it, what they are capable of and what they are not, and what is the contribution to its solution which HMG might make if they chose to. He is like a man who has to transport heavy material across a frail bridge, he knows just what the bridge will bear and loads his cart accordingly; there is an absence of guessing that is quite astonishing, and quite unlike MEW, for example.

When he and the housekeeper have put the adopted child to bed, and he has had his one-course dinner, he must read a great deal. Otherwise he could not possibly know all that he does. He never dines out. He said quite simply, 'Some people use the stimulus of social life, I don't.' It is just like a teetotaller saying, 'I prefer a cup of coffee.' I told you, I think, that he is ravishingly good-looking.

Often I say to myself, 'Why don't I ask for Syb to come out?' and then I think that in these times you would not want to be tempted away from the children and Chute. I can get on better without you than they can, although I miss you fifty times more than they would. Perhaps in October if I am still here *en poste* you could leave them for a month. It would be lovely. Think it over. I should have to go to immense subterfuge to get you to meet Salazar, he is as shy as a badger.

I cannot write more to you as I must get on with my official correspondence which is in a mess as usual.

All my love—David

1. *and* 2. Foreign Office officials.

[On 25 July I went home for a fortnight's leave, returning to Lisbon on 13 August.]

13 August 1940 Lisbon

Darling sweet—We had some adventures on the way out. Five minutes after our escort turned back we saw a German plane, but it didn't notice us as it was about to bomb a merchant vessel. Both bombs missed by about fifty yards; the ship was a mile from us. Then we turned sharply into a cloud and the German did the same. Evidently there was a bad raid on Portland later in the day, it looked lovely as we passed over the bay of Weymouth. I remarked the colour, almost peacock blue and very faintly barred with green.

Arriving here in this lovely place I suddenly had a passionate desire to cling on to life, to hug it and never let it go. I think our fortnight had been so marvellous, I was so happy to be with you, and Chute was so beautiful, and Lisbon and the Doctor are so absorbing, that I fell clean in love with living. How awful it is that thousands of people do not want to do anything again they have done before, or go back anywhere they have been, or kiss anyone they have kissed! How different we are! *J'adore la vie*, and there it is, and you are my life to a huge extent.

All my love in a hurry—David

15 August 1940 Chute

My dearest love—Well—we have had our first air raids! On Sunday as I was leaving Bournemouth they began battering the south coast—apparently doing little damage (this according to letters from residents and not only from the press). On Monday they were at it again and lost a lot of planes. Tuesday Nannie went out and as I was struggling with the young ones to get them ready for a walk—John sauntered in and said, 'They're having a practice, I suppose, I've just heard an air-raid warning.' But I always underestimate the astonishing accuracy of my eldest and just pooh-poohed the poor boy and off we went up the hill—and a good thing we did for we had a fine sight of it all from the pub. Half-way up the boys ran off—a stream of aeroplanes came over at great speed and presently the crumps began and columns of smoke rose over Ludgershall. We sheltered in the Cross Keys, front row of the dress circle—and applauded the performance. One could see the salvoes hit the ground in rapid succession and the puffs go up. Presently the Spitfires were overhead and we watched a chase—but the cloud was very low and one couldn't follow anything for more than a second or two.

During a lull we made for home. Polly, pick-a-back and the boys most demurely in single file. Our trio thoroughly enjoyed themselves and made a striking example of the insensibility to danger of the young. John and Simon were profoundly interested while our woman hopped about shouting, 'Here are the Germans, I'm going flat on my tummy like a soldier—Bang bang bang,' which made the boys laugh like anything. They got the military stores at Ludgershall and a few unfortunate soldiers. Nothing else of importance—and several planes were brought down.

All my love—Sybil

15 August 1940 Madrid

Dearest Syb—I write a note as I am in Sam's circus and performing night and day. Madrid is very hot and tension is running high. I don't doubt the Germans have been stung to fury by their failure to get Spain into the war. There is evidence on every side. They simply loathe our Portuguese efforts and are going all out to break our economic negotiations here. Provided the chaps at home are not influenced to rage by the disgraceful articles in the press which are paid for by Germany and designed to cause us to break off economic relations I think we shall weather this storm.

The Spanish Government is weak but not wicked. Our Labour politicians don't make enough allowance for this. We shall some day learn the elements of human nature, and then our policy will be more consistent, more far-seeing and more successful.

I am staying with Arthur Yencken who has been made a minister. This promotion he richly deserved. He has a wonderful technique for getting Sam, or his cook, to do what he wants. He first fires a sighting shot which isn't meant to hit the bull but to try the gun and the wind, and then he waits a little and puts in a deadly shot that never fails. I don't know anyone else who so uniformly splits up all his actions into two parts.

—David

17 August 1940 Chute

My dearest love—We've had a glorious week of sunshine and Germans—but the last two days have been quiet. The RAF have given them something to think about and the clouds have been too high. They get such a dusting even when it's overcast that they keep off on the blue days. We went swimming at Weyhill on Thursday—the pool is full of dead wasps and floating bits of this and that which if you're wise you leave unexamined—but the afternoon was gloriously hot—we had a picnic by the edge and the children adored it. Some bombs came down after tea and as they weren't so far off we beat it for home—but no one was agitated—the last thing I remember on looking back was the sight of a stout woman in a tight, flowered satin bathing dress with a tin hat on her head still dangling her chubby legs over the edge of the bath! You'd be surprised how soon one gets used to it—and the children don't give a damn. Of course we haven't had anything drop very near.

With all my love—Sybil

21 August 1940 Chute

My darling love—Our RAF successes must help enormously in maintaining Spanish indecision—the Prime Minister's review yesterday I thought first class—and it seems to have made a good impression everywhere and in fact I really don't think it could fail to impress—it was so direct, sober and confident. All this must help you. How hot Madrid must be! I remember how I used to linger in the cool of the Ritz hall, summoning enough courage to plunge out into the glare and dust of the Castellana where the sun would press through onto my shoulders like a hot iron.

Here the weather has completely changed and it is cold and bleak. Last night was like an evening in late autumn, all shivers and I had the light on for dinner.

We go bicycling and blackberrying and the riding lessons make a diversion. The raids go on every day—we have more warnings than bombs. The boys and I were in Andover for a morning on Monday which thrilled them—we went and stood near a shelter and watched the aeroplanes—no bombs—a splutter of machine guns and they were soon off.

Goodnight, my dearest dear.

I love you—Sybil

25 August 1940 c/o Conde de Albiz, La Granja

My darling Syb—I came here last night for a day in the country. Sam was emphatic that Arthur [Yencken] and I could have the time off, so we accepted Albiz's invitation and drove over the Guadarrama in a violet dusk that rapidly changed to the black sky and white stars of Castilian night.

The Albizes are a jolly family—six children, eight to twenty-one—and life in a large and jumbled house. Arthur and I have to have a guide to the bathroom, we should certainly lose our way.

After dinner we were swept along to the La Granja social club, now at the height of its season, full of Monarchists and 'quite a good crowd' as Albiz said in distinction from old fellows like Arthur and me. They were dancing to a victrola, about fifty of them, in dresses of cheap satin run up at home from a tuppenny pattern! This is what war does, but it doesn't matter. As always here there was an awkward tendency for the boys and girls to segregate and quip each other in bunches. Then came a 'prestigiator', the local conjurer, who performed the simplest tricks to the huge delight of all.

Did I tell you that in the royal letter to Sam HM[1] said good things about me and the audience? So it went all right. I am astonished at the *réclame* which the Portuguese treaty has in Spain. Here they all think the work done in Lisbon quite fundamental to their hopes of neutrality. When you make anything—like a child—you don't know at all how it will grow and what success it will have in the world. Other people have taken hold of our Portuguese treaty and done with it all sorts of things I never dreamed of. Realising this I am thinking out a new child, whose name shall be called Western Mediterranean or the Pillars of Hercules, who shall be born of the same parents and sponsored by the same godfather: with one extra.[2]

My windows are tall and open on a balcony overlooking the street at right angles to the Hotel Europeo (*viene la sopa?*). The air is full of sharp noises, 'Pepito' shouts one, 'Marianna' another, cocks crow, carts bang, and some argument about the price of washing clothes is attracting a meeting; now I hear a boy directing a car how to back, '*da la vuelta*,' he shouts, I can't get the answer but it sounds angry; some girl has begun to sing a *sevillaña*, whether to listen, or by accident, the others are quiet . . . it is a plaintive caressing tune that calls from woman to man with passion mixed with despair. Adoring and desperate at the same time. The village seems to like it, there is some applause; now a big jingling of bells which shows that a cart has stopped and moves on. I really love the Spanish life, not as part of myself, like life at home, but as something I have met, sniffed and accepted as good. I shall get up and stroll out under the trees in front of the Europeo with Arthur. We have a bundle of old *Times* to give to the English nannies—seven or eight—who are here with their 'charges'. They know we are coming and will be all agog. I might make them a little speech about winning the war. They like it and I want practice.

I love you with all my heart—David

1. After I returned in July 1940 Lord Halifax arranged for me to have an audience with King George VI. The King asked questions about Franco.
2. USA.

30 August 1940 Madrid

My darling love—We are in a worse patch here than I have ever known. It is just touch and go. The Spaniards are desperate, harried by the Germans on one side and our Blockade on the other. Strange to say as we move from one crisis to another Sam is gaining in authority and courage. I almost like him, I certainly admire him. His capacity for skating over thin ice and for conveying to the Spaniards that his personal vanity is the pride of a minister of our Royal Master is exquisite, and deceives them all.

This morning I persuaded him to put to the Minister of Finance in person our proposals for giving Spain a quota for oil. I primed him not to give way and not to fall for a request for a 'gesture of goodwill'. I was a good deal frightened; but he stood his ground admirably and defended with astonishing fertility our rather tricky position. When matters looked black and he had to depart—ever so slightly—from the straight and narrow path, he protested '*con toda franqueza*' that he was not a diplomat and did not understand the wiles of professional negotiation. It was as good as a play.

I have seen a lot of Frenchmen. They all say the same, 'Abuse the Vichy government as much as you like, but not Pétain, he is the sacred bull, against whom all shafts are useless and return to the breasts of their deliverers.' They are also unanimous in disliking de Gaulle.

I wish you were here. I am lonely among many good friends.

All my love, sweetest Syb—David

1–3 September 1940 Madrid

My darling love—I came home last night at 1 a.m. to find Arthur [Yencken] drunk. The extraction of a wisdom tooth had given him hell and I suppose he couldn't stand it any more. I don't see much of drunkenness. Arthur was waving in front of the chimney, legs wide apart, and Virginia Woolf's *Roger Fry* in his hand. The cover, you know, is a late self-portrait of Roger Fry with white hair. 'Looksh him all to peeches, usherly degenerate, a faish like a shloppy shpinshter, no bloody good to England or any womansh.' I edged him upstairs, but once there he took a nice leaning position against my open door, and continued to abuse all intellectuals. I went on undressing and finally pushed him into his bedroom, but when I came out of the bathroom he had got downstairs again. What for I don't know. We didn't mention it at breakfast.

It's Sunday evening. All day I've been working quietly and happily in a half-empty Embassy, and have walked slowly back along the Castellana to change for dinner with Sam and Maud. The sky is brilliant with a golden sun, the plane trees shining darkly. The air is clean and warm, and no smells; innumerable children muck in the gravel and the conduits that irrigate the trees, they look very poor and too often beg. They execute upon each other acts of incredible cruelty, one of six gouges the eyes of one of seven whose arms are round a baby he can't drop—yes, he did drop it, and blinded with his own tears lashes at the aggressor who goes down howling and slightly bleeding.

Poor Spain! One disaster has followed on another. The Civil War, a bad harvest, our war, another bad harvest. No exports, no tourists, no imports. Even the fishing industry, which supplied the want of meat quite admirably, has collapsed. Now they have no petrol for the boats because they sell their exiguous ration to private motorists at a huge profit. Profit—what a queer motive to have picked on as the giant employer of labour and provider of food.

My dearest sweet, I meant to write much more, but the American Embassy want me urgently. A kiss to the creatures, and all my love to you. When shall we have time to breathe and read books and make love?

—David

8–10 September 1940 Madrid

My darling love—I want you safe and sound when I come home. Often now I stop short in my thoughts and say, 'How is Syb? Is she all right? I wish I were with her and she with me.' The days when we shall be together will be more precious for this separation. I've no doubt we shall look at each other with curious eyes. Experience at the rate we are getting it must leave its mark, but it won't be an offensive scar, at least I know yours won't.

Did I ask you if you have heard of Pétain's motto, '*Veni, vidi, vichy*'??

Always the Continent asks the same question, 'If you win will you impose on us the same corrupting system of liberal-capitalist democracy; we can't stand another dose, the first nearly killed us.' I try to show them that I at least won't endorse the old game of French party politics, but they don't believe I am more than a freak. There is an opposition between a moral and a religious society that is slowly dawning on me. Justice is made for man, love for God. To be just is merely a matter of keeping contracts and carrying our rights and duties according to an earthly standard, to be religious is to love enough not to revenge, not to imprison for small offences 'as we forgive them that trespass against us'. In Catholic countries they put more value on love and less on justice, more on sacraments, less on sin. We have to borrow some of their conception of love, and they adopt some of our conception of justice: but in truth men are not limited creatures who can be moved into patterns according to laws which are based on just principles, they have a capacity for being and creating which depends on how much one asks of them. All history shows that inspiration, leadership, a cause are wanted to stimulate human beings who are naturally bad and lazy. The doctrine of original sin cannot be refuted.

My darling love, I kiss you and wish more than ever you were here or I with you.

—David

15 September 1940 Chute

My darling love—With every day the wind blows colder and whips the Channel into angry waves. We are all convinced that Hitler will try something—everything is assembled in huge array and he is pretty well committed to an attempt. But time is shortening and he must have counted on air mastery before he began and this, even the last fortnight has failed to obtain for him. So we sit and wait and wonder and are in good heart. There are well-authenticated reports that the first attempt was made last Saturday or Sunday—and the transports were sunk before half the journey had been accomplished. Hurrah. But one knows nothing for certain. In any case the church bells rang merrily in Andover and other southern towns and the Home Guard sprang to their muskets!

I've made the humiliating discovery that I'm no heroine in air raids! Not so bad when I felt I absolutely had to go to London to do my duty to Mabel[1]—but altogether a hopelessly apprehensive victim when I spent the day there (four days ago) for inadequate reasons and got thoroughly tangled up in the biggest daylight raid they've had. I sit in a stupor burdened by thoughts of you and the children—that widower, those orphans!! And with conscience nagging can only cravenly think of getting out and getting home. Too bad, isn't it? Motherhood's the devil. Grandnan and I watched a Hun sail over Hyde Park—the guns boom, booming in his wake. A few seconds later he dived and got Buckingham Palace with a loud noise. Poor King and Queen—twice in two days and they're as brave as lions.

—Sybil

1. The housekeeper at 17 Motcomb Street, whom we inherited from Jim Byam-Shaw.

17 September 1940 Chute

My darling love—Tomorrow is your birthday or as Father would correct—the anniversary of your birthday. I wish I was going to be with you, not that you are much of a man for anniversaries. All the same I would like to be there, if only to kiss and remind you that though *you* are now thirty-six, *I* am only thirty-five.

I find myself wandering aimlessly about—inventing jobs that don't really need doing—and then suddenly out in the garden, through the soft autumn rain one hears the thud of bombs dropping a few miles away and that sends one's thoughts flying to London and to all the people we love who are there. It's hell that they can get at London, but try as they may they won't be able to destroy it, the devils. I could spit in the eye and screw the neck of every one of them.

John Claydon[1] has lost everything and I am trying to move him and his old mother to the flat at No. 20.[2] Some of our windows are broken but not those in the flat.

Tonight on the wireless Priestley talked to the Londoners: 'Don't think of yourselves any more as civilians—for as civilians life is hell—you're soldiers and as battles go, it's not bad.'

Goodnight, my darling. I feel an awful slacker here—the only thing one can do is to turn Dean Farm into a refuge for the weary. Father comes tomorrow for a few nights. I love you and long for you.

Always—Sybil

1. A crippled shoemaker in whom Sybil had taken an interest since she was a schoolgirl.
2. Montagu Square.

17 September 1940 Madrid

My darling Syb—We are just keeping our end up here. Suñer is in Berlin and the Germans are making one big effort to drag Spain into the war. We try to show that such a step would be disastrous—how they would all starve. The background is the German propaganda that England will be beaten in a month or so. There is just a ray in the sky, showing that the Germans themselves are not so confident as they were. They have withdrawn their offer to supply Spain with rolling-stock, which proves that our bombs have been well aimed. Their economic commission leave abruptly today for Moscow, a destination singularly unpalatable to the Spaniards, where they will no doubt crawl to Uncle Joe for some more supplies. I certainly have the impression that the Germans will crack when the time comes and not slowly bend before our advancing strength. We have four to six weeks to go here in acute uncertainty and misery, never knowing whether the war party may or may not succeed in persuading Franco to come in. The Embassy are well led and well integrated and in a good humour. Our points of difficulty are Vichy and Morocco, and the reluctance of London to send Spain adequate supplies. However, I've dodged the last fence by calling in the USA. I'll tell you about it some day, it is amusing and ingenious and may do the trick, at least till the end of October. Get hold of Walton [Butterworth] and tell him I want some help, and Roger [Makins] will let him know in what way. Have them both to Chute. Lord! What a struggle it is.

Dearest Syb, I love you very much and miss you always.

All my love—David

20 September 1940 Madrid

My darling Syb—Your wire came yesterday, many thanks, and your letter of 15th today. I spent my birthday in feverish negotiations. The sands are running out and we have to resist the temptation to succumb to a fascinated paralysis. The way in which the Embassy is standing up to it, and the skill with which we are fighting our rearguard action puts heart into everyone. I doubt if HM has ever been better served by a mission abroad. Of course Portugal would go too, the Peninsular division has no basis geographical or military, that is why I went all out for the Spanish-Portuguese-UK Agreement. Countries which are in sympathy politically must form economic blocs or they will never resist the might of Central Europe.

We have heard nothing about an actual attempt to invade England, only news of vast preparations and great damage done to them by the RAF. When the BBC announced that Berkeley Square had been hit I'm sorry to say the whole Embassy shouted, 'If only they've got MEW.'

I dined at the Ritz last night and was set on by a bunch of the Castellana girls just back from their holidays. Why didn't I go out anywhere? What was I doing? And I realised that so short a time as six months had changed my desires. It must be so. As the war continues we shall shed first one extra and then another, always trying to preserve ourselves in vigour and purpose. I daresay it will become dangerous to hear soft music, and we shall run away from it for fear it turns us to self-pity and depression. Instinctively we reject bad food.

All my love, sweet, and I'm sorry this is a '*lettre de dix minutes*'.

—David

21 September 1940 Chute

My dearest love—Marylebone has suffered badly. Mummie and Daddy had a bomb on the doorstep last Wednesday. By a miracle they all escaped. All the mains burst, lights were extinguished—coping fell down, glass blew out and brickbats blew in. When the shattering roar died away Daddy's voice was heard through the gloom—'Anyone there,' 'Aye, aye, sir,' came the subdued reply—as Mummie and Ian got to their feet.

The maids got the worst of it in the basement but all were upstairs in a few seconds.

The main sewer burst—and Mummie says the worst part was spending the rest of the night in darkness—listening to the sounds and smells of escaping gas, trickling sewage and rushing water!

The fabric of the house stood up to the shock wonderfully. I do hope it won't get any more. Poor 32. We have had some happy years there and so much of the Dawson family history has been made within its walls.

The Hinches'[1] house got it when the back of Madame Tussaud's went down. I was in London that night and the roar was horrid. I think the tumbling crashes of falling masonry are the worst—the sound is so deadly and destructive and makes one seethe with rage that those bastards can commit such crimes against our London.

We've even had seven bombs in Chute, which thrilled the boys. John came flying into my room in the early morning crying—'We're in the front line, Mum, all the Morses'[2] windows have been blown out'!!

The young horrors imitate dive bombing, screaming bombs and siren warnings all day. It's their chief pleasure and, bless them, they don't worry about it at all.

This afternoon, by hook or crook, we must take our slippers off and go for a walk. It is Harvest Thanksgiving at St Mary's but Dr Freer is hard enough to face on a fine morning, one can't contemplate him on a bad one. The poor Vicar, he's lost his little paunch with worrying over ARP and the war. Last week was one too much for him—he got a sting from his bees and bombs from the enemy all on the same day. When I met him in the village that evening he couldn't raise a nod.

Good luck to you, dearest David—you are in just as much of a battle as we are—I love you very much.

—Sybil

1. Viscount and Viscountess Hinchingbrooke.
2. Admiral Sir Anthony Morse's house.

24 September 1940 Chute

My darling love—You know I offered John Claydon and his mother a home at No. 20? John's shop has been bombed and so his business is destroyed. This morning I received a letter from Mrs Claydon which is a miracle of simplicity and courage, it runs:

> Just a few lines to thank you for your generous offer. But I feel I would rather stay here. I would like John to go away for a day or two. We have a good basement shelter, where a few people come down at night and I feel God will take care of us. We manage to get sleep down there and I am expecting the boys home on leave soon. Also my nephew is coming to me as his mother is away. I would not like to know they had no place to come. But I am ever so grateful to you.
> With all good wishes. R. Claydon

Isn't it a classic? There's the true Cockney spirit and it makes one feel very humble and more than a little ashamed to be sitting in peace and comparative safety. They are in the very worst part of East London. I hope John will come here for a few days and have written to him.

There's a battle tonight over Southampton and all the freckled autumn sky is red with fires—while now and then the guns flash out like brilliant fireworks.

Simon gazed up at the aeroplanes speeding towards Southampton and said reflectively:

'Up there God must get a lot of bullets.'

'He throws them back,' observed Polly in a practical sort of way!

Our potatoes are nearly all up and look a fine lot. Harris has arranged a neat enclosure this year to prevent them from slipping all over the floor of the store house. The jam-making is all done and the remaining blackberries are dropping from the bushes. When we wake in the morning the valley is drowned in mist and there is dew on the lawns that have surprisingly sprung into green again—the early day bites a little to remind one that summer has said goodbye and we must pack up our cotton frocks, get out the moth balls and resign ourselves to the long evenings and the tasks of winter.

Goodnight, my darling dear—I love you always.

—Sybil

27 September 1940 Madrid

My darling Syb—We are all a bit cast down by Dakar,[1] altho' I must say for Sam that he has prophesied for a week that it would be a failure. People in England don't understand (a) de Gaulle commands no respect in French Africa (b) Pétain is a sacred bull (c) that we haven't won quite enough air battles to make the neutrals and the French believe our chances of victory are worth backing, and most important (d) the upper classes in France are still against a democratic revival in any form at any price. When I see you I will tell you the history of this affair and you will realise how foolish it was, and how, if they had shared my views about France and Vichy, they would never have tried it.

Sam has very definite ideas about the French Empire. He has always hated the French. I can find no solid reason for his aversion, it seems to spring from professional jealousy, as between slick politicians. He says the French Empire must disappear—that it is an artificial creation without the guts to live on its own. France will relapse into an agricultural third-rate power and her empire fall to pieces. He would therefore have no compunction about bribing Tom, Dick and Harry with promises of bits of the French Empire. I disapprove and disagree. The French can and will revive. Perhaps not in a form that suits our interests. That we can't help, we can make better or worse of it. Our error was to put up de Gaulle, who now ought to go and be replaced by Weygand. That has always been my idea.

We await Master Suñer's return from Berlin. Certainly his visit is important, and we must expect a big battle. Himmler is coming back with him, and I invented the gag 'Spain sent her leading

Statesman and Germany replies with a Policeman'! This is proving a popular number. I suppose that the Funk plan[2] for a new European order will be trotted out. I have got in first. I have written a pamphlet denouncing the false and wicked theories of this B. Funk and it is proving a best seller. When some more copies are available I'll send you one. The FO produced a wretched brochure by Henry Clay on the same theme, no punch and no talking points.

The news from the Lisbon Embassy is not too good. Dissensions, failure to keep contact with Salazar, jitters in the colony, all the old stuff which I thought we had cured in May and June. People are tiresome, they will relapse so easily into bad habits. I must visit them like St Paul and chastise them for backsliding. In the interval I fire an epistle or two.

Spain is not lost but the crisis is at hand and if we can stand the pressure for three or four weeks the whole country will come over to us. Dakar has hurt us badly. Bombs dropping on Gibraltar are too near to be pleasant. The fire is within a few inches of the Spanish powder magazine. Never mind, if we manage it, it will be all the more satisfactory.

Roger writes that he will come and spend a night with you when he can: encourage him.

All my love, my dearest darling Syb—David

1. De Gaulle in person headed a large Anglo-French raid on the French garrison at Dakar in West Africa on 23 September 1940, but Vichy had reinforced their ships and shore batteries. After three days of fighting the Anglo-French forces were withdrawn by War Cabinet decision.
2. Nazi plan for a kind of common market in Europe.

Begun 28 September 1940 — Madrid

My darling Syb—As I did with the Petersons, so I will try to describe to you Sam and Maud. Sam has a fine head and figure. A double-first at Oxford, he has been in the Cabinet for eighteen years, serving in more offices than any other living minister. He is the essential politician, extremely slick, extremely sensitive to atmosphere, and always working in terms of the personalities with whom he has to deal. His weakness lies in this training to keep in with his constituents and his party. His career comes first, although he is a patriot and a strong monarchist, and would be a statesman if he could forget himself. This is no bigger defect than a belief in God prompted solely from a desire to save one's own soul—in Sam it slightly corrupts purity of action and judgement, and, added to a lack of physical courage, produces bouts of hesitation and compromise that mark the limits of *a highly gifted nature*. His powers of negotiation are very high. After a minimum of briefing he grasps his subject, and opens a discussion with Spanish ministers in a firm and masterly way. If the subsequent technical arguments drag, or go badly, he becomes restive too soon, anxious for a solution, and has to be held back from the easy way out. When the main lines have been agreed he sums up quite beautifully, and everyone goes away happy and even exhilarated. Provided he has a first-rate staff and is not instructed to pursue an unpalatable case too long, he must rank among the best of ambassadors.

In private life he is all things to all men, and altho' he speaks hardly about other people he contrives to give you the illusion that you are an exception. His vanity protects him entirely from the censure of the masses, for whom, as far as I can make out, he does not care a fig, and I assume they know it. He has principles, and quite sound ones, but he gives the appearance of never rating them higher than some subterfuge that may suit the occasion of his policy. It is a nice point, but I believe he seems more dishonest than he really is. The Spaniards like him very much, appreciating his rank as an ex-War Cabinet Minister, and quite undisturbed by that element of Jesuitism in his character, which is so often found in their own.

Maud, Lady Maud the sister of the Earl Beauchamp, is the most difficult woman to value I have ever met. You feel that this sterile aristocrat (beg pardon, it may be Sam's fault) has important qualities, but you can't discover what they are. She is indefatigable, listens well, runs her parties well. You might order her from a catalogue ready-made, and be completely satisfied that the purchase corresponded with the short and inhuman description. She seems to be Sam's valuable partner in office rather than a wife, he relies on her a great deal in a business-like way, discusses his career with her every night, but I suspect in no different terms than he would use to Arthur [Yencken] and me.

We have had some pleasant meals together, these two, Arthur and I. Arthur is super-cautious, a realist who knows the moves of the game and yet keeps his eye on the distant object. He might become a very great ambassador but we shall know only when great authority has been given to him. Possibly it would go to his head. His wife, Joyce, is a darling and will save him. He is an Australian, with a slight inferiority complex (the FO, for some curious reason have never given him the CMG or any of those ribbons chaps like to have[1]). When the inferiority complex is drowned in glory great things might happen.

I liked very much the letter from Mrs Claydon. They certainly deserve all we can do for them. Why not re-condition that cottage in Honey Bottom and have a rest house? We could supply a good bit of food and firing. We know a number of people who could take a little leave now and again, and benefit enormously.

Tell Rose [Hinchingbrooke] I'm doing everything possible to get her father out of France. The old fool got drunk last week and slipped down a marble staircase in Cannes and broke three ribs so plans had to be changed. He really makes me mad, writing and writing that I'm doing nothing for him, and he living in the lap of duchesses and princes, and we stuffed with heart-rending appeals from the really poor and broken in France. Still I must be patient, he is Rose's father.

I miss you so much. I hate being alone, and I want to come close to you and sleep for a week, and listen or not listen to all the details of our life at Chute. Curious I don't ever think of Montagu Square. I want to be with you in our bedroom with the plaques[2] and to throw a log on the parlour fire, and to turn my chair after lunch half round to see the chestnut trees . . . and instead of that I must put on a white tie and dine with the American Ambassador —oh, hell!

All my love—David

1. He did finally get the CMG.
2. We collected Staffordshire wall-plaques.

1 October 1940 — Chute

My darling love—Your daughter is a trollop in the making—there can be no doubt of it.

This evening in the bath she suddenly squeaked out—'Look Simon—look round quick.' Her unsuspecting innocent brother obeyed—whereupon her hand darted out and tweaked his twee-twee good and hard! Imagine it.

Simon being male and therefore far more sensitive to improprieties than the coarser-fibred female—giggled first from sheer necessity and then hung his head, 'No, Mummy—I couldn't *possibly* tell you what she did.' 'Ha, ha, ha,' shouts our ribald young woman not a bit abashed. When I got them out on to the mat, Polly offered to rub Simon down while I dried *her*.

'No, no, no—don't touch me,' cries Simon. Once bit twice shy. And Polly rocked with laughter.

When did I write to you last? I think it was before my visit to Walton. He's got a charming cottage near Henley and the Flemings.[1] Tish[2] is there with her four children, living in Celia and Peter's house—and the pair of them (Peter is soldiering) make company for Walt who is very bereft.

We went rough shooting on Saturday in a cold wind and beneath a scudding sky. Lovely country. I had forgotten how seductive beech woods are, with their pale green twilight and tall shining trunks, rooted in a neat carpet of dried leaves—here and there a clearing, with a patch of fern and a white light beating through—otherwise no tangle in the wood.

The bag was tremendous—50 rabbits, some pigeon, 3 partridges, a pheasant and 4 hares. We came home to eat a huge tea and marvel that when bombs are dropping one can still spend an afternoon like that.

2 October

Michael Fleming it is now known is safely in Lille as a prisoner and Tish feels a new woman now that her long anxiety is over. He had a fracture just below the hip and it is hoped he is doing well. News takes ages—her last postcard from him is dated 15 July. She is longing to let him know—

(a) that she and the children are well
(b) that they are in England
(c) that she is getting his letters.

Wangles are strictly forbidden—she mayn't send a letter through a neutral country but she wondered if you would write the briefest of notes with these bare particulars.

When I told Daddy of this plan he was doubtful and said he

would on no account take the slightest risk of getting Michael into trouble. Will you be very cautious, my sweet, and if after making enquiries it looks a risky business—*don't* do a thing. It occurred to me afterwards that *you* are not unknown to the German authorities! And it might not do him any good to get a letter from you. You will be careful, I know. His address is enclosed.

Walt and I sat up on Saturday until the small hours and I pine to talk to you about many things that are not for transmission even by FO bag. And certainly not to anyone but you.

Goodnight, my dearest, darling love—I wonder, like you, and unless I take care sometimes a little mournfully, when we shall be together again. And then I remember all our happy years and am ashamed.

I love you—Sybil

1. Peter Fleming, author and traveller, married to Celia Johnson, the actress.
2. Wife of Peter Fleming's brother, Michael.

4 October 1940 Madrid

My darling Syb—We've had hell this week. Sam's got the jitters again, they come and go like bouts of malaria. When he heard Neville Chamberlain[1] was finished of course he wanted to rush home and pop into the War Cabinet—as if he had a chance, but he is blinded by vanity. And then my struggles with MEW are never-ending, Roger [Makins] is right when he calls them Sisyphean, only it is not the Germans but my own ministry who push the stone back again.

Poor Roger! he writes a long and very sad letter. The difficulties in the government are immense and we have to contend with a set of gents who are out for themselves at the expense of HM's interest. It is so hard to be run out by your own side. All will come right, but just now we could do with a little more common sense and a little less monkey tricks. Dakar has hit me hard.

I had two hours with the MFA today, 1–3 p.m. and then it was too late to join Arthur for lunch so I went to a little restaurant in the Plaza Mayor where I used to go with the Spanish Foreign Office boys last winter. Now deserted, and the patron and wife, and waiter, greeted me with tears of joy, '*El bienvenido*', so I sat down to sucking pig and peas and a bottle of wine on the house. Rather touching. Afterwards, there being no taxi for want of petrol, I had a three-quarter-hour walk back here.

Please send me my green tweed suit, the one with a waistcoat that has lapels. Ask Roger if it could possibly go on the aeroplane as I am getting very chilly; also a thick shirt—no, but I asked for that last bag.

All my love and forgive this wretched letter.

—David

1. Neville Chamberlain had been operated upon for cancer in August. He resigned from the House of Commons at the end of September 1940 and died on 9 November aged seventy-one.

5 October 1940 Chute

My darling love—Somehow or other you must keep the Spaniards sitting on their fence, it must be rather like propping up Humpty Dumpty. But we *must* keep Gibraltar and control of the Mediterranean, then the Hun will have difficulty in getting reinforcements to the Italians and our navy can continue to harry them.

Oh! We were downcast by Dakar too. Lord—what a pity. And it was the old story over again—too little and too late.

When condemning de Gaulle I think you should remember two things:

(a) that he has been for many years an intelligent advocate of mobile mechanised warfare. If his theories gained no recognition this was rather from the stupidity of his seniors than from any fault in himself.

(b) that we had to have a leader for Free France and he was the only one to present himself.

As for your advocacy of Weygand, this sounds interesting but too cryptic without further information. Even if possible—I would advance one grave objection—he's much too old.

Oliver Lyttelton is President of the Board of Trade. You may have something sharp to say! But I'm pleased. At least he is new, vigorous and comparatively young.

The curse of senility is still with us *vide The Times* today in announcing the appointment of Sir Charles Portal[1] 'at the early age of forty-seven'!! Poor old Neville—his number is up and we mustn't say any more horrid things about him. He's *our* sacred bull.

The French upper classes are right to turn their backs on the bureaucracy they knew. And we shall have to do the same—how I wish I could see my way through the fog, to the kind of order we must produce to take the place of the old helter skelter. But I can't—and sometimes I grow angry and impatient.

I love you very much, my dearest dear.

—Sybil

1. Chief of Air Staff 1940–5.

7 October 1940 Madrid

My dearest sweet—There are so many convulsions going on that I lament your absence more and more. First at home, there has been a row in the Cabinet about Spain, based on my complaints and hopes endorsed by Sam. Result victory for Halifax but only after what must have been a heroic struggle.[1]

Then in Spain: I was nearly torn to bits yesterday at the bull-fight because I would not stand up during the German national anthem. The *corrida* was in honour of a German military band of two hundred who, in uniform, have given a concert here. I ought to have guessed they would go to the bull-fight and stayed away. I went with Conchita de Olivares who is thirty, very fierce and pretty, and if she had not turned on the crowd like a tigress, until the police came, I don't know what would have happened. After things had calmed down a bit they said fifty *Falangistas* would lie in wait for me as I went out and do me in. That was jolly, wasn't it? We waited till the ordinary crowd had gone and were escorted out through the back door, so to speak. Afterwards I had to pull myself together and go down to the Ministry for a two-hour meeting on Morocco, which went well enough altho' I felt sick as a cat.

I don't deny that our Spanish policy is a gamble. It is designed to keep Spain neutral, failing that to arouse in the Spanish people a sense of resentment equal to the feeling against Napoleon in 1808. In 1805 every Spaniard hated us for Trafalgar, three years later all but a treacherous handful of the aristocracy were on our side. You read the 'Convention of Cintra'[2] and see how it worked. The time schedule in the twentieth century moves too fast to allow the necessary psychological readjustments to take place. That is our difficulty.

For the first six months after the Civil War the Nationalists lived in the glow of victory, doing nothing but thank God and congratulate themselves. Just when this convalescence was coming to an end and they should have started the work of reconstruction, Hitler's war began. At first very little commotion and no serious effects for Spain: indeed the memory of the huge profits Spain had made in 1914–18 encouraged the hope that this war would actually speed up reconstruction. This hope was false because a factory which suddenly gets a big order cannot take advantage of it unless it has enough working capital to advance wages and buy materials. The Civil War had stripped Spain of the stocks and capital required to take advantage of the European war. I made this my chief argument during the winter for asking the Treasury to make a loan to Spain.

Then comes the collapse of France and with it the swift realisation by all intelligent Spaniards that the present war, far from being an opportunity for Spain, is a calamity. They react in different ways. Some plunge into gloom and ask what reason there is to keep out the Germans. 'At least let us be on the winning side: faith and ideals count no more.' Others, and they seem to be the majority, say, 'We must obey one of two masters, Germany or England, there is no escape, which do we prefer?' and the answer to this question is *not clear* to the majority of Franco's supporters. They fear that a British victory will mean Communism throughout Europe. Any German ruler or 'new order' is better than that. The Europeans believe there is a fundamental distinction between Communism and Nazism: Communism and Fascism, remember, is a more Mediterranean antithesis. We may say there is no real difference, but that cuts no ice if these people believe there is. It is a plausible case. Europe wretched and devastated by the war, hungry and homeless, an easy prey for Uncle Joe's agitators. A quick victory for Germany would end this nightmare. So you see an immense struggle going on to decide whose victory would be preferable. For my part I think 90 per cent of the argument would vanish if we could win some substantial successes in arms. Egypt will probably be a turning point. The winning horse always looks handsome. Just now both animals are judged on their merits.

All my love — David

1. Minute from Churchill to Halifax of 29 September 1940 (FO 800/323 M154/40): 'I entirely agree with your letter of September 28 that we should delegate authority to our Embassy at Madrid to smooth the economic path, and settle minor blockade points out of hand. The Economic Warfare Ministry naturally do their best against the enemy, but they must be restrained, as you suggest, in regard to Spain. I would far rather we should pay our way with Spain by economic favours, and other favours, than by promises of giving up Gibraltar after we have won the war.'
2. By William Wordsworth.

8 October 1940 Chute

My darling love — The pigs arrived this morning — squealing and lively under a large net. Harris tucked them under his arm and bore them protesting to their new home. They've spent the rest of the day nosing round and grunting to each other uncertainly — I fancy they feel a trifle strange. It *must* be odd to have only one body to snuggle up to at night when you've been used to ten.

My darling David, I love you very much — in two days we shall have had twelve perfect years together, the rhythm is broken now, but there will come a day when it takes up its beat again.

— Sybil

14 October 1940 Madrid

My darling sweet — I sent you a telegram for our wedding day, I hope you got it, because I think it was rather creditable to remember! After a deluge for two days the sun shines brilliantly, and we have put the eiderdowns on our beds, not again to be left off this side of May. Arthur and I live a quiet industrious life, very methodical, breakfast sharp at 9.30, start for the Embassy at 9.55, lunch at 2, start again at 4. At midnight we listen to the news and then take the dog out, and so to bed. Of course we dine out sometimes and have people in, but our days are uneventful in the social sense. We get through a very great deal of work, and on the whole maintain an even rate of output, and do not get behind with our papers, but at the cost of no reading (except before breakfast) and very few private letters. It would be unwise and unpleasant to pass the whole of life in this way.

Our relations with Vichy have been worrying me, so I wrote a letter to Roger for his master's eye, which is very potted but a letter of more than one page doesn't get read. Logically there isn't any difference between sending food to Spain and sending food to unoccupied France—in fact both are partly-occupied countries in different degrees. The Germans come into the north of Spain and snap up eatables just as freely as they pass from occupied to unoccupied France. The Blockade is no doubt a great weapon, which in the end might bring Germany to defeat, but it is essentially negative, it stops Germany from doing this or that for want of something. Now there are occasions when *we* want to do positive things, win over this people or that province to our side, and the price we may have to pay for this positive addition to our own strength (as opposed to a negative diminution in the enemy's strength) may be to let a little food through the Blockade. It is necessary to weigh one thing against the other. Do we profit more by the goodwill of x Frenchmen or lose more by the addition of x tons of food to the supplies of enemy-controlled territories? MEW are in the awkward position of being responsible for the Blockade, and any departure from the strict rule necessarily weakens their system and their authority. I sympathise with them.

As you know, I think we have made a howling error over Vichy. To exaggerate a little, the French denied us three times and we should have forgiven them like St Peter was forgiven, for the very simple reason that working with Pétain we might have raised the flag in the French colonies, and working thro' de Gaulle it can't be done in time. Imagine if we now had Tunis as a base. Of course we should have had to be saints to forgive such a piece of treachery as the Armistice, but it should have been done. At least Pétain's value should have been recognised. That conversation I wrote to you about[1] which I had in Lisbon with Chastenet and Bressey takes on extraordinary significance looking back. We all talked instinctively, the sediment of history and of our ancestors was floating in our minds and coloured thoughts and language so deeply, that I doubt if any of us would today recognise himself if faced with a transcript of what was said. The note I wrote the next morning did not seem quite real. After three months it reads like fiction.

The faithful Roger reports nimbly that our policy is making headway at home. We don't mean to quarrel with the Departments and *we* are not in any sense jealous, nor do I think they are of us. If that is true we must find agreement.

All my love, darling sweet, and look after yourself, drink milk and sleep well.

—David

1. Letter never arrived.

Letter to Roger Makins at the Foreign Office

15 October 1940 Madrid

My dear Roger

Relations with Vichy

We cannot substitute de Gaulle for Pétain before the Near-East campaign develops, nor would it be wise to do so if we want to keep an unoccupied France and to turn it to our side. The Marshal is cherished as the only man who stands between ordinary Frenchmen and fears they dare not formulate. On 9 October he stated a theory of social reconstruction that is his own by conviction. The hierarchical form of the new system is no more our concern than Salazar's régime. We count on France as an ally for geographical, not political, reasons. The Marshal's personal authority should be sufficient to carry this theory into the experimental stage, but the more we cold-shoulder him the more he must rely on the approval of the Germans.

There are more Frenchmen every day who pray for our victory and look to us for some help in their struggle against German ideas. The French intelligence is finer than the German and could resist the corruption of physical defeat, if it is allowed to function with some hope of ultimate deliverance. A symbol of England is needed inside France. A scarecrow would be better than nothing, provided he was the official representative of HMG. De Gaulle is outside, over against his people, many of whom, feeling he does not share their sufferings, find his actions anti-French.

The test of our goodwill will be the supply of food. We are already allowing some ships to reach France. If we let any more through, surely it should be with a flourish of consent? Not very much food, not enough to endanger the Blockade, but enough to encourage our friends and confound some of the others. On this basis we could go to Vichy and save from the wreck of our relations something enormously worthwhile.

Treatment is everything. Take the example of the delegation with whom I am negotiating the Moroccan barter: their nerves are all exposed, they want a doctor not a diplomat. Can it be right to starve an invalid in the hope that he will, in yet greater misery, crawl back to you?

Laval and his like are scabs on wounds, inevitable but temporary, fascinating because disgusting, gangrenous if not disinfected. We are tempted to confuse the wound with the body that is hurt. Refer to my conversation with MM. Chastenet and Bressey in Lisbon and you will see that they suggested a double recognition: Pétain *and* de Gaulle. That treatment corresponded to a correct diagnosis.[1] A sense of dual personality is common enough among the sick. 'Today I do not feel myself; I am somebody else, but tomorrow I shall be my old self again': and so will France.

Yours ever—David

1. It was just at this time that Churchill was asking Weygand to abandon Pétain, which he refused to do.

15 October 1940 Chute

My darling love—I went a bit gay last week and ended on Saturday with a night excursion to Salisbury in a huge party, mostly military. (Not my cup of tea really but grass widows in rustic seclusion can't be choosers.)

After many drinks at the Kidstons[1] we set out in assorted cars to drive across the brilliantly moonlit Plain. Half-way we ran into a red warning—all lights out but we had the moon and she no rivals, shadowy groups of soldiers clustered beneath the trees and along the hedges, red lights waved and fire engines sped into the night—with caution we made our way—laughing a little, watching and waiting—above our heads the moon sailed serenely in a mackerel sky—in the distance one could hear a gentle but persistent droning. Such an exquisite night, how strangely men transform their lives.

We reached Salisbury without incident and launched upon such a pub crawl as you couldn't beat it if you tried. The Red Lion for a mixed grill and on to the Rose & Crown—too sordid and beery this, even for the gentlemen of the Rifle Brigade. From this delectable tavern to the Old Mill by way of the White Hart where sitting on an umbrella stand a pink-faced innocent in the RAF confided his latest love affair.

The Old Mill was a rustic affair, pretty sordid and suspiciously fifth-column, run by a French *émigré* and a wicked old woman (she looked) who fancies herself a second Rosa Lewis. We drank (not much for me) and danced to a piano played divinely by a tipsy Jack Tar. At 1.30 I suddenly giggled uncontrollably to general astonishment—I think they thought it was beer—but they were wrong, it was you. Suddenly I saw your face at *that* party and it was too much for me. My darling sweet, I *was* glad you weren't there.

On Sunday people came to lunch and tea and we heard some saucy bits of news from the RAF about their successes over Germany. The view is that before long the Hun will have to withdraw from the Channel Ports which practically do not exist any longer. And there is evidence (good evidence) that the continued and relentless bombing is having an effect upon the morale of idle German troops. Apparently our contact with the French coast for propaganda purposes, sabotage, etc., is constant. Every night the MTB[2] boys put ashore—do their stuff and dart home again. Not to be spread abroad this. I don't really think he should have told us.

He also said a good bit about our exquisite device for diverting the directional rays along which the German bombers fly—too neat for words this and explains some of their poor marksmanship. It's like laying a false trail in a paper chase, or watching a spaniel lose the scent and run round in circles. Perhaps he shouldn't have entertained us with this item either though the Germans must know we've got the dodge.

All my love—Sybil

1. Colonel George Kidston-Montgomery, DSO.
2. Motor torpedo boat.

18 October 1940 Chute

My darling dear—Two lovely long letters from you this week. I am horrified by the *corrida* episode—it turned me hot and cold and afterwards I simply couldn't concentrate on Simon's lessons and several times saw him looking at me strangely.

I am rather proud of you for sitting down and couldn't resist telling John [Wrightson] about it when he spent the night here two days ago—we decided over a bottle of champagne (the second—the first was corked, what a tragedy) that we should never have displayed such cold-blooded courage and would have half sat and half stood. 'No, of course I'm standing,' 'No, naturally, I'm sitting down.' A horrid and shameful example of English compromise. We gazed at each other, pleasantly mellow, and tearfully decided that while we were *very*, *very* cowardly—you were *very*, *very* brave. Whereupon a melancholy but sentimental silence fell and we both thought upon your virtues and our own failings.

As you know, I've always found it hard to follow you in the ideological chase. It may be hopelessly wrong to turn towards the left—but in abhorrence of Nazism, its tortures and tyrannies, it is easy to understand how this happens. I think we have got somehow to overhaul democracy and liberal capitalism so that it isn't such a come day, go day, selfish, greedy, haphazard business.

Everyone should have enough to live in comfort if not in security (we shouldn't expect too much of that) and privilege should not extend to the point of keeping others down. Nor should riches be used to the sacrifice of the poor.

I agree absolutely that the washed-out intellectual softie lefties are a real danger if they make headway with those in authority over us. But some lefties aren't softies and they might be led into the way of a new truth.

All my love—Sybil

18 October 1940 Madrid

My darling love—The change of ministers here looks very bad, two chaps who have just returned from Berlin put into key offices previously held by Anglophiles. Sam—'Coo-er, how our Sam does take on'—went to pieces yesterday morning. However, Arthur and I worked on him all day and now he is in a much better mood, and I don't think he'll run away.

I guess we are going to have a stupendous success with Suñer as MFA. Naturally we have to mask our superficial, and Sam's very real, disapproval of these cabinet changes, so I am holding up my economic negotiations until we know the new minister's economic policy—to Funk[1] or not to Funk. I *know* he won't Funk, but Sam has to be placated. Luckily Salazar asked the Portuguese Ambassador here to get me to come to see him in Lisbon on Sunday, so off I fly tomorrow to visit the beloved Doctor. I adore the prospect and shall have one of those delicious conversations that mean so much to me personally. The Spaniards can think things over while I'm away and they cannot complain about my accepting an invitation from the Doctor.

Good old Walton! He's a rare treasure and we shall be all right so long as there are a few Americans like him. We had another of the same kind here, Eric Biddle stayed last weekend with me, absolutely champion. We must draw South America and the Peninsula closer together, the Doctor's dream, and a good one, I have been pegging away at it with the FO since July. The USA are the people to give the party, and we can be like the old family nannie, leaning over the banisters to watch the young and old in their fine clothes, dropping a tear perhaps to think how sweet they were in the rubber bath.

All my love—David

1. Refers to the Nazi 'Funk plan' for the economy of Europe.

21 October 1940 Lisbon

My darling love—I am disappointed here. The relations we established with the Portuguese Government in May–July were really good. Now they are quibbling and crotchety. It's a one-man show and that man is so complex and gifted that he takes handling. Well, there we are, after three months of air battles he doesn't seem (I haven't seen him, this is what I gather) to believe in us as much as he did in July. What a pity you could not be here! The women of the Peninsula would regard you as some strange exhibit drawn from an inferno, and you could propagand the faith with enormous effect.

The Embassy has become an office, it is convenient, but I regret the Victorian ease of the drawing room. The new office building is nearly ready: very good.

The harbour reflects the blue of heaven, there go half a hundred ships, with or without navicerts,[1] who cares, they look so quiet and confident riding on the Tagus. I love Lisbon, but hate to think of the chances we miss here.

All my love and kiss for Polly—David

1. For navicerts see page 13, Introduction.

21 October 1940 Lisbon

My darling love—There must be a letter from you reposing in my bin in the Madrid chancery . . . Regretfully I saw the messenger put the Madrid bags into a car to catch the train. I wished I could have opened one and pulled out your letter.

Here we have a minor tragedy in the failure of Walford[1]—and he is *so* nice—to carry out his own good ideas. If the trumpet gives an uncertain sound who shall prepare himself for battle? And the sound is very wavering. His inability to express his own thoughts, which I have so often described to you, gets worse. He stumbles through a conversation like a man in a sack race, you feel the impediment between his ideas and his words as something physical, something you could touch with your hands. Do you remember that phrase in one of Walter Pater's essays, 'men and women, in their mixed and uncertain condition, always attractive, but always saddened by the shadow of the great things from which they shrink'? I have probably misquoted, but it applies to Walford, only his is not so much a shrinking as an inability to act up to his own sense of his own role. What a tragedy, quite a tiny tragedy, but exquisite in its completeness!

The framework of this mission is now so much better than the horse-and-buggy affair we found here in May, that the deficiencies at the top are illuminated in a glaring way. The Commercial Secretariat, which before did not exist, has taken root and is doing well; the Counsellor and First Secretary are admirable, the new office almost ready, and a new military attaché on his way. But poor Walford remains a little Secretary tutupping after Dr Salazar . . . It wouldn't matter if the whole government of Portugal were not a one-man show; as this is the case, and the Ambassador alone sees him, the effect is doubly bad. I wouldn't sack Selby because I like him so and he tries so hard, and he is so honest, but it is not in the wartime interest of HMG to be represented by someone who can't cope with the Doctor.

I've just had a long talk to Selby, damn it, he has all the right ideas, why on earth can't he put them across? It reminds me of Croce's theory of aesthetics which says that you can't criticise a painting properly, understand it properly, unless you can paint yourself. Between thinking and acting there is such a gap.

The rain descended in floods this morning and the aeroplanes didn't start, so I have an extra day in Lisbon. It is lucky. Salazar, who is away in the north of Portugal and won't be back in time for me to see him (I must respond to the friendly gestures of the new Spanish ministers without delay), sent the head of the economic department to talk to me about the relations between the Peninsula and South America. Salazar fears the dominance of the USA, the idea of the materialist dollar conception of life taking hold of the Catholic civilisation of the South American Republics fills him with gloom. I do not see why the result of the integration of the two Americas should be to sever connection between the Peninsula and Brazil. We shall have to do something constructive to prevent this.

Winston spoke well to the French. Gradually we are orientating ourselves to deal with invalids and not with healthy enemies. Not a word about the Vichy ministers, that was good. I spent yesterday afternoon in the French Legation here, rather looked askance at by our chaps, but I don't intend to be stiff or stand-offish with the French.

The Portuguese Government have been very kind in begging me to stay on here but, as I said above, to Madrid I must go. The front line is there. There may be an observation post in Vichy which someone should visit, but the main battle for the Western Mediterranean will take place, has been taking place, in Madrid.

Later again

My sweet Syb, how weary and flat I feel tonight, running about all day and embracing the ugly Portuguese. If you were here in some house or flat I should be putting my paper away knowing we were going to have a good gossip and a quiet dinner; as it is I must dine with the Spanish Commercial Counsellor, what an unnatural thing is this man-made society!

Goodnight, my love, sleep well in our delicious house, some day the fuss and sweat will be over and I shall take to keeping house for *you* and giving the children lessons and writing in the parish magazine. 'We are not to despise,' said Dr Johnson, 'soldiers who after many campaigns take life easy.' Not to despise indeed, I shall worship idleness.

All my love—David

1. Sir Walford Selby, HM Ambassador to Portugal.

23 October 1940 Chute

My darling love—I love it when you really get on horseback and go galloping down the wind. Your theories on our treatment and behaviour towards the Vichy government take the breath away at first but when one comes to think it over it's an impressive notion. And it is obviously true that we should have left the hand of friendship extended to Pétain—who is sincere within his limits—even if we wanted to retch at the thought of the other scoundrels who hang on his trousers.

Your letter to Roger on Vichy is simply excellent—I never cease to wonder at and admire your powers of condensation.

I suppose the very idea of sending food to France is unintelligible to our orthodox and unimaginative government departments. The Blockade is a kind of precious old friend who is practically sacred because he did the trick once before.

Our chaps in Whitehall aren't too hot on taking risks—or changing their minds. But your wife sees a big truth in the idea. I'm quite sure we ought to do as you say. But the struggle must be hard and very tricky especially from such a distance. You need to go for them yourself.

I am delighted that you do not take too gloomy a view over the Spanish government changes. Walt and I pulled long faces about Suñer and were rather afraid for you. Walt is absolutely grand—I like him more and more. I motored over there on Monday and he arrived from London by seven o'clock. We drank, bathed and dined and were down to the Brave New World by nine o'clock and didn't go to bed until the small hours. On Tuesday we set out in a white fog for London.

I came back a new woman having slaughtered my unnecessary apprehensions about our home town. My darling—I'm sure you would be surprised at the jaunty air she wears—as do her citizens. As for the damage, well, I was only in central London—but you still have to go looking for it. Of course there will be much more to come—but the back is broken. And anyway it is astonishing how many bombs drop in the roads—that makes it a bit awkward when you want to turn on the gas ring for breakfast or pull the plug—but it spares the houses.

All my love—Sybil

25 October 1940 Lisbon

My darling love—Still waiting for an aeroplane, I hope to go tomorrow. Not much to do these last forty-eight hours so I have been walking along the Tagus and thinking about our Spanish negotiations.

The world at large will see in the elevation of Suñer[1] and the dismissal of Beigbeder a victory for Germany. We may have all kinds of assurances from Franco and Suñer that no changed policy is intended, but Franco goes to talk to brother Adolf and the Falange rejoice. The world will take note, and the pro-German riff-raff in Spain will take courage. What then should we do? Accept the assurances given in private and continue our economic assistance as planned? Or should we bid up the hand? My instinct is in favour of the latter. I would like to screw Sam's courage to the point where he agreed that unless British subjects are treated fairly and unless the Spanish press adopts a more reasonable attitude towards us, economic help will be cut down. The risk would be that they would lose their tempers and say, 'Oh well, these English won't do anything for us after all. Let's take a chance and go in with the Germans.' Eighty per cent of the population would be against such a course, but states are ruled by tiny minorities.

Perhaps the issue turns on the USA. Without a big dollop of wheat from the USA we cannot hold out any complete programme of economic relief to Spain, and without bread the rest is frills. Unless then I could get the USA to march exactly hand-in-hand in raising the bidding I doubt if we should go forward alone. If I could get the US Ambassador to sing a duet with Sam I think we could and should raise the bid. The responsibility will be mine whatever we do.

The sun is out in a big blue patch between white monsters of clouds, the Tagus sparkles, and the air is clean. I can see the masts and rigging of ships for miles, a woman comes up the hill with a basket of fish on her head glittering like silver lamps.

All my love—David

1. Serrano Suñer was Franco's brother-in-law and head of the Falange, the Spanish Fascist party, whereas Beigbeder had been pro-British.

28 October 1940 Madrid

My darling sweet—I was due to go to Madrid by the 5 a.m. aeroplane on Saturday. Packing my bag at 10.30 Friday evening, 'ping' went the telephone and there was my beloved Doctor [Salazar] just back from his holiday: couldn't I stay and see him at 10 a.m.? We had two hours and traversed the whole situation, Portuguese, Peninsular, European and world. My note of the conversation pleases me but I dare not send it to you. I will keep a copy for the archives. Archives reminds me that Salazar greeted me, 'How are you, my young architect?' 'Architect?' say I. 'Of the new world!' Wasn't it nice of him? In spite of the ministerial changes here and the meeting between Hitler and Franco (at which Franco behaved extremely well) Salazar is not defeatist. He says we've now got the toughest diplomatic job in Europe but that we can still do it.

The train to Madrid, which I was to take instead of the aeroplane, went at 1.30 but I missed it as Selby insisted I stay to lunch. So at 3 p.m. I jumped into a small Renault with Robertson, my bottle-washer at Lisbon, to catch the train at the frontier, we thought at 8 p.m. The day was blue and white and we went fast across the bosom of Portugal and I was delighted with the peasants in their sheepskin coats, huge hats, and coloured waistbands, and all the business of farming on every side. The villages were very gay with washed blue, pink and green on the houses, very clean. At six we reached Estremoz in a blazing sunset to find our lights wouldn't work. Luckily we remembered that an ancient Anglo-Portuguese family by name Reynolds had an estate there. We found with great difficulty a rambling house, once the first cork factory in Portugal, with a huge grass lawn in the middle of a square of houses and outbuildings. Wonderful tiles on the walls representing some coarse scenes between nymphs and shepherds. Victorian furniture and photographs of Queen Victoria and her children, mostly signed. The house-party of nine men, nearly all English, clattered in from a partridge shoot and began to drink heavily and forgot that I wanted a car. Finally I got one and off we went in the dark, a hair-raising journey through a divine town called Portalegre—a more beautiful name you couldn't invent—we couldn't see much of the town in the dark but it had immense charm and a quite heavenly situation. I thought suddenly that I was glad it was dark, so is the world all round, in peaceful days we will go there in the light of day and we shall stay two or three days in a spacious coaching sort of inn and enjoy the gate to happiness—Portalegre.

On we went on a pot-holed road to the frontier station, reached it at 8.35 exactly *two* minutes before the train went. I had to sit up all night in a rotten old carriage, cold and fuggy, with a young officer who was pleasant company but very smelly. He had the most pathetic ideas about the future greatness of Spain, I couldn't help liking such unfounded and unquestioning faith.

Arrived in Madrid at 9 a.m. to find the place in an uproar of rumours. Had the Germans marched across the frontier or hadn't they? It seems some journalists got tight all night and invented these stories and then rang the embassies up to know if they were true.

Sam is very wobbly and we are having a sickening job to keep his courage up. Also my Commercial Secretariat lost all sense of organisation directly my back was turned. I don't think I am born to run offices, I cannot make my system work by itself.

I open every letter from the FO and MEW and leave yours to the last, like icing off a chocolate cake, and then gobble it up. You can't ever know how much I love your letters.

All my love—David

29 October 1940 Chute

My darling love—I am reading *Guilty Men*,[1] an indictment of our leaders during eight years preceding this war. There is one lovely phrase about your Sam. 'As Foreign Secretary Sir Samuel Hoare passed from experience to experience, like Boccaccio's Virgin, without discernible effect upon his condition'!

We've had lots of aeroplanes over today and this evening. Since dinner there's been a steady procession of Huns above the chimney pots. There was a to-do on the Plain this afternoon—but they drove them off pretty quickly and no harm done.

Dearest David, here is all my love.

—Sybil

1. By Peter Howard, Michael Foot and Frank Owen.

1 November 1940 Madrid

My most dear love—I've read again your last three letters, all of which I received within three days. If you didn't write so well I shouldn't speculate on how far we may travel apart in this twilight. But when you describe London craters or your spree in Salisbury, and I am wrestling with State Papers, I want so much to see and hear and touch you to make sure that we live in one and the same world. I catch myself looking at the children's photographs, and spinning to myself all sorts of dreams about how they are and what they will be, and suddenly I hear myself say, 'Are they real?' 'How do you know?' 'What proof have you beyond the urgent fancies of your imagination?' 'You *are* sure that you and Sam are going to call on the minister, to talk about this and that, but how do you know that these creatures are there, are alive, are yours?'

Reality, I think, is relative, and altho' 'out of sight out of mind' applies only to shallow affections, it is true that everyone tends to lose faith in the reality of absent things. One of the tests of civilisation seems to be how much we are prepared to shape our lives in response to claims, loyalties, passions, and so on, which arose or arise from persons or things we can no longer verify by their actual presence. To the religious, I suppose, God is the essentially absent but desirable motive.

I'm glad you were interested in my Vichy theories. So was Roger. You must be reading all sorts of stuff about Pétain meeting Hitler, and surrendering to Hitler. Don't you believe it. It is not true. The old man is playing a cunning game, and must have been touched at last, at five minutes before midnight, by the messages from the King, from Roosevelt, and from the Prime Minister (how clever it was of Halifax to turn me Royalist at that psychological moment!). He is leading the Germans up the garden path. Hitler's great coup has failed. He thought that we had so insulted the Vichy government that he could collar the French fleet and bases in the French Empire.

I'm sure he's failed and as the realisation of failure dawned on him he has begun desperately to conciliate the French people whose growing loathing is a serious menace to the morale of the German troops in the occupied area. There has been, since the day the Armistice was signed, this great question of policy: 'Shall we try to get the French Empire back into the fighting line through Vichy or through de Gaulle?' For months I was almost alone in saying 'through Vichy' but I never stopped saying it, or was dismayed at my isolation. Now I am joined by enough of the great ones to know that my ideas might be victorious. Armand du Chayla, the counsellor at the French Embassy here, has been staunch all through, I owe him a great deal, and I clung to the knowledge that he knew the Marshal better than anyone else I was ever likely to meet. You see, my sweet, the great thing is to know your own mind and stick to it. My letter to Roger, of which I sent you a copy, was my supreme shot, the sands were running out, and I knew I had one more, and only one more, chance; it worked. I do feel that if all comes about as I have optimistically prophesied above, it will be a modest, but real, contribution to history.

We are getting on nicely with the new Spanish ministers. They make no bones about their sympathies being pro-Axis, but they admit that economic necessity forces them to put their sympathies below the need to import wheat. If we, and the USA, don't send the wheat, they will try to get some food (what a hope!) from the Axis, or at least shift the responsibility for hunger by entering the war. The Spaniards are up for sale and it is our job to see that the auctioneer knocks them down to our bid. I don't mind an inescapable blackmail. We know where we are, and can act accordingly. We should not be where we are if we had not had all these weary months of economic negotiations.

Did I tell you that, on my suggestion, we are trying to get Cathleen Queensberry out here with her paint-box? We want to flatter in oils some of the Spanish ministers.

All my love, dear Syb—David

3 November 1940 Chute

My dearest love—In one of your letters you said, 'I wish you were here. The women of the Peninsula would regard you as some strange exhibit drawn from an inferno.' Walking this afternoon in a whacking great storm along the causeway and down through Limmer I thought how right you were in this. I'm sure in other countries people picture England as some vast and seething furnace of war—all bombs and bangs—blastings and disaster. If only they could be here for a day they would open their eyes and see the plough harder at work than ever over new furrows. The rain falls on lush fields, cows graze, pheasants cry out in the autumn woods, the washing blows in cottage gardens, women have babies and children kick stones to school. If you meet the Vicar by the village scrap dump he will dwell with modest pride upon his honey crop.

The other morning out shooting waiting for the beaters and the birds, Peter Fleming waved his arm across the sky, embracing the valleys and the golden woodland and said with a sigh, 'If only they could realise this overseas—they think that it's all gone—and if you tried to tell 'em they probably wouldn't believe it.' They might even think us callous and careless of the war—but they wouldn't be right there—we've just absorbed it into the fabric of our lives, along with all the myriad other things that make up that long eventful procession from the cradle to the sod.

Darling, when you come home you may find a hearty, back-slapping, hard-drinking, pig-sticking Poona wife. Won't it be horrid? I'm leading more of a shipboard life than ever—drinking with the RAF, dining out with marines (and their wives!), eating curry with Anglo-Indians. But there you are, what can one do but live and laugh with whoever is around.

Darling, Roger on paper sounds a bit depressed about Spain—is that just Roger or are you keeping your spirits up artificially?

Between you and me (and a million others) our dear FO should be scrapped, scrubbed, brushed, dusted, disinfected and begun all over again.

Our friends are all right. But there's enough dead wood about to depress even their cheerfulness and resource.

All my love—Sybil

III

Tangier and North Africa

November 1940–February 1941

3. Tangier and North Africa

On 3 November 1940, without warning, the Spanish Government annexed the international zone of Tangier, which lies across the straits from Gibraltar. This illegal seizure was generally believed to be the work of Serrano Suñer, Franco's brother-in-law, who had replaced the pro-British Beigbeder as Minister of Foreign Affairs. Suñer, head of the Spanish Fascist Party, the Falange, was a close friend of the foreign ministers of Italy and Germany. He trumpeted his belief that Germany was sure to win the war and therefore Spain must hurry up and join in the spoils of victory. Knowing that he was intensely disliked, not least in military circles, the British Embassy in Madrid had taken his appointment less seriously than did the Cabinet in London. Tangier was not annexed to please Hitler, it was done to show that Spain deserved and would claim more territory in Africa.

The international zone had been administered by officials representing the contracting powers, Belgium, France, Holland, Italy, Portugal, Sweden and the United Kingdom. Were these officials, now dismissed and out of a job, to receive compensation from the Spanish Government, and their countries' interests to be respected? The Spaniards offered nothing. The French and the others, except the British, protested but took no action. Our Embassy in Madrid was told to insist on compensation and, if this was refused, to use the Blockade to cut off supplies to Spain—a fearsome instruction at a moment when we knew that Hitler was increasing the pressure on Franco to come into the war. However, after lengthy, but quite good-tempered exchanges, our threat prevailed, the Spaniards conceded what we asked, and Sir Samuel Hoare enjoyed a chorus of praise at home and from the diplomatic corps in Madrid. It will be seen from my letters that he hardly deserved this applause. He had been so afraid of driving Franco to invite the Germans to enter Spain that he wanted us to give in like the other signatories to the Tangier statute. Arthur Yencken and I managed to persuade him to stand firm.

After the resolution of this crisis, during which I had learned much about North Africa, London gave me permission to go to Tangier. The Embassy needed to know more about the economic and political situation in Spanish Morocco, and a deal had to be completed with French Morocco, where the Arabs were clamouring for sugar and green tea and the British wanted to buy phosphates. But there was something else to go for. Robert Murphy, the United States Consul-General in Algiers, had been in correspondence with me about the chances of making a war trade agreement with General Weygand, Pétain's Delegate General in charge of all French Africa. MEW refused to believe that any such agreement was possible, so I played down this objective for my visit.

When I arrived in Tangier I found everyone, including the British Consul-General, expecting the Germans to occupy French North Africa within a matter of weeks.[1] I could discover no hard evidence to support these fears. Then Murphy turned up, bursting with ideas and optimism. He repeated what he had said in Lisbon, that Weygand passionately wanted the Germans to be defeated and could be persuaded to give the Allies, in exchange for a limited supply of goods through the Blockade, the political and military advantages we had begun to envisage in our correspondence. He described the economic situation in French Africa as on the verge of collapse. There was no time to lose and, if trouble broke out, Weygand would go and the Germans would come in. Perhaps Murphy exaggerated the crisis, but what was I to do? I was on my own with no colleagues from any of the Departments, political advice was not available as it would have been in Madrid or Lisbon, there were no local businessmen worth consulting, the bag service was poor, it took days to get London to answer telegrams and my own Department was against aid for the French. I could not get a visa to go to Algiers, but Murphy was ready to post between there and Tangier. On this basis I joined in the negotiation with Weygand. Even in war this was an extraordinary situation; nowadays with the telephone it would be unthinkable. My letters to Sybil on the subject are exceptionally discreet mainly because I had to be very careful about security. Tangier was riddled with agents and the British Legation had not had the resources to install the security measures which had been adopted in Madrid and Lisbon.

Our Consul-General in Tangier, Alvary (Joe) Gascoigne, was in a quandary. He had not been fully informed. In Madrid we knew more than he did about affairs on his doorstep in Spanish

1. See Murphy's *Diplomat among Warriors*, p. 83.

Morocco, and in Lisbon we were always talking about North Africa to Frenchmen coming in and out of Vichy France. He did not know what HMG's policy was towards the French. He refused to say if he thought the extension of the flexible Blockade which I was trying to bring off in North Africa was either sensible or possible. He looked and behaved like a well-bred gun-dog when his master goes off in directions to which he is not accustomed. Public business apart, he and his wife were very kind to me. I must have been a great nuisance to them, seeing so many odd characters at such odd hours, and putting a strain on the cypher clerks. Grateful for his hospitality, I sent him from Lisbon three dozen of the very best port I could find. This did move him to loud and hearty thanks. After the war he was our Ambassador in Moscow.

The key figure in this drama was General Maxime Weygand. In October 1940 Marshal Pétain appointed him the French Government's Delegate General in the North African colonies, responsible, not to the Cabinet, but to himself. His instructions were to defend Algeria, Morocco and French West Africa from attack from any quarter, that is from either the Axis or the Allies; and to put down subversive movements against the Vichy government. The Germans had agreed, under the terms of the Armistice, not to occupy the French African colonies so long as they remained loyal to Pétain, and to allow the French armed forces of approximately 100,000 men, stationed in these territories, to be kept intact. By this arrangement, in his hurry to defeat Great Britain, Hitler left the French a big card in their hand. He soon had reason to regret his mistake. He would be denied the use of the African ports so long as Weygand, with his exceptional experience and skill, maintained order in the territories, and by so doing gave the Germans no pretext for invasion. At last, in November 1941, Hitler turned on the pressure and Pétain was forced to recall Weygand, but by then it was too late, the British had re-equipped their forces, the Russians were in the war and the Americans were about to come in. A German attempt to occupy French North Africa would have met with formidable resistance.

After the war Weygand published his memoirs in a limited edition now difficult to find (Flammarion, Paris 1950–7). In the volume *Rappel au Pouvoir* he describes his relations with the British and American governments in the winter of 1940–1 when Murphy and I were negotiating with him an agreement to permit limited supplies to reach North Africa through the Blockade. It is interesting to see how well my letters tally with the General's memoirs, and in particular to consider whether Weygand's fidelity to Pétain was to our advantage, as I maintained against the supporters of General de Gaulle in London.

No doubt the British bombardment of the French warships in Oran and the failure of the expedition to Dakar helped to stifle movements against Vichy in North Africa, but these events did not shake Weygand's hope that Germany would be defeated.[1] It must be said that in the months before Christmas 1940 the British Government misunderstood both Weygand's loyalty to Pétain and the value to us of the policy he was pursuing. Churchill wrote to him in October and again a little later suggesting he should act independently of Pétain and come out on our side. Weygand did not answer these letters, knowing, as he says, that Churchill would appreciate his loyalty to the man who had given him his command. Then in March 1941, after the British Government had changed its tactics and was on the point of agreeing with the Americans to let Weygand have limited supplies on conditions which Murphy and I were to discuss in Washington, de Gaulle intervened. His uncivil letter asking Weygand to join the Free French was left unanswered, again for reasons of honour, but this time Weygand made the striking comment which I translate freely:

> The bad timing and certain miscarriage of such a proposal were alone sufficient to rule it out of court, at a time when the resources at the disposal of General de Gaulle were insignificant, when England was not in a position to mount the forces necessary to support us in North Africa,[2] when the United States was not in the war, and when Russia was still marching in step with Germany. This is what one has to remember. To have followed the programme suggested by de Gaulle would have been the surest way to draw the Germans into our North

1. All good Frenchmen wanted Germany to be defeated but not all wanted England to win.

2. Admiral Leahy, United States Ambassador to the Vichy government from December 1940 to April 1942, told me that Weygand had said to him: 'If the British come to North Africa with four divisions I will fire on them. If they come with twenty divisions I will welcome them.' Leahy prints this remark in his book *I Was There* (Gollancz 1950).

> Africa, as they had so often threatened the French Government they would do if we showed ourselves incapable of maintaining our authority there.
>
> *Mémoires*, vol. I, page 459

After Weygand's rebuff Churchill insisted even more strongly that our policy must be to keep the Western Mediterranean quiet. He was not going to allow political antipathies to prejudice the conduct of the war. This did not please many important people in London who were all for encouraging a revolt in the French colonies. First among the critics was de Gaulle, whose broadcasts were aimed at the total destruction of Pétain's authority. No Englishman can understand the events of 1941 unless he can recollect or imagine the irreconcilable clash between our hope that all Frenchmen would resume the fight with de Gaulle at their head and the absolute necessity to keep everything quiet on both sides of the Straits of Gibraltar. Weygand correctly appreciated the military situation. So did Cordell Hull, the American Secretary of State, who writes in his memoirs:

> We were not ready in 1941 to send military supplies to North Africa; nor did it seem wise to us, since this very act might provoke a German invasion of the French colonies.
>
> *Mémoires*, vol. II, page 1039

Weygand in his account of the negotiations with Murphy and myself says that by the end of October 1940 the shortage of oil ('*L'Afrique du Nord est un pays de motoculture*') was becoming critical. He explained the situation to the Americans and some weeks later was told by US Consul-General Mr Cole that the United States was ready to exchange certain products with French North Africa provided it was done with the agreement of the British, and therefore they must first know what were the intentions of the French Government regarding the independent status of their African territories. Weygand replied that it was in the interest of the British that North Africa should not starve. Only if the territories were calm and the economy ticking over could the danger be avoided of an unwarrantable intervention by the Germans.

From December onwards Weygand pursued these conversations with Murphy, for whom he was to entertain the highest regard. They concluded that the main obstacle to an agreement was the hostility of the British under the influence of de Gaulle. That being the position, Weygand asked what were the conditions which the British Government, supported by the Americans, would insist upon if supplies were allowed through the Blockade? This question could not be answered without serious negotiations. At first the French Government refused to allow the talks to take place in Algiers. It must all be done in Vichy. Weygand objected to this. The British, he said, had to be a party to the deal, but they had no representative in Vichy. Murphy was advising him that no agreement could be negotiated unless I came to Tangier and took part in the talks. While the row with Vichy was being settled, Murphy and I were working on a text. On 11 February Weygand was given our first draft about which he writes, 'I was able to thank Mr Murphy who had taken a significant step towards our agreement in talks he had had with Mr Eccles, the representative of the British Minister of the Blockade.'[1]

Murphy and I had discussed both the volume of supplies and the conditions to be attached on a much more ample scale than the State Department was expecting. We were taking something of a gamble, but Murphy reported that Weygand was confident of success, because Pétain, who had seen much of me in Madrid, had told him that I could persuade the British Government to make an agreement satisfactory to all three parties. For his part Murphy was sure that President Roosevelt would agree.

Murphy presented our second draft to Weygand on 18 February. A provision had been included for the delivery to the British of the neutral ships interned in French North African ports. Murphy and I put this in to give Weygand something to strike out. This he did, and on 26 February he signed all the other conditions, including the establishment of a network of American observers at the ports. On page 486 of Volume I of his memoirs, Weygand prints the text of the draft agreement which had still to be put to Washington and London.[2]

1. Weygand could not know that the Minister, Hugh Dalton, was against any economic aid to French North Africa.

2. In his book *Vichy: Two Years of Deception* (Macmillan Company, New York, 1943) Léon Marchal, then Director of Commerce for French Morocco, (see my letter of 6 January 1941) writes: 'Contrary to a very

What would have happened if either government had turned it down, preferring to back de Gaulle to raise a rebellion against Weygand? Murphy and I would have been in disgrace: that would not have mattered, but with French North Africa in growing disorder who would have kept the Germans out? Seeing how far I had gone beyond my instructions Murphy and I decided to present the agreement as entirely his responsibility and not the result of our joint efforts. He would then have a better chance with the State Department and I could tell London that it looked certain the United States Government would go ahead. Events justified the modest deviation from the truth which we employed. Once the British Government accepted that an Anglo-American deal with Weygand was worth a try the thoroughness with which we changed our policy was admirable. As will be seen from Sybil's letters, from this time forward British opinion about Weygand, and Pétain behind him, was less hostile and more understanding of their efforts to keep North Africa quiet. All those, and what a large and distinguished company they were, who had been against allowing any supplies through the Blockade to French North Africa, should have asked themselves whether in the early months of 1941 it would have been in our interest if the Western Mediterranean had gone up in flames. Weygand's account of what took place between us is accurate, and his argument that we were right to support his efforts to maintain order in the French colonies is sound. We gained the time to win the war in the Mediterranean.

---

widespread conception there exists no written document which can properly be described as the Weygand-Murphy agreement.' This is true. The text printed by Weygand was a draft that had still to be approved by Pétain and by the British and American governments. It never was by the last two. In Washington on 24 April 1941 we accepted the main propositions of the draft but thought it in no one's interest to have a definite text. As far as I know, the British Government never asked for a final text.

Marchal says that when it was suggested to Weygand he might undertake to break with Vichy, he observed: 'It is not at my age that one becomes a rebel.' I do not believe that Murphy ever made such a suggestion. We were agreed that nothing good could come of our negotiations except on the assumption of Weygand's loyalty to Pétain.

4 November 1940 Madrid

My darling love—Every day a new snag and a new danger. I do not want to say to myself, 'This can only end one way, in war between Spain and England,' because such a conviction would half-consciously bias all my actions, and make more probable the result we try to avoid. However, I am on such terms with the Spaniards that I now discuss openly with them the prospect of war. It is better so. We do great wrong in concealing from each other tragic results just because such events are horrible to contemplate. It is far better to talk openly than to drift cowardwise into reality by a kind of mutual agreement not to speak of it. Father teaches me a lesson here. You know his refusal to face up to illness in his own family. I will not be caught that way with Spaniards, who, in a diplomatic sense, are my family.

I do not know how much the newspapers at home will tell you about today's events in Tangier. The Spaniards have seized the Tangier zone. Why? Not at the Germans' request in order to prepare a base for an attack on Gibraltar, but because they must do something to justify to themselves their Civil War. When bread is lacking men desire, more than ever, to prove to themselves that they do not live for bread alone. A little glory, and they can put up with hunger. This pathetic little explanation is so obvious here, and yet I feel that the result of their poor little coup may be disastrous.

Do you know, my sweet, why it is so desperately hard to explain to some men why other men act the way they do? If you could answer me that I should be a wiser and a more confident man. In the last few days I have spoken to a number of French and Americans hot from Vichy. All agree on one point: the Marshal is untouchable. Think of Mistinguette, how those legs, which once twinkled so divinely, never lost their enchantment for the French public. No matter if the revue in which this bygone creature appeared was a hotch-potch of flops. The theatre was crowded, and the lower limbs cheered to the roof. So it is with the Marshal, the male Mistinguette of beaten France. Never care that the vehicle in which he is presented is the most villainous contraption. He is, and will be, cheered till he dies.

Yesterday (Sunday I mean) we snatched a half-day's shooting. Sam and Arthur and I worked in committee from ten to twelve and then set out for the Casa Valdes estate in Guadalajara. You

1. Sybil and Polly, 1939

2. Sybil, 1938

must imagine a windless autumn day; not a cloud in the sky, the poplars by the river yellowing at the tip like gigantic torches or the feathers of a Brazilian bird. We climbed up to a keeper's hut on the peak of a tableland from which we could see the Guadarrama forty miles to the north and the Sierra de Toledo fifty miles to the south. Our lunch was spread on a trestle table under the last leaves of an acacia grove; we ate and drank too much, and proceeded to a rolling country of rock roses and broom across which rabbits were driven by excruciating yells of '*hay va*', 'there he goes', from a patchwork of beaters of all shapes and colours. The Embassy shot very straight and earned rounds of applause. We returned to a blood-red sunset, 'the blood of Christ streams in the firmament', and a crescent moon. A dish of tea and we went gingerly down the winding hill to the valley and main road. We reached the Embassy at 8.30 and found the Tangier telegrams. I noticed that this extremely serious news had little or no effect on Sam or Arthur, so protected were they by the divine day we had just spent in the open air. Aren't human beings attractive? The way they respond to the pleasant things? Put them on like an overcoat or mittens? Feel comfy, and smile rather stupidly at insults? We belong, I so often feel, to an agreeable race, I hate to see so much death and destruction of young men.

I started negotiations with the representative of French Morocco this morning. Lord! How we sniffed each other, like cats. I'm afraid he's defeatist, damn the propaganda services of this world, can we ever hope that truth will overcome lies in an age when so many means of spreading filth exist?

All my love—David

8 November 1940 Chute

My dearest love—Today I was taken to Salisbury in someone else's car and on someone else's petrol. The day dawned fine and clear with a white frost and the four of us set off in high spirits like elderly children who've been promised a picnic.

Phil Mason, Ursula Drew, Rosemary Maddock and your wife—all Greek to you, but a nice trio of respectable British women.

We shopped, lunched, shopped again, crying out to each other in triumph when we found a pot of marmalade, pressing our noses against the windows and exploring any ancient monuments that came our way.

Do you remember St Thomas's church? It's lovely—very stout and plain—built of great slabs of pale grey stone and decorated inside with a most unusual fresco. A monument to Christian virtue rather than a work of art—in fact it's hideous but we gazed on it with respect.

10 November

Your super letter of 1 November arrived yesterday. It is difficult indeed not to grow apart in this twilight. Life has become such a makeshift affair—the objects and the persons to whom we gave allegiance and love are vanished out of our lives—and though they will surely return one day, in the meantime the urgent preoccupations of existence enslave the body and deaden the mind. More and more one finds onself 'making do' with the second best and being as merry about it as possible. But you are always in the very near background for me—I have only got to lift one corner of the curtain and there you are in full possession of the stage—but I don't do it too often for it lays bare my loss too devastatingly. It is noise and bustle about a dozen jobs all day—and only in the evening I allow my thoughts to wander and then I drive them forward into the hardworking, happy future that waits round the corner.

I believe we will look back on this winter as the turning point in our fortunes.

Roger says there is a growing restlessness in France and agrees with you that the French are loathing the Germans more and more—though he fears they are still apathetic and not at all vocal—that the scoundrels in power can put it across them.

He agrees also that Pétain is *au fond* an honest man but he is old and must be tired and the danger is that the bad hats may make rings around him letting him see very little of their schemes until everything is practically *fait accompli* when they wave the document for signature and cry, '*Votre honneur est sauvé, Monsieur le Maréchal.*' Roger is obviously in sympathy with most of your Vichy views and thinks very little of de Gaulle—though he considers we were right to make use of him. The trouble is the General is now a bit big for his boots, 'Le Général de Gaulle', which doesn't go down well in France and complicates any possible relations with Vichy. Somebody, when asked the other day what he thought of de Gaulle, replied, 'The General has a head like a pineapple and hips like a woman.' Roger has a lovely Dakar story too. Apparently while we were preserving the most terrific secrecy over the whole expedition—whispers behind barred and bolted doors—the officers of Free France were raising their glasses nightly at the Coq d'Or, '*A Dakar, à Dakar*!' they cried—while a goggle-eyed waiter scurried out to the telephone!

My dear darling, if only you had been here—but Roger says you can't be spared so I keep my hopes pitched low—I love you always.

—Sybil

Letter from Roger Makins

9 November Foreign Office, SW1

My dear David—Thank you for two more admirable letters; far from writing too much your letters are eagerly awaited, and help me enormously. I'm very sorry but I send you such scrappy and inadequate replies, but just lately I have been completely swamped with work. Sam and I have been telegraphing madly—I hope to some purpose. Nearly all our information on a short view not discouraging, but I do not trust it too far. There are two questions, is the bribe big enough? And will the Americans play? You know well the difficulty of increased assistance from the home political point of view: but we have our £2,000,000 for the next five months and the UKCC[1] are now using your authority to lose £1,000,000 for food purchases in Spain. (This plan has been invented to cope with the obstruction of the Ministry of Food, whose attitude is well demonstrated by the recent talk about buying raisins in the Balkans. Price originally asked 55 shillings; Ministry of Food refused to pay more than 50 shillings; UKCC would have bought if allowed. Price now 100 shillings and Ministry of Food asking for *dollars* to buy raisins in the USA!) The idea is that UKCC will re-sell to Ministry of Food at prices which will enable them to stick to their maximum price orders. The snag is shipping (much the most serious aspect of the war at the moment), otherwise there would I hope be no obstacle to buying the oranges.

Tangier has been tiresome: I should have liked to be a little stiffer with the Spaniards over what they did, even if they were out to forestall the Italians. The Americans are very annoyed with them. We can't negotiate alone with the Spaniards about the question in the absence of the other parties to the Statute—we can only say that as far as we are concerned we are agreeable to the Spaniards running the show in Tangier in practice, as the French did before, but that they must guarantee certain things and must impose no more *diktats*. I don't think there is any hurry to pursue these 'discussions' with Suñer as proposed by Sam.

I hope you are right about Vichy—I mean that we are winning. I am not quite so confident. We are trying to do the right things now, but late, and we have heavily handicapped ourselves. That 'creature' de Gaulle is getting much too big for his jack boots and is quite capable of mixing in rather delicate relations with Weygand. I will not promise to shed a tear for the Marshal—but I understand well enough the place which he shares with Mistinguette in the hearts of the French people. He alone stands between them and a total loss of self-respect.

I have taken advantage of a very kind invitation from Sybil and am going down there this evening for a night. I will discuss the winter clothes crisis with her. Unfortunately I rather unthinkingly sent off some large parcels without realising that they would not go by air, and they are now on their way by sea. This was before you asked for the aeroplane to be used; it's awfully difficult to get anything on to the plane.

I must go on with my military duties.

Yours ever—Roger

1. UKCC: United Kingdom Commercial Corporation set up to trade in neutral countries on behalf of His Majesty's Government.

Letter to Roger Makins at the Foreign Office

10 November 1940 Madrid

Dear Roger—A risk exists that ignorance of the economic situation, and of the possible Anglo-American remedies, might give the Falange a chance to push Spain into the Continental bloc before our help arrives. Therefore Sam agreed that I should inform the Spanish Generals of what we are doing.

Archie James[1] took me to General Aranda this morning. He is very pro-British, too much so to make me confident he can do what he says, or be left to try to do so by the Germans. He said that recently a group of Generals had told Franco Spain could not afford to waste time on internal politics, theories of organisation that mutually cancelled out, etc.; the only chance of salvation was administration first, economics second and foreign trade in the forefront of economics. When Spain had recovered somewhat they might again be able to afford the luxury of a little politics. The military do not define their terms very well, but they possess the only shred of common sense in a fool's purgatory.

I explained to him the idea of 'guaranteed rations', feeling as though I was lecturing on an extinct species, and led up to the financial bankruptcy of Spain and the immediate necessity for fresh credits, sterling and dollar. The questions he asked were pertinent, although his knowledge of the nature and size of Spain's deficiencies was sketchy.

He then informed us that the Generals were fed up with Suñer, that they wished to reduce him to a head of department, and stop this nonsense of incipient dictator. Accordingly it was probable, within a few days, that three or four Generals would enter the government. He looked for a combined Defence Ministry under himself, with military heads of the three Service Departments. He would take charge of administration and orientate Spanish economic policy in our direction instead of the present rudderless higgledy-piggledy (his gestures and language here were delicious). The guiding principle would be anti-Axis.

I said this sounded fine. For our part we should carry on with our economic talks, and if the United States Ambassador received satisfactory assurances, I saw a successful issue in a few weeks. Naturally, whoever happened to be the ministers at the time when these agreements were signed would be able to resolve a large part of Spain's economic difficulties. Speaking in Moroccan French, he said, '*Je comprong vortre pwong.*'

Yours ever—David

1. Wing Commander Archibald James, Air Attaché at HM Embassy; later Sir Archibald James, MP.

11 November 1940 Chute

My darling love—I was afraid Tangier was bad though I didn't realise the full extent of it. Do you mean that for the moment it is a harmless little coup—but later on if the Germans persuade the Spaniards to fight, Tangier can be used disastrously against us?

I still believe in you—so does Roger who wishes you could be cut in half and shared between Lisbon and Madrid—and so hope still springs in me that in spite of every appearance to the contrary peace between Spain and England may yet be saved.

—Sybil

12 November Madrid

My dearest Syb—We cannot go on for long at this pace. The whole Vichy-London negotiations and exchanges are now done thro' us, and on top of the Spanish situation, which is steadily thickening with difficulties, it is too much. Arthur and I are so tired every night we can hardly drag ourselves upstairs and have twice dropped off together down here in the library.

Against this very bad background there has been much of interest and importance going on. Especially I shall always remember my conversations with Marchal,[1] the Director of Commerce for French Morocco, who has been here to make an agreement with the Spaniards and with ourselves. He insists—oh! how rightly—that what binds England and France together as peoples is a common conception of the value of human life and the civilised uses to which human endeavour should be put. During the last twenty years the political forms which characterised the French governments, and the politicians who made use of those forms, were aberrations from the common ideal of life which we both long for. 'Nothing,' he said, 'can now stop the French people from turning to you and praying for your victory, except a belief that you prefer these deviations and these shameful sidetracks rather than the way of life that is our common ideal. If you support the old French politicians, Madame Tabouis, Pertinax & Co. then,' he said, 'you will have to have your revolution before we meet again on the common path, and have it you will.'

I'm so glad you had Roger. Without him we should not have kept the Germans out of the Peninsula, he is one of the five to whom this is due, Salazar, Sam, Arthur, Roger and I, all necessary to each other.

Sam has gone to Portugal to see Lothian[2] and afterwards Salazar. It is an interesting move and impresses the Spaniards. I shall try to get to Lisbon at the end of the month. The air services are very irregular now, bad weather, etc.

My darling love, what would I give to be with you for a week? Our life here is so hard, always arguing and scribbling and making sorties to this or that ministry, there is no comfort in it. What you do with all those military creatures I can't think but I would gladly be there to see.

The Moroccan delegate has just come in to say goodbye, with enormous emotion, he and I have hit it a crack, we have felt the possible tragedy of a rupture with France so deeply and silently, that when it came to '*bon voyage*' we could hardly speak.

All my love—David

1. Léon Marchal. For reference to his book see note on page 190.
2. The Marquess of Lothian was British Ambassador in Washington. He died a few weeks later.

Letter to Roger Makins at the Foreign Office

14 November 1940 Madrid

Dear Roger—I ask myself what are we trying to do with French Morocco? I suppose
(a) to keep the tribes quiet
(b) to obtain certain Moroccan products for our own use
(c) to make friends with the Moroccan authorities convincing them that our victory is certain, is their victory, and is something for which they must fight.

Now how can we hope to achieve (a) and (b) without (c)? If the Moroccan authorities are not with us, what chance is there of the smooth working of the economic agreements or tranquillity among the tribes? The exchange of goods and our attitude to the Moroccan authorities will either reinforce or paralyse each other.

When a crisis overtakes the Vichy government, e.g. the Germans occupy the Mediterranean ports, Pétain dies, Italy sues for peace . . . what will French Morocco do then? Exactly what Weygand, Noguès, Marchal & Co., want it to do. It will be a question of *la volonté des chefs*. If you agree with this, you will let me have my chance to prepare these men for the invisible event. You can't marry a girl if you throw stones at her window, out with the guitar and a bunch of roses.

Marchal said that the Germans have no immediate economic interest in Morocco (cobalt excepted) because the products are only transportable by sea; their interest in Morocco is subversive. If there is social trouble it will be easy and worth their while to take over to restore order, and if there *is* trouble the French authorities will turn to Vichy and Laval and not to London and de Gaulle. Anyone who doesn't recognise this as true doesn't understand how weakened, injured, guilty and remorseful men behave.

But if after fourteen months of war our people find it 'reasonable' that commercial firms should collect a balance of £150,000 of debts rather than renew relations with Morocco, I give up in despair. It is a way of thinking that has no sense of values behind it and no knowledge of the effect of such stipulations on men in the state of mind in which Frenchmen are today. Marchal is quite ready for a liquidation of debts on both sides; for instance, he claims that some Moroccan firms hold stocks of tea, paid for, in the United Kingdom. I don't know the details and didn't press him as I wanted first his goodwill and afterwards his account books.

It is Morocco which can bring pressure on Vichy to play with us, and not we who can bring pressure on Vichy to make Morocco play. If we make a sharp distinction between Morocco and Vichy in the matter of blockade, we gain three advantages. First we prove to all parts of the French Empire, with very little risk of goods going to the enemy, that friendship with England is possible and valuable, second we prepare Morocco for the crossroads that are approaching, third we guard against the Spaniards or the Germans entering Morocco on a pretext of quelling trouble.

Yours ever—David

14–15 November 1940 Madrid

Dearest Syb—We are pulling out of the rough water and I see signs, tiny signs, of another move forward in our relations with Spain. We have had a foul six weeks at the beginning of which the British Cabinet was inclined to write Spain off as lost, but Arthur and I wouldn't have it, although Sam saw some reasons for throwing in his hand. The Spanish public are recovering from their fright that Suñer's advent to the MFA would mean a swift entry into the war. In restaurants there is less food than ever but more cheerful faces. The Taranto action[1] will give a powerful push to this growing optimism. There, you see, I am cheerful again.

The Moroccan negotiations are all but complete. I think that in Marchal I have a friend for life. He says that we must come and stay with him in Rabat just as soon as we can. What would you give for a lazy week in the sun, on the terrace of a long white house, looking over the bougainvillias at the sea? One day we will go.

The French are rushing into our arms and all my hopes will come true if we keep our heads, avoid incidents, and remember that they are weaker and unhappier then we can ever guess. When did I tell you that my plan was to substitute Weygand for de Gaulle? Ages ago, wasn't it? I'll tell you what is happening in Vichy. The old gentleman met Hitler and agreed a number of subjects for economic and social collaboration, such as railways, currency, prisoners, foodstuffs and propaganda. For each a joint commission was set up and in no single commission on any single detail have they been able to reach agreement. The Marshal never toyed with the idea of giving up the fleet or bases in North Africa. It was just a dirty lie put out by the Germans to make us strike first and push France into war with us. The history books will bear me out. Against the deluge of rumours and anti-French caterwauling from home this Embassy stood fast, and I think we shall soon be proved right. A curious feature is the sudden popularity of Spain in France. It seems that the French are everywhere saying, 'Franco wouldn't let Hitler in. Hooray for Spain.' Public opinion swings this way and that, but this is certainly an odd *volte-face*. We have only to knock Italy out before the spring, and I believe we can do it if the Germans wait much longer to come down the Balkans to her assistance, to make absolutely sure of Spain and to be able to choose our moment for that campaign which is so dear to my heart.

Here is what a friend of mine tells me who lunched tête-à-tête with the German Ambassador yesterday. Von Stohrer said, 'The New Order in Europe will sweep away all this; no more silver on polished tables, no more flunkeys handing soufflés light as a cloud, no more wines and cigars, we have to realise that the Führer is going to make a new order of equality between all men; gladly we shall accept this sacrifice, it is time we realised that all men who love their Fatherland are equal.' Well, my sweet, this is pure Bolshevism. The Fascist Party is finished; and I bet you that the Nazi Party cannot stand alone, to Uncle Joe [Stalin] it turns. Our victory is in sight. Have no fear. I had a week or two of hell here keeping the Germans out and our friends calm, but it is over now.

I wonder how you found Roger, I shall have to wait till next Tuesday to know. I have kept him informed of every turn and twist in the game, no one shall ever accuse me of hiding my hand from the Secretary of State. How are the prophets belied! Today dawns with the news that Suñer is again on his way to Paris and Berlin. I rather think the immediate cause of his precipitate journey—he only broke his dinner engagement at 8.30 p.m. last night—is Tangier. The Spaniards have made asses of themselves in Tangier. I cannot go into details for lack of time, but the possible consequences are very grave. Also I smell that the Spanish Generals are out for Suñer's blood and may give him the KO in his absence. We shall have an amusing weekend.

Sam, the pink rat, no sooner gets to Lisbon than he says he is going home. Running out, without having had the guts to tell Arthur and me before he left Madrid. We have telegraphed to ask him to come back. What an ass he is not to see that his success here is phenomenal and that we all need him. My God! we need him, and not only the Embassy but every Spaniard who wants to keep out of the war. I suppose he was going home to say, 'I won't go back to Spain unless you promise me the Viceroyalty!' and I hope they would have called his bluff but, if not, I hope they would have promised him India, as any price is worth paying.

Arthur and I reflected last night on how unscrupulous we should become in our old age. What do you think? I only know that I could not have done what I have done in the last year without a peaceful sense that it was right by standards other than my own interest. What star guides Sam? We none of us know. Damn it, I like him and admire him very much. How complicated is the world!

All my love and I long to see you and have you near me.

—David

1. On 11 November the British sank three Italian battleships off Taranto.

17 November 1940 Chute

My darling love—Thursday was very noisy—guns all night long and a continuous drone of Huns overhead on their way, as we realised later, to brave and unfortunate Coventry.

The raid there was appallingly severe and the people bore it with the greatest fortitude. This isn't newspaper stuff—John [Wrightson] arrived down on Friday and told us a bit about it. Apparently they ran out of water—in spite of the city's excellent supply—for the fires were so many and the lack of means to extinguish made the night pretty hideous. In the morning troops were poured in and heaven and earth were moved to clear up, feed and house, succour and comfort the homeless and wounded. The King, of course, was there in a trice. He's grand, that man.

All my love, dearest David—Sybil

17–18 November 1940 Madrid

My dearest love—I think your description of Wiltshire in war and mine of a mission abroad would make an amusing duet, and that we must string them together, and read them at a sitting, because it is astonishing how the evolution of events and ideas comes out when you take a big bite at papers written seriatim. I've just read the four gospels, in the order of Mark, Luke, Matthew and John, and the grasp you have of Christianity as a whole is quite extraordinary. I put Matthew way down the course. He was too regional, so much less universal than the others.

You need not worry about marmalade. You are the wife of the

marmalade king. Yesterday I bought the entire crop of bitter oranges, offering two shillings a case more than the Ministry of Food had authorised. I couldn't let the Germans get them, and we have authority to lose some money for special purchases. So 350,000 cases will be consigned to the UK because I threw £35,000 on the table to clinch the sale. The joke is we can now have the oranges consigned to MEW, if I like, and if they were to cut out the middlemen I daresay marmalade would be cheaper than ever. In quieter times I would love to play this game.

Sometime soon I must go to Lisbon and look up my Doctor. We have such a special affection for each other. Everyone recognises it as something odd but real; and now I think there will be no more heart-burnings when I announce my wish or his wish for a meeting.

Sam comes back this afternoon, and Arthur and I dine *en famille* with him and Maud. I will tell how he got on with Salazar and Lothian in my next letter. We need Sam here. He is symbolic. All Spaniards who want to keep out of the war rally to him. One learns much about symbolism in public affairs.

All my love—David

20 November 1940 Chute

My darling love—We're still living on the excitement of Taranto and are all impatience for the next fillip. I am so afraid the Greeks will break for lack of material and aeroplanes—like the unfortunate Finns. Oh dear—what a long tale of unpreparedness it is. But we are obviously giving them all the help we can. If only America would speed up production. Apparently there is such a big gap between producing some of the new weapons and being able to turn them out in large and useful quantities. And according to many this gap isn't narrowing as fast as it should considering the resources at their command.

As for Spain, are you sure she will still hold out? The ice may be thin but it just won't crack. They *can't* want to face another war—and your persuasion combined with our successes in the Mediterranean must make them doubt a swift victory for the Axis, even if they don't yet doubt the 'victory' itself. And you'll be enchanted to hear that I'm genuinely coming round to your view of Pétain. I don't believe he will do the dirty even if he does mistrust democracy and believe that France should pay for her sins with a new discipline, albeit German. A more fundamental morality will restrain him from the final treachery.

I'm so glad always to hear you talk glowingly of France and our common cause. I find myself often as its champion. So many thoughtless people have caught the habit of saying, 'Oh, we'll have to declare war on them in the end'—they just don't *see*.

All my love, sweet—Sybil

21 November 1940 Madrid

My dearest Syb—Friday morning and no London bag. I rely more on your letters as time goes on. We are nearly sunk here, the awful process of demoralisation by corruption has begun to work in the Spanish ministries. Tired and miserable, they are ready to give in like Roumania. The USA could have rallied the position, but because of a series of unfortunate incidents—provoked by the Germans to embitter Spain's relations with America—it looks hopeless. I told you it was the last shot, but the gun is jammed and the trigger won't pull.

I think we are all to blame, but especially the Service Departments who ought to have made their voice heard, and swept aside the hesitations of the civilians in offering the inducements which would have kept Spain neutral. How important to the conduct of the war is the neutrality of Spain? I can't say with any expert knowledge, but I know that if I were fighting in the Eastern Mediterranean my heart would sink if I heard the Western door shut with a clang. And not only my heart, but the hearts of all the French, who put their rising hopes in our cause. How will they feel, trapped and surrounded like Czechoslovakia? For all these reasons we should have gone straight ahead, generously and boldly, buying the neutrality, yes, and the goodwill, of the Peninsula. I never doubted it could be done, I never wavered in my advice or in my efforts, but we are beaten by the old gentlemen and the modern ideologists, who place personal fears and fancies before the King's interest. God forgive them, they lay upon us and upon millions of Spaniards an appalling burden. I might try to make one desperate appeal in person in Whitehall, but the hour is late.

As we walk to the Embassy in the morning we see an ever-increasing number of men, women and children picking over the dustbins and the slop pails standing on the kerb. As they spy a bit of potato peel among the filth, they eat it, and stuff into sacks garbage too horrible to describe. Today the wind blew over her head the black cotton dress of a young woman sifting some ashes: she had nothing on underneath, and I think was arrested for indecency. What will happen to these people if the Germans come in and Spain is blockaded? They will die. We could have offered them food and so life, and if the Germans did not allow them to have it and invaded Spain, then at least they would have died knowing they had one friend in the world. I could weep for shame at the miserable mess we make of our lives and our duty.

If all this happens it will enter deep into my being and I shall never again be the same man.

All my love, I love no one but you and never will.

—David

[I went home for consultations on 28 November to ask for more supplies for Spain. MEW opposed further aid but the Foreign Office carried the day. It can be seen from the letter which follows from Hoare that the defeat of MEW at this juncture was crucial.]

Letter from Sir Samuel Hoare in Madrid to DE in London

6 December 1940 Madrid

Dear David—Many thanks for having put our case so ably and successfully in Whitehall. It has been worth anything to have you and Ellis-Rees in London during these critical ten days. I wish all the same that you could have been in two places at once, for we have had here the most eventful chapter since my arrival. First, my very heated interviews with Suñer, and next the economic offer.[1] Madrid, as you may imagine, has gone from the extreme of depression to the utmost limit of elation. Having convinced themselves that everything was all wrong, they have now equally convinced themselves that everything is all right. If we are to prevent a reaction, we must move quickly. This is why I have been pressing for two or three ships to bring wheat from Canada.

Carceller[2] is sending his people about Madrid saying that he has done a brilliant coup with the British and that it is the British who helped to smooth out the American trouble. Our stock therefore for the moment has gone very high, perhaps too high.

Come back here as soon as you can for we need you badly in the war of movement that has now developed.

Let us know as soon as you arrive in Lisbon and come on here as soon as you can.

Yours—Samuel Hoare

1. The supplies and credits which I had obtained in London.
2. Spanish Minister of Commerce.

17 December 1940 Lisbon

My dearest sweetest Syb—They told me to be at the office in Poole at 8 a.m., at 9.10 they rang the 'London' to say that I must come at once. We were off at 9.30! Fighter Command were anxious to see us go, the morning was clear as crystal and not a cloud to hide in.

I love coming home more each time. You are always more worth loving: curious isn't it that the clock should do more than stand still, even go backward. We are lucky indeed that this is so. I shall make huge efforts not to stay away so long again.

Lisbon was at its best when we landed at 4 p.m., a rich warm colour from the declining sun lit up the shipping riding on an almost dead calm.

I go on to Madrid at dawn on Thursday. Sam had written to me here begging me not to linger. He's right. Madrid is the front-line trench.

The news from Vichy continues to be reassuring. You see the abused and despised will come right and have their justification.

All my love, darling—David

20 December 1940 Chute

My darling dear—It was funny, I just knew I was going to get a letter from Poole and the thought kept me cheerful all through a long day on the Canteen. When the washing-up was over your telegram came through to Nan's and I scuttled home on a wave of relief (absurd, but there it is) as sure as one could be of anything that there'd be an envelope on my desk. And there it was. Dear David to send me a message. I read it a great many times.

Roosevelt never wraps things up in fine phrases, does he? He just hits Mr Everyman's nail on the head. 'If your neighbour's house is on fire you don't open negotiations with him for the sale of your hose—you lend it to him.' Thus in a few simple words, history is changed.

He's a splendid fellow for reducing difficulties—and how he must annoy the Jonahs and the economists since by doing so he makes their elaborations look absurd. And probably reduces their tidy arrangements to chaos.

With all my love, darling—Sybil

21 December 1940 Madrid

My dearest love—I am already angry because I know I haven't the time to write you a decent letter. I have sent you no Christmas present, I am simply bewildered by all there is to do, and am doing nothing for you who are more important than all the foreign policy in the world.

In Lisbon things are bad in the economic field because our negotiations have been carried on by silly methods. There is only one man in Portugal and with him Selby made no progress. We may be able to start again with Campbell.[1] I did all I could to impress on the Portuguese that a great man was coming.

Here in Madrid everything would be all right if it were not for Tangier. That disgusting little man Suñer keeps breaking his word to Sam, and as we in England believe in the doctrine of the collective responsibility of cabinets, what he says and does is what the Spanish Government says and does. In fact, all his colleagues are against him, but not yet able to kick him out. We don't want to fight to the death on the issue of Tangier, because this issue unites all Spaniards in their common desire to prove to themselves that they got something out of the Civil War in the way of extra territory. This is a bad ground on which to say: 'You give way or we cut off all food supplies,' and yet Suñer's action deservedly provokes the wrath of the House of Commons. A nasty business. A little later and we will pick an issue on which to give him a real jolt.

I dined with Sam and Maud *à trois* my first night. She is—they say—growing her hair again! Isn't it sweet at her age? She had on a nondescript dressing-gown sort of dress in dark purple with an immense silk scarf in violent orange wound all over herself like a boa-constrictor. Quite absurd. Sam was in huge form, very slippery and amusing.

All my love—David

1. Sir Ronald Campbell had been HM Ambassador in Paris and was now coming to Lisbon as our ambassador to Portugal.

Christmas Eve 1940 — Madrid

My sweetest love—I'm now conducting loan negotiations with the Spanish Government, Tangier negotiations with the Spanish Government, disposal of colonial surpluses with the Portuguese Government, commercial negotiations with Vichy, commercial negotiations with French Morocco. There you are: five balls in the air at once. It's quite impossible, and my hair is coming out in handfuls.

The disappearance of the Viscount[1] from the FO is a heavy blow, I felt wretched all day. He resigned, as you know, just after I got home, but Winston wouldn't let him go. When Lothian died it was clear that all the Gerry Villiers of the world would jump at the chance of putting him in cold storage till the peace! He has immense qualities, an unrivalled faith, but inadequate force. Dorothy [Halifax], I suspect, keeps him going. Often he must wish to retire to his books and his prayers. For him the conflict between this world and the next must have taken the edge off the political struggle. He'll be very good in Washington and perhaps will develop a legend there that will ensure FDR making him president of our delegation at the peace [conference].

In the British official news announcing the cabinet changes there was a sinister emphasis on 'no more appeasement' need be expected now. Appeasement is so often the misnomer of 'understanding', not necessarily giving way, but a knowledge of the limits to which we can go *given our military power to take strong action* at that particular moment. Today our military power is increasing in the Mediterranean and I am carefully bidding up the hand step by step with the victories in Albania and Egypt. The Italians evidently believe they can hold Bardia, for they are making a great song about the certainty that we shall not capture it. If we do I expect the rot to set in quickly.

I listened with admiration to Churchill's speech. As a performance it was marvellous. In taste I wondered. It made this clear at any rate, that we can make no peace with Italy and save Mussolini. He must go. I ask, however, if we should not be wiser to let the Italians come to this conclusion by themselves. If anything is capable of rallying them it is the appointment as Secretary of State of the author of sanctions coupled with a personal attack on Mussolini. Still, the PM has many more chances of judging the state of opinion in Italy than I have.

Tomorrow is Christmas Day. It is nearly midnight and I am too weary to go to the midnight mass to which the English Catholics in Madrid have invited me. I struggled all the afternoon, four hours without a break, with the compensation we are demanding from the Spanish Government for our officials who have been dismissed in Tangier. It is very unfair to wish this filthy negotiation on to me, but as there's no one else, I must do it. It means working all tomorrow.

Christmas Day

Your letter has come and one enclosed from Saxton Noble, my only friend who writes to me by the Christmas bag! How grand it must have been to see John and Simon together at Oxford. They do us credit, I feel, and if we lost other things we could point to them. I hope to see Halifax in Lisbon, but don't know if I can make it, it depends if Tangier is finished. From Lisbon I shall go to North Africa. *Que vida!*

All my love, darling Syb—David

1. Lord Halifax had been made HM Ambassador in Washington and was succeeded as Foreign Secretary by Anthony Eden.

Boxing Day 1940 Chute

My dearest love—Christmas is nearly over. All about England tomorrow morning countless mothers will be waking with a sigh of relief—and many too, with tears that the stockings are emptied and they were not there to hear their children's cries.

We had a day of scrambles, as usual. Simon chose to collect a temperature of 102° on the Eve so he was in bed. I tried to console him for this—but he thought that *I* was worrying! and turned the tables on me with, 'Oh, don't worry, Mom—it's really quite all right—I don't mind a bit—I really quite like being in bed.'

We got over the stockings nicely in a grey, green mild December morning—then breakfast and presents. No tree—unless you count a tiny one for Simon's bedroom. Eleven o'clock was with us before the last parcel had been admired. Polly fell so violently in love with the doll we gave her (Annabella Eccles) that it was the hardest job to get her to look at anything else.

Away to St Mary's—which proved to be colder than it's ever been before and a round dozen of us shivered through the dreariest service that imagination could conceive. The dear Vicar lost himself in the middle and there were several agonising moments of atrocious stumbling!

Out we tottered, rubbing our blue hands and stamping our dying feet, and there was a conspicuous lack of Christmas uplift.

3 p.m.—and his Majesty—rather tired—rather lifeless—rather flat—but touching and probably went slap home to the heart of the Great Proletariat.

Then out into the black-out for Christmas evening. Anyway the boys enjoyed it, especially a game of shove-halfpenny played in two teams with half a crown for a prize.

John's team won in spite of *me* and the Captain pocketed the cash and, magnanimous in the hour of victory, remarked to his mother, to the huge amusement of the company, 'You weren't too bad, Mum, after all. You got one or two. I was glad to have you, you were quite useful on the whole,' and was quite disconcerted by the roars of laughter.

Midnight and in bed. 'Goodnight, Mum—it *was* a super party. A super super party. I wish Daddy had been there.' (Don't break it to him that Daddy would have hated it!)

All my love, dearest darling—Sybil

26–28 December 1940 Madrid

My dearest love—Here we are in 'crisis total': no settlement over Tangier, no further economic help for Spain. I agree with this intransigent attitude, but I doubt if London knows the risks we are running. This risk is worth running because the Tangier hold-up can be clearly traced to the discourtesy and stupidity of Suñer alone, and we have, I think, been able to fasten the blame on him. This is a big gamble, because if the blame were not concentrated on a man whom 95 per cent of Spaniards hate, they would turn against us for thwarting what they consider their natural deserts, i.e. the absorption of Tangier. Our position is weak because the other six signatories to the Tangier Statute, France, Portugal, Belgium, Holland, Sweden and Italy, have given in and told the Spanish Government they can do what they like.

London, I surmise, know that we are on the point of a big diplomatic success in Spain and they are unwilling that Sam Hoare should have a facile success at the expense of the British interests in Tangier. Perhaps they don't know the risks they run in this pleasant game of getting something back on one of the Guilty Men.[1] Anyhow the game doesn't frighten me as I think we can play the hand successfully, but it is exciting, if not criminal, to walk so near the edge of the volcano.

The German Ambassador sent a message to Franco yesterday that the war was about to take 'a favourable turn'. Germany and Russia are agreed on all points and will shortly begin a joint attack on Turkey and Persia. I don't know if this is to frighten Franco from coming to terms with us about Tangier, or if it is true. If the latter it proves (a) that Germany has abandoned Italy, (b) that Germany's need for oil is urgent. You will remember that I told you some months ago that if Italy dropped out, the Nazi Party would be obliged to re-insure with the Communist Party. There can be no other move in the war, and I hope our Chiefs of Staff realise it.

The skies are blue here but the cold intense. Food is steadily becoming scarcer, eggs are 9*s.* a dozen and almost impossible to get. Small chickens fetch 15*s.* apiece. I do not know where it will end, because the Spaniards will never be able to organise or be willing to submit to a system of maximum prices, so that in a month or two's time we may be paying anything for anything. I could get 10*s*. a lb. for the butter that is sent me from the Embassy at Lisbon.

The Tangier negotiations swing this way and that. They don't frighten me, somehow I am sure of a good issue. I hope it is not 'overweening pride'.

Goodnight, sweet—David

1. In December 1935, as Foreign Secretary, Hoare made a pact with Laval which enabled Mussolini to partition Abyssinia despite Emperor Haile Selassie's appeal to the League of Nations. He was considered guilty of appeasement.

29 December 1940 Chute

Dearest love—As far as we are allowed to judge from our BBC news affairs between Vichy and England look promising. I hope that presumptuous donkey de Gaulle won't pop in with any grandiloquent manifestos and so touch up tender spots.

The Marshal [Pétain] is a brave old man and what an astonishing degree of influence he seems to have. What did you think of the PM's broadcast? It came across very well and was loudly acclaimed. At the moment it was such a surprise—like a blow between the eyes. Very clever. Perhaps the Wops were too astonished to jam it in time.

My darling—there is all my love and thoughts—I feel happier just now about your chances than I have ever felt. We're on the up-grade.

—Sybil

30–31 December 1940 Madrid

My darling love—There is no fresh news since I last wrote. We continue to walk the Tangier tight-rope. Progress is slow but not unsatisfactory. The hold-up in our economic assistance for Spain, due to our desire to secure the rights of British subjects in Tangier, has shown conclusively that this Embassy leads the diplomatic chorus in Madrid. Sam is besieged by ambassadors and ministers begging him to find some solution, as Spanish neutrality depends so exclusively on what we do. This is all to the good, and is a queer contrast to the abysmal state of our prestige last Christmas. Sam and the RAF may divide the honours, with the rest of us standing in the back row.

Archie James being sick of the 'flu, Eugenia J. and I went to lunch by the river at Aranjuez on Sunday. The night before the frost was cruel, every backwater in that strong and silent Tagus was frozen over, and huge white scarves marked the cuts in the vertical banks where the little streams come down. The sun struck through the winter branches a thousand colours off the frosted leaves on the iron ground. The smoke from the chimneys was pencil-straight and the world seemed a garden of shining metal, immovable, bloodless and still. Eugenia, a sensible girl without frills, talked very little, and I was glad, for silence best suited this midday truce between the sun and the ice.

Your letter written on Boxing Day came in today. I see it all, the scramble and the fun. Did I tell you about our Christmas? Maud did the supper party to the staff too beautifully, they had never had such a spread in their lives, a sit-down supper properly served, and curiously the *pièce de résistance* was not the turkey but scrambled eggs and truffles, which were served first, after soup, I mean. I had not realised how scarce eggs are.

Roger has written me a long letter about the change of Secretary of State; he and William [Strang] worked with Anthony Eden at Geneva, and are keen on the combination getting back into its old stride. I still heave a sigh for the Viscount [Halifax]. Here it is all hands on deck to try to clear up that wretched Tangier mess. You know I can always find some consolation in most difficulties, and I do think that in this case, if we make a really good agreement over Tangier, and my secret hopes are rising because I've nobbled the negotiations[1] and am doing quite nicely, then the world will have an example of the way England can stop snatch and grab, can stand up to 'aggression' (poor little Falange!) and secure for HM's subjects better terms than any other nation will get for theirs. It would be a salutary lesson. In the meantime it is really awful to see starving people all round and feel that we are holding up their bread supplies. No doubt the greater good includes the lesser evil.

What about 1941? I went to a dance at the Turkish Legation last night, champagne and jewels such as you seldom see in Madrid.

At midnight on 31 December you have to eat twelve grapes while the clock strikes. If you don't finish them in time you will not be happy. I found myself with the Duchess of Sueca and we bolted our grapes, beautifully prepared in little wicker baskets, kissed and wondered what 1941 would bring.

The world is weary of the past,
O let it die or rest at last!

Shelley, to my ear, quite shamelessly borrows the music of the last page of *King Lear*; there is a melancholy beauty about his two lines, that might undermine a doubting heart, and must touch the bravest. St Augustine would call it heresy. There is no rest for the servant of God, and no world without a struggle.

All my love, sweet—David

1. The British Embassy got fed up with the prevarications of the Spaniards and Hoare said that as no one wanted to go on trying to get what we wanted except me, I could do it by myself.

New Year's Day 1941 Chute

My darling love—A letter from Roger this morning. He is rather sad at his Lordship's [Halifax] departure across the seas and prophesies that he will be a greater loss to the Cabinet than they now realise. I wonder how Sam will react to Anthony Eden. Roger predicts an increase in captious-ness! And his sympathy is with you! For himself he sounds quite hopeful and says it will be like the old days when he and AE struggled at Geneva together.

It will be a struggle all right. I'm longing to hear what you think of the changes. You must be in for a difficult time in any case—France is like a volcano—rumbling day by day and one opens the paper every afternoon fearful lest it will hold the first indications of an explosion.

One thing is very amusing and particularly so when I think of the views you've held ever since June. In the summer the Marshal was constantly referred to in the press as 'that aged and senile figure'. He has now become: 'the dignified and isolated figure of Marshal Pétain, etc.'

—Sybil

4 January 1941 Madrid

My darling love—No bag today. Evidently the weather is too bad for the seaplane. What a difference it makes to me to have to go another four days without a letter! We are in the last stages of the Tangier negotiation. You know how hardened I became to last-minute hitches a year ago, now I am quite a seasoned campaigner and tell Sam and Arthur in the blandest way, 'Don't fuss, it will all come right in a day or two.' Over this particular negotiation I've never had any doubts, we shall obtain substantially what we want. You see, it's like meeting a girl at a party and knowing at first glance that you could if you would before the evening is out.

The Spaniards in their FO with whom we are negotiating are typical 'cut flowers', that is my name for professional diplomats. They have no roots. I love the grace and beauty, but it isn't enough. You want knowledge and resolution.

Think you I can a resolution fetch
From flowery tenderness?

No, of course you can't.

As soon as the negotiation is over I shall make arrangements for North Africa, where the prospects are improving,[1] and will, I think, be greatly assisted by the success of HMG in securing the rights of British subjects in Tangier and by the miserable failure of Vichy to do the same for their nationals.

All my love and a kiss to Polly—David

1. I cannot think why I did not tell Sybil about the correspondence I was having with Robert Murphy.

7 January 1941 Chute

My dearest love—Darling, I was most interested and amused by a portion of Dr Dalton's speech on the Blockade:

'Yes, I know we have been criticised on the ground that Spain constitutes a hole in the Blockade and that we have been too generous to the Spanish Government. But I am convinced that less generous treatment might have played into Hitler's hands and deprived an impoverished Spain of any independence.'

CONVINCED mark you.
What a triumph for you, my sweet,

All my love, dearest David—Sybil

Begun 6 January 1941 Madrid

My darling love—I've had two days in bed with a streaming cold of the kind that evokes your bitterest comments. A comedy has gone on as Sam wanted to wobble horribly over Tangier and kept sending Arthur to and fro with messages and pleadings. But I was able to draw the bedclothes over my head and say, 'No, not if you want my approval, if you want to placate the crocodile do it on your own responsibility.' Arthur was torn between loyalty to Sam and mild admiration for the younger generation.[1]

Today I came down to lunch as the two Spaniards most concerned with North Africa were coming. One of them, Figueras, the Secretary-General to the Residency at Tetuan, always said to be one hundred per cent pro-German, is a very formidable figure in Spanish politics. I asked him what the Arabs would do when they realised the defeat of Italy and the semi-defeat of France? (All Spaniards think that *qua* Africa France has lost the war whatever happens.) After some hesitation he said that the British and the Spaniards would have to 'protect' North Africa between them. Well, what about Morocco? He looked to the unification and independence of the three zones, Spanish, Tangier and French. The Tangier incident was important because the Arabs saw in it a step towards this independent Arab state, which Spain alone would give them. I didn't like the sound of this, but to humour him, I said that British colonial policy lay half-way between the Metropolitan-controlled, market-seeking policy of the French, and the noble vision of the Spaniards who thought nothing of money but only of the natives. We also worked towards self-government, but our rhythm was more cautious. He purred. He was sure that the tribes in all the zones hated the French, and loved the Spaniards (which is not true), and that the end of French influence was in sight. He looked to one strong and independent Morocco from Melilla to Agadir, the trusted ally of Spain! That vision must, I thought, be related to the fact of the British Empire. If that Empire was to endure, and I gave him a tip on that score, then we could no more play about with abstract formulae, our communications would have to be guarded, we should need the Mediterranean highway open and secure, and once we had cleaned up the Eastern Mediterranean (he hated the phrase '*estamos limpiando el este*') we must either find an ally in Spain, or think several times before the fate of Morocco was decided on the lines he desired. He said, quite pathetically, 'But it's all so difficult, when I was in Berlin with Suñer they said they were certain to win the war, and we must orientate our African policy to suit their book, but maybe it is you who will win.'

This kind of discussion shows how fluid neutral opinion is, oscillating between the consequences of a German or a British victory. It is an admirable moment to convince them how our victory is in their interests, when we are cantering home what we say will not make such an impression, because they won't have to make any effort to believe it.

Thinking ahead I would rather have the French in North Africa than the Spaniards. For this reason: unless the French come in and share our victory the war will end with an England disgusted with the Continent, too weary and too poor to care about Europe, and that will be an unmeasurable disaster for civilisation. The French will only fight again through their Empire, and through North Africa first and foremost, and then only if we back them up.

We cannot—God! How I wish we could—trust the British public, composed as it is of uneducated heroes and educated asses, to take on single-handed the mastery of Europe, and yet, when we have won this war, with our blood and our guts, that is the role we shall have earned for ourselves. Of all the tragedies I have ever read or imagined none touches the possibility of our refusal, after such a war, to accept the leadership of Europe. To come back to France: unless she is with us before the end comes, how shall we preserve our European connections? And if, as Sam is always urging, we should not hesitate to give away the French Empire—Syria to the Turks, independent Tunis and Algeria, Morocco to Spain, etc.,—how can we still have an ally in Europe strong enough to stand with us against Germany? All the more reason to recreate France. In power politics the Peninsula—which we could secure at the price of Morocco—would be a poor exchange. You see that as our Spanish policy succeeds there may be a temptation to push it too far, i.e. at the expense of France;

and I, who could score a big triumph by underlining any success we may have here, will have to be the brake on my own child.

I have treated you to a long exposition of North African politics, as I want you to have some background for the coming negotiations, and to know why I have stood out so firmly over Tangier. Tangier is a vital step in the game of securing Morocco for the French, and not as Figueras said, for the Arabs, at least not for many a year.

I'm off to Lisbon on Friday and shall take the aeroplane to Tangier early next week. I'll write and perhaps telegraph to you from Lisbon, a farewell to messages, except an occasional telegram. The Tangier affair has been a great education in North African politics and I'm very glad to have been through it.

Marshal Pétain is a wonder; I am glad I stuck up for him in the dark days. He is preparing now for the final blow, the occupation of all France, which is imminent, in my view.

North Africa will then have to decide, and if it decides to fight the war will be shorter by many a month. All this I foresaw, and made the phosphate-sugar agreement with Marchal on this supposition, against everyone in London, except William, Roger and the Viscount. What a world of myopia! My dear, sweet Syb, what a pity we are not handling the map together, I can only report to you, and not very fully at that. I want to see the Arab kingdoms and taste their savour, I'm sure I shall know more, understand better, about Spain afterwards. Sam is coming to Lisbon on Sunday and we shall have a big conference with Campbell.

All my love. I love you very much—David

1. By the time this letter was finished the Spaniards had given in and we had concluded the agreement on Tangier.

11 January 1941 Madrid

My darling love—Here we have a new burden, the Vichy chaps have sent a huge project of economic import which I can't handle, as I'm off, but I must digest it and send it home with comments. I wish Charles Stirling would come out and deal with Vichy. I'm not the man, they all suspect me at home of being in the Marshal's pocket. It isn't true, but I've served my turn with Vichy, and now they'd better have someone who was not so vociferous in the summer to undertake the negotiation. Africa for me. It's so personal and so important, I know no one else can do it, and any sound negotiator can deal with Vichy. Sam and I couldn't motor to Lisbon today, the snow is too deep, at least it has frightened him completely. I shall go tomorrow with someone else and hope to get through without an accident. I must see Campbell on Monday and the Doctor [Salazar] on Tuesday. Thursday or Friday I shall fly to Tangier, and start my adventure. Marchal is coming, God bless him, between us we'll do it.

Love—David

Begun 14 January 1941 Lisbon

My darling love—Malcolm Thomson and I had an awful journey here through ice and snow to the Portuguese border, and then a bad car smash 30 km from Lisbon. I was not driving at the time. Nothing except a shaking, and I am in excellent spirits. Things are as usual in a proper mess here, it will be a mystery to me all my life why our affairs in Portugal went so badly during the last half of 1940. Campbell has an uphill job, but I think he'll get round the Doctor. It's wonderful to get back to sun, warm sun in the middle of the day, and good food. Toast for breakfast made of white bread, you don't know what that means, but you will. And coffee too, delicious. I'm here four days and have no lunch or dinner untaken. Lisbon gives a warm welcome.

Now begins my great adventure. The preparations have been made, slowly and carefully. Marchal is in line, so I believe is Noguès, but I can't tell till I see him. The great complication is Spanish Morocco. Tangier is the middle of the Moroccan see-saw, on which I shall try to balance holding the French and the Spaniards on equal terms. I think it can only be done by perfect candour, telling them both that Germany is their enemy and that the time for local quarrels is after the war. I expect to go to Tetuan on Sunday for a couple of days to talk to the Spanish High Commission, and then go back to Tangier, and start off towards Rabat. I'm in a dreamy state about it all, and don't know what the problem will look like when I get there. I've done my best to read up the history of Morocco, but I can't say how it will help under present circumstances. I don't, of course, believe that institutions or habits ever change very fast, wars or no wars, so that reading is always worth while.

Four and a half hours with the Doctor! What an innings and how I love him. I have had four telegrams from Eden today and three from Sam, I simply can't do everything, and the Doctor says I must come back and settle the economic problems here.

It's not popularity I've earned: it's the reputation of being able to swing the Departments at home, and all the world is hungry for decisions, and for responsibility taken and taken gaily. That's the point. Oh! my love, how queer it is, when are we most ourselves, in bed, at home, in the air, in the Doctor's parlour, walking along the causeway, reading by the fire? Who knows? Oh! what a dusty answer gets the soul . . .

All my love—David

20 January 1941 Tangier

Dearest love—The only way to write to you is in journal form as the bag goes once a fortnight. Tangier is heaven. After the snow and ice and filthy food of Madrid, here blue skies, warm sun, the enchanting straits of Gibraltar, and French food. Yes, and something else: a huge bathtowel such as I haven't had since Chute. How can rich people ever be mean about bathtowels? It shows a fundamental ignorance of civilisation.

The Mediterranean is going to blow up. I feel it in my bones and I am afraid that this letter may not be on its way to you before the explosion occurs, and so you won't believe that I prophesied correctly. It must blow up. Germany can't leave Italy to perish, and the weather is too bad for a Balkan campaign before mid March or even mid April. So what? Occupy all France and have a go at us via the French colonies—I mean Algeria and Tunis? Of course they would need to take Malta first.

Last evening I spent in Tetuan with General Asensio, the Spanish High Commissioner for Morocco. His house and his office are in one large modern Moorish building, vulgar courtyards with Derry & Tom's fountains. I liked him. He is hard and handsome, and so obviously struggling to maintain some Spanish prestige with the Arabs when all the promises made in the Civil

War have had to be left unfulfilled. Up to now he has been under German influence, but I used on him the same arguments—only more concise—which had proved so effective with Garcia Figueras. I reported that conversation to you in a previous letter.[1] He listened with growing attention and I could feel him saying to himself, 'Well, after all Great Britain is not negligible: I must look out.' I did not get much change out of him, no commitments regarding their relations with the French, but he said he would think it over and send me an emissary to Tangier. Gascoigne came away depressed, but I was quite satisfied, because I saw the immense effort the General had to make to adjust himself to England victorious after such a long dose of German propaganda. Gascoigne said, 'You did well but you can't shake him, nothing will come of it.' And today I come back from lunch to find that his chief of staff is on his way from Tetuan to see me. I am waiting for him now. Here he is.

Later

The problem here is how to be sure that both native populations, i.e. in the Spanish and French zones, remain loyal to their rulers, and how to make friends between their rulers, who now dislike each other 'more than somewhat'. Usually I negotiate with one government, sometimes with two, as in the colonial products agreement between UK–Portugal–Spain, but I have never had a double native problem underlying the European negotiation, nor two European governments on such bad terms. My present idea is that the only way quickly to build a common front in North Africa is to feed the natives with British goods, letting them know where the stuff comes from: this will increase the growing swing of Arab opinion to our side. Both Spaniards and French are afraid of the natives, the one because they have not carried out the promises made to the Moors during the Civil War, the other because a defeated France has lost prestige in Arab eyes. If then we can bribe the natives with food to show strong signs of a pro-British attitude it will greatly influence their masters. To make friends between their masters means to exchange assurances between Weygand and the Spanish generals. A delicate and unpromising negotiation, but not, I feel instinctively, impossible. There you have the lay-out of the 1941 Moroccan situation.

27 January
Writing to Sam about Tangier economics I described the situation as follows: 'The international régime flourished on the leisure and luxury of a world at peace. When holidays were the rule, the pigsticker and the sunbather paid tribute to the revenues of an artificial enclave, which produced nothing for export but a few tons of vegetable fibre and a handful of tortoises. In times of war the fruits of idleness have vanished. In their place, four thousand Spanish soldiery batten on the zone, and some fifteen hundred refugees of different nationalities have left their homes to pass here a frugal and bad-tempered existence. Nothing remains of the former gaiety but the weekend party from Gibraltar, composed of a few dozen military, who, with a courage that does credit to their profession, leave their money if not their hearts in the places of pleasure.' Sam will laugh, I'm sure, and it will do him good. Later on there are two other Edward Gibbon-like sentences, which I rather like: 'Faithful to every hint and whisper from enemy-controlled Vichy the authorities in Rabat watch with a fascinated gaze the ruin of the wealthiest province in the Empire,' and 'The Tangier black market in exchange deserves a notable place in the history of unhealthy institutions. Behind the counter in every other shop in the main street sits the Jew, recording on his blackboard the struggles of a world in decomposition to send help or to run for safety from one barricaded area to another.' I described the artificial limits of the zone as 'a frontier drawn by an international pencil'. The international experiment failed, was bound to fail, because we only work well when our traditions and our characters are satisfied. I don't believe in a menagerie of administrators, representing half a dozen countries with half a dozen foreign policies and half a dozen hates and hopes. Idealist slop, far away from the stuff of which the world is made.

I've seen many French from their zone of Morocco, not very honest, not very brave, not very far-sighted, one and all unhappy, selfish, guilty with an agonised desire to be saved. I wish I had been brought up a Jesuit. There is no single path to salvation, some of them will respond to eloquence, some to money, others to honour, love hate, fear . . . we must keep open all the doors.

Darling, suddenly the courier is off with the aeroplane which is making a special trip. So here goes a rotten letter that I would have ended up better. I am taking some risks here, and feel the need of more communications with Roger. I hope all is well in the FO *re* this business.

All my love and I cry to think that you too are not looking out at a blue and sparkling sea, with Gib faint in the distance.

Kiss Polly—David

1. 6 January 1941.

25 January 1941 — Juniper Hill, Burnham, Buckinghamshire

My darling love—Oh! What a day in the Great Metropolis.

I took Grandnan[1] off to a meal at the Dorchester and gave her gin and ginger beer and her old eyes sparkled. She wanted to know who everybody was and said to me afterwards, 'Well, I did enjoy that—and the gin makes you feel ever so good.'

In the evening Roger [Makins] and Bill Elliot came in. Roger had had a spate of telegrams from you and seemed pleased with things in general and hopeful of future prospects. He says the Americans are delighted with the prospect of the Viscount and he thinks that his Lordship will enjoy the whole business enormously—as he has a tremendous talent and affection for parties.

We both decided over our cocktail that you—my sweet—are having a lovely war—all aeroplanes—secret plans—intrigue and excitement. What an excursion into diplomacy. But you recognise your luck without having to be reminded of it. And I feel like Roger—glad and confident that you are playing the hand. Yesterday morning I found Victor[2] on the doorstep of the Dorchester and we talked a bit. Harry Hopkins[3] is a big success with the North Country industrialists and promises to return home more Anglophile than ever. There is a great deal of enthusiasm for Wilkie's[4] visit. He's bound to keep the Presidency warm for himself, so it must be a good thing to make contact with him early in the day. I came back here feeling a new woman after my excursion and return home tomorrow.

—Sybil

1. Grandnan had been my nanny when I was young.

3. David, 1942

4. Chute Farm

5. David, John and Simon at Chute, 1939

2. Victor Cazalet, MP, Conservative member for Chippenham since 1924.
3. President Roosevelt's personal representative.
4. Wendell Wilkie, Republican candidate in recent American Presidential election. Roosevelt had sent over his defeated rival to meet Churchill.

2 February 1941 Tangier

My darling love—The French are desperately disappointing. They have lost their place in the history book; if anyone is ready to forgive and forget it is I, and when I get them in a room I can convert them, but down there in Morocco they are just as selfish, dishonest and cowardly as any bunch of civilised people have ever been. It's horrible to see the ruin of a great nation. They have it in them to recover. I know they have, but my God! they've sunk low. Still, I cling to my ways of peace and patience; if I spat on them like Gerry Villiers I might as well go home. I will not be dragged down by their sin, I will keep my eye on the end of the road and refuse the dirty sidetracks that are so easy to take.

In Tetuan I have a huge welcome from the High Commissioner; with the Spaniards I can get on. They've won their war. It may have been rather a squalid little civil war, but they won, and they've a sense of personal dignity. They're simple too, and love life for the sake of living and not only for money. If I were an Arab I should infinitely prefer a Spaniard to a Frenchman as protector. In some queer way Spaniards and Arabs alike think I may be a saviour to Morocco. They treat me as HM's personal representative, there's no accounting for it, and I make no effort to argue about it, I have few enough weapons to fight with, and if these people like to exaggerate my role and I do not abuse their confidence, what does it matter? Talking to an emissary of the Glaoui (the Pacha of Southern Morocco) who came five hundred miles to see me, I could feel the agony of the Arab world as it hopes and fears for the outcome of the war. How the Italians have murdered them and the French exploited them! Mussolini the Protector of Islam! It's laughable, he's more hated by the Arabs than the violator of their children; as for the French banks and politicians who have stolen their land and their wealth, their history is too sordid to be told. Lyautey[1] was grand. After him the disgusting politicians of Paris put in one blood-sucker after another, and now what happens? The tribes pity the French a little, and are—I really believe it—ashamed to cut such despicable throats. If the French were worth fighting I believe the Arabs would move. Perhaps that's an exaggeration, but it's half true.

All my love—David

I hope my telegram for your birthday arrived.

1. Marshal Louis Hubert Lyautey was the great French colonial administrator of Morocco before and during the First World War.

Letter to Roger Makins at the Foreign Office

3 February 1941 Tangier

My dear Roger—In talking to Marchal I struggle not to commit you, but you must realise we are dealing with drowning men, who catch at straws and think them spars. With the Spaniards it's different; they may be underfed, but they've won their squalid little war, and spiritually they're healthy.

Behind Marchal's conversation revolves a dim company of soldiers, sailors and officials, acting a piece the sound and sense of which only reach me in disjointed phrases. The stage is dark, it has no safety curtain, the noises off don't fit the speeches. Shadows and whispers indicate the role of Weygand the priest, the blackmailed Noguès, Monick so intelligent, and Bataille so obstructive. What's the play about? Is it a military drama or a bargain between merchants? You won't tell me, Washington is uncertain, the French wait for a lead, having lost their way completely.

Was Murphy right when he said, 'Those boys in Rãb't have gotten their hearts all warmed up, and we just must take a chance on them'? If I saw those boys face to face, I could tell you. That they are ready to be seduced into fighting again, I think probable. Some spark is needed. It ought not to be so, but they are *égarés* and selfish and frightened to a degree unbelievable until you've seen a few. And after all, whom do I see? The best of them, those who dare to come and talk.

The argument to which they respond quickest is this: you will lose your place in the history book if you don't fight before we've done the dirty work for you. Unless you come in soon, we, in our battered island, will forget all that happened before the Armistice. We shall acquire a feeling of indifference, if not contempt, for those who did nothing to help. The Americans will come in, and together we shall make an Anglo-Saxon peace. You can't afford that, and those of us who love the European tradition don't want it to happen. This gets them every time. They will never fight for anything but themselves.

Some say we could make sure of North Africa, and Spain too, if we offered France the pickings of Tripoli and Libya, while France agreed to give Spain the Sebou line as frontier to their Zones. It's an immoral plan, and one that would outrage the Arabs. The Arabs are awake. Here is an example.

Yesterday, among piles of cushions, I had two hours' talk to Moulay Arbi, the headman of Glaoui. Moulay Arbi is about forty, immense and negroid, very well informed, and speaks beautiful French. His theme was simple: the Arab world had one intelligence service and therefore one soul (Whitehall, please note): certain through experience that we treat native races better than do other protecting powers, nothing but the Arab fondness for military success could weaken their preference for the British. German victories had made the Arabs feel that, if the Italian murderers and French thieves were driven out of Africa, at any rate they could respect the incoming Germans. Immediately we began to advance in Libya, their hopes rose that we should be masters of all Africa: and now they are 80 per cent on our side. I had heard that in French Morocco the Moors were loyal to the French. 'We pity them,' he said, 'that is the only kindly feeling we have towards them.' He went on to recount the villainies of Paris bankers and politicians who, after Lyautey's departure, sent a series of bloodsuckers to rob the Moors of their land and to capitalise on the Bourse the resources of their subsoil.

Laval had told Glaoui via Epinat that the Germans would respect all the mineral companies in South Morocco, as a reward for Glaoui's loyalty, except the phosphate mines, which had been promised to the Germans. See how they work, all of the crooks, Laval, Epinat, Glaoui and Noguès!

Moulay Arbi asked why we made no propaganda among the Moors; especially, he was astonished that we had kept mum about the tea and sugar we were financing in exchange for the phosphates sent to Spain. We had only to let the Moors in Tangier know what was happening; they would do the rest, spreading the news south and east. 'For me,' he said, 'you need make no propaganda; I know there is a university in Cairo, that the Nile is dammed to irrigate the plots of the Egyptians, that you have stolen no land in Iraq: the natives in Morocco want to be your allies but they hear so little of what you are doing.' I said I would think aloud. Could it be that he wanted us to sponsor the independent Arab movement, to fan revolt against France, or at least to promise a change in the Protectorate after the war? Why should we do that? This was a tough world in which it was unwise to chase too many objects at once. Our first object was to defeat Germany, and to persuade the French to fight again. If the Germans attacked North Africa, we should expect the French to resist, and again to become partners in the war. Did he think the French would resist? They had always said so, he answered, but it depended on Weygand, the French were in a pretty poor condition, they would need to be inspired. He would ask me something: if the French did not resist, what then? To avoid this one, I took an instinctive plunge. 'Have you said anything to the Americans about this possibility?' He blinked and blinked, and replied very gently, 'When Mr Murphy saw the Sultan, it is possible HM did not confine the discussion to Blockade matters.' We left it there.

I asked him also about the Spaniards. He thought they would go in with the Germans (i.e. give bases in Spanish Morocco), if threatened with invasion of Spain. I said I disagreed, and what authority had he for his information? The French army believed it. 'Pooh! Pooh!' said I, the French, those pathetic creatures he had been describing to me, what confidence did he have in their opinion? He said if I would tell him solemnly that there was a chance the Spaniards would resist, it would be an extremely important piece of news. I told him to turn his intelligence service on to the job and learn through them how matters stood, and in a week's time to let me know the result.

Lisbon sent me the summary of the Doctor's reply to our economic proposals. I thought it satisfactory. I hope you do. It was his own drafting as far as I could judge. There's no reason, there never has been any reason known to us, why the PG and ourselves should not co-operate satisfactorily in working the Blockade. For many years I shall look back with pleasure on those four hours with the Doctor last month. We made such a tremendous sweep, as the communiqués say, of things present, past and future.

Yours ever—David

6 February 1941 Tangier

My darling love—I'm in a feverish lull while my friend Marchal has flown to Vichy to consult Pétain. Everything here depends on what is happening in that unwholesome place. I still think that in the last resort the Marshal won't let us down, but in the last few days the news has been confused, perhaps I should say bad. I firmly believe that the fact the old gentleman knows what I look like is having its effect. He's too old to make new contacts and puts a bigger value on those well established. It's queer to think that between General Wavell's troops and British West Africa we have no representatives except the consuls here and at Tetuan, and nobody but myself empowered to negotiate with a rabbit. Lucky DE wriggling his way into a front seat again. I'm lonely though, and on very delicate ground. One moment the Americans are tremendous supporters, the next they take offence at something we do in Washington, and pipe down here as part of the reaction.

Bags being so infrequent I have to bombard Roger with telegrams. I can't forget how minutely the Duke of Wellington reported home the details of the first Peninsular Campaign. They take it all in very good part in London, but they must be watching to see if I drop a brick, it's only natural they should be, the professional *v* the amateur; after all, it's a bit tough on them to find an outsider pulling one of the plums out of the diplomatic pie. What is diplomacy? In cynical moods I think it is nothing more than guessing what is certain to happen, and getting the credit for bringing it about. In December I was mad at those inter-departmental meetings for not having the historical and human foresight to drop the rigid Blockade with grace, because events would make breaches in it, whether they liked it or not. Why didn't they know that Americans are the sort of people who must send milk to children? Why didn't they know that Roosevelt can't let Morocco disintegrate for want of supplies (i.e. can't give us the pleasure of testing the 'join de Gaulle or starve' theory to the utmost limit) since the Atlantic is a vital interest of USA and if USA ever came into the war the Moroccan and Senegalese ports would be their first and most important bases? Sad, isn't it, that beautifully educated men should be so ignorant? What the hell is the matter with our public schools and universities?

8 February
I don't know what is the matter with me here but I don't write to you as much or as easily as I want to. The place is relaxing and the moment is tense. I fret a great deal and am pretty miserable. I want someone to talk to and to be comforted by, and you are not here. There are several idle women who declare their passions in a straightforward way, and if I thought I could possibly derive any pleasure or profit I would go to bed with each of them once. But in advance I know I should be disgusted, and feel suicidal afterwards. Today was perfect, hot and still, flowers and leaves growing as you watch, I went out to lunch on the western coast with an old lame lady, by name Jessie Green, who has lived here sixty years. Her father was our minister here in her childhood. She speaks Arabic perfectly, keeps, or rather kept, an antique shop with nothing in it that was nice for sale. Once she had a furious affair with a FO chap *en poste* here, and never married. She taught me a lot about local conditions, and told me to take a mistress, in this climate she said one must, or go mad. 'But,' I said, 'I, the real I, doesn't want a mistress, my bloodstream might aspire to such things, all of me that I care about, doesn't want one.' 'Poor little public-school boy,' was her answer. Perhaps it's the spring, and such long periods of over-thinking and of time passed in celibacy.

The signal for depression in me is always some success in the negotiations. 'Forlorn in success', 'the strong wind of success blew out my dreams', 'Failure is God's freedom to mankind', phrases like these occur in T. E. Lawrence's *Seven Pillars of Wisdom*. I wish I had the book here, he was dealing with Arabs, and like me he was a lonely negotiator, and he despised the Whitehall end of his mission; despised it much much more than I do, but I can sympathise. Then he became friends with the people he negotiated with and I advance in that direction with the Spaniards. Yesterday I heard that Marchal had persuaded Vichy to separate the Moroccan from the French franc. He did it because I asked him to. I wanted Morocco to stand on its own legs and not cling to a sinking ship. The effect throughout North Africa will be excellent, but it plunged me into gloom. It's the tension that relaxes, and we cry as easily when we see the bride come down in her going-away dress as at any funeral. I miss the bags so. Roger wrote regularly and I could feel how far they supported me, and when to draw in. Now I'm cut off, and all the more so because the Viscount and I understood each other, and really I know nothing about Anthony Eden. For two weeks there has been nothing in the telegrams to indicate the degree of approval which they feel. Sam has sent me a charming wire of encouragement, and I hugged it with real joy, but from London nothing.

10 February
I read through the pathological pages of this letter and thought to burn them and begin again. But I won't because I am happy again this morning. Yesterday I laboured to produce for the FO a clear exposition of the enormous risk being run in giving me instructions to present French North Africa with nothing less than an ultimatum. And suddenly the bits came together in my mind and I saw the situation, and saw it whole, and now it's fixed for ever on paper to Roger, and I know what is right, and they can comment at their leisure—after the event if Marchal returns here on Wednesday.

All my love—David

14 February 1941 Chute

My dear sweet—I'm engaged in a colossal, wordy and apparently endless correspondence with various baby departments of the Ministry of Agriculture. All about our precious porkers. We are allowed to keep one whole pig for household consumption every three months. But we shall have to kill them both together owing to the food shortage and as Harris says: 'Tisn't any use to linger one on until May.' Short rations, poor fellow, and he wouldn't fatten but only run to muscle and scrawn. So we propose to have a wild fling with all the food we can muster, cram it down their willing throats until mid March and then slay them both—eat one and sell his brother to the Government Meat Supply. A bit of cash back—that appeals to me in these hard times. We mean to keep another pair through the summer—when barley meal isn't so essential and garden produce is plentiful as an alternative. Then we can accumulate our cereal ration and use it en bloc at the end of the summer to fatten them and kill them off in October. Again keeping one and selling the other. Then comes the problem. How to keep a winter pair—when green stuff won't provide an adequate substitute for meal. After much thought—I've arranged with Withers at his kind suggestion that he sow some barley on our old potato strip three-quarter acre and we take it over. He will stack and thresh it with his own and we should with luck get six sacks off it. Making 12 cwt. This should provide a solution. I'm determined to keep porkers next winter—willy nilly. The poultry problem is a teaser too. No one is raising sittings. Always the same cry—no food for young chicks. So I've had to buy (in advance for May delivery) twenty-five pullets at six weeks old at (hold tight here) 4*s.* 6*d.* each!! Harris says it's cruel—but what is one to do? What a domestic letter, my sweet.

I love you very much—Sybil

Begun 15 February 1941 Tangier

My darling love—Marchal's return from Vichy was the signal for a tragic series of conversations in which the depths to which France has sunk were plumbed. It's awful. The whole French Civil Service has gone to pieces, and is demoralised with fear and corruption. At meals they can talk of nothing but the Germans, 'The Germans say this', 'The Germans have done that', 'The Germans will do this'. In the ministries they dumbly wait, doing nothing all day in expectation of the sack. Pétain only just survived the Laval crisis.[1] He almost yielded, and I think he knows that his end is fast approaching. He is both weaker and stronger than he was. Weaker in relation to his ministers, stronger in his personal courage. He might easily take risks to annoy the Germans, as he feels the end so near, that he wouldn't have taken a month ago. It is reasonable to cock a snook at the world on the last day of life. I hope HMG will be *sufficiently sensitive* to realise this precious twilight and to play it up. Weygand, too, is in a precarious position, he hangs on the Pétain thread, if the Marshal went the

French Admiralty would have him out in a twink. I feel I ought not to tell you just how the negotiations are going, although it is a sad deprivation for you and me to restrict our conversation. The Germans won't allow me a visa to see W[eygand], and I am maddened by their refusal, and W's acceptance of it.

Today there is cinema sort of tempest, thunder and lightning and crashing trees, water spouts down the hills and pools in the hollows. The sun is shut off by a curtain of rain, anyone who ventures out today has my sympathy. All the Tangerinos say they never knew such weather in their lovely paradise, but I don't believe them, I expect it's like this every February.

We're on the edge of a colossal failure, and the only way to stop it would be something equally colossal. The most obvious move would be for the Comte de Paris[2] to declare himself King of all Frenchmen, to do it in Algiers, and to couple it with war on the Germans. The less obvious way is to carry on into Tunis if and when Wavell reaches the Tunis-Libya border. Heaven help us to do the right thing, and to do it in time. Why did I come to Africa? I invented the negotiation and forced it on the Departments, against their will. There was something instinctive, some compulsion outside and deeper than my ticking brain that drove me here. Before I came home in November, and when I was home, I was in my inner heart fretting to get to Morocco. If the history of the war is fairly written that blind urge will deserve a sentence. We've very slender chances now of getting the French to fight in time, but we'd have had none if I hadn't come; not one chance in a million. The wise don't search for the key to life, they don't ask why the butterfly is marked with a lovely pattern, or why the moon dies once a month, and yet it is an endless speculation that haunts and holds the human mind. In these days of supreme difficulty, I think so much of Chute and the quiet to which I will return and share with you. Ambition is puffed out by the strong wind of the tempest.

—David

1. Pétain had dismissed Laval in December 1940. The Germans reacted strongly, see note to my letter of 21 April 1942.
2. Orleanist pretender to the French throne.

18–19 February 1941 Chute

My darling love—On Saturday I went over to see Walt [Butterworth] at Merrimoles. He got back from the States ten days ago and had hoped to find you in Lisbon—where they told him you were in Tunis! (They were moving a bit fast I thought.) However, he saw Murphy[1] who had been with you and had apparently had a long talk to you and this made some sort of contact. Murphy had been to see Weygand and brought back the message that the General did not consider himself irrevocably bound by the Armistice terms. This and no more. But I felt we could draw some encouragement from it and so did Walt.

But I expect you know this and a good deal more as well. In America, it seems, they too often see the British as a nation holding its breath in expectation of an overwhelming and deadly blow. Braced (if it were true) to meet the shock with courage but with a rigidity that could only prove fatal. Walt was disturbed by this 'open-your-mouth-and-shut-your-eyes-I'm-prepared-to-take-it-so-come-and-hit-me' view of us and started in to preach the gospel as soon as he arrived. 'I told them—they'd got the British all wrong. Here was a nation bred to independence—only dimly aware of its peril and quite unperturbed by it. Sufficiently conscious of the threat to its liberty to be determined to defend it in a perfectly stolid commonsensical way as part of the day's work. No heroics—no breath-holding—just plain slogging at the job as the only possible thing to do.' There is a tendency to regard us as the last Maginot Line—backs to the wall and all that. The honest and well-intentioned Yankee doesn't spot the difference between moribund France and an England still convinced of her place in the history books.

All my love, my darling David, I wish you were here to share this lovely day and watch the garden moving.

—Sybil

1. Murphy's visit to Lisbon was in between the first and the second drafts of the agreement we sent to Weygand.

Begun 23 February 1941 Tangier

My darling Syb—Do you form a habit about getting up when you stay in new places? It takes me about a week; and then when I enter the bathroom, with one hand I put on the light, with the other run the cold water in the basin, walk to the windows in the shortest way and draw the curtains, picking up my sponge on the way back to the basin (since it was left in the bath the night before) and begin cleaning my teeth. Everything falls into an order which can be performed with no mental effort so that I am free to think about cabbages and kings. Here I am not called, I wake up about 8.15, doze till 8.30, shave till 8.45, read the New Testament till 9 a.m., breakfast in bed, and am down in the Chancery between 9.30 and 9.45. Reading the Bible, if only a few verses, every day, influences me in many ways. I think I see the effect in writing to Roger, for example, the huge secret is simple language to express complicated ideas, mysteries if you like, and an emotional cadence in the sentences that wrings the heart without you knowing it.

—David

24 February 1941 Chute

My darling love—Your long letter of 6 February gave me a kind of melancholy pleasure. When you're lonely, to read that someone else is too is of inestimable comfort. And when it comes to your man missing his woman so much that he flirts with the notion of going to bed with another one. Why—even that has its consolation. But darling David—all the same—don't take a mistress—don't listen to that old Jessie Green. She gets a great deal of vicarious pleasure from her persuasions—as well any of us might, were we old and lame with one warm memory that is cooling year by year—struggle as she may to keep the chill off. It isn't that I'd mind so much your going to bed. I should try a good deal not to—since I've learnt that my own bloodstream can be pretty troublesome, so how about yours? But you would very likely fall in love. Knowing you—I think you would. And that would be quite unbearable. So don't, please—or everything will be spoiled and we shall never want to see the African spring together.

I wish you weren't so cut off and your letter (at the beginning) sounded so mizzy that I had made up my mind to write Roger a careful little note to tell him to send you more letters. Then you ended quite gaily—having got a long letter from him. So now I'm in no doubt and shall probably hold my hand. Don't worry that your work is not appreciated at the office—nor that they are suspicious of you, nor that they keep watch in anticipation of a false step. I don't believe in any of this. They are all straining every nerve to make the thing 'Go'—and know only gratitude towards anyone who helps. I always put out a feeler whenever I can and heard both from Walt and Bill Elliot how well you are considered to be doing.

I asked Bill if they had talked about Spain and he said no. The evening was spent touring the Balkans and Turkey. I gather that the Turk is causing a good deal of anxiety—so far no amount of ginger can persuade him to declare himself. There is a fear too that the German encroachment on the Balkans is planned to coincide with a Japanese attack in the Pacific. And apparently there is a pretty breathless hush in the courts of Whitehall.

Write to me as often as you can—I love you and do want you so much.

—Sybil

IV

Washington

March–June 1941

4. Washington

I went home for a fortnight after Tangier and then spent a few days in Lisbon before going to Washington to discuss Tangier, North Africa and Vichy France. The three months in Washington seemed deliciously romantic, like a summer holiday sandwiched between two hard spells in Spain and Portugal. By the beginning of 1941 we could see that it would soon be difficult to find the shipping, the wheat and the raw materials to fill the quotas we had agreed with Spain. America was the only place to which we could look for help. I was sent to Washington to see what could be done. Agreement was reached on the principle of aid to Spain but the details and the particular cargoes were a never-ending problem to be skilfully handled by the MEW section of the British Embassy in Washington.

My second objective was to explore with the United States Government the conditions which would justify economic aid to the French. On this controversial subject both governments were groping for a policy. We had heard that the Americans were toying with a proposal to send relief supplies for children and old people in metropolitan France.[1] I was to tell them that in a total war such charitable gestures had no place. Pétain's government in Vichy was too weak to give us anything worthwhile in return. French North Africa was a different proposition. There General Weygand had enough independence to do something positive to help the Allies, if he wanted to.

The reader will have seen from the Introduction to Part III how Murphy and I had worked out a plan to offer supplies of such materials as oil, binder twine, whisky, cigarettes and silk stockings, all calculated to boost French morale, in return for help from the French in preparations for an Allied landing somewhere

1. In his book *I Was There* Admiral William D. Leahy, US Ambassador to Vichy, tells President Roosevelt how much Red Cross supplies did to increase the goodwill of the French public towards the USA. He adds, however, the significant comment that there was no effective means by which the Germans could be prevented from taking out of France the equivalent of whatever the Red Cross sent in. Spain was a different case. There the Germans had no power to commandeer supplies.

in their part of Africa. Murphy had the brilliant idea of asking Weygand to accept twelve US vice-consuls, whose official duty would be to check that the goods allowed through the Blockade were all consumed locally, and not sent via France to Germany. In reality the consuls' main job would be to collect information and to organise resistance to the Germans and support for an Allied landing. We were to say to Weygand, 'No consuls, no supplies.' When I reported this draft agreement in London, ministers were sceptical, and I had to insist that since the Americans were determined to send critical supplies to French North Africa (I knew Murphy was determined but was uncertain how far the United States Government was behind him) we must make up our minds what we should require in return for allowing these goods through the Blockade. It was generally agreed that Weygand was not in a position to give us an undertaking that he would act independently of Pétain. On the other hand Murphy's vice-consuls pointed to Anglo-American joint planning for action in French North Africa, and with the French as well, to the extent that Murphy could persuade them to take part. Co-operation of this kind assumed that the United States was coming into the war. How the State Department would react to this assumption I was left to find out when I got to Washington.

A few days before I arrived in New York, Murphy had seen Lord Halifax, the British Ambassador, only to be told that an Anglo-American agreement with Weygand, such as he was talking about, was not a starter. This was an unexpected blow, described by Murphy as follows: 'In my conversations with Lord Halifax he manifested the greatest doubts about the possibility of co-operation with the French in North Africa, and he gave me no encouragement or support.'[1] Halifax's damper depressed Murphy and sharpened the quarrel inside the State Department between those who were ready to prepare for entering the war and those who wanted the United States to remain a benevolent neutral. Who, the officials asked, was right about British policy, Halifax or Murphy? Murphy replied that the answer depended on what I was coming to say. On arrival I had no idea that the British Embassy had just taken a position contrary to the purpose of my mission. When I explained the proposal which I was instructed to make to the United States Government, the Embassy staff (but

1. *Diplomat among Warriors* (Doubleday, 1964), page 88.

not Halifax) were more than a little put out. They thought the proposal unworkable and me an interloper. They had been given no hint that my discussions with the United States Government had been prepared by three great Americans—General 'Wild Bill' Donovan, at that time President Roosevelt's special adviser on the military strength of the Axis, John Winant, American Ambassador to London, and Robert Murphy. On separate occasions either in London, Lisbon, Gibraltar or Tangier I had put to each of these men the case for the flexible use of the Blockade. Murphy summed up his conclusion, which was shared by the other two, as follows: 'Eccles understood how to make effective use of economic concessions, which was the most formidable weapon the British had in 1940–41.'[1] If the Departments in London had grasped this formidable weapon when France fell we might have secured great advantages from the Vichy government. Now in 1941 it was getting late. When in February Donovan and Winant had canvassed the flexible use of the Blockade with the State Department the response had been very feeble, mainly, they said, because the Department knew so little about economic warfare. By contrast the idea was an instant success with the President. Mr Roosevelt asked to hear more about it as soon as I reached Washington, and no doubt this was the reason why Cordell Hull, the Secretary of State, pressed Halifax to bring me to see him.

Halifax had helped me before the war, and as Foreign Secretary he kept the belligerent MEW in order when the War Trade Agreement negotiations in Madrid were making slow progress. In Washington he and Dorothy Halifax, who very much liked Sybil, gave me a great welcome. He was amused, thought it something of a joke, that Cordell Hull was so eager to see 'the young man from Spain'. The interview took place on 2 April.[2] The conversation opened with a ready acceptance by the Secretary that unconditional aid to metropolitan France was not worth considering. Turning to North Africa I said how much we admired what Murphy was doing in Algiers and how valuable his contacts were with the French leaders. If the United States Government approved in principle of Murphy's draft agreement with

1. *Diplomat among Warriors*, page 88.
2. See W. N. Medlicott, *The Economic Blockade* (HMSO/Longman, 1952, 1959), Vol. II, page 348, for a reference to this interview.

Weygand the British Government would co-operate and I was instructed to discuss the conditions on which limited quantities of scarce goods would be allowed through the Blockade. It went without saying that in return we must secure action from the French helpful in the prosecution of the war. The Secretary agreed and said very firmly that the gamble ought to be taken because it was so important to us to gain time. He then discussed the conditions we had proposed in the draft agreement[1] with Weygand. These would be studied in the State Department and I would be welcome to join in the talks. Halifax thought the interview had gone well but that nothing much would come of it.

Donovan and Winant had arranged for me to repeat my story at the White House, where Harry Hopkins, the President's principal adviser, saw me about twice a week. Hopkins liked working in a large four-poster bed (he said Abraham Lincoln was born in it). On two occasions Mr Roosevelt came in for a few moments to hear how we were getting on. The President used a phrase that made me jump: 'You are talking of this operation as a curtain-raiser to a military adventure.' He looked at Hopkins: 'Agree?' 'Yes,' replied Hopkins. I said nothing. It seemed odd to be conducting the same negotiation in the White House and in the State Department, where Hopkins was much disliked. I never discovered how bad the communications were between them. Donovan said that was how things got done in Washington and I was damn lucky to be selling my goods at the two best stores.

When the State Department had made up their minds under what conditions aid should be given to the French in North Africa, Sumner Welles[2] called a meeting which is described by Murphy in his book as follows:

> 'On 24th April Under-Secretary Sumner Welles announced that it had been definitely decided to go ahead with the much-delayed agreement . . . I was assigned to Algiers as a sort of High Commissioner . . . Welles then called in David Eccles, who was waiting in an adjoining room, told him of the American decision, and asked for comments. Eccles explained that sentiment in London had changed and that the British Gov-

1. Murphy had put our draft to the State Department as entirely his own. He and I thought this would give it a better chance than showing a British hand in the text.
2. Under-Secretary of State.

ernment probably would agree now to include even Dakar in our co-operation sphere, an idea which would have been hooted down a few weeks earlier.'[1]

Sumner Welles had asked whether the negative response of the British Embassy to Murphy, when he had raised with Lord Halifax the possibility of a deal with the French, still represented the view of HMG. He knew quite well that it did not because this had been made clear to the Secretary of State and at the White House, but he wanted his officials to hear it from me. I said how encouraged we were that Murphy was to get all the resources he needed. Then Welles came to the scale of the proposed Anglo-American co-operation and asked that Dakar should be included. I had no instructions about Dakar, but, being an amateur, that is, someone who in moments of crisis finds it easier than professionals to break the rules, I accepted. The Embassy muttered, the military rejoiced, and Halifax said that co-operation on this scale was 'probably worth a try'.

The published American accounts show that the meeting on 24 April was considered a significant step in the run-up to entering the war. Certainly it put an end to the paralysing quarrel inside the State Department on the use of economic aid to secure concessions of military value. But I feel sure that in relation to French North Africa the United States would have had to do sooner rather than later what was then decided. The war was moving so fast they could not have dithered much longer.

In the background Donovan's advocacy was invaluable in convincing the White House to act in North Africa. He contributed more than anybody to the British cause. His imagination and eloquence, his courage and persistence were used to the utmost to persuade his countrymen that, in spite of one reverse after another, Britain would hold on and win in the end, but at a disastrous, irreparable, cost if the Americans did not join in the battle. He invited me to make my home in his house (which now belongs to Mrs Katherine Graham), and there on the porch at the back we worked on the memoranda for the President which led to Donovan being put in charge of the Office of Strategic Services,[2] which proved so valuable in the war.

1. *Diplomat among Warriors*, page 88.

2. Similar to our MI6 and SOE combined, covering secret intelligence and special operations.

Now, forty years later, knowing better than I did then the jealousies of Whitehall, I understand how my daily contacts with the leaders in the United States administration made the Embassy increasingly restive. They could not keep track of me, but by the middle of June they knew that the North African policy was off the drawing-board, the State Department were recruiting Murphy's consuls and economic action was going forward. The Foreign Office, no doubt prompted by the Washington Embassy, started to fuss about the situation in Portugal: Salazar was fractious, the commercial side of our Embassy was in deep trouble, I must go back at once. I showed these messages to Hopkins and Donovan who used unprintable language to describe what they saw as a trumped-up pretext to get me out of Washington. They proposed to ask for me to stay, even if it meant appealing to the President. But no, I said, Sam Hoare told me that in public life, it is always best to leave the stage before you are ordered off. I installed Ian Fleming[1] in my place in Donovan's house and took the clipper to Lisbon, sad to say goodbye to such wonderful friends, but confident that Murphy had everything under control.

1. The author of the James Bond books, then serving in British Naval Intelligence.

Letter to Sir Samuel Hoare

23 March 1941 Lisbon

Dear Sir Samuel—I was very sorry that the booking on the clipper made by the State Department did not leave me time to visit Madrid. It now turns out that I could have come as the clipper was due to start on Saturday and day by day has been put off as it is delayed coming in from America. Now it is expected tomorrow, Monday, and our departure will therefore be Tuesday.

The Saving telegrams enclosed with this letter give an account of my talk to Dr Salazar yesterday. He was patient and resigned and showed some signs of being harassed. What he said about the Blockade seems to me good sense and I am quite hopeful that Dr Dalton will take another step in the right direction, especially as Noel Hall[1] is sending home some hot criticism of the superabundant details which Blockade work is putting on this mission.

Last evening I saw the Spanish Ambassador and told him that I was going to the United States of America partly to discuss possible assistance to the Peninsula in the form of such commodities as wheat and cotton. He wished me every success and said it would be a very valuable thing to bring American aid to Spain. I told him that unless our Loan Agreement had been signed, it would be very difficult to start discussions for American assistance. He is going to Madrid on Tuesday and promised to press for the signature of the agreement. He said he hoped he might have an opportunity to see you while he was there. It seemed to me that he may have something he wishes to tell you because he winked and chuckled a good deal while he was talking on this point.

He then gave me a lecture for half an hour on how to prevent sabotage in munition factories, which I found exceedingly boring and of no practical value whatever.

I will let you know how I get on in Washington. Please give my best wishes to Lady Maud.

Yours sincerely—David Eccles

1. Professor Noel Hall, who was going to Washington as chief representative of MEW.

Telegram drafted by DE from HM Ambassador, Lisbon, to the Ministry of Economic Warfare

23 March 1941

When he received Mr Eccles yesterday Dr Salazar was in a depressed but not defeatist mood. He spoke sadly, without a trace of bitterness, of the increasing pressure to which he was being subjected, and in particular repeated his belief that the machinery of our Blockade was unnecessarily clumsy, and seemed designed to irritate neutrals as well as to injure the enemy.

2. Mr Eccles argued that the inconveniences suffered by the Portuguese as a result of the Blockade were not serious in themselves and were insignificant in comparison to the troubles of occupied and belligerent countries. Dr Salazar admitted that the Germans would not invade the Peninsula for purely economic reasons. He did feel, however, that HMG quite failed to appreciate the changed conditions under which the Blockade is being applied today compared with 1914–1918. Bullying and pinpricking tactics, which had succeeded before, only played into the Germans' hands in a world where nationalism had grown so fast and the technique of German propaganda had so immeasurably improved. If we lost the sympathy of the Portuguese, would our blockade methods in his country have been justified? We were, he said, a queer people who thought straight on first principles and then gave ourselves every imaginable handicap in carrying out our policy. Our plans to help neutrals in economic distress, and in danger of being dragged into the German camp, were absolutely right. In the application of this policy, which was essentially to make friends, we had lost our famous common sense and employed the wrist-twisting dodges of schoolboys. Mr Eccles said that the machinery of the Blockade was under constant revision and that Professor Hall was that day investigating with HM Consul-General a number of specific complaints.

3. Mr Eccles thinks that Dr Salazar is feeling his own position less secure. The responsibility for the inevitable troubles of war conditions is laid at his door, and the Germans lose no chance to suggest that he could be firmer with us if he wished to be so. Sir Walford Selby used to insist on the points of resemblance between Dr Salazar's position and that of the Austrian Chancellor, Dollfuss.

4. Dr Salazar may be right to draw attention to the different conditions in Europe today compared to 1914. There are now two bullies each twisting a wrist of the unhappy neutral, and it is neither so obvious that the British bully is the stronger of the two, nor, and this seems equally important, does the British bully have the same right to domineer as he did in the last war. We have enjoyed for some years the luxury of pretending that all nations are equal, a fallacy which has no place in a world devoted to reality, and now in time of war we cannot rely upon an acknowledged priority among big and small states which is the foundation of disciplinary action such as the Blockade tries to impose without the sanction of force.

In the last war the Germans were comparatively remote from the Peninsula, on the other side of the Allied armies, now their soldiers are on the Pyrenees, their agents in every town and province, their propaganda in every house, printed, spoken, filmed, broadcast. They seize on every restriction of economic activity and explain it as due to the Blockade. This propaganda is the more readily listened to because nationalism has developed so strongly, and because the bullying of a small power by a big power is not so natural as it was. Further, the state has assumed in recent years a much greater control over all forms of industry, finance and commerce. An autocrat like Dr Salazar, whose personal conception of neutrality and of his responsibility towards his people is unshakeable, resents the contradiction implied in the neutrality of the state and the unneutral attitude which we, by Black List methods, force on Portuguese individuals and firms. He feels that in exacting information from a firm in Lisbon, and possibly asking for guarantees that the firm should cease trading with the enemy, we are asking these things of the Portuguese State, and that such practices square badly with our claim to be fighting to maintain the independence and sovereignty of small nations.

In his heart he knows that strict neutrality has no meaning in modern war and that spotless sovereignty will have no meaning in modern peace, but he is an obstinate man, who cherishes the reputation and independence of his country, so largely his own handiwork.

5. For particular points raised by Dr Salazar see my immediately following Savings telegrams.

Letter to M. Henri du Moulin de Labarthète, Chef de cabinet to Marshal Pétain at Vichy

25 March 1941 Lisbon

My dear Henri—François Panafieu[1] carries this letter to you and with it my best wishes to yourself and your wife. I would like so much to see you and to renew those pleasant conversations we had in Madrid. Now we should have more important things to talk about but I have no doubt of the value we should derive from an exchange of ideas.

January and February I spent in Tangier discussing with Marchal and Murphy the economic problems of North Africa. Then I went to London for a fortnight and am here for a day or two on my way to Washington where our Tangier talks will be resumed. I think that we all, Marchal, Murphy and myself, have a common object, which should make certain agreement between us. We all want to maintain the independence and vitality of the French Empire. This seems to me to be an aim which no one can dispute and, therefore, I am optimistic about the results of our coming conversations.

You will know, however, that we have had too long experience of the subversive activities of the Germans to regard the infiltration of German commissions, experts, etc., into the French Empire as a movement which can easily be stopped or made light of. In taking a serious view of the German designs upon North Africa, I know we are acting in the interests of France as well as of ourselves and of the United States.

We shall win this war. There is no young man or woman in England who can contemplate defeat. To be defeated is not an idea which enters into the consciousness of our island population, and I can assure you that you would only need a few days in London to catch the faith in our ability to outlast the Germans and, with America, to achieve a complete victory. I can quite understand that in France you may have doubts about our ability to win. Put away these doubts and you will not only be making the right estimate of the outcome of the war, but the very fact that you in France believe in us will shorten the war and make possible a European peace on reasonable lines.

We do not want a purely Anglo-Saxon peace. Such an instrument would leave the Christian tradition of Europe at the mercy of the New World. You and I both want to preserve the best of the Holy Roman Empire and everything that Greece and Rome have meant in our history. We shall only be able to do this if France is there at the peace conference, taking that part in planning the future to which her history entitles her. When that moment comes, nothing would please me more than the hope that you and I should meet at the making of our New Order, and on a larger scale renew those attempts to develop the friendship between Spain and our two countries at which we worked last winter.

Please give my best wishes to your wife and, if you should see him, to Armand du Chayla.

—David Eccles

1. Counsellor at the French Legation in Lisbon; the letter was read by Marshal Pétain.

26 March 1941 Chute

My dearest love—On Monday Walt and I set out for Bath and after long detours over the Plain, which was lost in mist and swallowed by the softest of grey skies—we arrived to find lunch very elusive with the Admiralty in command at every hotel. However at Fortts an excellent meal was found—Walt insisted on champagne! And to our astonishment the list boasted a Krug '25. After lunch we bought some socks, then climbed up to the Circus and wandered along the Crescents, so elegant and secure in the quiet afternoon.

Almond blossom and forsythia tumbled about the gardens—pert and brilliant against the unfledged trees—there were even pansies blooming in the beds. The day wore on and after a sentimental sigh or two we took the road to Bristol—the farewell pilgrimage was done.

Poor gallant Bristol—how sad and bold and brave she is. We had tea and then walked round the worst of it. Most touching of all are those notices—put up over heaps of rubble and a twisted girder or two, 'Louie—Hairdresser—reopening here shortly.'

One rather touching thing—in a flower shop we asked to write a card and after some hesitation the woman produced one with a black border—saying quietly, 'I'm afraid I have only these just now.' As though in Bristol there could be no other need for flowers. It made the tears spring. Then home through the black-out—rather flat and weary—since all the laughter was over and goodbyes are pretty wretched anyway.

—Sybil

Letter from Roger Makins at his home address

28 March 1941 30 Chester Terrace

Dear David—There are many pitfalls in your present journey, and the question of supply to unoccupied France the thorniest and most uncertain of topics: already we have had one or two small breezes here and the wind is variable. If I may offer a word of caution I would not stay in Washington longer than is necessary to place the Professor [Hall] on the straight and narrow and to hold the essential discussions with Marchal, Murphy and the State Department about North Africa.

I wonder how the Americans strike you: they are just beginning to feel and assume their responsibilities as a really great power and I am afraid they will misuse their strength. American imperialism may be very dangerous to Anglo-American relations and more dangerous is the prevalent tendency to strip us to the bone. It is shortsighted, psychologically as well as economically, for it will provoke a reaction here which will in the end be unfavourable to American interests. Talk to Dean Acheson[1] about it. We do all the fighting and are being deprived of our liquid assets while the occupied countries hibernate with their store of riches safely blocked in the USA!

No raids for a week and spring in all the parks—but the clash of interests and personalities in Whitehall almost shakes the fragile blossom from the trees.

Yours ever—Roger

1. Later Secretary of State.

31 March 1941 Washington

Darling sweet—What a life! We arrived at NY at 6 a.m. and there was a secretary from the Embassy, the New York Consul, Bill Donovan, and Marshal Field;[1] the last two to meet me, very grand, and lots of reporters. Peter[2] was snug in bed but kindly sent a message asking me to telephone later. I went back to Marshal Field's apartment and he and Bill told me they had 'laid on' FDR[3] and as soon as he gets back from the fishing I'm to start in and do my stuff. Bill has been saying all sorts of nice things about me, and I can tell already how much difference it will make.

American power is most impressive. The number of cars, of factories, of dollars, of people, of noises, etc., all combine to say, 'We are the mandarins of the world.' They are guilty about the war. They'll come in soon. I shall certainly ask FDR when he will send marines to Casablanca. He is a sublime figure here, everyone, of all parties, feels that he represents the vastness of the USA. It is marvellous that in so selfish, jumbled, corrupt and undisciplined a menagerie the keeper should have such control over his animals.

Wednesday 2 April

I was summoned to the White House this morning by Harry Hopkins.[4] It's a thrill going in through the gate and up to that famous porch. When inside the most terrific negro waiters seize hold of you and whisk you upstairs. Hopkins was in his bedroom. He said that FDR wanted to know all about North Africa. The Secretary of the Navy was with him. I said my piece—three quarters of an hour—and they were most helpful and saw the real point at once. So I believe that we have a fair wind for the big plan. The President is to think it over and then I'm to go back again. In the meantime I had hours and hours with the State Department. They're a poorish lot, and woefully ignorant. However I shall work on them and with help from above they'll soon be where we want them. The Viscount [Halifax] is amused and sceptical, he lectures me in the typical Whig tradition that 'politics is the art of the possible' and that in this sinful world you can't get much done, and it doesn't matter much if you can't. He's a devitaliser but he won't devitalise me. He told Charles Peake[5] that it was odd how I kept my end up, and wouldn't give him any peace, but that he rather enjoyed it.

The Viscount and I had an hour and a half with Mr Hull today. Things are moving. We shall soon be in the thick of a negotiation that may lead anywhere.

All my love, darling dear Syb—David

1. Owner of retailing empire based on Chicago.
2. My brother.
3. Franklyn Delano Roosevelt, the President.
4. Hopkins said the President told him to see me before Halifax and I met Hull.
5. Halifax's devoted assistant, later Sir Charles Peake, HM Ambassador to Athens.

4 April 1941 — The Dorchester Hotel, London

My darling dear—I came up two days ago largely because Bin[1] had decided that I must meet the Doctor. (By the way 'the Doctor' is now dropped in favour of *Mr* Dalton—so read, mark and learn.) We dined at 20 Chester Square and oh! how spruce it has become with the descent of Bin.

We had a delicious dinner—Mr Dalton, Sam Courtauld,[2] B and G and self. Mr D was my neighbour and by the end of the evening I'd been conquered. He talked a great deal about you—always seductive as a topic—and was at great pains to allay any doubts I might have about your position *vis-à-vis* NH [Noel Hall] in Washington. With that superb ambiguity—of which the over-educated public servant is always a master—he managed to convey in a series of generalisations that it had been absolutely necessary to push NH sufficiently far up in the hierarchy to serve the purpose that he'd been sent there for: 'Butler[3] and the rest of them were inclined to think they could manage the economic side for themselves—but I know they can't and was determined upon my own representative and that representative had to go sufficiently armed for the purpose—but that isn't going to affect David who is only there for a specific purpose and will be allowed to play his hand freely—etc., etc.'

Then he told me he had been afraid that you were a trifle touché by the whole affair—and had therefore taken great trouble to talk the whole thing over with you and hoped thereby to have put things right and laid your doubts to rest. Then he turned suddenly to me and asked: 'Now tell me—did I succeed or not?'

At that I quizzed him ever so little, and answered that he had—which is indeed true, though it cost you an effort—but I hope I left him with a small question mark hovering somewhere.

He has, like Gladwyn, great hopes of your success and does not see in the least why with the proper American support North Africa should not be treated and maintained separately[4] from Vichy.

Neither of them believe that France will declare war—there will be repeated 'incidents' in order to placate the Germans—but no more. I can't tell you the nice things Mr D said about you—or the honours he means to win for you! 'David moves so quickly that sometimes I feel I'd better tie him down to the table leg or we shall both be flying out of the window.'

Keep safe and well, dear love—Sybil

1. Cynthia, wife of Gladwyn Jebb.
2. Industrialist and art collector.
3. Nevile Butler, second in command at the British Embassy in Washington.
4. This is the measure of the change in British policy brought about by my discussions with Murphy.

Begun 9 April 1941 Washington

My darling love—I can't describe the rush here. The US Government is in a fix. It is more than half committed to war and it isn't able to act as tho' it were at war. Foreign policy is neutral in its legal form; yet the Lend-Lease Bill is as unneutral as it can be. The bulk of the Americans don't want to fight anywhere but their Service departments are building up armies, navies, air forces, and they begin to want to use their toys. I think it will come this way—some incident between US marines and the enemy. Perhaps at Dakar. I am working on FDR to send a squadron to Dakar and/or Casablanca. It would have a huge effect on the French. The French must have been fired by the Yugoslavs. It's not possible that the decision of that small country to fight, when the crack German armoured divisions, which had smashed the great French Army, were ticking over on their border, it's not possible that such a decision did not move many Frenchmen to the depths of their emotions.

US opinion is in a queer nervous state. They are our *fiancé*, and 'in the frigidaire' as we used to say, nervous and irritable. We must get them to bed as soon as possible. They want to know what sort of world we are, and they will be, fighting for, passionately they do. At this distance from the fight they can indulge such fancies day and night. For us the noise of battle has drowned theoretical aims. It's a good thing to think ahead when they are still calm. I welcome it. So I think does the Viscount, but he doesn't quite know what line to take.

Darling Syb, you are having the worst of our war. I will make it up to you as soon as ever I can. I love you very much. Dorothy Halifax continually impresses on me how attractive you are and how fortunate I am. Quite true.

All my love—David

Begun 13 April 1941 Washington

My darling love—I've had a heavenly day. Easter Sunday, I had made no plans and at breakfast rang up Dean Acheson to ask where the Butterworths' country house was. 'Two miles from ours and we're starting in an hour.' What incredible luck! The roads and gardens are splashed with blossom of astonishing brilliance, forsythia, magnolias, cherries and daffodils out underneath, all together in a rush. And such cherries as you've never seen before. Washington cherries are mostly pink, every shade from a faint blush to a crushed strawberry, and such beautiful willowy shapes. Near to I prefer apple blossom.

Driving back to Washington in the evening I was stupefied by the number and size of the cars, four lanes on each road bowling along head to tail at 40 mph. For the first time I realised we were not the richest people. This revelation gives a new edge to patriotism, it is better and purer to love the second-rate, and I understand now how little nations can be so touchy and tender about their position and independence. Spain and Portugal and the Arabs are so old and so tired beside these people. Here they are so frisky and foolish and powerful. For they are very foolish very often. They never wait to hear the answers to their own questions, so they learn little of wisdom. They love themselves ecstatically and gape at the world in a trance of self-satisfaction in the spring, under the cherries, with a million Buicks on the road and the President going to church, and Eleanor[1] making tea for ambassadors' wives . . . You must be gentle with these young creatures, you couldn't hate anything so easily pleased and so easily depressed. They take all our setbacks so tragically. Washington is full of little Chelsea-like houses, old and rambling, two servants, damned bad ones who won't clean your shoes, eight to dinner once a week on cold soup, meat salad, cheese and fruit, cocktails and whisky. Lots of talk, very little sex, few jokes and no great wealth in evidence. Solid middle class. I could stay here two months always learning and always educating. They don't know how to look at the war as a whole and I try out all sorts of wiles to catch their imagination and unleash that will to direct action, to fight, because if they don't we can't win outright. The news from Libya and the Balkans has depressed them very much. They want to feel we shall win but not easily and then they'll help us to the full. If they think we can't win they lose heart and this could easily happen. So I want to direct their attention from the fighting to thinking about our common war aims, to the marriage contract without which I don't think we will get them to bed. I use all the arts I know of and often catch myself saying, 'If Syb were here I wouldn't dare to talk in this way, she'd think it bogus,' but perhaps it isn't entirely bogus. I've a new way of talking about England and our future which grows quickly in the hotbed of war and foreign capitals. No doubt it needs pruning and I should love you to be here to do it.

North Africa gives me uneasy moments. You know how I tried to impress the people at home with the dangers of German penetration in Morocco and of German propaganda among the Arabs. Well, the German success in Libya has put the searchlight on these warnings, but it's too late to do anything concrete except fight in North Africa. Always, always we're too late. Isn't it maddening?

I am leaving John Foster's[2] and going to Bill Donovan's. There will be much chit-chat in Washington but I shall have a daily line to FDR and probably see Harry Hopkins continually.

Kiss Polly and Simo'. Love to you, sweet.

—David

1. Wife of President Roosevelt.
2. Sir John Foster, QC, legal adviser to the British Embassy in Washington.

21 April 1941 Washington

My darling love—I send you the draft of my response to FDR's invitation to state in two pages the present position of Anglo-American relations with France. I will improve it. You can see that the situation is as bad as it could be. Unless the US come in quickly we can't hold the Western Mediterranean. I have persuaded the Viscount to put this on his personal authority to the US Government. No one but I had dared use such language to them before. Now his lordship has done so with surprising success. We wait to see Winston's reaction. I didn't want the PM to put the case to FDR either in a personal message or thro' Halifax acting on his instructions. It is much better that we here should do it out of our own guts. When the Viscount came back from seeing Hull this morning we lunched together—he was like a man transformed, radiant with hope. Hull, instead of biting his head off, said that this was obviously the only thing to do to save the situation, but would the American public stomach it? It's queer that this should be the vital moment in Anglo-American relations and that the initiative should come from the Western Mediterranean. Truly I have all the luck.

The war has come to the point of absolute crisis. We can't win if the US doesn't come in. They won't come in if we suffer more reverses. They are essentially commercial, their money must go on a horse that has a reasonable chance. The total collapse of France and the French Empire might easily cause all America to despair of us, and then the worst would happen. God! It's a struggle. Nothing in Spain or Portugal ever came near it.

Later
My draft paper on France is likely to be a political sensation. The State Department are in a twit. The question is now posed in the strongest light and we must see what happens. Wouldn't it be heaven to know the President's first reaction? Perhaps I can find out thro' Harry Hopkins.

Every night a dinner party. Congressmen, Senators, old trouts and some pretty women. Too much food and gin, lovely jewels and an ocean of silly chatter, but some good moments. If only the news from the Peninsula wasn't so bad I'd feel better.

All my love, Syb—David

Draft by DE on
Relations between the United States of America, France and the United Kingdom

Written on 21 April 1941 for Lord Halifax to see before submission to President Roosevelt

1. Anglo-American policy towards France has been vitiated by an over-estimation of the French Government's liberty of action. It was useless to beg, bribe or bully a government to exercise an authority they did not possess. It was equally useless to starve a sick people in the hope that they would crawl back in a still more miserable condition.

2. The Germans wrote the Armistice, as a temporary document, in the belief that the bases they were securing would be adequate swiftly to defeat England. This calculation proved wrong. So they are now forced to demand the French Navy and bases in French North Africa. If Pétain refuses these demands, Hitler will use force. He is preparing to do so.

3. The Vichy Government does not represent the French people. The government feels the full force of German pressure which is concealed from the public. Pétain's bargaining power, always doubtful, is fast disappearing. The overwhelming presence of German troops, the need for food, and the critical position of the French prisoners of war made it impossible for him to resist the demands for economic collaboration. The French fleet and the French Empire were the only weapons at his disposal.

4. The fleet has lost its value as a bargaining counter. It is dependent on the will and ambition of a man who believes Germany must win the war.

5. The African empire, less dependent on personal whim, was Pétain's only card; but the arrival of German troops in Tripoli and German experts in Morocco have destroyed its importance. Weygand is no longer capable of carrying out his instructions to defend North Africa against all comers.

6. This is the present position. Nothing can save metropolitan France. The Germans are masters there. The fleet is doubtful. The French African empire—at least the vital ports of Casablanca and Dakar—can still be saved. All the rest is as good as lost.

7. The degree of collaboration which France will concede to Germany is governed by one permanent and one fluctuating factor. First, the Germans could occupy the whole of France at any time they wish. Second, the belief among the French people that Germany or England will win the war varies with the military situation. Public opinion in France is the only restraint upon the pro-German inclinations of a government—Pétain and Weygand excepted—which is convinced Germany will win.

8. Anglo-American initiative must concentrate its entire effort on North Africa. The French Empire is so tightly controlled by the Vichy Government that independent action by Weygand is not to be expected. The Vichy Government will only, at this eleventh hour, be moved to accept the consequences of military intervention by England or the United States in North Africa if French public opinion is electrified by the hope that Germany can be defeated. Only direct action by the United States will provide this shock.

9. Economic assistance to metropolitan France or to French North Africa is no longer adequate inducement to Weygand to resist the German demands. He must invite, or be forced to accept, British or American troops.

10. If the appraisement of the situation given above is accepted the choice lies between asking Pétain to receive British or American troops and sending an unheralded expedition to seize Casablanca and Dakar. If it is thought that Pétain or Weygand would communicate to Darlan[1] our request to be invited into North Africa,

then action must be taken without warning. It is possible that Pétain, knowing that his end is near, would have the courage to open the door to our troops before the curtain falls.

1. Admiral Darlan was Pétain's Prime Minister.

22 April 1941 Chute

My darling love—Here during the last week or two it has been hard to keep up one's spirits. Though we all knew the dangers of that gesture to Greece and the impossibility of making any other decision it has been horrid to watch the double retreat in Libya and the Plains of Thessaly.[1]

It was an honourable choice, however, and everyone feels that our name would have been mud if we hadn't taken it.

I dissect every morsel of American news that appears in *The Times* and read behind the utterances of FDR the reflections of my husband's influence! Once I've had a letter from you this is even easier to do and I'm simply thrilled to think you've been to the White House—talked with Harry Hopkins and Cordell Hull—and harbour great hopes that by now you've seen the President in person. I'm glad you're to stay with the Halifaxes; they're so kind and you will do him good—he absorbs a little of your energy and this amuses and invigorates him. I've watched it happen. And since your minds are beautifully in sympathy it doesn't irritate him to be bullied by you—it's just an entertaining exercise in dialectic. He's a bit of a devitaliser—that's the only trouble—but one doesn't have to worry about that with DE. I'm glad to report that he's a success—when I tried to pump Walt he pulled in his horns and wasn't having any—which left me wondering. How lovely that some parcels are coming. We've been entertaining these holidays and my! how the stores dwindle.

Oh—my darling, I do miss you very much—come home to England on your way if you can.

With all my love—Sybil

1. The British sent troops to Greece at the end of March. The Germans attacked on 6 April and broke the resistance of the Greeks and the British.

24 April 1941 Washington

My dearest sweet—I was awfully interested to feel the effect of Mr (thanks for the tip) Dalton on you. Look out. I went through that stage. He has great qualities well produced and easily recognisable. The war teaches one what are the fundamental requisites for the management of human affairs. First, that it is 'human' affairs we have to deal with; not only statistics and money and material wealth. How much does HD realise that? The Blockade is the finest experiment in human-cum-material acrobatics that this man ever had to handle. Second, that human affairs are sometimes predictable but not with a rational technique; you can't tell who is going to fall in love with whom, but if you've a good nose you can smell it out almost before the parties concerned have realised it themselves. There is a swing, a rhythm, a pattern in history that those who stand away from the newspapers and the day-to-day buzzing of the machine of government can comprehend. Nothing can happen that will destroy that pattern, that is a limiting factor. Hitler, for example, could not absorb the national characteristics of Poland, Belgium, Yugoslavia, etc., try as he might. Those things endure. The pattern is, however, pretty large and the colours and fiddly bits can be chosen and varied by the clash of human wills and human events. The problem is to judge how far you can go without offending the major pattern and yet mould the details to your own liking. Whitehall is so incredibly ignorant of the human limitations and human possibilities of the world they try to govern. I think men are much worse and much better than the nineteenth- to twentieth-century politician has given them credit for, and if I ran the foreign policy of HMG I should ask foreign nations to do things that fitted with the heights to which I knew they could climb and I should avoid asking them to do things which the baseness of their natures *always* made it impossible for them to contemplate.

25 April

Yesterday I had a tremendous interview with Sumner Welles, he had with him two heads of Departments and Murphy, and I faced a barrage of questions on Spain, France and North Africa. The Viscount had agreed that I could talk quite straight on the understanding that neither the FO nor himself were committed in any way. I led to the conclusion that unless the USA takes military action in the Western Mediterranean before many days are over the Germans will be in Casablanca and Dakar. Welles is pretty nasty on the surface but efficient and I should think much more agreeable on further acquaintance. The substance of his unwillingness to see the situation as it is is an age-old dislike of pulling British chestnuts out of the fire. I did not attempt to dodge this issue, insisting plainly that we had no troops to spare for North-West Africa, but the chestnut was as much theirs as ours. They could not afford to have the Germans less than half the distance from Brazil than the US is from Brazil. We rocked in argument, if you know what I mean, trying not to fall and not to give way. In the end he gave in, admitting the case was fairly put, but saying that the question of military intervention must be discussed in another place and at another time, i.e. with FDR. I do not think I could have got more at this interview, the issue was forced right up to the point of decision, everyone knew where we stood and the responsibility for the answer was squarely placed on the US Government and accepted by Welles.

When I came back and was having a cup of tea with the Viscount he said, 'It sounds pretty encouraging, I hope you didn't compromise me in any way.' 'Oh! Edward,' said Dorothy, and we talked of something else.

Dearest Syb—there's no time to write to you any more. So here's my love. The war is something of a mistress but I shall chuck her the minute I can.

—David

27 April 1941 Chute

My darling love—Yesterday we were all asked over to the Gwynnes at Perham for a picnic lunch—the children, six altogether between ten and fourteen, went to the miniature rifle range where a kind 2nd lieutenant gave our two their first lesson in rifle shooting. The other four were extraordinarily good shots and June Gwynne quite exceptional. She can pick off a cardboard man on a cardboard horse two inches high without a second's hesitation! John took to it like a duck and his last rounds found the bull again and again. The coach was delighted with his pupils—

pronounced them promising and we're all to go again tomorrow and Tuesday. Huge excitement as you can imagine.

I wonder all the time how they are taking our reverses in America and pine for your letters and opinions. Some people mutter that we have made a mess of Greece—that we should have concentrated on the defence of Egypt—that now we have undergone a double failure and face a double danger.

But it can't be so. If we'd deserted the only small champion of liberty in her hour of need our name would have stunk in the history books. This is what comes of backing England and defying Juggernaut they would have said. No, no, we just had to do something about it—like sharing your lifebelt in a rough sea even though you know it won't keep both of you up. We shall all feel better when it's over and the men are out. At the moment it's just like sitting in the dentist's waiting-room.

All my love—Sybil

2 May 1941 Washington

My darling love—Americans don't like putting anything on paper. They use the telephone or telegraph; and most of their written contracts are so badly drafted that half the intelligent young men here become lawyers and have the fun of untying the knots.

I have tried to direct all I am doing to one end: to get the USA somewhere and as soon as possible into the war. At home MEW still bother about Blockade niceties, tons of this and bales of that, pinpricks and sand-in-the-works, apparently oblivious that the great tragedy of the civilised world is mounting to its climax. Tonight I have sent Dalton a long personal telegram, telling him that little things must be sacrificed to big things, and that we cannot expect an administration and a general outlook, which has been conditioned by years of deliberate non-intervention in Europe, suddenly and easily to proceed in the opposite direction. We have to make them our partners in small things and work as quietly as we can without tripping up on the way to the big plunge. They won't work for theoretical reasons. They must actively join with us in doing certain things, feeding Spain, holding out a hand to Weygand. If only MEW had realised long ago that food is a weapon, and not something to be locked in a cupboard so that no one, whether *friend* or *foe*, can get a sight or a smell of it. The errors of our past hang like night between us and the dawn of tomorrow. I do not doubt that the darkness will lift, and lift in time, but it's a cold and dangerous business in the interval of waiting. The very luxury and peacefulness of the Maryland and Virginian scene are irritants to the state of stern resolution and drive that is required by all engaged on this enterprise. I don't know what to make of the changes in our Cabinet. Leathers[1] is a good man, another Lyttelton, and should be a huge improvement at the Ministry of Shipping. Dalton must be rocking, no man can defend a bad policy in times like these. The pity is he would push a good policy with equal success. Why he never saw how useless the old-fashioned blockade is we shall never know. God blinds all sorts of men. I want very much to come home. At present it is out of the question because I am the midwife of the new policy of the US Government in the Western Mediterranean and I must stay with my child for the month. Beyond that I am carrying the main attack on the State Department on the general issue of fight or not fight. Everyone, Bill Donovan, Welles, Frankfurter,[2] Lippmann[3] —all say I must stay till the US has fired the first shot. Ray Atherton[4] told someone in my hearing that I was the only Englishman who could dictate the foreign policy of the USA and remain as much liked afterwards as before. There comes over me an agitated sense of power which I like and dislike at the same time. It must be so, because they behave to me in a way that shows they recognise this *at first sight*. That is so odd.

America is about two generations behind the stage where its people could assume their responsibilities. They exercise less power in the world than their resources entitle them to do. France after 1918 exercised more power than her resources entitled her to do. Perhaps one fundamental requisite in international relations is that such a disequilibrium in power and resources should be recognised and corrected. Here it is a matter of education. Isolationism is really a sign of immaturity. Nothing worse, and nothing easier to cure as the sense of adult power grows, and it is growing fast. I love them very much, and enjoy enormously their puppy-like shoves and bites and rough and tumbles. The Viscount doesn't feel that way. He has so much to lose, such a burdened tradition and habit. Remorse, sorrow for the past, passionate attachment to this or that possession (Chute excepted) mean nothing to me. I want the future. America is the future to a great extent, and I can easily love anything that promises to bulk so big in my own ideas and action. A year or two ago I should have been bored with a bunch of Congressmen talking the wildest nonsense and drinking like fishes, now I embrace them all with the most genuine enthusiasm. There are many moments in this place when I ask myself if you would recognise the hearty and gay playboy that was once your studious and sulky husband.

Now I want you to understand this important fact. *We* might be unable to win a convincing victory in this war. *America* cannot be beaten. She is on the road to power politics and imperialism such as the world has never seen. And if, by a series of mistakes and muddles, her help did not arrive in time to save us from a bad peace, then in a few years, and not very many, America will go to war with Germany and smash her to bits. That is a solemn prophecy which you can record and repeat as much as you like.

I have a huge fear. The peace of the world can only be secured if we and the USA pool our arms and make the rest of the world obey the international law we propound. To do this successfully we must have a common morality between the USA and the UK, and if we alone go through the experience of war and blood and tears our people will emerge with a character and a soul so different from the American soul, which would not have passed through fire, that I doubt the chances of getting on together well enough to rule jointly the wide world. I want these people to suffer now, and to suffer in a way as nearly like the way our people are suffering as possible. I want them to be bombed and killed and starved, for the peace of the world it is necessary.

My sweet, goodbye—David

1. Lord Leathers became a friend after I returned to London.
2. Felix Frankfurter, Associate Justice of the Supreme Court.
3. Walter Lippmann, distinguished American writer on international affairs.
4. Ray Atherton, head of the European section of the State Department, had been a friend of mine before the war.

4 May 1941 Juniper Hill, Burnham, Buckinghamshire

My darling love—These are touchy times and one giggles whenever there is a chance. But it's a funny thing, you can get used to misfortune just as you can to bombs.

Greece and Libya made us all very short tempered a fortnight ago, now you can almost hear the deep breaths being drawn all around that the Greek thing is over and so many men safe. It's as though a nursery whisper were in the air—if at first you don't succeed try, try, try again. Everyone seems ready to jump up to the third try—Dunkirk—the Peloponnesus—surely we shan't have to swim for it the third time!

How enchanting of Dorothy Halifax to remind you of me! I bless her for it—though I'm sure it isn't necessary, for I do believe you love me and miss me often. My dearest love, you are always in my heart and that helps a lot in this long separation.

With all my love—Sybil

On the train The Old Farm, Great Horwood,
8 May 1941 Bletchley

My darling love—Your remark upon the decreasing bargaining power of Vichy seems sadly well timed—the news was out last night that an agreement had been reached between Darlan and the Germans—certain concessions to the French but no mention of the other side to the bargain. So I suppose it's bound to be bad. It can't be otherwise—can it, with such a combination of weakness and scurrility?

Winston made another splendid speech yesterday. His robust courage and sober confidence must impress the New World and urge them on.

It's rather a sad reflection that democracy, which is undoubtedly a generous, noble conception of government, seems at the same time to make man lazy and self-satisfied—it doesn't easily inspire faith and fervour—or the will to defend and if need be die for the institutions and the way of life in which he puts his trust. Democracy is a stodgy dish, it needs a lot of stirring. I'm getting near to Oxford in the train. It's a bright cold morning and one pinches onself to remember that it is still only seven o'clock. Two youths in bright blue suits have come to share my third-class carriage. They are very talkative and cocksure and are on their way to buy clothes for themselves in Oxford and there is a lively discussion as to which movie they should patronise. The spires are in sight and the spirits of my two friends are rollicking high, they may burst out of the carriage at any moment.

My darling dear—I don't really want you to be homesick—yet in my heart I hope you are a very little bit—I love you so much.

—Sybil

8 May 1941 Washington

My darling love—You know my habit of falling in love with each new experience as it comes along, poor David's enthusiasms, so temporary and so exhausting while they reach their short-lived climax—well, America is the last and biggest of these pashes. I like the way they take life so seriously, nothing is make-believe, the two chairs and the hearth rug in between really are a boat, and we are sailing for Australia, and don't you dare say it's only a game in the nursery after a tea of corn bread and maple syrup. I like the way they talk: 'Why David, that's a dreamy idea,' 'Does Colonel Lindbergh[1] say he stands for America first? I tell you, sir, he stands for America next.' And then Bill Donovan's speeches: isn't there something alive and throbbing that catches you by the heart strings and makes you feel good, a bathe in cold water and a furry towel to rub with? From whatever cause, good or bad, such enthusiasms come, come they must if one is to get the best out of people with whom one deals. To understand equals to love. A very old rule and not to be broken even in these disastrous days. Why was Peterson doomed to be a failure in Madrid? He couldn't like the Spaniards, not one of them. That was an obstacle no brains, no subtlety could overcome.

I came up on Friday to stay two nights to meet Bill Donovan's big business friends for a 'tonic talk'—Bill and I giving alternate doses.

I could never describe the hospitality and real love that is given to me here. Perhaps anyone like me is symbolic of the things they want to do for all England. To give me a meal is to vote for convoys. To put me up is to send an expedition to Dakar. I float through American life, a bubble, reflecting the lights of England, nothing substantial but something effective. Here in New York the big men are isolationist, most of them, as Bill says, 'There's nothing more scared than a million dollars but two million.' Money. It gives you chances to do lovely things. To take a £22 return air ticket Washington to New York, to spend £20 on a dinner for two in a fairy's room in the Milky Way, to have bright jewels and soft furs. Oh! I don't know sometimes what I care about most, or how I can put aside the less important to stick tight to the work that is coming. To look over one's shoulder, just occasionally, to that distant and dazzling life is not a crime but it's nearly a mistake.

Ah! well, all my love is yours, now and ever—David

1. The trans-Atlantic flyer believed Britain would lose the war.

18 May 1941 Chute

My darling love—Your wife is very gay. Two dances this week! One at Barton Stacey Camp among the military men. Very tough and very gay. Wooden huts hung with Chinese lanterns, a pine wood floor and rickety arm chairs in down-at-heel chintzes—the other at Bill's[1] aerodrome. Very exquisite streamlined building—smelling like a ship (the most luxurious sort of ship) green leather armchairs of immense depth and size—lovely food—long rooms, floodlit from the ceiling with tall graceful Georgian windows, oak fireplaces and satiny floor to dance on.

Beautiful creatures in blue to dance with. The most fantastic scraps of conversation:

'May I dance with you now, please, you see, I take to the air at ten o'clock.'

'It's very lowering doing this on lemonade.'

'Goodnight, Mollie—see you soon. I wish I hadn't got to go but I've an appointment with the enemy.'

Then beyond the windows, shrouded now with long, soft green curtains, rise the strong voices of aeroplanes on the move—hum, hum—they circle the aerodrome and are off into the twilight. The band strikes up and those who have no rendezvous with the foe take to the floor again—there is a great deal of laughter and popping corks and those who have departed are forgotten.

It was such fun. Bill sat in a corner with me and pointed out the celebrities. 'Do you see that long, loose, filleted, pallid long-haired creature over there?' 'I do—before the war one would have said interior decorating by day—the ballet with Cecil Beaton by night—oh! my dear, too divine.' 'Exactly,' agrees Bill. 'Well, he's our best pilot, brave as a lion, absolutely tireless, volunteer for anything and an excellent officer.' Gosh—I'll never criticise anyone again. It isn't safe. 'Do you see that one? Oxford don, aged thirty-six, crawled into the service by the back door on all fours. Couldn't keep him out. Now he's a rear gunner and *my*, what an eye!'

A round, pink, plump, fair person goes past—one can see him in a white starched overall behind Sainsbury's counter in the High Street. 'Look at him,' urges Bill. 'Made an officer the other day, twenty-two, comes from Camberwell and as tough as you make 'em.' There he was in his beautiful new uniform and as happy and at ease as anyone could be. At 2 a.m. I took the road for home—past the winking lights and the aerodrome—under a black sky, criss-crossed with searchlights nosing after a particularly active Luftwaffe. The night before we only got home at 3 and I crawled into my lovely chilly bed at 4 a.m. So today your wife wears a dissipated air.

Later

Two Free French men came to tea. In the British Army and stationed at Tidworth. Bill and Ro[2] came over too which was angelic of them and brought Pamela Jackson.[3] I was grateful for their presence—for with Syria and all, the poor creatures must be feeling more than usually uneasy and miserable. One of them is obviously of a sensitive nature and, in the midst of lively conversation, will suddenly fall silent and one catches in his eyes a desperate look. More than once he wandered off by himself and we watched him stand alone at the edge of the garden staring out over the fields.

I feel frantically sorry for them with their khaki—their rusty borrowed bicycles and their borrowed names—it must be a nightmare of anonymity—bewilderment and distress, only it doesn't end with morning. Poor old Pétain—he's done for, isn't he?

Air-Marshal Joubert said last night, 'They'll be the only recorded case in history—a people who get their country given back to them after being beaten by both sides!' *L'affaire* Hess[4] was a lark, wasn't it?

Goodnight, my dearest love, and many blessings—I love you very much.

—Sybil

1. Air-Marshal Sir William Elliot.
2. Sir William and Lady Elliot.
3. Daughter of Lord Redesdale, Pamela *née* Mitford, married Derek Jackson.
4. Rudolf Hess, Hitler's Deputy Führer, flew into Scotland alone, on an unauthorised mission, to persuade Britain that Germany would win but that Britain could have peace with Hitler in return for the previous German colonies.

18 May 1941 — Washington

My darling love—I hear that in ten minutes a 'man' is off to UK in a bomber and he will carry this to you. I wish I were coming with the letter. Yesterday—Saturday—I spent all day with the Under-Secretary for War, and I do believe there are some here who would fight at once. Only we must keep at them, and never think that *our* difficulties will be enough to make them take the plunge. Rather the reverse: they won't back a horse that's sick and going worse every mile. So it's a problem to tell the truth, to keep up their spirits and to get them in. Their Civil Service hasn't the slightest idea what energy and drive is wanted. They might *administer* war in some fashion; but never *make* war. Luckily they have got into the Civil Service some good chaps from outside who are rapidly taking charge of the outlying departments, but it will need war itself, and a big shake-up, to extract from this country a quarter of the energy and output of which it is capable.

I must stop as the bag is closing and I have to lunch with Norman Davis, a clever, vain old man, who was a roving ambassador and now plays foreign politics with the Red Cross; a gargly hoarse voice and a twinkle in his eye. I like him and he has helped me a lot. His heart is in the right place and he can be counted on to push 'help for Spain' which has few friends here.

Sweet Syb, all my love—David

Letter to Norman Davis,
Chairman of the American Red Cross

19 May 1941 Washington

Dear Mr Chairman—The good news you gave me about relief for Spain means that many of the Spanish people are going to learn in time who are their friends.

2. Such action is of the essence of the struggle we are now engaged in. For we begin to see the true character of the war. It is a civil war, fought to decide between two ways of life. Inside every nation opinions are divided on the great issue. We must strengthen our friends, put heart into the waverers and defeat our enemies.

3. The Spanish people suffer and are hungry. Yet the pro-Axis element in the Franco régime, aided by numerous and well-placed German agents, have never ceased to obstruct the help which our governments have been anxious to give. So it is clear that the Spanish Quislings, like all Quislings, care more for their foreign tutors than for their own people. The Spanish Civil War goes on, and will go on without end until the Nazi poison has been stamped out. For such reasons I want to stop thinking of the war in terms of homogeneous nations, lined up on one side or the other, labelled 'belligerent' or 'non-belligerent'. It is not as simple as that. All the world is our battlefield. The Germans are in action every day and in all lands. We must go after them, overtake them, and throw them down. Just because there is this civil struggle going on inside all countries the fortunes of the war may change very quickly.

4. If the Germans occupy the Iberian Peninsula the last door on the western shore of Europe will be closed but, even if this did happen, we should still have friends inside in the dark, whose number and energy would greatly depend on how we are going to treat them now.

5. Germany would derive such great advantage if she controlled the harbours of the Peninsula and the Straits of Gibraltar that the fact she has not done so already is significant. Hitler plainly does not relish the idea of an opposed occupation of Spain. He hesitates to attack Spain because:

(a) He would have to admit that the Axis had lost a so-called partner.
(b) The effect on Italy and France would be serious. They would see a Latin and Catholic state in conflict with the New Order in Europe.
(c) South America would be touched through racial and cultural ties.
(d) Hitler reads history and knows where Napoleon's power was first sapped.
(e) The lack of supplies in Spain, especially oil, the dependence of the Peninsula on seaborne imports, the shocking state of the railways, etc., would make a campaign costly and difficult.

6. These considerations which have kept the Germans out of Spain are our opportunity. Can we plan a counter-infiltration by trade, by relief and by propaganda? Keeping the door into Europe open till we are ready to use military means? For this would be needed a project engineer, ample resources, and a central authority to execute the plan.

7. Trade is the simplest form of counter-infiltration. Buy as much as we can from Spain. To spend one dollar is better than to lend five. The producer talks about the customer, but the debtor keeps quiet about the creditor.

8. Credit to Spain is scarcely a commercial proposition, but nor is any money spent on the prosecution of war. The working capital of Spain was destroyed in the Civil War, and without credit the country's production cannot recover. They need cotton, agricultural machinery, fertiliser, etc. The rate at which such supplies reached Spain could be controlled so that stocks could not accumulate as a temptation to an invader.

9. Buying and selling have a high publicity value, and a vital part of the plan would be to tell our friends in Spain what help was coming and from where. It will be many months before any large quantity of goods could reach Spain from the United States of

America; but a statement of our objectives is needed right away, carefully put about among Spaniards who would spread the news, rather than forced into the limelight. Where the press has been so long muzzled whispers travel fast. It would be a mistake to insist on a major change in the enemy-controlled press, which is an exhaust pipe that allows Spain to blow off the pressure of German steam, and to appear pro-Axis, a necessary disguise until we can promise our friends adequate military assistance to oppose the German Army.

10. Relief, which your great organisation is sending to Spain, may be resented by a few quixotic persons, whose Castilian honour is stronger than their common sense; but the poor, the hungry and the sick will be grateful. Your friends may be dumb, but they will fight savagely anyone who takes away the precious help they were receiving.

11. Spain and Portugal stand or fall together. Portugal is an Atlantic state with colonies she can only keep if the British and American navies control the ocean. Today these colonies badly need a market for modest surpluses of peanut oil, copra, sisal, corn and coffee—perhaps to the tune of $10,000,000 per annum c.i.f. Lisbon. This problem haunts the Portuguese Government. All these commodities Spain wants but cannot pay for. The British Government have already lent Spain money to purchase a part of these surpluses. Would it be possible for the United States Government to take up this triangular salvage operation and to finance the import into Spain of these goods which can easily be carried in Portuguese ships? I earnestly commend this plan of aid to you. I believe the Portuguese would supply the shipping to Spain on credit and that Dr Salazar would welcome a growing American interest in his colonies and islands.

My thoughts having carried me much further than I intended, I am sending a copy of this letter to the State Department.

Yours very sincerely—David Eccles

20 May 1941 Washington

My darling love—I feel like a gossip with you. Let's start on the Donovans and see where it leads to. Bill loves Ruth Donovan but she's a sad woman (white-grey hair, good figure, blue eyes: fifty-five). His brilliance and agility leave her too far behind to be happy. They had a daughter of twenty-two who was killed last year in a motor accident while Ruth was away on a cruise. I think that when she returned she felt that her one real tie to Bill had gone. Perhaps he made allowances for Patricia that he had grown accustomed not to make for Ruth. Patricia must have had plenty to say for herself. The house is full of her photographs, she looks honest, obstinate and warm hearted, as though she had played Rosie's part in Wimpole Street. I wander into her bedroom, which is just as she left it, to borrow her books. She read much modern poetry. Some of it is good. I like this description of Long Island luxury 'in the empty heaven of our times', and I found a poem beginning

> Ask not for freedom if you fear to weep
> Or dream of peace if terror makes you start

It's always easy to hit upon scraps that suit one's mood. I should invent them if I didn't find them.

What a big part preoccupation with some catch in a song must play in shaping actions and works of art. We are penetrated by a tune like sugar by a drop of water. I think Shakespeare was, more than you might suspect. For instance, I've only just noticed how seriously, skilfully and repeatedly Hamlet uses the word 'heart'. Perhaps it is one of the secrets of the play. Surely that is ample evidence that 'heart' meant something tremendous to Hamlet. Somewhere else Shakespeare asks

> Tell me where is fancy bred
> Or in the heart or in the head?

Hamlet answers the question once for all. It suits my philosophy —if it's worth so grand a name—that Shakespeare should come down heavily in favour of the heart, and against the head.

Sometimes I wish we had never met, never kissed, never spoken to each other. Then how much more I should have to say, how much more to offer you now than at our first encounter! Imagine it. What would happen if we still had to have 'our first and fatal interview'? Would the world stop for me? Have we changed so much, relatively to each other, that we should be more distant now than we were? I don't think so. What is here now in flower was there in seed. I should look more closely and listen more intently and be rewarded more generously for my pains. Do you think I could make you fall in love with me? Quickly and fiercely? I would try hard enough. Whenever any woman—English, Spanish, Brazilian or American—makes love to me I always—yes, always—ask myself if you would fall again, if I could have some effect like this on you. I know we love each other very much. NO doubt about that. But the rush of desire, the inescapable need to find out what someone is like, how should we deal with that if we had still to have our 'first and fatal interview'? Does such speculation please you or do you find it silly? I think it pleases you. And I base my hopes on the idea that if someone is attractive to two or three people, he is in bloom, and would be attractive to all if he chose to try. And how I would try if I met you for the first time!

26 May

The reaction of the US to our naval losses round Crete, and of the *Hood*,[1] has been very bad. Why do they fear death more than the consequences of defeat? That question—you remember Gordon put it to himself at Khartoum—is the simplest form in which patriotism can be expressed. I spent Saturday night on Frank Knox's yacht in the Potomac. Knox is Secretary for the Navy. He pretends to be very bellicose, 'coats off, punch 'em on the nose' stuff, but he isn't really, he's a politician trying to give a show of war when in fact he desires to keep out. Knox *et praeterea nihil.* Here's an anecdote that struck me. A coloured doctor of eminence came to Knox to ask him to let the negroes play some part in the US Navy. Knox, who found the doctor a highly educated and interesting man, had to explain to him why it was impossible to admit coloured men in the Services. 'If I posted you, a first-rate doc, to the US ship *California* you'd have a hell of a life.' 'I have already,' replied the negro.

I was so pleased to get your telegram. Sometimes I want to communicate with you instantly, and I have a wish to break the telephone on my desk because the wretched thing won't call you.

I must stop. The US must come into the war. We must live together again. There you are, in order of importance.

All my love—David

1. HMS *Hood* was sunk on 24 May 1941.

29 May 1941 Chute

My darling love—I remember old Norman Davis well. He's a bit of a humbug and as you say very vain. I've had him on Louvain and Brussels in the last war. But he's an interesting old boy—though rather a back number who is thrown a bone here and there to keep him happy. I once heard a fairly straight and frank 'American Commentary' on him! Hence my impertinent remarks.

We have been and *are* plunged in the midst of a ferocious war weapons week. So far we've taken £1,500 from the three villages (Chutes), isn't it good?

Last night we took a tank (with soldiers) and a band round Upper and Lower Chute and Cadley and collected in stamps and certificates more than £500 and only crept exhausted home to dinner at ten o'clock. Mrs Collins and Co. were so elated at the success that I couldn't resist sending you a cable for a contribution. I put in £35 for myself and the two children. And mean to do some more for John. We keep as busy as we can.

The Americans are very disappointing to us over here, quivering with eagerness to see them take a plunge or two, they seem incredibly cagey. Stir them up, my darling—you can do it if anyone can. To me they seem a queer gang (and gang they truly are) ready to shoot each other up for love or drink or dollars—prepared to commit any of the nastier crimes to which their newspapers give the grossest publicity. But fight in the cause of freedom and democracy? No, sir. Why, they might lose tuppence halfpenny. Oh! It's hard to keep patience with them—more especially when one remembers the hard things they said about us in '38. Why, they're as soft as a feather pillow themselves—in spite of all their saucy, brittle, bright, bold chatter.

I pin my hopes to you, dearest David—while I wonder, and how I wonder, when I shall see your very dear face again.

I love you—Sybil

1 June 1941 Chute

My darling love—Thank you so much, my sweet, for sending £100 to Chute. Mrs Collins was so excited that she told the world—and when I went down to discuss with her whether 3 per cent Defence Bonds were the thing to buy with this princely sum, she had your cable snug in her capacious bosom and declared she was keeping it for ever—as a memento! The old lady has had a huge kick out of this week and the work and excitement it has brought her have helped a lot to ease the blow of old Collins's death. He departed in April—practically without warning—and horror of horrors—*not* in his own home but in Winchester hospital where, as his daughter says with gloomy relish, 'The specialist said he could do nothing for him.'

Crete is apparently nearly over and we have run through the entire emotional gamut during the course of the operations. The pattern is always the same—hope, doubt, hope again, then a horrible period of anxiety and increasing gloom, then a really bad attack of depression as failure has to be admitted. This is bedrock. Once everyone has bitten on to the fact that we've been defeated again, spirits begin to rise!! It's really very extraordinary—but there it is.

I miss you so much and am terrified that you're going to come home just as I'm elbow deep in raspberry jam at the Preservation Centre. Darling—sweet David, you have all my love.

—Sybil

4 June 1941 Washington

Darling sweet—The war looks bad from here. Sly whispers, thoughts of defeat, idle or unprofitable hours, distract and corrupt Americans from the great trumpet of our cause, which they would hear so much plainer above the din of battle once battle were joined. We should fuss no more about American opinion. It is as united behind the President as it ever will be. If he gives them a lead the people will follow him; if he doesn't do so soon the people will cease to respect him and America will back out of the war. Why does he hesitate? Because he is not sure of public opinion? Certainly not, he knows it well. Because he has not made up his own obstinate mind on what is right to do? Nonsense, he made it up two years ago. He's sick at heart and sick in body, and, listening to the true stories of how unprepared the USA is for war, he shrinks, in his invalid state, from exposing Americans to fire and death until they have more weapons. That is the analysis. *We* may be old enough to retreat again and again and still to keep up our courage and fight on. I suspect that FDR feels the USA is not, *as a nation*, sufficiently tough to stand reverses; or rather that his political prestige and the Democratic Party could not stand reverses. So he wants more weapons before he begins. I don't see any other explanation.

I think he's wrong. Wrong technically, because if the USA came in and merely used their fleet it would be an enormous help, and what is perhaps more important, they could then double the output of munitions and ships here, which is the real danger point; and he's wrong absolutely because he underestimates the effect on us, on Germany, on the occupied territories and on neutrals of the USA entering the war. The Americans don't grasp the power their resources entitle them to in *world* affairs. They are like a provincial millionaire who doesn't know he could buy up Mayfair if he chose. We in this Embassy act like lunatics on this last point, carefully concealing from the United States Government how strong they are and disputing silly points of precedence. To win the war we must hand the world on a plate to the USA, they'll vomit it up in due course, and we will have it back again. It is utterly absurd not to realise the facts of a very simple situation. We shall really lose control over our destiny if we let the USA fight us for it, winning every time little by little, no, we must roll with the punch, and come back without much difficulty at a later stage. In short, my view is—if we have any hesitations about how to win the war we shall lose the war.

One should distinguish between the American genius for improvisation, for planning something bold and moral to deal with an awkward situation, and their ability to carry the plan through. In the realm of foreign politics—and especially foreign economic policy—they've had no practice; deliberately so since they kept out of Europe and pursued Free Trade. They can plan and carry out the production of a million motor cars, but that's due to practice. We have had much practice in economic agreements (not so much as Germany) but we're somewhat fossilised in planning. The result is a tendency to accept the American plan and grossly to overestimate their power to carry it out. They are just like children. Suddenly they decide to go for a lovely picnic, and the idea is first rate, but they forget that Mother and Nannie must cut up the sandwiches and collect the tea things; all this takes time and trouble which annoys the children, even sometimes to the point of losing their desire to go at all. Over my Weygand negotiation they have never lifted a finger to cut up the sandwiches and to collect the tea things. I've had to do everything. An odd bit of behaviour that occurs when different generations combine to carry out a joint picnic.

All my love—David

5 June 1941 Chute

Dear love—Sometimes one loses touch with reality in the midst of this anxious adventure. The old world is crumbling so fast that even the things that one used to love best or mind about the most no longer assume the same importance. I often wonder what our life will be like when the war is over—and what we shall be like too. People say to me, 'I hear David's having a whale of a time,' in the way people do. Washington on the eve of war—reckless—romantic—its opportunities irresistible. If a whale of a time came my way I should embrace it—neither for reasons of love nor for the lack of them—but just because the days and one's hopes are often leaden-footed and happiness is to be captured if, for a moment or two, she shows her face. Nothing really matters beyond winning the war—and Crete for the first time has instilled a horrid doubt as to whether we've really got the hang of the thing. Unpreparedness is one matter, sterility of ideas quite another. Are our soldiers perhaps like your MEW idiots—ostriches with their heads in the sand?

Of course you're right—this is a war between ideas rather than peoples—very few have grasped that, just as it seems that not enough have yet grasped the significance of the aeroplane. In London one senses an undercurrent of disturbed thought—half expressed—barely admitted. But this latest, fatal adventure has shaken the steady confidence that until now everyone has determinedly displayed.

Oh—my darling David, I wonder if we shall ever know the same happiness again.

All my love—Sybil

10 June 1941 Washington

My darling love—I love your letters, you are writing better and better, don't strain yourself to keep up any standards, just go on as you are. If I could stand with you at our bathroom window and look down on the garden and up at the chestnuts I would cry for joy. I see plenty of beauty here but it isn't ours, and its power to comfort is limited and sometimes nil.

We've had a tremendous two days on France. On Monday the Viscount was away writing two speeches—he does too much of this—Butler[1] was off graduating his girl and the next man on leave. A huge storm burst in the shape of ten telegrams to the US Government from Leahy.[2] So down I had to go to deal *in nomine regis Britannici* with the whole bunch. I think the result was good, and pleased the Viscount on his return. Then dinner with Hopkins, and an all-night conversation. The President must find some overt acts to provoke the Germans and to reassure us and inspire his own people. I think he will. There are two which I am specially sweet on, but I cannot tell you what they are.

I pine to have you here, although I don't think the married couples in the Embassy do half the good we runabout fellows can do. The war is totalitarian and is a wife. One needs a mistress, but not a wife, and I would keep you as a mistress and what heaven that would be! The posting from place to place, the sitting down to talk and staying half the night, the drinking and the scheming and the rhetoric and all the hurly-burly of this huge game of shove and push—this doesn't fit domesticity. It suits a wild affair, like a dash to a Maryland hayfield and a literal 'roll in the grass', a fierce and momentary battle, no regrets, no sentiment. But to be quiet with you, and love you gently and for long days at a time, no, it wouldn't be easy in such a snatch and grab atmosphere, *but* it's all I have to look forward to, and without it as a dream I should fold up and become bloody and useless.

All my love—David

1. Nevile Butler, HM Minister at Washington.
2. US Ambassador in Vichy.

17 June 1941 Chute

Dearest love—Last Friday the Sykeses, Frank and Barbara, appeared in the afternoon with a car[1] already nearly filled with suitcases and fishing rods, picnic baskets and bottles of ginger pop. Into the modest spaces still left over I in turn squeezed a noble accumulation of sausage rolls and shortbreads, of grapefruit juice and chocolates and finally myself. We drove away in high spirits and reached Upton-on-Severn without mishap or incident in time for dinner.

Mrs Child was waiting on the doorstep of The White Lion, her arms outstretched in welcome. In I plunged with cries of, 'Good-night, ten o'clock then, in the morning,' and away drove Frank and Barbara. Within all was as usual. I had my slip of a bedroom with its shiny linoleum dotted with treacherous mats—downstairs the bar was as noisy and cosy as ever—dinner was presently served to the wireless, Mrs Child hovering near with endless assurances that the salmon came straight from the Severn. Oddly enough it tasted precisely as though it had. After a bath I fell into bed and a dreamless sleep.

It's hopeless to sit up on such expeditions. When I am at home surrounded by familiar things I can get on well enough. But put me down in a strange inn among unknown faces and I miss you unbearably—miss the comfort of your presence and the fun of sharing the excitements of a journey, however unimportant and brief. So the only remedy is bed—and thank the Lord I can always go to sleep whatever else I can't manage.

The fathers' match. Gosh, was it cold. An icy blast blew from every angle and we wrapped ourselves in rugs like papooses and clapped our purpling hands with a fine pretence at enthusiasm. It was a merciful release when all ended very properly in a draw—and we could totter on stiffened legs to tea in the car. After tea—and what those lads can put away—we took a little walk, then said goodbye and scuttered back to our respective roosts.

On Sunday—chapel—and afterwards to view an exhibition of the boys' pictures. John then bashfully confessed that one of his had been chosen to form part of a collection which is to tour the English schools. And there, lo and behold, was his name written up in the catalogue amongst other illustrious infants. The picture I couldn't see as it had already gone—but it was called 'Ship in a River' and I presume was sensational! I gave him a big pat on the back from both of us and told him you would be very pleased.

All my love—Sybil

1. To take Sybil to Abberley, John's preparatory school.

Letter from Roger Makins[1]

20 June 1941 Foreign Office

My dear David—I did not answer your telegram by telegram for a number of reasons. First of all it arrived corrupt . . . Secondly, knowing Sir R. Campbell he would certainly not appreciate my explaining to you why one of his principal advisers was going back to Lisbon! Thirdly, I couldn't give my reasons in any case, and finally it is not, alas! for me to direct your movements . . .

For weeks past Ronnie Campbell has been crying out that he cannot carry on without someone to take off him the burden of the economic work which at present he is obliged to deal with himself with the Doctor, at a time when he ought to be free for major matters . . . MEW feel that Lisbon has been rather cheated of your services in the last few months.

I take a more selfish view. I regard you as a Guards Brigade to be thrown into the fray where the need is greatest. Unfortunately I didn't command you and have to share you with another Ministry and two other Departments of this Office. I have been scrupulously fair. David Scott has seen all your letters from Washington, so has William [Strang] . . . all are of the opinion that you have set the ball rolling as nicely as can be expected in present circumstances . . . as you have presumably fully indoctrinated the Embassy, the latter ought to be able to keep the ball in play.

All is not well in Lisbon. The Portuguese Government is faced with a critical decision, for us it is vital they should take the right one.[2] We have reinforced the Embassy but the Germans continue to make headway. We must recover the lost ground . . . do what you did in Madrid and Washington, get hold of the Portuguese who see and know the Doctor, talk to the Doctor himself, inject confidence, and at the same time take some of the strain off the Ambassador . . . There is more to say but it is better that Arthur

Yencken should say it than that I should put it on paper . . . I suspect that you prefer not to go to Lisbon, but I am quite sure that for the time being you can get more results there than in Washington. I know what a lot you did there, but in the last analysis the flux and reflux of American policy and opinion will not be determined by individuals, or even a group in Washington. The drift of policy is much stronger than any individual influence in a vast agglomeration like America . . . none of us think that your return home is essential at the moment . . . certainly as far as Spain is concerned I wish the future was a little brighter as it is very stupid of the State Department to blunder into the trap laid for them by Suñer. They have also been very clumsy with the Portuguese (this is another job for you to close the gap again).

Yours ever—Roger

1. Makins is saying (a) Sir R. Campbell was not doing well with Salazar and (b) the Embassy in Washington thought I should leave the job to them.
2. The decision concerned allowing us to use the Azores as a base.

Letter from the Viscount Halifax to DE in Lisbon

24 June 1941 British Embassy, Washington

My dear Eccles—One line to thank you for your note. I hope you will have a good trip back.

We shall do our best to look after the things on which you have been working out here, and I am quite sure it will be very useful indeed for you to see how minds are working in the Peninsula and at home, and you will no doubt be able to judge from that end where it is most useful for you to be.

I shall look forward to seeing you back here before too long.

Yours sincerely—Halifax

Letter to Roger Makins at the Foreign Office

24 June 1941 Lisbon

Dear Roger—I enclose a memorandum on the new agency which the President is setting up to co-ordinate strategic information. You will see that Bill Donovan is the co-ordinator and will guess that I assisted at the pre-natal stages. Bill offered me a copy of his paper to the President but I thought it better the DNI[1] should have it. In order not to break the continuity of collaboration between us and Bill on this subject, I have installed Ian Fleming in my bed at Bill's house. He knows much more about the details of intelligence work than I do.

Bill left Washington directly he had seen the President on 18 June. I caught him up in New York next day when he gave me the account of the interview reported in the enclosed memorandum. He offered me any job I liked in his organisation.[2] There is no winter in his generosity.

Yours ever—David

1. Admiral John Godfrey, appointed Director of Naval Intelligence in 1939.
2. I went for a long walk up Fifth Avenue wondering if I should accept this offer. Then I thought of home, and all my friends in Europe.

Memorandum by DE sent to Roger Makins

United States Government
Co-ordination of Strategic Information

1. Colonel William J. Donovan submitted a memorandum[1] to the President in the first week of June advising him to set up a co-ordinator of strategic information, responsible directly to himself as Commander-in-Chief. Copies of this memorandum were sent to Mr Hull, Mr Stimson, Mr Knox, and Mr Edgar Hoover.

2. Colonel Donovan's paper emphasised the need to analyse, comprehend and appraise *in one place* all information pertinent to the plans and resources of potential enemies, whether this

information were collected at home or abroad, either directly by a new organisation or through existing departments. It was held that 'accurate, comprehensive, long-range information' was necessary to make 'the war-plan of 1942'.

3. The President consulted the State and Service Departments on this project.[2] The departmental intelligence sections all advised against a single co-ordinator. Mr Hull, Mr Stimson, Mr Knox and the Under-Secretaries of War and Navy advised for Colonel Donovan's plan.

4. On 18 June the President entrusted Colonel Donovan with the post of co-ordinator. The following points were agreed by the President at this meeting:

(a) the co-ordinator shall report direct to the President and have access to him at any time;

(b) the President will instruct in writing each department of government concerned to place at the co-ordinator's disposal all existing and future information which the department possesses bearing any relation to the war;

(c) the co-ordinator shall plan and execute through his organisation all external publicity and propaganda; (*Note*: the President asked Colonel Donovan to take on internal morale as well; he refused.)

(d) the co-ordinator shall recommend to the President all action of a subversive nature to be taken abroad, and shall be responsible for its execution either directly or through existing organisations;

(e) the co-ordinator will collect and analyse all information bearing on economic warfare. He will recommend to the President direct both the economic warfare policy of the USG and the allocation of the carrying out of this policy through existing departments of government.[3] In the first instance it is not intended that Colonel Donovan's organisation shall itself execute economic warfare policy;

(f) the co-ordinator will recommend to the President general strategic plans for the conduct of the war; (*Note*: Colonel Donovan asked the President if he intended to keep the strategy of the war in his own hands. He said yes, and that a totalitarian war must be planned by civilians.)

(g) the President asked Colonel Donovan to set up a committee to study economic plans for the post-war period; (*Note*: this was an unexpected addition to the co-ordinator's duties; Colonel Donovan accepted.)

(h) the co-ordinator will be advised by a board composed of a representative of the State Department, the heads of the War and Navy Intelligence, the director of the Federal Bureau of Investigation, and certain other co-opted members; (*Note*: Hamilton Fish Armstrong is likely to be one; Henry Field is to have the Middle East Bureau.)

(i) the co-ordinator will be financed by the President's secret fund;

(j) Colonel Donovan obtained a written promise from the President that if the USA enter the war he may resign his post and take a command in the field.

5. The President asked Colonel Donovan to pay particular attention to civil war character of the present struggle. He would like to go all out in subversive activities. Colonel Donovan asked if he would use food as a weapon. The President said he was tired of hearing that Holland or Belgium were starving, such generalities meant nothing. He wanted someone to say: 'This town in Holland has 20,000 inhabitants, 500 of them are organised to resist the Germans, if we give them so much food, money, arms, etc., they can start a revolt.' In a case like that, which had been carefully studied, he would give anything which Colonel Donovan recommended.

24 June 1941 Lisbon

1. Donovan had asked me to help draft this memorandum.
2. I am not certain if the FBI were consulted, but think it likely.
3. I persuaded Donovan to insist on this.

V

Portugal and Spain

June–November 1941

5. Portugal and Spain

After the excitement of Washington, dealing daily with the heads of the United States Government, the blockade difficulties in the Peninsula seemed dull work. It was the usual story of MEW wanting the Embassy to harass Portuguese firms for insignificant deals made with German agents. Nothing of great importance happened, and my wish to get a job in London became stronger every month. For these reasons I have cut the correspondence drastically during this period.

Letter from Roger Makins to DE in Lisbon

26 June 1941 Foreign Office

Dear David—I hope you are still not reproachful at us all for directing your reluctant steps back to the Peninsula. The outbreak of the Russo-German war has made ever more difficult our efforts in Spain and Portugal, and I fear memories of the Reds may be more effective than German money and threats. What does the Doctor [Salazar] think? Is he tempted by the possibility of exorcising the spectre of Bolshevism and the menace of American materialism at the cost of accepting a place in the new order?[1] I imagine that he is strong enough to resist, but there are many in Europe for whom the temptation will be strong. The attack on Russia is far the most interesting thing that Hitler could have done and it is bringing a rapid re-alignment of forces; as for the Japs you can almost hear them thinking—they are thinking so hard.

Yours ever—Roger

1. Hitler's new order envisaged in the Funk plan.

28 June 1941 Lisbon

My darling love—I'm settling down here to a few weeks' hard work. Chiefly staff reorganisation and smoothing away the friction caused by working the Blockade. I don't think there's much in the Portuguese complaints about the Blockade, here and there some bad manners on our side and some silly pinpricking, but if we were obviously winning the war there wouldn't be a murmur.

29 June

I spent Saturday night 270 km away near Mertola in south-east Portugal on a pyrites mine in order to see a man who has been abusing the Embassy here and MEW for harsh and ill-judged treatment of the Portuguese. His complaints didn't amount to much and I think the sting has been removed. On the way we saw some marvellous flowers, great clumps of oleanders as big as haystacks, all pink with blossom, hedges of plumbago whose debutante blue I find very touching, I thought of our sterner ceanothus, then cystus, acres of them, and a yellowish sort of rock-rose, I don't know its name. One could enjoy Portugal very much. The smells are good, more resin-y than Spain, and always more green to comfort the eye. Sam and Arthur are calling to me from Madrid. I am very gloomy about my return.

Write often, not necessarily at great length, as the bags are very frequent, and I would rather have a few words with you several times a week, than many once in ten days. Some of your letters must be in America, they'll come back in time.

You tell Roger that if I don't get two weeks' leave during John's holidays I'll never speak kindly to him again.

All my love, darling Syb—David

30 June 1941 Lisbon

My darling Syb—We can thank the war for a small consolation, that it has taught us both to write better. You don't have the discipline of drafting telegrams. I think it's the finest exercise in lucid writing the world can give: the subject is always important; thought is given by several minds to the matter in hand; your audience the other end is the top flight of contemporary society. All along the line keen eyes are watching, and ruthless comments are written by the bright and ambitious who see a chance to prove their wisdom and wit. 'What does this mean?' is Ronnie's [Campbell] short but shattering phrase that I see almost daily, applied especially to the telegrams from Washington where the contagion of American idiom has corrupted without capturing our people, and the hybrid is always ugly and often unintelligible.

Love—David

1 July 1941 Chute

Darling—Nannie has been away for nearly a month and we've measled all the time. Simon is about and very well again. Polly got up for the first time yesterday and seems fine—though her eyes haven't completely cleared. Harris is off with lumbago. So I rushed in a frenzy from blanket baths to bedding-out and in my vast confusion of labours practically took a thermometer to the hens. Through all this welter shone the ever present hope that soon, very soon, I should see you—as I weeded and planted—bathed, soothed and scolded—I told myself all the time that I was weeding and planting so that the garden should please you—bathing, soothing and scolding in order that the children should be well by your return. This helped a great deal—so perhaps my visions, however false, did me a good turn. But when your letter came yesterday I must confess I was rather dashed. But recovery is swift—it has to be. The eggs have still to be collected—the washing hung out—the housekeeping arranged. Mrs Austen was even more downcast than I. She had been killing the calf in imagination ever since your cable. Though I'd done my best to dull her certainty—having in my bones a horrid premonition that our Russian allies would impose a strain upon the bonds of friendship—however ancient and well founded.

But it was no good. She even baked a plum cake on the sly (and used up our last almonds) and then was compelled to produce it with tears for Simon's and my solitary tea yesterday!

I love you and perhaps—who knows—this surprising life may take another twist and you'll be at Bristol or Poole before the summer's out.

—Sybil

Savingram No. 251
En clair telegram from Sir R. Campbell to Mr Eden
By Bag

2 July 1941

Opening a conversation yesterday evening Dr Salazar welcomed Eccles back to civilisation. He looked on the Americans as a barbaric people illuminated not by God but by electric light. Were we not afraid that the world after the war would be run by the USA with a strong dash of Communism? This was a horrible prospect for Europe.

2. Eccles suggested that Dr Salazar's dislike of a single and

dominant system diverted his attention from the inescapable choice between the mastery of Germany and the mastery of the Allies. He must choose between us and he should not permit himself or his friends the luxury of hope that a compromise is possible. He asked how we could possibly win the war outright. The German Army could not be beaten. Eccles wondered how many Portuguese had said the same about Napoleon's army. There were many other factors in modern war besides mechanised divisions, and it was strange that Dr Salazar should insist so exclusively on material forces.

3. He returned to the dangers of our partnership with the USA and the USSR. Eccles asked him if he had read the American Constitution, a document patently inspired by Christian ideas. *Mein Kampf* and the Nazi doctrine would be a poor exchange. Eccles twitted him with speaking of the Americans as crotchety old men talk of boisterous and tiresome children. It was surely wrong to condemn a child for being young. As for Communism Eccles thought it was a spontaneous disease likely to flourish anywhere where extreme poverty, bad government and an agitator were to be found. There was nothing mysterious about it and neither the UK nor the USA would be frightened by the Russian bogy. Dr Salazar replied that we should be so weary and battered after the war that Communism would have an easy prey. Eccles thought that exactly the opposite was probable. It was true that this war was causing material damage in every corner of the UK, but if the last war had done so we might have made the spiritual effort necessary to assume the responsibility of our victory. Today the British people were passing through an experience too intimate and too molten to define clearly their war aims. Dr Salazar must be patient and not lose faith in the possibility of unpredictable events.

—Campbell

8–9 July 1941 Madrid

My darling love—Here in Madrid all is violent and fluid and only interesting in parts. I half hate and half love this place now. The Embassy runs well, far ahead of Washington and Lisbon in organisation, originality and efficiency. Sam is on top of his work, and needs only regular doses of courage and an occasional new idea. A wonderful performance. I had a huge welcome from all here. They were so pleased that I had left America to return to their squalid surroundings that I was quite overcome. Particularly in the Ministries I have never seen such warmth and affection. As for Madrid society I have taken a violent dislike to it. I arrived Saturday afternoon and went in the evening to watch a polo match at Puerta de Hierro because I felt sure I should see all my out-of-school friends at once. There they were, exquisite and idle, flannels and flowered dresses, parasols and jewels, gossiping and drinking and abusing everyone not in their world and a good many in it, having stayed up all last night, now planning a party to stay up all this night . . . they have learned nothing from the last war, the Civil War, or this war . . . nothing at all. I much prefer the middle class of America to these rancid aristocrats for all their grace and lovely eyes. The Americans play our rules, or very nearly, but how can we cope with Spanish life? Listen. Two young ladies, *Y* and *X*, seized upon me, '*Ola Davido, venga aqui el bienvenido.*' I sat with them and they asked me to join them in exploring some dance and song place that opens at 3 a.m. 'Before that we can drink and dine at someone's house, it doesn't matter where, and the Domecqs expect us for breakfast.' I excused myself on account of work. 'Oh! but you're impossible, it's outrageous you come back from America and here in Madrid is your girl, and you won't come out with us tonight.' 'Well,' I said, 'there is a war and I didn't know "my girl" was in Madrid.' 'Monstrous man,' they shrieked, 'you have the most beautiful creature in Spain wildly in love with you and you don't even know where she is.' . . . *Y* broke out, 'What's a war compared to life, and what's life but love? In our war our men always left the firing line for a woman they loved, they went back quite soon, were slightly punished, were killed, but they didn't mind because they had lived . . . but you, you mind about all the little and the stupid things, you're always wrong about life, trying to be mildly happy for years together, instead of wildly happy once in a way, oh! you mistake the essence of this passionate and bloody world.' 'Really,' I answered, 'you have learned a lot since we met.' 'Oh! yes,' said *X*, '*Y* has been to Cordoba with a poet, it was wonderful while it lasted but he wouldn't hurt her, so she got bored and came back.' 'Quite true,' *Y* replied unmoved, 'and David wouldn't hurt me either.' *Que vida*! I used to like them, and tried to play along, I who am so bad at parties, but now I can't any more, and I must creep home to my only comfort.

I can put this in a Madrid bag. I daresay you'll get a Lisbon letter—I'll be there tomorrow—before this arrives.

All my love—David

11 July 1941 Lisbon

My darling love—I have had two letters of note: one from the Viscount saying he wanted me back in Washington as soon as possible, and another from London agreeing in principle to my transfer to FO but asking me to wait till I come home 'shortly', to fix the details. There is apparently a fight going on at home over my body—USA v. Peninsula. I have a huge sentimental attachment to the Peninsula but the work here is now more or less caretaking—except the reorganisation of the Lisbon Embassy which is much weaker on the economic than on the political side. The war will be conducted from Washington and now that I know I have only to make the personal push to be sent there permanently I don't want to go. Winning the war is the first object, the second is to be ready to take a share in building the peace. I see that from the educative point of view I have learned pretty well all there is to learn in the Peninsula. Conversations with Salazar are always instructive, but apart from that I have sucked dry the experience to be gained here. In America there exists a day-school for all future government, and I must say I hanker for the unequalled training which contact with the US Government would give: still I don't want to go. I would rather mix in the political scene at home. I don't want to be out of touch with our own people and problems. It is very difficult. I will come home open-minded and we will talk it all over at leisure.

You see, the economic policy of the war has got into a mess. It has been pretty clear for six months which way things were going. The world's shipping was so rapidly decreasing that it was only a matter of time before this physical limitation would silently do half the work MEW had been making such a fuss about. Of course we have still to see that the dwindling shipping available is not all used for the import of products which the Germans want; but this is much easier now as the neutrals will not part with shipping space, which is needed for their own people, with anything like the alacrity they used to when they could bring in more than we allowed them for their own consumption. We used to spend our time fixing quotas, now we should spend it filling the quotas. This is a sound development if we use the opportunity wisely. Before we had to restrict trade, now we can appear as the Father Christmas who helps to find such supplies as can be shipped. In other words there is a big chance to turn from destructive to constructive economics. This comes at a fortunate moment. Hitler is proposing his New Order, and a pretty thin affair it is, if we take it to pieces. Against this we were offering the sour grapes of the Blockade, now we have a chance to offer help, constructive help, and to show vividly the difference between life under the German order and life in our orbit. To work this out needs a touch of genius and a truce to inter-departmental squabbles. I doubt if these pre-requisites are to be had at home. Therefore, with a sigh of regret, to Washington we must go. It would be better to work out the new world in London. We are Europeans and America is very remote. But I doubt if it is politically possible to do so in Whitehall, we are too near the battle and too entrenched in old-fashioned formulas.

Give Polly a big kiss and Simo' whatever he likes to have as a sign of affection. I shall be with you in a few weeks.

All my love—David

Letter from Arthur Yencken, HM's Minister in Madrid, to DE in Lisbon

12 July 1941

Dear David—I had a talk with Sam yesterday about your future movements. He is delighted with your visit here, and encouraged that you will spend a few weeks in Lisbon, but quite convinced that the infiltrating panzer thrusts that you represent can now most usefully be employed in Washington. Encouraged by me he has written in this sense to Anthony Eden.

I think our show here is now running on an even keel, will hold the ground gained, and keep on pushing in where opportunities occur. Occasional visits by you will always help us greatly—don't forget that—but Washington now looks as if it ought to be your house.

As regards MEW, Sam and I agree that it would be unwise for you to change over to the FO. The move would create a prejudice and we think it more useful that you should keep your card of re-entry into MEW. For you status is not an issue; it does not really matter under what mantle you pursue your delightful ways.

Hastily written but not hastily thought out.

Yours—Arthur

Letter to Sir Samuel Hoare from DE

12 July 1941 Lisbon

Dear Sir Samuel—I want to tell you how extraordinarily glad I was to see you again. And how sorry I shall be if my Madrid days are numbered. On my return here I found a charming letter from the Viscount asking me to return to Washington as soon as convenient. My immediate plans are to send Robertson[1] home on Tuesday with a number of questions to discuss with MEW, which are not very important taken singly, but put together represent a fairly extensive modification in the present application of the Blockade in Portugal. He knows more about details than I do and I feel he would be a better advocate in London in the immediate future than I should be, so I shall stay here until he returns at the end of the month. Then, I will go home.

Apart from the details which Robertson will take up in London, there remains the big problem of how to shift the emphasis of our economic policy from restriction on the trade of neutrals, typified by the Blockade, to supplies and shipping and exchange of goods between areas which are near each other, and therefore transport between them is easier. We must now concentrate on filling quotas and no longer on fixing them. It seems clear to me that unless the utmost ingenuity is used in re-routing the dwindling shipping at the disposal of the neutrals, they are going to suffer very much from another year or more of war. Of course, the occupied territories are going to suffer more, but our business is to draw the maximum distinction between the life in German-controlled territory and life outside. It is this constructive policy which will put heart into all those who hate the Germans to continue the war passively or actively. I wish I could think that in Whitehall there was more vision and as much capacity for building a new world as for walling up a bad world.

I would only go to Washington with a light heart if I were really persuaded that there and nowhere else could our New Order, and in particular the part of it which deals with the Western Mediterranean, be worked out. I am not sure of this. I have a feeling that if HMG would trust a few of my generation who have seen the absolute necessity to offer some constructive alternative to Hitler's Order, they should really work out their plans as the Economic Department of the Foreign Office and not have to take a room in Washington for this purpose. We are Europeans and the Americans are very remote. But if our Foreign Office will not take on the responsibility of working out a new policy, or cannot do it because of political difficulties at home, then to Washington let us go and there do our best, in a soil not perfectly suited to the plant, to construct a new Europe.

Yours very sincerely—David Eccles

1. My assistant on MEW matters in Lisbon.

16 July 1941 Chute

My darling dear—Your letter from Madrid has arrived—how remote your life is from mine. Those black-eyed ladies and panting beauties—the aeroplanes, the aides-de-camp, the gold braid and dinner parties—the speeches, the celebrities, the hurly-burly of great affairs—jewels, lovers, conversation, statesmen, politicians, rogues, food, drink and—finery, all jostling together in a vast and dazzling kaleidoscope. Sometimes I leave your letters unread until the wheels of the day have caught me up into their revolutions—otherwise I'm robbed of concentration and calm and only spit fire at Simon when he stumbles over his reading book.

I have a good Polly story for you. The other night she gabbled her prayers in a more than usually disgraceful way. Nannie took her to task and said that God didn't like being talked to so hurriedly. At which our young woman observed: 'I don't see why he should mind, it takes him less time to listen.'

All my love, darling David—Sybil

20 July 1941 Chute

My dearest love—What lovely stockings! I gasped with joy when they fell in a silken heap out of the extraordinary official-looking envelope. I'm sure the Germans aren't allowed to send their women silk stockings labelled 'On Adolf's Service'.

I'm sad that you are probably to go back to America. For though you say you will return 'open-minded' I think I see that your mind is made up. Here, the thoughtful, the practical, the energetic and the knowing, all are beginning to talk in terms of an American-made peace, of an American-controlled future—they may try to throw in a word for England now and then, by way of comfort to themselves and consolation to their audience—'England will supply the wisdom, the experience,' etc.—but it doesn't ring true—half of them don't believe that England will supply anything. We shall struggle painfully with domestic reconstruction while America blows a trumpet call to the world. I oppose this view with angry obstinacy fortified by the conviction that at any rate I must have Mr Winston Churchill on my side. But I expect it's a losing fight and you and the rest of them have seen the unhappy truth. If you have, then it is certainly right for some of the best brains to depart and take up their stations in what is to be the new hub of the universe—for only thus will Englishmen be able to influence the course of the future.

I love you and think about you.

—Sybil

21 July 1941 Lisbon

My darling love—I am sitting in the Ambassador's car at Cintra waiting for Roger's [Makins] aeroplane. I long to see him. Perhaps he will bring some message from you. Yesterday I was bathing in the pool where we used to go with the Duke of Kent last year, and some silly woman said, 'Oh! but Mr E can't be married, it isn't true.' They often say this and I feel furious as a captain does who is taken for a corporal. I ought to bear about me the marks of twelve years with you. If I am still a virgin in appearance I am insulted. I lack some medal or scar to which I and you are entitled. What can I do about it? Living the war is like riding in a sleigh in one of those Russian forests, pursued by wolves. One by one you throw out your belongings to lighten the load and then I believe you start on the horses and finally on your friends. You reach home naked and alone on foot. The throwing-out process has reached the stage where my pre-war luggage of ideas and habits has almost gone, and my wartime friends are in considerable danger. I should hope that as this process of stripping continues the essential I, the married-to-you I, will appear clearly. We shall see soon enough.

The Latin races hope the Russians will be beaten but not too quickly or too cheaply. I daresay a good many of our people feel the same. The Americans who do not have any close contacts with Russia or Russian Communism (they had in the USA the good sense to know that Communism is not a specifically Russian product) wouldn't mind if the Russians beat the Germans. They won't of course, so it doesn't matter *qua* the war, but it does matter very much *qua* the peace. Communism is a bad smell which comes naturally when the drains of a social structure are blocked—when men of talent cannot rise and when wealth and poverty are too widely separated. You can remove the smell if you keep the drains clear, but if you pay too much attention to the smell you may, and this is the danger, get used to it, and think of ways of liking it because you have forgotten it is unnatural and should be removed.

—David

Letter from Sir Samuel Hoare

22 July 1941 British Embassy, Madrid

Dear David—I was very glad to receive your letter of the 12th and as you may imagine, I very strongly agree with the views that you expressed in it. Indeed, I had already written a despatch to London in which I impressed much the same conclusions upon London. You may also care to know that I wrote a personal letter to Anthony in which I told him that whilst you were very valuable to us in Madrid, and perhaps even more so to Campbell in Lisbon, it seemed to me of paramount importance that you should return to Washington where you evidently made such excellent personal contacts. I am afraid that since you left Madrid things have been made much more difficult by Franco's speech.[1] London reacted as you will have expected and Anthony was evidently anxious to make a counter-attack in a statement in the House. I have strongly advised him not to tie himself up as to the future, but to content himself with a statement of the facts and that our future policy must depend upon the conduct and action of the Spanish Government. A direct issue with Franco now is just what Suñer would like, and if we want more time for military operations, it is essential to avoid it. As I have not yet received an answer to my telegrams I do not know whether or not Anthony agrees with this view. In the meantime, Irving and Ellis-Rees are sending to London a Memorandum upon the present economic position, and emphasising the new factors, namely,

(1) the problem of filling, and not fixing, our quotas;

(2) our own dependence upon Spain for various commodities, the details of which you already know.

I may be wrong, but I have the feeling that after a week or two's commotion over the Franco speech, we shall get back again to economic talks. None the less, there is no doubt that Franco's speech was, from everyone's point of view, indefensible and has greatly complicated the position.

With all good wishes.

Yours ever—Samuel Hoare

1. Suggesting all belligerents should cease fighting and make peace.

23 July 1941 Lisbon

Roger and I had a huge gossip, most of which must wait till I see you. He was very tired, but in possession of those trenchant faculties that make his the most incisive mind I have found in his service. He would be the ideal head of the FO, and will be, only he may be really tired by that distant date. There is something about the really good Wykehamist mind, cool, lucid, yet ardent, the sort of mind that in the Middle Ages preached, planned and plundered on the Crusades, something which the Etonian never has. The objectivity of the Etonian mind so seldom embraces the idealistic, the pathetic and the illogical side of the human spirit. It rejects mystery. The Wykehamist is inclined to love mystery too dearly. Roger and I naturally discussed the Peninsula, Washington and my future. For the first we are both resigned; the long day is done and we are for the dark; we worked hard and not without success during the day, almost made the sun stand still in his course, but there are some events that are beyond all control. The campaign in Russia will decide the timetable, and as that ferocious medley may swing this way and that for a time unguessable we left direct forecasts to wiser people.

Washington, he agrees, is the most obvious place for me. He seems to have half arranged it, subject to a number of conditions regarding the exact job, which I suppose the Viscount on his visit to England would have to decide. But I don't want to go. The reasons are complex, and not for a letter. One is that I am European, and would remain so.

I feel from your last letter that you sigh sometimes to think that I have wandered so long and so far from your life. You need have no fear. The scars I have earned are only skin deep and are rapidly disappearing; I dipped my bucket here and there in the diplomatic world but was not refreshed either mentally or bodily. I want to be with you and to stay at home, if possible for the rest of the war. Go to bed tonight knowing I shall be with you.

My love to those creatures, I am very fond of them, and very much more of you.

—David

27 July 1941 Chute

My darling dear—Your letter of 11 July from Lisbon is my last. You sound weary and I long to get you home. The walled garden is almost at its best—the phlox are coming out and the daisies and gypsophila make glorious splashes of white among the purples, the yellows and the reds. If you don't hurry up the monarda will be over and you always had a taste for those shaggy crimson heads. The roses have never been as good—you've always shaken your head over that border—this summer I think you would nod it.

I love you—Sybil

29 July 1941 Lisbon

My darling love—Ian Fleming is here and I am trying to arrange that he should go to Tangier. He came straight from Washington where I had installed him in my bed in Bill's house when I left. He told me a sad tale of the jealousy which I had aroused in a section of the Embassy. What a bore these things are, and how they complicate our work! Except for Noel Hall I thought I had been pretty successful in keeping them all sweet. The Viscount was too kind, he helped and hindered me; but on balance helped. Dear precious Syb, you perhaps don't realise that I have to pay heavily in some quarters for my wartime career. The FO are all right, I have always served them with a pure heart and they must know it by this time. The others, the amateurs and the minor departments—there has been and will be trouble without end. 'We, brethren, veterans in warfare, may have fewer enemies, but enemies we shall always have.'[1] It is this disgust at the rivalries of men that may effectively keep me from pursuing the great game of public life.

I spend so much time working that I never arrange my private affairs and constantly run out of toothpaste, etc.

All my love—David

1. Saint Augustine.

Savingram No. 325
En clair telegram from Sir R. Campbell to Mr Eden
By Bag

6 August 1941 Lisbon

The Spanish Ambassador[1] discussed with Eccles at length this morning the present position of the war and of Anglo-American relations with Spain.

2. His Excellency emphasised that the Spanish Nationalists hated Communism and were glad of a chance to square their account with Germany by sending a small force to fight Russia. The Germans on the other hand had only attacked Russia in order to destroy the Russian Army. Their pretended crusade against Bolshevism deceived nobody. His Excellency was sure that the Russian campaign was proving more costly than the Germans had anticipated. Eccles suggested that whenever the Russian campaign ended it was now certain that Germany's ability to export would be seriously impaired by her need to replace damaged or lost material and by the falling off in supplies obtained from Russia. This strain imposed on German industry would be further increased by the growing power of the Royal Air Force attacks. Since the Ambassador agreed with this forecast, Eccles pointed out that the moment was ill chosen to lean on Germany and to risk the loss of Anglo-American supplies. He made a special point of petroleum products and the raw materials which could alone come from the dollar and sterling areas.

3. The conversation then turned on how seriously General Franco's speech of 18 July ought to be taken. The Ambassador made it clear that he thought his brother had gone too far, that his remarks were for internal consumption. Eccles replied that the external effect was no less for that, and that while he could understand putting all one's money on a horse within a yard of the winning post, this was a bad moment to plump for a German victory in the way in which General Franco had done. The Ambassador asked if neutral opinion was really shocked. Eccles painted as gloomy a picture as possible. His Excellency said that he had intended to go to Madrid in the near future and that he would put forward his journey and take the first opportunity to speak to General Franco and find out if there was any way of

clarifying the situation in the direction we should desire. Finally, he referred to the extreme difficulty which all European statesmen found of learning the truth about events inside and outside their countries and earnestly asked that no opportunity be lost to explain in private the dependence of Spain on seaborne imports.

—Campbell

1. Nicolas Franco.

Letter from Reves Childs, US Minister at Tangier, to DE in Lisbon

5 August 1941 American Legation, Tangier

My dear Eccles—As you are aware, I transmitted to Bob Murphy the message contained in your letter of 25 July and I sent you a brief telegram in reply which he asked me to convey to you.

He has now written me more at length as follows:

> I would appreciate it if you would let him know that I am satisfied that the effect thus far of the arrival of the initial shipments of supplies under the economic plan is most favorable and helpful from every point of view. You might say to Eccles that I am certain that the General [Weygand] really has developed along the right lines lately. Obviously the economic plan is not solely responsible. The Russian campaign has adjusted everyone's idea, not least of all the General's. He is now convinced that Germany is not going to win this war. That conviction is most important. It makes the task so much easier. Support of Weygand I feel is the right line even though one could wish that he had more political ambition. Please tell Eccles to turn on his charm on some of these doubting Thomases when he gets to London. The investment here is costing them not a farthing and while we don't guarantee dividends we consider the plan a splendid speculation which risks nothing.

Unfortunately I don't have more time to write you at length. The courier is leaving in a few minutes . . .

As you probably know by now, we arranged the Tangier blocking of dollars just as we desired. Dollars held by Spanish nationals were removed from the general license issued to Spain and their unblocking made subject to special license from the United States Treasury.

We miss you very much over here. My wife joins me in very kind regards and in the hope that you may look in on us soon.

With best wishes, I am,

Very sincerely yours—Reves Childs[1]

1. Reves Childs was a firm friend who arranged for me to meet at the US Legation in Tangier those Frenchmen who preferred not to come to the British Legation.

8 August 1941 Chute

Darling love—I've shut the boys into the book room where they are make-believing at enjoying themselves with an album, a pot of paste, and a collection of swops that must be arranged in as tempting a way as possible. I know their hearts are with the swimming pool—their thoughts pinned to all the exciting things they might be doing if only the weather would dry. This afternoon I take them out to tea and then go on to Andover to do the weekend shopping. Here is John's report. He is full of life and engages me in all sorts of conversation. His history this term seems to have interested him very much. 'We "did",' he says, 'from the Industrial Revolution to the European War.' 'We did it'—oh, the superb ignorance or indifference of youth for all the joy and bitterness and pain that those years represented for mankind—as in their turn do all the pages of history. Last term, between 3 May and 29 July, that chunk of the agonising struggle was satisfactorily polished off the slate.

No letter from you for quite a long time.

With all my love—Sybil

17 August 1941 Chute

My darling—I'm a bit soggy today having crawled into bed at five o'clock with the dawn streaking the sky—after the Rifle Brigade dance. It was enormous fun and preceded by a dinner of unbelievable luxe—with champagne and all! When you get down to it a good deal of the luxe was ingenuity but the result was grand and there was no deception about the champagne! And what chic! I could have worn my green satin Eva had I not been too cowardly—thank goodness for my three bracelets. We danced without a pause till three. Such make-believe evenings cheer one up and shed a rosy if slightly bogus glow—and leave a memory or two to chew on. A little glamour goes a long way.

With all my love, dear David—Sybil

Letter to Dr Salazar from DE

20 August 1941 Lisbon

Your Excellency—I am writing to thank you for your kindness in giving me so much of your time yesterday evening. Two matters of great importance were raised during our discussion. The first is the possibility of chartering French ships for service in Portuguese trade. I enclose a list of the French tankers which we believe are at present in Mediterranean and North African waters. The company which owns the *Frimaire* and the *Vendemaire* is said to be in financial difficulties.

The second question concerns the production of wolfram in Portugal. I should like to draw Your Excellency's attention once again to the extreme gravity of the present situation. His Majesty's Government cannot remain inactive when deliveries of this metal to Germany are known to be vital to the steel industry, which produces our enemy's tanks and guns, and makes possible the continuation of the war. As I said yesterday, we do not wish to engage in a commercial battle *à outrance* with the Germans on Portuguese territory. The results might well be disastrous. Therefore, it was with great relief that I understood Your Excellency to be willing to study the position urgently with a view to working out some scheme that would effectively reduce prices, and so production.

As soon as I reach London discussions on wolfram will begin, and I should very much like to ask my friends to hold their hand until Your Excellency has reviewed the situation; but as the delivery of wolfram to Germany is of first-class importance in the conduct of the war, and the situation in the mining districts is rapidly getting out of hand, Your Excellency will appreciate that if the Portuguese Government can devise means to curb the upward course of prices, those means, to be effective, must be put into practice without delay.

I have the honour to be, with the highest consideration,
Your Excellency's most obedient Servant—David Eccles

[At the end of August 1941, I went home for leave and consultations. Some letters on both sides, written following my return to Portugal, have been lost. My letter of 13 October 1941 is the first after the break.]

13 October 1941 Lisbon

My darling sweet—I've been working desperately at the North African business. The French are very amiable and if they could they would give me a visa; as yet I have not popped the question. We are at the point where they know I want something but aren't sure what. I've written to Wallace Murray in the State Department so that they will be prepared for my visit to Africa.

There's not much gossip here. The Italians are very low. I saw Phillips, the US Ambassador at Rome, on his way to Washington. He left Italy a week ago. He said Mussolini is loathed bitterly up and down the country. Everything is funereal and he never conceived such gloom and misery. He's against bombing the centre of Rome. I think he's right.

The Germans here say that they will have Moscow before the end of the month and that the big impediment to their advance is having to feed so many Russian prisoners.

14 October
I'm becoming very American. I lunched with four of them today,

including the American Minister to Portugal[1] and Mr Biggers on his way from London to the USA. The latter gave us a very amusing account of Beaverbrook's journey to Moscow. On the way from Archangel to Moscow their aeroplane was fired at by Russian AA batteries. On arrival Beaverbrook wired Winston, 'Whatever you do don't send them any AA guns, and if I can't settle with the guy (Stalin) I'll have to return to Archangel by train.' Hence the quick settlement, says Biggers.

The US Minister told me that when the draft is called up in the States a very large percentage have bad eyes or teeth or something and are thrown out. The government doctors then order them to go back to their native village, find a *local* doctor, and get cured at the government's expense. 'I guess,' said Mr Fish, 'that the man sitting on the lid (FDR) figured the docs hadn't had enough out of the New Deal and this is how he spreads the dough around.' Aren't they astonishing? After all, why not do this? When you think of it it's rather a clever dodge. Tell Daddy how the GPs' votes are culled in America.

The wolfram business goes from bad to worse, the Germans have now sunk a Portuguese ship carrying wolfram to the USA to warn this wretched little country ('You can't,' says Ronnie Campbell, 'expect a kitten to behave like a tiger') that they mean to stop at nothing to secure wolfram for themselves and to deny it to us and America. We are getting near a shooting war as you can see.

PS. Later: we find it was untrue that the ship had any wolfram.

15 October

I have been wondering if Rab[2] has put you on his committee yet. The social services depend on first principles; what kind of citizen do you want? The answer is emphatically *not* just a lazy, well-fed, well-washed, movie-going creature with no home life or rather no domestic responsibilities. You must begin by grasping what men and women can do and want to do. In *The Oxford Book of Christian Verse* is John Donne's poem 'The Litany': one verse begins

> From being anxious, or secure,
> . . . Good Lord deliver us.

That's the point. We don't want to be either anxious or secure, but both at once. It is fairly easy to construct a political pattern on either the principle of security—Socialism, equality of wealth, social service, subsidised houses, etc.—or on the principle of anxiety—living dangerously, power politics, lust for glory, Hitlerism. You see both principles are more or less clean cut; but mankind demands a mixture and that means planning in opposite directions. John Donne analyses our nature in nine words. It has taken me a long time to realise that this is the bottom of human nature, and if you accept the Christian thesis that moral progress is possible, and men can be made better, then what the true part of us wants is right and should be encouraged to develop through our social institutions. In other words the Christian cannot regard the state as solely a remedy for sin, a policeman for our bad nature, but must regard the state as the vehicle through which our good nature can express itself and without which it cannot express itself.

When therefore you examine projects for social services you must pass them through the test of (a) does the best in us want this service? (b) will the service promote the love of man for his neighbour? The second is perhaps the simplest single test you can use. By 'neighbour' I mean your family as well as your *voisin*. If you give children free milk how can you see that farmers, distributors, school teachers, children, parents have to work together to realise this common service? You must bring them all in. Much of course can be done by explaining to all of them how they are co-operating, but I should agree with Salazar (e.g. Salazar won't let the Portuguese workmen be housed in flats. He says that separate houses cost more but are morally worth it), that to spend a little more time and money to make them all *take a hand* is worth while. Looked at from another angle this is the doctrine of 'work and pray'. The politician has to grasp that the type of society which he builds will condition how the citizen works, and how he works will condition how good he is, and how good he is will determine how happy he is.

All my love, darling Syb—David

1. Bert Fish.
2. R. A. Butler had been appointed President of the Board of Education in July 1941.

17 October 1941 Chute

My very dear David—Your first letter came this morning and I read it greedily. I haven't said anything to you in mine about my horrid state of mind because I want you to forget it. It was a disagreeable episode and I've banished it now—though it was disquietingly real and vivid at the time. A nasty exhibition of unbridled egotism.

You are wonderfully patient, my dearest David, and I know you to be right. Our lives must run apart—physically though not in thought—during these volcanic years. My duty is to be here and in my heart I've always known it. Perhaps perversity played the greatest part—I wanted to believe that you needed me and missed me—I had begun to doubt both—unreasonably you may say, but there it was—a nasty gnawing thought like a 'worm i' the bud'. I wished to know that you were unhappy and lonely without me—so that we might be miserable together!

Lord—how idiotic and lopsided one can become!

Anyway, I am quite happy again—settled to the task of holding the fort, against all who might threaten it—for it is as you say the rock upon which is founded the unity and strength of our family and our love for each other.

There will come a day when we will be together again and I haven't any longer any doubt of the endurance of our partnership.

Sometimes I wake in the night and lie trembling at the knowledge of what is happening to Russia and with dreadful foreboding for ourselves. We may not love their Bolshevik state—but it is their creation, cruelly earned and now in deadly peril of being fearfully and totally shattered. It must be agony for them—and it might come to us. I toss and turn until sleep is the conqueror. And with morning and the smell of good coffee the Russians recede and England seems as sound as a bell.

With all my love, dearest David—Sybil

21 October 1941 Lisbon

My darling love—We have had no bag in for nine days and I'm beginning to fret for a letter from you. I am in the middle of the wolfram racket, it is most unpleasant, but we must somehow deny such precious stuff to the enemy. I can't exactly tell how badly the Germans want the metal which is now £5,000 per ton against £150 before the war. If *we* paid vast prices for something, you could be sure that the price was a measure of our needs; the Germans on the other hand are very corrupt, and a big part of an inflated price may be due to Goering and other brigands making money for themselves. Our boys in MEW are too theoretical, they look at a lot of figures about previous stocks and rates of consumption, and produce a policy of pre-emption which is sure to bring the German armament industry to a standstill in so many months. But it never does. The calculators forget the elasticity of man under pressure. He substitutes there, he collects old scraps here, and the production v. consumption picture changes completely.

22 October

The other day an isolationist American, passing thro' Lisbon, came to see me. He thought the war was criminal folly. Why didn't we realise that nations rise and fall? We'd had our day. We should depart, as many of us as could go, to Canada, Australia, etc., and leave the UK a barren appendage to a German Europe. I shut off my attention and saw the shape of England, as it is stitched in the sampler over our dining-room sideboard. How I love the arm of Cornwall, the bulge of Norfolk, and there's Wiltshire snug below the centre of gravity! Then I began to see bits of it. The river and St Cross at Winchester, and our fields falling away from the edge of Limmer. What was the American saying? We should abandon England—'Why not? It's only a museum and a cabbage patch.' I didn't argue as I wanted to preserve that warm feeling—*ce souci tendre*—that was half asleep inside, not to wake it into action, but to hug it quietly. He seemed surprised at no reaction. 'Say, can't you put a smile on your face?' 'Why, yes,' say I, 'but I was too grateful to you to be amused, one is so seldom really happy.' I expect he thought me cuckoo.

I love you very much and think of you as often as I go to bed and get up. Kiss the children.

All my love—David

25 October 1941 Lisbon

My darling love—What with work and the travellers who descend upon us I'm out of breath. Attlee[1] came with Arthur Jenkins,[2] a really first-rate miners' MP from Pontypool, Roger [Makins] and an ex-Victoria and Albert secretary. This last fat and trying so hard, just like Leigh,[3] but no attraction, a man of middling virtue and no great scholarship as far as I could tell. Jenkins was a fine fellow. We argued for hours on individual freedom, profits, how to avoid unemployment, etc. I can get on with enthusiasm, however badly supported by knowledge, far better than with profound knowledge if it is unsupported by enthusiasm.

Attlee, the Deputy Prime Minister of the United Kingdom, is a bit of a puzzle. I gave him, Jenkins and Roger dinner on Thursday and had a very good chance to try out the form. He's *tired* and shy and very afraid of making a mistake. Result is that he retires behind a set of clichés that give a dead-alive tone to all he says. (For example: 'I say the people of England want security: security first and very little besides; why, I remember when I was a lad'—all politicians were 'lads', queer, isn't it?—'walking with a girl of twelve and saying, "Well, I must be going home to tea now," and she said, "I must go and see if there is any tea in our home." And that's what security means.')

You have some difficulty to get him away from the public-meeting-in-a-poor-district stuff. I tried him with the lines from Donne's 'Litany',

> From being anxious, or secure,
> . . . Good Lord deliver us.

He said, 'Donne lived in the seventeenth century, that has nothing to do with our days.' That's a pretty poor answer for the Deputy PM. He thawed towards the end of dinner and we had an interesting talk on subversive activity among the French workers, altho' he would interpolate bits from Jaurès and other pre-last-war French Socialists.

He didn't seem to have any love for Dalton, which surprised me; as for Jenkins on the Doctor [Dalton], he was quietly but effectively damning. I don't see where the Trade Union mind and the opportunist Socialist intellectual mind can meet—except in expediency. After dinner, which was very expensive as these great leaders like champagne, Roger hissed in my ear, 'Worth every escudo, jolly good show, valuable, valuable.' What a racket it all is!

Yesterday I had a real treat, compared with which the other visitors described above were dull. Louis Mountbatten walked into my office and said, 'We must have a talk.' We went out to lunch and had three hours without a breath. He's been sent for from the USA, where he had command of the *Illustrious*, to go home for a most exciting job. Last weekend he was staying with Roosevelt, tonight he will be with Winston at Chequers. I'd always heard he was the best of our younger sailors (forty-one), but I never suspected he was quite outstanding on *any* subject. People say complimentary things about semi-royalties to show they know them, and instinctively one discounts such praise. In this case no one had said enough to me. This man *knows* how to fight and *wants* to fight. Does that seem to you pretty trite? It is the first time I've ever met an officer of whom I could say this in the full meaning of 'Knowing how to fight *our* war in the conditions of the world *as it is*, and even *as it may be*, and not always thinking of conditions that are dead.' Admiral James Somerville and Admiral Andrew Cunningham probably 'know how and want to fight', but I have only met the first and he's an operational officer, not a planner. 'Wanting to fight' is rare among staff officers. They take too many courses, they learn, like undergraduates reading philosophy, too many 'buts' and 'ifs', and in the end they do nothing. We are doing nothing today. Mountbatten will change all this. You see. This is an extraordinary man with the *instinct* and the *industry* necessary for modern warfare. He asked me if I would agree that he should ask the PM to get me out of my present job to become his economic adviser. I said he could if he felt that the conduct of the war would benefit. He replied that he had had such write-ups of me as made him suspicious but now he was for it. I pointed out that the Western Mediterranean policy was in a difficult and interesting stage, and as the USG[overnment] had fallen for my idea of a special economic mission to the Peninsula, *I* ought to see this manoeuvre through. He suggested a combination of his job and my present one. We agreed to let Winston decide between the two. I think I must have a very good press in the White House.[4] I certainly hope so, as the American businessmen can hate him as much as they like, but the man 'sittin' on the top of the lid' is the greatest long-range statesman alive today. He said some extraordinarily interesting things about the conduct and outcome of the war to Mountbatten but I can't put them in this letter which I intend to send by safe hand.

I wait eagerly for more account of your social studies. How often do you go to London and what do you do there? Roger said that Rab told him he was very glad to have got hold of you, evidently he was casting about for someone and, quite rightly, saw his chance when I suggested you. I asked Attlee how poor he thought we'd be after the war. He hadn't any idea. He murmured something about so much repair work to do, and when I said, 'Where are the raw materials coming from?' he talked about Australia and New Zealand. There's no particular reason why he should have thought about it, but it is interesting to know for certain that he hasn't.

Mountbatten, of course, wants me to come home as soon as I've done Tangier. That is in a fortnight's time. The Ambassador certainly won't let me go unless superior orders come from London. The only thing I can do is to go straight on, and see if anything turns up. You mustn't get excited. There will be a solid wall of opposition from the upper-middle class of Whitehall.

All my love, dearest Syb. Keep at it, and we shall flourish together.

—David

1. Clement Attlee, Prime Minister 1945–51.
2. Attlee's Parliamentary Private Secretary and father of Roy Jenkins.
3. Sir Leigh Ashton, Director of the Victoria and Albert Museum.
4. Mountbatten afterwards told me that it was Roosevelt and Hopkins who had advised him to get hold of me.

30 October 1941 — The Dorchester Hotel, London

My darling love—The old address and quite a pretty room with green wallpaper and pink covers on alas! two beds. I would always rather they found me a single room, one feels lonelier than ever with that empty second bed. But then in any case I always feel so much farther away from you in London than at Chute—perhaps beds make little difference. Henry Drogheda tells me that you went to Tangier on 27th and should be back in Lisbon by tomorrow—'Though,' he added, in the Henry manner, 'it would never surprise me to learn that he'd been found weeks hence disguised as a Sheik in Fez.'!!

I dined with the Lithibys, we all went to a Spanish restaurant in Barrow Street, and ate a paella that reminded me of the Estudiante at Alcala de Henares. Moules in it, too—but happily no ill effects. Oh! it was cold as January but there was comfort in the thought that those damn Germans must be a whole lot colder.

Darling—I love you all the time and think of you and long for the moment when I see you again.

—Sybil

30 October 1941 Tangier

My darling love—Didn't I once describe Tangier as blue and white, fresh as a clean sailor-suit? It is just so today. The enamelled waters of the Mediterranean glide between the Rock and Africa into the wide arms of a sleepy Atlantic. There are sea-lanes in plenty, curving paths of a lighter blue, and above them a few dazzling gulls dipping and twisting in the clear sunlight. I'm in the garden, under a fir tree, all is quiet and faintly smelling of herbs. Dragonflies stab the air without noise, and a mouse has run three times along the wall and back again.

If in after years we take an October holiday let us come here; only never to work. At great heights men's lungs and hearts fail them, so in Tangier by some iron rule of our nature, their kindness and common sense wilt and give place to unbelievable jealousy and stupidity.

A tragedy is being played here by the British, American, French and Spanish officials, all of whom, I suppose, long for a Christian world at peace. So great a common desire should lead at least the first two to work in harmony, and both of them to try hard to get on with the others. Instead there is a passionate attempt by the Americans to get on with the French, to the point of base appeasement, a corresponding hatred of the Spaniards by the Americans, and no close contact or mutual confidence between the Americans and ourselves. Whose fault is this? Tangier's, I say. It is in the air they breathe and poisons their dreams at night. And it is so obvious that busybodies arrive from Gibraltar and try, behind Gascoigne's[1] back, to 'put things right'. And then occur hopeless confusion and lamentable indiscretions. The busybodies are reprimanded, much as you punish a housemaid who pinches a little cash from a guest who always leaves a pile of silver on his dressing-table. Good Mr Gascoigne leaves the political cash about and outsiders come, and, very wrongly but rather naturally, pick it up.

Once in Tangier you fight to keep your mind clean and your emotions quiet. If one stands aside and looks coldly at the human forces at play the complexity of the material and of the interests— of the Americans, who want to dominate French Africa without fighting, and with complete disregard of the Spaniards; of the French who want to keep their empire without further material loss; of the Spaniards who have aspirations to control and misgovern more of Morocco at the expense of the French; of the Arabs who want to be rid of all Europeans and to run their country for themselves; of the Germans who work ceaselessly to corrupt the French, the Spaniards and the Arabs, setting them all against each other so that Germany may take over North Africa with no organised resistance; and of ourselves who should have no object but to beat the Germans and should contrive not to appear to have any other object . . . all this hotch-potch surges and bubbles and occasionally spits out of the pot. A very strong character and a very nimble brain are required to watch and taste and pull the best out of such a stew.

4 November

Murphy has been with me for four days, invaluable and pleasant days. If only we could be together in French Africa how well we should run the campaign. He believes in Weygand; and even if he didn't he would have to act as tho' he did to have any chance of success in stimulating the old gentleman to resist the Germans. They don't see this at home. The material (human nature is fundamentally bad) and the spiritual (human nature is fundamentally good) ways of handling people always conflict. After 1918 it was open to us either to try to make Germany *incapable* of fighting or *unwilling* to fight again. We tried both and failed at both. The same thing in North Africa, you must either give Weygand a chance to come over to us, e.g. give him some supplies on tick, or blockade and attack him with guns and aircraft. The middle course is fatal. It is true that every time we act ungenerously towards him we may avoid a danger, e.g. petrol falling into the hands of the enemy, but we also lose an opportunity. I am on the side of opportunity and against danger. One must gamble resolutely, and if with enough resolution then we shall win through.

I have no more time, the bag goes back to Lisbon so soon. I love you very much and think of you always.

All my love—David

I expect I shall spend the weekend with Gort.[2]

1. HM Consul-General in Tangier.
2. Lord Gort, VC, Governor of Gibraltar.

9 November 1941

The White Lion,
Upton-on-Severn

My dearest love—The Sykes and I left Chute on Friday before tea time and travelled slowly, from respect to the dwindling petrol ration (8 gallons now) through the deepening sunset and the hills and valleys of the west to Worcester.

We found our sons waiting anxiously in the drive—if one is a second late they smell disappointment or disaster. Away we went for our picnic—built a fire, fried bacon, eggs and chips. The boys, who looked blooming, consumed incredible quantities of fruit salad, cheese, shortbreads, chocolate, sausage rolls and orangeade and at 1.30 we dashed back to prepare for the first of the school plays. There were four of these. John took the lead as Mr Pepys in *The Fire of London* and was astonishingly good as that bumptious, overbearing and dogmatic individual. He was completely disguised in a gigantic wig and elaborate brocade coat and I shouldn't have recognised him apart from his voice. Afterwards when I congratulated him he said, 'You see, that's the only sort of part I'd be good at—I'm only any use at ordering people about.'

Chapel this morning at half past ten. We thundered our psalm and prayed with vigour—the hymns swing along and the choir sang a descant most beautifully—then we rose to 'God Save the King' and departed to criticise and admire the art exhibition in the gym. 'Mummie, look, that's a still-life by Graham senior,' the voice drops to a whisper of awe and incredulity—'He's going into *oils.*'

Off we went in the car once more to a very decent pub in Ludlow where they produced the best roast beef anyone had tasted for months and larger lumps of butter than appeared seemly. But as Frank observed, 'We're very far west—and in the west they don't hold with rationing.'

Back to tea—most delicious—with a fine home-made currant bun of phenomenal softness and size. We had a sitting-room to ourselves with a bow window hung with lace curtains and overlooking the tumbling river where some white swans flirted among the rising trout. The fire was warm, the chocolates seductive and it was hard to go in time back to chapel at 6.30. The boys grow rather subdued as the miles diminish but they are much happier now than when we used to leave them. The harsh apprenticeship is over—at half term we now return a pair of veterans—lordlings who view with cold and distant eye the red-nosed snivelling of the smaller fry—who at the dark and cold back door bury their mournful faces in their mothers' coats and play the part our own sons played a year ago.

Dear John—I love to see him at school in the world he has had to make for himself and where I have played no part—I see him in flashes as a stranger and then can judge him fairly to be a good chap.

Oh! I do hope it won't be long before you can come too and we can share it together.

—Sybil

10 November 1941 Gibraltar

My darling love—Lord Gort is just what I expected, bustling, attractive, strict and unhappy. Intensely interested in the political side of Mediterranean strategy, chafing at the lack of direction from home, suspicious of Sam's 'appeasement', he welcomed the chance to get hold of me and try to knock out something definite in the way of plans. He had my hero, Admiral Jimmy Somerville, waiting here for a staff talk, and directly after lunch on Saturday we settled down to four hours without drawing breath. We are all agreed that a definite line of action should be taken in North Africa and on what that line should be. How satisfactory that is! To find generals and admirals willing and anxious to go ahead on a straight course. Nothing will happen, we feel certain London will turn everything down as usual. The ABC is always the same. To beat us the Germans must strike south on the Narvic-Cape Town line; our empire defence is east and west along the Mediterranean. The enemy may have gone off east now but that is only to be free to go south later. On the other hand we can only get back at him from our east-west base, the north shore of Africa; besides, as Gort neatly puts it, the fish always dies from the tail, kill him in Libya and then in Italy and the gangrene will mortify upwards into his heart. I wish I could write to you in detail.

There are some new faces here, Admiral Sir E. Collins and Major-General Sir C. Jardine, both very good chaps. Who, as Dr Johnson might have said, does not relish the company of commanding officers? After diplomats, what a healthy change, and how readily they listen and how honestly they explain their difficulties and objections! If I'd been in uniform during this war I could never meet these men as equals, the lounge suit is the only passport.

I went to church with Gort this morning. Just as he enters the door an ADC hands him a pound to be put in the plate, a regular institution which amused me very much. The service was like chapel at Winchester, appalling hymns about the empire, 'ruling pine and palm', 'the lesser races of the heathen'. Very good army prayers, not a bad sermon on the Epistle to the Hebrews, and tempestuous singing, no good the organist piping down in the melancholy verse of 'O God our help in ages past', the men wouldn't have it, they went on roaring away like a football match; some of the choir winked at their comrades in the gallery (officers in the stalls, other ranks aloft), just like school.

Afterwards I went and drank sherry in a mess. One flight-lieutenant, about twenty, wound himself up and said to me, 'I say, sir, you know everything, sir, at least that's what I'm told, sir, how long is the war going to last?' Deadly serious he was, so I didn't like to be too flippant. 'Well, what do you think? Not less than one and not more than two years?' 'Two years . . .' long pause . . . 'I see, two years, well, I can't hope to last two years, can I? We lose 5 per cent a month, you know. Oh well, anyhow I've nothing much to look forward to, still, I would have liked to see it through.'

(Apparently his calculation is correct; he can't hope to last two years.) It makes you think.

If Gort, after all he went through at the hands of the French last year,[1] can still have hope in Weygand, and still press me to pursue our policy of cajolery and confidence in him, then it makes the vindictive little men in London look pretty cheap. The war teaches you more and more that the man who sits in his Whitehall office loses his sense of proportion and is far inferior in judgement to the man in the field; only the knowledge of all the factors in the situation is usually denied to the man in the field, therefore he seems to make silly recommendations because he is partially in the dark, but the instrument which he applies to the facts at his disposal is far superior to the Whitehall instrument.

Tomorrow I go by car to Seville and the next day from there to Lisbon, in time, I hope, to avoid the revolution in the Spanish Government which we all think inevitable. Franco and Suñer are done. That is my conviction. Will the generals be any better? We shall see but from the British point of view it is by no means sure.

All my love, sweet Syb—David

1. Lord Gort had commanded the British Forces in France.

Letter from Robert Murphy to DE in Lisbon

13 November 1941 American Consulate, Algiers

Dear David—On my return from my brief, pleasurable and instructive visit with you at Tangier, I have had the additional pleasure of reading your letter of 16 October, enclosing yours of 13 October to Wallace Murray.[1] I congratulate you on the clarity of your exposition as well as on your treatment of the subject matter.

I have had opportunity since my return to talk about these matters with General Weygand and his assistants. I am very much encouraged that progress along these lines may be possible. I have no authority to advance any views as to Peninsular participation[2] in the North African plan because I have no indication whatever from Washington as to their wishes. However, I shall hope to have news soon.

The present moment has a good deal of touch and go in it, but there is little novelty in that.

It was grand seeing you.

Sincerely yours—Bob

1. Wallace Murray was in charge of Africa in the State Department.
2. I had suggested triangular trade between Spain, Portugal and her colonies, and French North Africa.

Begun 15 November 1941 Lisbon

My darling love—I wrote from Gibraltar to you an account of conversation with a pilot from the *Ark Royal* who was calculating his chances of survival, I hope he's safe. She was a fine ship with a big legend. Jimmy Somerville didn't want to go out on that expedition, he was as nervous as a cat before he started.[1]

Here in Lisbon is a man Burckhardt, who was League of Nations High Commissioner of Danzig.[2] A very agreeable Switzer. A few weeks ago he was in Berlin dining in the company of a German general, who began to abuse the Swiss press for articles unsympathetic to the Nazis. B said nothing. The General grew angry, in a few months these dirty little scribblers would be put up against a wall then B would see what snivelling little rats they were. No answer from B. 'What,' said the General, 'you don't even defend yourself, you haven't a word to say!' B replied that he was wondering what would have happened in 1919 if the Swiss press had been unfriendly to England, would any British general have bothered to raise a finger in protest? A long pause. The German snapped out, 'You're right. We're bloody provincials.'

B also dined with Bernsdorf and four other old German diplomats. After dinner they watched an air raid on Berlin. In an interval of quiet the five of them agreed, 'We wish we were dead: there is nothing to live for.'

The Portuguese press published in huge headlines a statement by Brendan[3] that a convoy of a hundred ships had arrived in the UK and that such an event was worth more than any victory in Libya. I wonder if he really said it. Such a disastrous effort is unlike him. Here the reaction was awful, what it must have been like in North Africa I dare not imagine. Whether he did say it or not, consider the implications:

(a) we are starving and must have imports above everything else. So the Battle of the Atlantic is not going well;
(b) we are so soft we prefer imports to victories, full shelves to captured positions. This is an appalling line to take.

Think of the effect on the Arabs. (Of course he may think he was bluffing the enemy that we aren't going to attack.) Mountbatten wrote me a very acceptable letter after he had been back a few days. We shall see more of him and I'm sure he's a winner. I would like to have watched him read a statement like the one I quoted above. He would be wild.

It is hard to explain the steady increase of German influence, economic and political, here in the last four months at a time when their chances of winning the war have been patently upset by the Russian resistance. The answer may be as follows: first, the Portuguese fear invasion much less than they did and they calculate that Germany, even if victorious, will satisfy her territorial ambitions in the east, leaving the western fringe of Europe alone—this lessens the hatred of the Nazis and puts the Portuguese off their guard; second, now that the Russian leak in the Blockade is closed the Germans are much more anxious to buy at any price Portuguese products, and are distributing here every week larger and larger sums. The Portuguese are beguiled by such easy profits. Third, the Germans have torpedoed one Portuguese ship and threatened to sink the lot if the Portuguese Government don't behave tamely. The PG haven't got a navy fit to convoy their ships so what can they do? If they were clever (and indeed also honest) they would ask us, their ally, if they should declare war on Germany. This would put us in a hole, as Portuguese neutrality has advantages.

If the Americans will play with us now in full partnership we can produce an economic campaign in the Western Mediterranean that will greatly embarrass the enemy and will, I think, enable us to occupy all the key positions before the shooting begins in this area.

No answer yet to my request to come home. I don't think they want to be worried about North Africa. Opportunism is our policy and we shall muddle through as usual. We shall always be fools and the Germans will never be gents. In the immediate future the key is in Libya, if that door is opened you will see astonishing results.

All my love, my dear sweet, I wish so much we were in peace and at home.

—David

1. The *Ark Royal* was sunk on 12 November.
2. Dr Carl Burckhardt was in Danzig at the time of the German attack on Poland.
3. Brendan Bracken, Minister of Information.

19 November 1941 Lisbon

My darling love—Attlee was here again on Monday. He wants to like me. He finds it difficult, but his miner-MP PPS[1] has no inhibitions. We get on a treat. I want to be at home with the political ball in play. This foreign service is a hothouse affair; unreal and I chafe exceedingly.

Definite news about Weygand.[2] At least he behaved like a gentleman and refused to give the enemy the use of the Tunisian ports (the cranes in Tripoli are all bust and you can't unload tanks without cranes). I always said W was a gentleman. He wouldn't resign. He had to be pushed out by a band of traitors who will swing from lamp posts when the Paris mob gets at them. My chances of getting home are now nil and I must settle down to work in the Peninsula. I shall spend a week with Sam who most affectionately bids me stay with him and Maud, and then I shall go back to Gibraltar and talk again to the soldiers and sailors. It will take me a few days to get over Weygand. We had a good man for the asking but we hadn't the courage to ask, and now it is too late. My dear love, it is hard to be so disappointed but I shall get over it. I am nearly always alone against HMG and being proved right in the event is such a miserable consolation. Now we must pray for success in Libya and that if our men arrive on the Tunisian border they will be able to patch up some arrangement with Juin,[3] or whoever is in command, and go right on to Morocco. If W had been there they would have had a royal welcome.

All my love—David

You haven't cut your hair, have you? I dreamed it and woke shivering.

1. Arthur Jenkins.
2. Pétain was forced by the Germans to dismiss him.
3. General Juin was thought most likely to succeed Weygand.

19 November 1941 Chute

My darling love—After a long silence—letters from you have been pouring from the postman's bag.

Beside the fire last night I had the news of Vichy's dissatisfaction with Weygand—and this makes me hope that Gort, yourself and those few others who are perceptive enough and brave enough to struggle still for the old man's friendship and confidence are justified in your belief that his courage and resolution may yet be revived. Surely this North African campaign will provide you with something to argue with? Weygand must be wavering, if only ever so slightly—or the Germans wouldn't be bullying Vichy about him.

The Americans sound disappointing—no concerted action in North Africa. Perhaps the British can now carve out some propaganda and policy of their own on the basis of having taken the military initiative—which in war should give one the right to call a tune or two, even if the Americans are in the audience.

With all my love—Sybil

VI

Lisbon Again

January–August 1942

6. Lisbon Again

Towards the end of November 1941 I returned to London. The Peninsula was behind me. I was well satisfied to settle down in London as head of the new Pre-Emption Section of MEW. The objective was to outwit the Germans in the scramble to buy up strategic goods in neutral countries from which exports to the enemy were possible. HMG had not been very clever at this costly, at times unsavoury, business. We needed a strong organisation to harmonise both the departmental interests in Whitehall and our own purchases with whatever help the Americans, who had come into the war on 10 December, were willing to give us. I had collected an enthusiastic staff, who were coming to grips with priorities and markets when the wolfram[1] negotiations in Portugal turned sour. The Treasury, who had to provide more and more money to pay for the metal, demanded that I should be sent out to retrieve the position. The Embassy in Lisbon moaned about Dr Salazar's bloody-mindedness but thought he might listen to Mr Eccles. The Foreign Office agreed, I gave in and Sybil was very much upset.

1. Wolfram was a metal used to harden steel against bullets: it was used in the making of tanks and other weapons of war.

Letter from Sir Samuel Hoare to DE in London

16 January 1942 British Embassy, Madrid

Dear David—With your knowledge of what has been going on in Washington you can well imagine our local difficulties here. At last, after months of delay, the State Department have sent Weddell[1] their memorandum.[2] You will, however, see by the telegrams that we have immediately sent to London that we consider that it is a most unsatisfactory document. It is based upon the entirely erroneous conception that the Spanish problem is an economic problem and that we are supplying Spain with goods in order to get back Spanish goods in return. No doubt we want Spanish goods and we will do our best to get them. The real justification for supplying Spain with the necessities of life is not, however, economic but strategic. London has sent both Washington and us excellent strategic appreciations of the position, but it seems to me as if none of our people in Washington have ever told the real story to the State Department. I cannot imagine why Halifax has not himself taken it up with Roosevelt. As it is we must endure constant delays and misunderstandings. The only way to remove them is continuous insistence upon the strategic needs of the war. It is certainly a strange turn of the wheel that has now made the Ministry of Economic Warfare our best friend. It shows that Dalton and yourselves are vigorously attempting to keep our policy a realist policy. For all this I am most grateful to him and you.

It would be a tragedy now if for economic reasons things went wrong in Spain. Anti-German feeling is everywhere increasing, the opposition to entry into war is almost unanimous while Suñer and the Falange are becoming every day more unpopular. The tide will go on running in our favour provided we do not have a European catastrophe in the war and provided most of all that we do not give our enemies the chance of saying that we are starving Spain. These are truisms to you and me, but it seems that they need repeating several times every day of the week.

As to your own affairs, I fear that we must regretfully abandon the hope of seeing you back here in the near future. Might it not, however, be a good thing before you take up your new and important post[3] to come here for a short visit to check things up? Our purchases here will inevitably become more difficult in the face of German threats to sink Spanish ships trading with enemy countries and there is now added the complication of greater American purchases. This being so, I think that it would be a very good thing if you could come here for a few days and assess the position upon the spot.

Let me now end by sending you my best wishes for the New Year and my thanks for all that you have done for this mission in the past.

Yours—Samuel Hoare

1. US Ambassador in Madrid. Hoare did not get on well with him.
2. As far as I can recollect this US paper suggested we should do barter with Spain and allow nothing through the Blockade that was not matched by our purchases in Spain.
3. As head of the Pre-Emption Section of MEW.

5 February 1942 Lisbon

My darling love—I think every few hours of you and clutch at my conscience because I am not writing to you, but this place is a pandemonium. I have on my hands our wolfram negotiations, the USA's wolfram negotiations, our own tin requirements, the Spaniards' tripartite negotiations for tin with Portugal and with us, the tripartite negotiations between France, Portugal and ourselves for the release of French oil tankers for Portugal, a desperate bid to get the French to put their merchant ships outside the Mediterranean before the Germans requisition them, all these and a dozen internal worries; B's girl who is to be sacked, the wickedness and body-odour of our new registrar, the inhumanity of the chief statistician, the arrest of fifty pigs which were being sent from Portugal to the Governor of Gibraltar, a bad gaffe in Madrid—it is awful to be plunged again in such a stew. I used to like it. I still enjoy negotiating with ministers and ambassadors, but the office work here is wretched compared to London, where I must be as soon as I can. I shall have to go to Madrid, but only for two or three days, probably at the end of the week.

I wonder what you are doing. I do want you to be satisfied with your life. It is yours and I fully recognise is not just an annexe of mine. This has always been my view. You should have your own results and not live or wilt by my efforts. The children are of course a huge result of a kind that I can only love, but not approach.

It is strange to have orange juice for breakfast and a pile of butter balls on the tray, and to see the shops crammed with fruit and asparagus. The last you would love.

Events in the Pacific and Libya have shaken Peninsular faith in our victory. This is a curse as we need to extract more from the Portuguese than before. Ronnie[1] did marvellously over Timor[2] and only got a belated and grudging pat from the FO. He is upset. Gratitude is so easy that I always marvel at the scarcity. Sam howls from Madrid. He is extraordinarily persistent, making one of his staff call me up daily. I shall succumb.

Here the most frightful scandals. Everyone sleeping with everyone else and being catty about the others. What a nuisance sex is! Why can't we mind less? I mind very much, but I also see the point of celibacy. Only as Saint Augustine says you can't withdraw from the world, instead of acts you have horrible imaginings which are too revolting to contemplate.

I love you very much and count the days to my return. Kiss the creatures.

All my love, dear sweet Syb—David

1. Sir Ronald Campbell.
2. We were unable to help the Portuguese defend Timor against seizure by the Japanese.

7 February 1942 Lisbon

My darling love—Time is so short that I send you a copy of a letter I have dictated to Jack Troutbeck[1] to amuse him about the wolfram negotiations. I'm enjoying the mêlée now that the issue is fairly joined and I have Washington and the little twerps here lined up for battle. The preparation of a big negotiation, the assigning of rôles to each member of the side, the prevention of crossed wires, the multiplication of effect by combining two unlikely people as allies, this is the fun of the business and I'm such a pro now that I revel in it like Diaghilev must have revelled in a new ballet. It's extraordinary how quickly experience builds up into a sort of rule-of-thumb by which you can judge in a second the value of this or that move. I wish I had Father Joseph's gift of 'ravishing conversation', then indeed the end would be in sight and the wolfram as good as on shipboard. Today we are lying low after the American *démarche* of yesterday and the sweetest of notes from HE to the Minister of Economy last night.

I had a huge go at the French this morning to try to persuade them to put their oil tankers outside the Mediterranean before the Germans grab them; which they surely will if the French are so silly as to leave them lying about like cash in a hotel bedroom. I tried my old line that ships are in the English bloodstream and that whatever else the French may give to the Germans they must stop short of ships or there'll be an explosion in London. Conversely, if they put their tankers out of reach in a West African port, our joy will be immense and an atmosphere most favourable will be created for future negotiations. It went pretty well and they have sent Vichy a hot telegram.

All my love, sweet—David

1. At the MEW in London.

7 February 1942 Lisbon

Dear Jack—The wolfram negotiation is settling down to the classic pattern which has been found most likely to succeed. Discussions with the Minister of Economy had begun without adequate preparation in other official quarters. I believe in an approach from all sides at once, and in finding a different point to rub in through the Ministry of Foreign Affairs, the Minister of Economy's secretary, the Head of the Mines Department, the Minister of the Colonies who has a finger in every pie, the US Legation, etc. All these people are now converging with their separate and different titbits on Salazar. We must not enter the final round until we are ninety per cent sure of winning.

The Ambassador and I play a duet, my foot on the loud and his on the soft pedal. I bludgeon and he poultices. He has a beautiful line, to be recommended in all discussions between a big power and his little ally. 'We are friends. In the course of friendship one friend has often more need of the other's help than vice versa, but time passes, and as surely the rôles are reversed, and he who gave must now ask. We now ask you, Portugal, for a trifle of wolfram; the day will come, who knows how soon, when you will be asking us for much more than a few tons of concentrates.' Our eyes glisten, and our voices choke. It is so blessed to give. But then if that does not succeed, we have to threaten, and I have to do the threatening, the scourge is come temporarily from London, the sympathetic ambassador is here for good. I don't exactly say, 'If you give your wolfram to the enemy, we shall cut off your oil.' I put it rather, that if we do not get as much wolfram as hitherto, an atmosphere will be created in London and Washington so unfavourable that it will be useless to discuss other economic questions for many a day. After I've been particularly tough, I make the Ambassador send a charming note by hand to the Minister regretting our differences of opinion and appealing to the ups and downs of a centuries-old alliance. It's too moving.

The game has some funny moments. And none better than the thought of 'my staff working late into the night' in Washington, and the Viscount penning wolframic messages to Mr Hull, and all the time the US Legation here incapable of understanding a word of their instructions, bewildered, begging us to draft for them, Mr Fish[1] seizing his telephone 'to give Ron a buzz' (i.e. to call up HM Ambassador), the Counsellor[2] reminding him that 'speech is not secret', the Minister saying, 'But hell, if I can't understand it, how can the boys listening on the wire?' The Counsellor: 'Sir Ronald will understand it, though;' the Minister: 'I guess he won't, but he'll sound as though he does.' This buffoonery goes on all the time, and if we work late at night in Lisbon it is certainly not wolfram that engages our attention.

Yours ever—David

1. Bert Fish, American Minister to Portugal.
2. The Counsellor at the American Legation.

Letter from General Lord Gort, VC

14 February 1942 Government House, Gibraltar

My dear Eccles—Thank you so much for your letter and enclosures which I have read with much interest.

That you had little luck in pressing the views we discussed when you returned to London is rather dispiriting. We are woefully late starters in this war and I agree with you that we may live to regret our failure to formulate and carry through a constructive policy in French North Africa.

If you have an opportunity to come this way once again before you go home for good I should be delighted to see you at Government House.

Yours sincerely—Gort

14 February 1942 Chute

David darling—Our fortunes are at a low ebb, aren't they?

A young New Zealander was here today and it was sad to see how little faith he had in England behind his good and pleasant manners.

Singapore,[1] Libya[2]—you can put them down to 'supplies'—anything you fancy. But the battleships[3] sailing unharmed past our front door—oh! that was a knock-out.

The PM has done his best this evening. But it doesn't quite go. The hardships—the disappointments and the dangers that we must undergo because of our unpreparedness, the defection of an ally,[4] the needs of our other friends—these can be readily understood and accepted. But willy nilly, doubts of another kind creep in to fill one with disquiet.

The PM is a giant, but not a colossus. He needs some inspiration to revitalise and renew his own great powers. Yet he seems to reject any search for the men who might supply it. It looks as though Stafford Cripps[5] has played his cards well in staying out for a bit. What is the betting that he will come in with a rush presently when the PM has to throw the hungry pack another bun?

Your stories are good. Wolfram by day and fornication by night—your colleagues must eclipse in gallantry all other competitors in Dr Salazar's raffish capital.

Much love, dear David—Sybil

1. Singapore fell on 15 February and 60,000 surrendered.
2. Rommel recaptured Benghazi and Tobruk.

3. *Scharnhorst* and *Gneisenau*, the German battleships, sailed up the Channel despite British air attacks.
4. Siam (Thailand).
5. Brought back from being British Ambassador in Moscow and made Leader of the House of Commons and Lord Privy Seal.

13 February 1942 Lisbon

My darling love—All day I have resisted invitations to dinner because I wanted to write you a letter that has been generating in my mind, and now I have finished my first meal alone since I left England. Omelette, braised ham and mashed bananas with cream!

Ought I to stay in Lisbon for the rest of the war? I never wanted to and now I shudder at the idea but—

(a) the Ambassador is not well, terribly overworked, and he leans on me for advice of every kind;

(b) the Commercial staff, always a make-shift, is now patently inadequate: negotiations are more difficult, the Americans are with us now, untrained and flat-footed partners, *X* . . . is weakened by his love affair, the Consulate and United Kingdom Commercial Corporation are more than ever out of hand;

(c) Spain has a remarkable ambassador in Don Nicolas Franco, from whom we can derive many advantages but he won't open his heart to anyone but me;

(d) in a real crisis—and we shall have many—I can always exercise an influence over Salazar. If the Ambassador were sick or away this would become of great importance;

(e) in Lisbon we can rebuild our relations with France; and, believe it or not, I have now a unique and recognised position with the French. High and low they come to *le jeune M Eccles qui a tant de sympathie pour notre pays souffrant.* Yesterday the French Minister said he told Darlan that I wanted the French to put their tankers outside the Mediterranean, because he thought it would impress the Admiral.

The last reason for staying here is the only one that touches my heart, and, wounded though it is, I have decided not to give in, and not to fill a post which dumbly—because all these people look on fascinated and in silence—they want me to accept.

In MEW there is no adoration, very little applause and much

opposition. But it is England. And the time has come to leave the flowers of a foreign mission for the jungle at home. It is a great searching of heart but it is right because the will and capacity to win the war among our own people need stiffening.

MEW will not allow the French to export to the US French books even though they will send none printed after the Armistice. The reasons are (a) that the French would acquire some dollars; (b) that they fear some propaganda would be included. I think this is monstrous. Are we to cut off the study of French civilisation? Are we to run Europe after the war with the Americans ignorant of the culture she developed? These offensive details of the Blockade make me mad, and I am ashamed of our mean and degrading folly. What is the life we are fighting to preserve? How can we 'degenerate so from the natural dignity of man'?

Darling Syb, I imagine you digging and delving and mending and perhaps reading a little. The war is bleeding us. We are losing some of our strength, but not at the same rate, nothing like it, as the enemy. You are my strength to whom I will return as soon as I possibly can.

All my love—David

Begun 17 February Lisbon

My darling love—I didn't tell you in my last letter that the negotiations couldn't be going worse—on the surface—the Minister of Economy is as obstinate as a mule and he will not budge an inch. I find it difficult to gauge how much of their intransigence is due to Portuguese bloody-mindedness—their natural obstinacy, and passion for legalistic formulae behind which they shelter their tuppenny-halfpenny pride and weaknesses—and how much to direct German pressure or even to a desire among certain official elements to pay us out for Timor and to give the enemy a bouquet. All these elements enter in. The last is not negligible. The Latin races of Europe are terrified of Communism and now they freely talk of the necessity to save European civilisation from the Bolshevik deluge. They welcomed the attack on Russia because they thought we should win the war anyhow and the Germans were giving the world an extra bonus by knocking out the USSR *en route* to their own defeat. Now they see the Russian menace as worse than the weakened German menace, and you must remember that the Spaniards *were actually* fighting Bolsheviks on their own soil only three years ago, and that the Axis and Portugal helped the Spaniards to overcome the Russian attack. Now the rôles are reversed, and the Axis is in mortal danger from the Russians; it is therefore not surprising that there should be a wave of sympathy for the Germans, who in their plight do not look nearly as odious as they did in their flush of unbroken successes. The way to handle this situation is to show the Latin races—France, Spain and Portugal—where their advantage lies, to disabuse their minds of the idea that we are going Bolshevik and very firmly to announce that we are picking up sides and they must choose between us. If you look at the map of the world, and imagine it coloured black for the enemy, red for us, and white for the undecided, you will, I think, see that Turkey should be pink, Sweden and Switzerland grey, and that only the Peninsula, France and the French Empire have any claims to be white (certain South American countries are pink). This means that the object of our diplomacy—i.e. the white part—is very small and it is therefore a mystery why we do not bend every effort on this comparatively modest problem, modest I mean from the point of view of the number of decisions to be taken and the personnel to be picked to carry them out. I shall never understand how we can be content to criticise the French instead of trying to construct a new France on our side, and I know with absolute certainty that the history books will be terribly hard on us for our inaction.

19 February

Now the Japanese have attacked Timor and anything can happen. One always thinks of the worst—namely that the Japs shall overcome our wretched little force and then hand Timor back to the Portuguese. The position of the Portuguese troopship now on its way with troops to relieve our force would be comic if it weren't so serious. I should like to hear the conversation among the brave officers and men when they know the Japs are in Timor already. I think the vessel will develop engine trouble. Perhaps all the senior officers will stumble on each other in the dark bowel of the ship, with spanners in their hands, ready to throw them into the turbines.

There is some chance of a safe hand. I will shut this letter, if this chance is not realised I'll write another as well. I love you very much and am comfortless and uneasy and want you very badly.

All my love—David

26 February 1942 Chute

My dearest love—I experienced a dreadful pang at the first sentences of your letter [of 13 February] where you consider staying in Lisbon for the rest of the war. I read on in haste and uneasiness and found solace over the page.

Of course I think of ourselves a little (women, you once told me are like good pears—and good pears aren't good without a little sun to warm them) but I also think of your future and the place at home that you should take before long.

I'm perfectly convinced that some are right to prefer the hazards and the rivals in the Derby to the awestruck competitors of the Pony race who, mesmerised and humble, would be half inclined to hand you the stakes before the flag went down. Even in the few weeks that have passed since your departure the tempo and the temper have changed at home. One has quickened, the other has hardened. This process I am certain will go on. I see it—at a later stage—flinging down the old barriers that so often in the past have impeded progress and discouraged initiative—and across the gap will vault the owners of untried and vigorous minds to take up the challenge. I would like to see you in that advance. And if you come home, you'll surely be there.

There are sour looks, yellow eyes and little praise at MEW—but these are directed at you by the Old Guard—not necessarily old in years but prehistoric in prejudice and thin-blooded from the meagre diet of timid tradition upon which they have been raised. The country is getting wise to these blokes, as Mason would say. Poor things, they've done their best—they haven't really understood—and neither have the rest of us. But the people are cruel when they are frightened and there will have to be a Whipping Boy.

You have a new Master[1]—I know nothing of him—do you?

The Andover Council have given me a job with the new Nursery School for young children of factory workers and it's thought wise to go to London and see several others at work. So off I go—with a full programme. I hope I'll be able to make it enough of a job—if not I shall chuck it and look again.

My very dear David, I wonder about and dream for you, love and long to see you and hear your voice again.

—Sybil

1. The third Earl of Selborne was now Minister of Economic Warfare in place of Hugh Dalton. As Viscount Wolmer he had been Parliamentary Secretary to the Board of Trade 1922–4 and director of cement, Ministry of Works 1940–2.

26–28 February 1942 Lisbon

My darling love—Here I live very simply on about £1 a day which covers the running expenses of the flat including washing, water, telephone, wine and spirits. Not bad, I think. I wake up at eight, having slept like a top. Shave, get back to bed, orange juice, a biscuit, the New Testament and the Portuguese papers. Dress at 9.15, go to the Embassy at 9.45, after inspecting the household books. You'd laugh, but I make quite a show of interest. Lunch out most days. Today with Winant. How magic is contact with a great man! We had lunch quietly and then went to Queluz[1] and walked for two hours round the gardens and woods. There is about Winant a simplicity and a directness that is cool and clear as running water, purifying what it touches and leaving everything better than it was. Much of what I shall tell you of his conversation is, of course, only for you.

He was one of the PM's[2] critics. He felt that the PM didn't understand the weight of the public's uneasiness and he, Winant, wanted Oliver[3] back more than anyone. Apparently the Beaver[4] blew hot and cold three times, first he said he would take the job but only if he could sack anyone anywhere; the PM refused; Beaver said, 'OK, I go'; then he said he wanted to stay in some other capacity; then he said he was too sick to stay; then he was quite all right. Finally they got fed up with him.

We had a huge talk about France and the occupied territories. I explained how the western fringe of Europe was trying to make both ends meet inside the Blockade by taking in each other's washing, and by doing some barter trade with the Peninsula; and how if the war lasted some years—it certainly will, said Winant—these improvised exchanges might yield a stabilised level of life, very low but enough, and that the people concerned might adapt themselves to this humble existence, forgetting the need to win the war. This was a tendency in being. What ought we to do about it? Encourage it, let it alone, or attack it? Certainly not the second. Then it must be (a) or (c) and we must make up our policy and act vigorously and go through with it to the end.

Winant was deeply interested. He saw at once that the crucial question is the effect on the morale of the working classes of pursuing either (a) or (c). Dalton, he said, had always failed to understand human values, and his policy had come near to being a disaster. This was a surprisingly strong attitude for Winant to take. He agreed with me that there is a real danger of drifting into peace, if we allow the occupied territories to tie in their economies too successfully. Why fight any more? You see how appallingly difficult it is to decide. Do we make men our friends and ready to fight again by helping them with their daily life, or should we set brother against brother and see children die that a residue of desperate fanatics might murder our enemies on dark nights? Tell me, darling, what you think.

Winant said, 'I like your dependable inspiration; they liked it back home; they liked it in the White House, and I will speak to Mr Roosevelt of what you say.' I found that a most endearing compliment and was vain and very pleased.

We talked of Pétain. Winant feels he is an obstacle to the revival of France. An old matriarch who keeps her sons under. They look to him, vaguely trustful, and do not make the effort to face the truth about themselves. They are a generation looking for a sign but no sign shall be given, and it is Pétain who gives them their misplaced faith in miracles. I stuck up for the Marshal as usual. 'Yes, yes,' said W, 'the trouble is the old man is admirable in his unsuitable way.' Just now the Japanese successes and our precarious position in Libya have profoundly modified the Continent's betting in the race, and there are in France a big bunch of pessimists who feel we can never win. If only I had been to Vichy! With what authority I could now put forward a policy!

Oliver will be here tomorrow and I shall have much to tell him. Winant said the only person in England who wanted Oliver in the War Cabinet at home more than he did himself was Dame Edith![5]

'What a grand old person she is!' he exclaimed, but he knew that women are braver than men in this war; without a doubt; they help British airmen to escape from France and Belgium, going against the prudent wishes of their men at the risk of their lives; in England too Winant prefers the female to the male gut, and why is this so? Because men are over-educated and their natural reactions are braked by too much thinking as a result of an education of scepticism, faithless and selfish; whereas you, you poor females, who have untutored instincts instead of trained minds, smell right from wrong and act at once instead of calculating the advantages. Sound stuff, I thought, and based on the idea that the natural man is good. Winant believes this, but thinks that in the last twenty years the Anglo-Saxon race have greatly overestimated the virtue of our generation, which is bad almost everywhere where money and the higher education have had a chance to corrupt.

Later
I have been with Winant again this afternoon. He saw Salazar last night, and he told him that if Portugal declared war on Japan she would be much more popular in the USA than if she declared war on Germany. 'Why?' said the rational Doc. 'Can't say,' replied Winant, 'just don't like those Japanese.'

The Doctor appealed to him to send American goods to the Peninsula to keep Spain and Portugal out of the arms of the Axis. Salazar said the English had taken too narrow a view of the Blockade and had not realised the wider implications of giving life to the Western Mediterranean, independent of Central Europe, even if it did mean that a trickle of stuff got thro' from the Peninsula to occupied Europe. Winant fell for this. And who am I to take exception to that? I agree with the Doctor that constructive economics were not Dalton's strong point and that his band of smart young men had so much energy that they called the economic tune in Whitehall. Our government has been wrong in regard to the Blockade, to foreign trade and finance, and in failing to plan military operations with the help of economics.

Winant wanted me to spend a year here organising the economies of the Western Mediterranean. I could have an American colleague and the two of us would be in charge. I suggested Walton Butterworth and he said he liked Walton but he was impossible to work with. He hadn't a friend in the US Embassy when he left. Everyone resented his independence and his scheming ways. I was surprised to hear him speak so strongly. One must look out, it is necessary to suffer one's own generation.

All my love, sweet Syb—David

1. A pink palace on the outskirts of Lisbon.
2. Winston Churchill reshuffled his Cabinet on 23 February 1942.
3. Oliver Lyttelton was coming back from Cairo to become Minister of Production.
4. Lord Beaverbrook, Minister of Aircraft Production 1940, Minister of Supply 1941.
5. Dame Edith Lyttelton, Oliver's mother.

4 March 1942 — Lisbon

My darling love—Oliver[1] was in huge form, and Moira, altho' coughing badly, excited and gay. 'What are you doing here?' shouts Oliver on sight, 'I thought I should find you Minister of Debris or something when I got to London.' 'So did I.'

He was reasonably confident about Egypt. Rommel has lost so much stuff. Oliver thinks him a wonderful tactician but a very poor general. He stuck his neck out unpardonably five months ago and lost two thirds of his men and equipment, including 14,000 men at Halfaya who surrendered for one casualty on our side. In fact if Rommel were a French general he would now be on trial, and if he were a British general he would be on his way to be Commander-in-Chief in India.

The trouble on our side was and is unbalanced equipment. We have the right number of light pursuit tanks and not enough heavy tanks, but if there are no heavy tanks to win the battle, there is nothing to pursue. Same with guns. Our artillery are numerous and excellent, but no good without enough anti-tank guns to protect them, and these we haven't got.

Whose fault is all this? Oliver says the War Office. There each branch gives its order to the Ministry of Supply, and that Ministry, particularly under a routine businessman like Duncan,[2] goes on the principle 'The customer is always right, and had better be lied to rather than be contradicted'; i.e. they try to produce the aggregate of the War Office's orders, which is impossible, with the result that all the orders are in different stages of fulfilment, and no military operation is begun with balanced equipment.

Oliver wants to take a drastic line. He kept asking me, 'Is my job on?' Meaning, 'Shall I have enough power, and even if I have will the Whitehall boys let me do it?' Of course I said everyone was looking to him as the man who could and would be allowed to do it. He has no faith in the calculations of the senior staff officers who are always studying out-of-date battles. He proposes to tell the army what weapons we can make, to make them and let them plan their operations, not in theory, but on the basis of what is available. In the last war Lloyd George refused to make ammunition for coastal guns, because he didn't believe in invasions, instead he made HE [high explosive] for the artillery to cut wire in France. Result we won in France.

Oliver has the lowest opinion of the leading personalities in the Ministry of Supply, and of the Beaver in particular. We went through their names. Some changes will occur. He hates Dalton with ferocity. Says that Dalton's opposition to relief for the Greeks nearly brought a major crisis in the Middle East.

The PM, like all great men, does not believe much in 'security' and is wildly indiscreet on the telephone. He rang Oliver up in Cairo: 'Ish that you, Oliver my boy? Wantsh you to come home. Needsh young blood here . . . You know that man who was CIGS, name beginsh with D[3] etc. . . .'

There's no doubt Oliver will try to control all economic matters, but, as he says, it is not easy to sit on top of existing departments. The Ministry of Supply, Ministry of Aircraft Production, Board of Trade, etc., have their traditions and large staffs of jealous civil servants; who will Oliver have on his staff to control the Sir What-Nots below? You remember the crashing failure of Sir T. Inskip as Minister of Defence. Oliver is alive to this and means to stake a big claim with the PM. One of the most interesting complexes will be to see if Tommy Brand can work for Oliver, he ought to be his right-hand man.

We had a lovely lunch: the Lytteltons, the Campbells, Winant and I, and afterwards walked along the cliffs for a mile or so talking and sniffing the sea breeze. Winant is still here, the weather in mid-Atlantic being foul. I see him every day. He is reading Oliver Cromwell's speeches and Carlyle's essays. The wicked would say he is thinking of the White House as a suitable home. He liked Kipling very much and through Kipling he came to like Beaverbrook. Beaverbrook is evidently a man who can exercise much personal magnetism and make people forgive huge sins. He is of the '*C'est affreux mais je l'adore*'[4] type.

We had another talk about France. The Vichy government have sent a remarkable telegram[5] to their legation here. Let me go back a little. For six months we have been trying to get the French to put two oil tankers outside the Mediterranean and in the service of Portugal. A week ago when all was ready to sign they made an impossible last-minute condition which I didn't even bother to report to London. Instead I went and harangued the French Minister and his Counsellor on their lack of courage and common sense, and I pointed out that Franco-American relations were so bad that they ought to jump at any chance to give London and Washington a small proof that Vichy was capable of doing something sensible in our direction. They telegraphed all this to Vichy and Darlan replied that the matter had been referred to the Marshal who, having been impressed by Mr Eccles's arguments —this was said twice—would do what Mr Eccles asked. Now the remarkable part of the telegram followed the decision and certain instructions how to carry it out: Darlan went on to say that if the USA broke off relations with France (i.e. took Leahy away) the Pétain government would collapse, chaos and blood in the streets would follow, out of which only Germany would profit. Think what power for the shaping of Europe is in Roosevelt's hand, for Winant and all of us here agree with the facts as stated in the Vichy telegram. Obviously we must not precipitate a revolution in France until we are ready to turn it to our advantage. What does that mean? That we must be ready to land a force in France and another in North Africa. We are not ready. We haven't the ships, let alone men and equipment. Then we must keep Pétain on his perch for he keeps the Germans at a short distance, i.e. out of North Africa, and so Leahy must stay in Vichy. This is the cold strategy of the game, but there are a growing number of left agitators in France who, for internal political reasons as well as pro-Ally sympathies, are making Pétain's life difficult; further, in the USA the friends of these agitators (all of whom the Vichy government calls Communists) are working hard to get the USG[overnment] to break off relations . . .

I can't go on as the bag is closing.

With a large kiss—David

1. Oliver and Lady Moira Lyttelton.
2. Sir Andrew Duncan was Minister of Supply 1940, President of the Board of Trade 1941 and Minister of Supply again in 1942.
3. Field Marshal Sir John Dill, CIGS 1940–1.
4. This remark was made to Sybil and me by a lady on an Italian beach surveying her toe-nails, which she had just painted green.
5. The French Minister allowed me to read this telegram and to make notes.

4 March 1942 — Star and Garter Hotel, Andover

My dear sweet—No letter from you yet. This morning I had an insane desire to send you a cable—but washing up the breakfast things and sweeping the larder, I recovered—one simply must not fall to such craven-hearted expedients. Simon helps me in the kitchen of a morning and I enjoy his cheerful piping as he wipes the tea cups (not without casualties) and patters up and down between cupboard and frigidaire. Polly imagines herself invaluable as well, but her energy is spasmodic, she is more at home with conversation.

I come into Andover most days as the equipment for the wartime nursery is arriving and in a cold and grey little room, looking on to a brick wall and a broken pipe, I count vast numbers of drab institutional blankets together with more cheerful heaps of turkish towelling bibs, dusters and nappies. Sometimes the association of ideas is so strong that I almost see myself in a mackintosh apron clutching a squawking bundle and lift my nose to sniff the dusty air as though I might find upon it the fragrance of Messrs Johnson's powder, mingling amiably with Vinolia soap.

5 March
Oh! David darling, what a heavenly surprise this morning. With the letters (two from you) came a smart brown paper parcel with a Dorchester label. Thinking, 'Drat, more washing left behind', I left it languishing on the carpet and composed myself to the longed-for letters and it was only when Simon had quite worn himself out with pleading into my deaf ears that I let him get busy with the scissors, only to hear him exclaim a moment later—'Oh! Mum—*do* look, some pretty blue stuff.' Then we got down on

our knees without delay. Dear David—you are a sweet—and it's quite the loveliest stuff that has greeted my wartime eyes for many a long day and I shall adore wearing it—knowing that it was your choice.

I feel with every letter that you are anxious and in doubt about your future. The negotiations must be hellishly hard and hedged about with every kind of complication, psychological and Timorous. These people at home are apt to be cagey about your endeavours. Pay as little attention as you can. Gladwyn once said to me, 'David is out of reach in a world of pure theory.' He was only laughing and as he is capable of thought himself I attached nothing to the remark. But these Henrys and these Charleses are mere plodders with their eyes bent on the ground, fumbling their short-sighted way from one day's task to another. They mistrust thought because they are incapable of controlling it and know not into what thorny thicket it may lead them. So quite naturally they are made jealous and angry by the spectacle of another venturing out where they themselves dare not tread.

I love you very much and think of you with longing.

—Sybil

7 March 1942 Chute

My dearest love—What a morning! Two letters from you and two of your best. I never read them while the washing-up is still to be done but hide them under the silver salver in the dining-room while I pile the trays and hurry to my drab task, hugging a cosy feeling inside, that keeps me in a rosy glow all the while I bend above the sink, shaking the soap powder with a sparing hand into Mrs Austen's admirable hot water.

Tomorrow I go off for my week in London. I have a full programme and shall spend each day in a different War-Time Nursery—picking the brains of their leaders. 'National Nurseries' Mr Bevin[1] wants us to call them—as a small piping note on the trumpet that bids us pay heed to the new communal, state-controlled life that lurks round the corner. It seems that the Mothers of England still prefer 'the neighbour' to 'the Nursery'. The English still cling to home and castle.

8 March
Do you sometimes wake in the night with the fear that Englishmen have gone soft and woolly? With the weakening of our belief in God do you suppose morale and courage grow feeble too? Try as you will not to believe it the fear creeps in that we do not fight as we used to do. Our men march backwards and we are told that lack of tanks and planes account for these movements in the wrong direction but sometimes one wonders if that can be all.

Darling dear, I love you so much and in London I shall miss you and need you more than ever I do here, where each room and corner in the garden bear witness to a life we made together.

—Sybil

1. Ernest Bevin, Minister of Labour and National Service 1940–5.

9 March 1942 Lisbon

My darling love—Sam and Maud [Hoare] are here. Rather weary, and looking older and talking older. They dined with me alone last night, Sunday supper, on soup, mock whitebait (they each had two helps), and cold meat and salad. Quite nicely done by Robertson's primitive domestics. Sam said that history would record three great mistakes in the first two years of the war:
(a) Mussolini's decision to enter the war;
(b) HMG's decision to withdraw our Embassy from France at the time of the Armistice;
(c) Hitler's decision to attack Russia under his own command late in the autumn.
Sam is quite convinced that (b) was equally disastrous for history as (a) and (c). He thinks, it is music to my mind, that half the wretched state of Anglo-American-French relations, and more than half the collaboration between Vichy and Germany, is directly due to our breaking off diplomatic relations in June 1940.

Sam is going to give up his Commercial Counsellor, Stanley Irving, to come here. Irving was CC in Paris with Ronnie [Campbell], and is one of the best men in the Commercial Diplomatic. With Ellis-Rees in Madrid they scarcely need him. If this comes off I shall have made my own presence in the Peninsula superfluous. First I built Sam's staff, and got the Treasury to second

Ellis-Rees for the duration, and put Noel Lewin there as his bottle-washer to be quite sure the groundwork was well done. Now if we get Irving for Lisbon I can put on my hat. This is suicide of a kind, because here I can manipulate a reputation and a local experience of some note; and all the evidence goes to show that since I left London Henry and Charles have been nibbling away at my job and have already succeeded in reducing it to third-rate proportions. So that back in London all the struggle is to be fought again. But I must leave this place and take what comes.

I spoke to Sam about all this. He says there is nothing that will satisfy in the Peninsula and he would not advise any other course than to go home. There he thinks Oliver should take me under his wing. We are going to have another talk about the best way to manage this. Sam hears that Dalton is in disgrace and on his way out for ever, certainly one doesn't see what political support he can have, and yet if they pushed him out of MEW why did they bother to find him another job?

I read this morning the epistle to the Philippians. It is superb. What courage in adversity! I think it is my favourite of all that came from that white-hot pen; no, I think he probably dictated his letters, and revised them orally, the language is spoken, not written.

My love to you, dearest Syb—David

14 March 1942 Lisbon

My darling love—When your letter arrives it is like turning on the light after I've been trying and gradually failing to read in a darkening room. There are things one can't imagine, and shouldn't attempt.

Whatever reverses we may be having the Germans are bleeding faster than we. Think of a casualty list of 5,000 dead a day. On our side we have two keys to victory, the one moral, the fact that all Europe loathes the Germans, the other material, the volume to which Allied production will grow. There can be no end but victory; but I don't want to see us disgraced in the process. That is the fear that gnaws a little at the vitals. War ought to produce heroes—I remember Beigbeder saying to me, 'In war people do worse and better than was possible in peace'—well, I want to see some of the heroes, not in courage only, though that is the most refreshing sight the world can show, but in brains and character. Where are they? The world is like some vast palace, Versailles perhaps, inhabited by savages, who kick the gilt off the chairs and make messes in the corner. It is the monstrous gap between 'the earth and the fullness thereof' and the way in which we use it; that is the giant tragedy of our days.

I have been talking to the Portuguese about sovereignty. What does it mean today? Can we be independent, any of us? Let them look at South America, their friends there are giving bases to the USA, and tying up their products, and Brazil looks nearly at war. Portugal can't play the ostrich among nations and get away with it. They have a lot of money here, millions and millions of idle dollars and pounds, but they can't buy anything with their money. The sellers won't sell because their goods are needed for our war effort, or there isn't enough shipping. The freedom that came from having the world's market at your disposal if you could pay cash, has gone, and with it the possibility of conducting your foreign trade on a private basis; now you must make inter-government arrangements about everything, and a very humiliating business it is too, when you are the weak little neutral, rich but not allowed to use your money, in face of ogres like the USA. All this is particularly repugnant to the Portuguese who hate to be embarrassed. Portuguese men stand and quarrel on the pavement for ten minutes, as to who shall sit on the right at the back of the taxi. A married man will never see a girl alone in public because it would do *him* damage if he were talked about. They have a mortal dread of being talked about, of spotting their white sheet, and all the time under cover they commit purple and puny sins. In fact a more selfish and timid race of men I've never known. The war brings out the *worst* in them.

Sunday night

I'm very low again. And want you very much. All these people, they mean so well, they do their best, but it's such a miserable affair (Ronnie excepted). I have produced one of my eggs. This time a forecast of the trend of life in Western Europe during this year—you will remember I talked to Winant about it—how I miss him—and now that my child is born, after much trouble, I feel empty, depressed and terribly anxious about the way it will be treated in this rough world. I enclose a copy.

I hope you do not think such a plea, which I put forward with all the passion I am capable of, is wild nonsense, for it is placed in your hands, with my love.

—David

Memorandum for Dr Salazar by DE
Lisbon, 13 March 1942

Economic Revival in the Occupied Territories of Western Europe

Economic warfare was designed to deny the enemy materials useful for the conduct of the war, and this the Blockade has done and will do with considerable success. It was also hoped that the Blockade of occupied territories would stimulate a spirit of resistance to the invader which would require a large army of soldiers and officials to control. However, the Germans did not hesitate to withdraw divisions from garrison duty in Western Europe when they were needed in Russia, and it is generally agreed that the volume of economic collaboration which the enemy has received from France has continued to grow in spite of the Blockade. This paper attempts to review the apparent failure of this aspect of our economic warfare policy.

Since the collapse of France, the occupied territories of Western Europe, Vichy France and the Peninsula have been learning to live within the Blockade. Economic life from Antwerp to Dakar is being stabilised at a low ebb, which with a few exceptions, e.g. the cities of Belgium, is not too low for survival. Human nature is sufficiently adaptable to make shift.

2. Although the standard of life may still be falling in certain places within the occupied territories, this paper is not concerned with the decline itself but with the rate of the decline relative to the powers of adjustment of the population. If people can learn to live on their own resources, without seaborne imports, more rapidly than their standard of life decreases, then the Blockade of Europe, whatever other effects it may have on the Axis, cannot stimulate the occupied territories of Western Europe to resist the enemy.

3. The Germans withdrew food from the industrial workers of the occupied territories and of Vichy France, and then offered something to eat in exchange for their labour. This technique has been successful, because the conquered were stunned by defeat before they had been physically or morally hardened by war; but now the occupied territories are recovering from the shock and are making little experiments in a new life, much as an invalid wobbles when he first gets out of bed. This tendency is clearly seen in Lisbon. Up to six months ago visitors from the occupied territories spoke only of food shortages, now they ask for industrial materials and continually refer to projects for the production or exchange of manufactured articles.

4. Every day there are fresh signs of this economic convalescence. Belgium offers manufactured products against Portuguese sardines; France exchanges sulphate of ammonia for Spanish oranges and Portuguese sugar; France charters tankers to Portugal; Portugal sends packing materials to French North Africa, which enables African products to go to France; in North Africa coal mines are being developed, and throughout the area under consideration alternative fuels to oil are being actively investigated.

5. France is the economic barometer of the area under consideration. Her food supply is improving and French resourcefulness will find ways of increasing industrial output. On the other hand, if Marshal Pétain's government fell, chaos would result, the Germans would have a chance to occupy French North Africa, and possibly the Peninsula would be involved. This situation would be of no advantage to us until we are ready to invade the Continent. In the meantime, what should we do? Stand aside, hinder, or promote economic exchanges between the nations of Western Europe?

6. If we try to hinder this attempt at survival, will the masses understand our motives? Supposing the Belgian Relief were cut off unless the barter of Belgian products against Peninsular food is stopped, or pressure put on Spain to cease trade with France, or French North Africa completely blockaded, what then? By frowning on the attempt to stabilise life inside the Blockade, are we likely to make more friends or more enemies in the countries where one day our armies may have to fight? It would be rash to

neglect the rule that men and women, when treated badly, behave badly.

7. If the war were going to be finished quickly, there would be little gain in encouraging the tender growth of economic revival, but if, as the Prime Minister tells us, the fight will last for years, we must take stock of this trend. It is possible that, without our help, these people will arrive, by taking in their own washing, at a state of degraded but tolerable existence. The brutality of the invader and the tradition of liberty may do much to preserve the national spirit, but will that spirit be proof against years of disappointment and the fatal ease with which human nature adapts itself to misery?

8. A long war, our own supply needs, and the desire to keep material as well as moral contact with areas where we may one day have to fight, all suggest that we should patronise this revival in Western Europe. A war in the Pacific makes it necessary to lay hold of all the available production of Europe and Africa, and strategic and economic considerations now combine to stimulate our trade with Spain and Portugal. The prosperity of the Peninsula will overflow into the occupied territories. We might even want to extract via the Peninsula certain products of North Africa, France and the occupied territories. If we set our faces against the economic revival of Western Europe, we shall certainly do so at some expense to our own supply position, and at a loss of sympathy to our cause which will differ from one country to another.

9. Transport in the occupied territories and from French North Africa to France requires the consent of the Germans. At first sight, therefore, it would seem absurd to encourage a traffic which is under German control. But if this traffic will develop whether we like it or not, and we expressly condemn it, the resulting material benefits to the occupied territories will be credited entirely to the Germans. On the other hand, it must be obvious that the Germans will not want the exchange of goods to develop to a point where it cuts into their own supplies of the labour and products of Western Europe, whereas we would very much like this to happen. Our interest, therefore, is to do the opposite.

10. In the last war wherever a Belgian was fed without having to work, he refused to work for the enemy. Have the workers less

courage in this war? If they began to work for the Germans it was because there was no other way of feeding their families; but it would be dangerous to believe that some of them will not get used to their new masters.

11. There are two types of action now open to us if it is decided that, being unable to stop the convalescence of Western Europe, we should try to make use of it.

(a) We can discreetly encourage specific proposals for the exchange of goods within the area under consideration, when our approval is asked, and it appears that no serious damage to the conduct of the war would result. For example, if Belgium gets tin from Portugal she is ready to send the Portuguese tin-plate, and it is therefore useless for His Majesty's Government and the United States Government to believe they can hold up to ransom the Portuguese canning industry by refusing to supply tin-plate themselves. In fact, there is no more vulnerable animal than the dog in the manger.

(b) We can take the offensive and say to the occupied territories and especially to France, 'If you will stop this specific form of economic collaboration with the enemy we will give you this concession.' For example, if the French agreed to put their merchant fleet, including tankers, outside the Mediterranean, such an act would be worth a considerable price—perhaps 50,000 tons of copper sulphate with which to save the wine industry of France. Already the French are saying that a year from now they will have discovered a substitute preparation with which to spray the vines.

It would be clearly understood that in the majority of cases where we put a proposition to an occupied territory we should expect refusal. The result, however, would be that the people concerned would know that it was the Germans or their own collaborationist government who were responsible for their failing to get whatever concession had been offered by us.

12. To sum up: the question of how to treat Western Europe can only be judged by making the effort to recall all that we know about human behaviour. Your Excellency will not need to be reminded that the natural instinct to do good, even an acknowledged power to tell right from wrong, have never proved sufficient to cause men to behave well; men and women must continually perform works consistent with these principles or

their faith dies. The great danger that confronts us is a possible failure to invite the people of Western Europe to perform a series of acts which would illustrate and sustain their faith in the way of life for which we are at war. Until we are ready to ask them to die for us, at least let them see that we are helping them to exist.

N.B. The above paragraphs were written before the RAF began to bomb factories in occupied France. This common-sense action would be more easily explained if at the same time His Majesty's Government were making a concrete offer to the workers: 'Stop working for the enemy and we will feed your children.'

16 March 1942 Chute

My dearest love—Your letter of 9 March was here when I got back on Saturday. I'm so glad things are going better—or *were* going better with the wolfram negotiations—one is half frightened to express relief at any piece of good news nowadays, it may so easily be nothing but a mirage.

Sam is probably right in condemning our withdrawal of the Embassy from France after the collapse, but I suppose it is difficult to judge the extent of the horrible paralysis and degradation of those last days in Bordeaux—our vain struggles to rally the failing friend, the bitter arguments, the useless recriminations—and almost impossible to measure the effect that these things must have had upon the people who suffered them.

I can understand anyone bearing an undying contempt for Pétain who saw him cringing and bleating through the final hours and our people must have longed to get away, be sick, wash their hands and faces, put on their hats and go home. So that's just what they did. Whether history will condemn them or not—I cannot say. We can probably rouse the real France just as well without attachments to '*les hommes d'Armistice*' as we could with them. The trouble is we don't try much. Even Roger who is very wise, while believing that re-created France is essential to the peace, sees no way to go about it.

Come back to London and make a REAL name for yourself—of course they don't *want* you—you're a trouble-maker—and it will be a struggle to overcome the opposition but you'll do it—

you always do the things you want—and there's going to be bags of room for trouble-makers before this thing is over.

All my love to you, very dear David—Sybil

19 March 1942 Lisbon

My darling love—The Portuguese Wholesale Grocery Association calls me up every day to know if we can help them to institute a food rationing system. I have asked the Ministry of Food at home to send out literature, but of course it doesn't come with the bags as they are. The Portuguese won't be able to use our cards, etc., as they can't read or write, but it will amuse them to have something to chatter about. I'm astonished how few of them can read. The other day a messenger boy of fifteen came to my flat with a parcel addressed to the man above; I said, 'Don't you read?' He replied, 'Not every day.' Quite solemnly; a charming answer.

The Portuguese care a lot about life and manners, but not as the Spaniards do, bravely and optimistically, here timidly and pessimistically. For example, I know an old girl of sixty, once gay and attractive, now 'putting up a good fight', who took a taxi and after a few yards the driver turned and asked, 'Aren't you Madame . . . ?' 'Yes, I am.' 'But how you've changed; how dreadfully old you've become, you were so lovely ten years ago when I used to drive you, it was a real pleasure, but now . . .' She tried to comfort him, '*Mais, mon ami, les années passent . . . il faut se résigner . . .*' But he wouldn't be comforted, and she became the brave one trying, but without success, to make him take a brighter view. At home she told the story to her maid, who has been with her many years, and all the consolation she got was, '*C'est vrai, Madame, vous avez beaucoup perdu.*'

All my love, darling Syb—David

22 March 1942 Lisbon

My darling love—Beaverbrook brought a bag and in it your letter. What awful couriers you employ! He's horribly depressed, the jaundiced old impresario. Says the Labour Party is finished, there are only Communist and Pink Conservatives now and many more of the former than the latter. British patriotism consists in sporting a photograph of Uncle Joe. Ronnie and I didn't answer back. He would have had us commit suicide, but we won't even to please him.

Comparisons come always to the mind. I thought of Winant and how healthy he was and how unhealthy the Beaver. Yet Winant liked the Beaver. I'm glad you have had my letters about Winant. We have to take a pull at ourselves just now, look around, and see who are our real friends, and cling to them.

I wish you were here, we could go out and sit in the sun before dinner and have a good gossip. Now the bag closes and I must go to a hotel and drink with Henry J. Labouisse, American Metals' King.

All my love—David

27 March 1942 Lisbon

My darling love—Your London letter and the next one from Chute dropped unexpectedly from grey skies today. Roger's party must have been great fun—I wonder, he doesn't do much without forethought, if he's trying to persuade the Private Secretary that I am not so bad, and what better dodge than to use you as the honey-cake for Cerberus? Roger makes my diplomatic life possible and Ronnie restores my faith in professional ambassadors. Both have complete power to see their work naked, without a shred of prejudice or ambition to cover the truth, or such of it as is visible to the human eye; this doesn't mean they always choose to do the strictly honest thing, irrespective of their own or other people's shortcomings, Ronnie makes exquisite allowances, Roger jumps the ditch in one not so exquisite leap, but if they do something a little queer it is only after seeing the absolutely right course and deliberately reshaping it in conformity with this degraded world. They remain masters of end and means.

I believe we shall be saved by Winant who went to FDR and insisted that America does what I told him was absolutely vital to our negotiations—that is to treat our Doctor as a gentleman, giving him supplies unconditionally and then asking for the wolfram settlement, etc. . . . bread on the waters. Ronnie says simply,

'No one but you could have persuaded Winant to do it; we needed some luck after Timor.'

Last night I dined with Peter Calder, once *Daily Herald* correspondent, now Political Warfare Executive in charge of propaganda, etc., concerning our raids in Western Europe. What a dismal tale he had to tell of missed opportunities and service jealousy and senile timidity! Can we have a second front this spring? Imagine what will happen to the last tatters of our military prestige if the Russians beat off the Germans while we do nothing. But the old men say we must sit still because we haven't the ships to lose in a series of raids from Narvik to Biarritz, so we cannot draw off any German divisions. We must conserve our supplies and maintain our rations. Calder speaks not out of anger, but as I do about these things, out of humiliation. He agrees completely with my paper on the economic future of Western Europe—you see how one can always agree with Socialist or Tory provided the argument is clear and sound—but he says no one at home grasps what total warfare is, they cannot see that the preparation of the road to Berlin is just as important as the military operation along that road.

The very difficulty of these negotiations, even their apparent failure, has brought a good many people to realise that luck is not my only asset. This is good. I told Eddie Playfair before I left that for once I did not think we could succeed, the scales were too heavily weighted. He made a mouth but he paid attention and the unswerving support that Ronnie and I have had from the Treasury has been a solid comfort, so different from the vapourings of Berkeley Square [MEW].

I meant to continue this letter with an account of a three-hour conversation with Dr Salazar, but there is no time now. The Doctor has a horrid respect for the enemy and some budding doubts about us, and more than budding fears of Russia. Oh! dear, if we don't look out we'll be the *tertium quid* of the three Great Powers, and Russia much nearer to us than the USA. The USA want a lead about the new Europe and we give them none. Have we lost all initiative? The desire to lead must come before the capacity to lead.

All my love, I think more often of you than before in spite of work.

—David

4 April 1942 Estoril

After working all Good Friday I still felt very stuffed up with my departing cold and I decided to spend the weekend at Estoril.

My suite is lovely and spacious with a terrace overlooking the sea, today green-grey under a sullen sky. I open all the cupboards and imagine your clothes there and the time you would have taken to unpack them, how you would have put the beds together, sent for an extra table in the bathroom (and why didn't they clean away the wrapper from the last guest's soap?) and filled the hollow vases with flowers. Below the casino are patterns of orderly beds stuffed with blooms:

Each regiment in order grows
That of the tulip, pink and rose.

I don't fancy them very much, the hills behind are far more attractive, there you have the buttery smell of the gorse, whiffs of rosemary, and the two kinds of rock-roses, of which the white with yellow centre has it over the all-yellow every time, and then for blue the gentian has the first place in any country, and in the streams are islands of shining white dots, I forget the name, they are everywhere in Spain and in Morocco. The little irises about four inches high and a yellow half-poppy, half-buttercup, make a wonderful mixture in the damp places.

After lunch with Eric Biddle, Louise Campbell came—who does the prisoners-of-war parcels—and we went for a twelve-kilometre walk, discussing our children and her work. You would like her, she is so clear-headed, and she never, in the two years she has been here, has been accused of any sort of flirt. A great relief.

All my love—David

Easter Sunday 1942 Chute

My dearest love—It's March and April all in one. The winds tear and shake the groaning house, while by night the owl's spring cries sound above the tempest. Then it rains in squalls of a ferocious intensity—which, the heavens be praised, don't last long or they would pound our newly-sown seeds from their beds.

The chestnut buds are swelling and the sycamores show points of green. Simon reports constantly on the birth of a new daffodil. Ken Turner[1] is here for Easter and we took the whole brood to church at Ludgershall. Polly was an angel of good behaviour. Happily she found a loose screw attached to the pew in front within easy reach and this provided the most excellent and not particularly noisy occupation for the sermon. In the porch—while we waited upon a prayer before going in—she whispered commandingly to Ken, 'You must remember to take your hat off. Men always do.' This caused an unfortunate convulsion among the boys and at the worst possible moment.

We are preparing a surprise for you. I may not say what. But it involves an enormous amount of energy and activity together with the use of some very murderous tools. A combination which John and Simon find irresistible—and Polly isn't far behind. I don't know how far we shall get before your return—or how long I shall be able to sustain their enthusiasm. But in the meantime 'the secret' provides a perfect solution to the Easter holiday problem, through the days that hesitate between spring and winter.

All my love—Sybil

1. An American doctor.

10 April 1942 Lisbon

My darling love—We had an amusing incident on Tuesday night. Admiral Sir Andrew Cunningham,[1] wife and flag lieutenant dined and afterwards went to take off at midnight in a flying-boat for the UK. Just as they were all set to go, plop into the Tagus tumbles another of our flying-boats with engine trouble and the Duke of Gloucester and seven generals and admirals in uniform. This party should have been interned for coming so dressed to a neutral country. So in midstream they changed aircraft and left the Cunninghams in the lurch. They got off next day. He wants some leave and then the Pacific.

The British Empire is gone, as a structure of children supporting a luxurious and rather easy parent it is finished. Why not say so? Don't let's waste time crying about it, but set to and work out some brother-sister relationship to take the place of the father-child relationship, and include here and now the nations of northern and western Europe in the new deal. We must convince ourselves, the Americans and our so-called Allies what it is all about. And I feel *more than* a doubt whether we can put forth the energy, we and the Americans, required to beat Germany and Japan unless our peoples have a much clearer deeper hope of the decent sort of world for which we are fighting. I've listened to all the stuff about 'we must win the war first'; for a time I was taken in by it because I thought we *could* win the war first, that is, comparatively *quickly*, but I see now this is pure balls, or any other expression you think strong enough to describe the excuse given by the feeble-minded for having no idea what the war's about; and my God! it simply isn't true, we have reached a point of danger where we know that we cannot beat the Axis quickly and that we cannot beat them at all unless our shabby faith is polished bright by some revolutionary change in our conception of the new world. The Americans are quite ready for this new world. They know so much better than we do, since they have 3,000 miles of ocean between them and an invader, on what flimsy moral grounds the struggle is being carried on. Personally I find no great difficulty in grasping the ground plan of a new society. Obviously the principle of equality of opportunity, in education, in health, in trade, in access to raw materials, is one plan. Another is the abandonment of individual sovereignty, the pooling of security, and acceptance that no state can defend itself alone . . .

I must stop as the Ambassador is calling for me and the bag will close before he is done.

All my love—David

1. Hero of the battle of Cape Matapan, in March 1941, in which most of the Italian Navy was sunk.

12 April 1942 — Lisbon

My darling love—Did you know I was a fishmonger? I am up to my neck in buying 750,000 cases (100 tins each) of sardines. What a job it is as the Ministry of Food only want to pay £3 a case against the ruling intra-Blockade price of £6 upwards.

My sweet Syb—I do so wish we could share some days

together especially in this divine introduction to summer, you can't imagine how beautiful the Tagus and the Atlantic are in these four weeks from now till mid-May. But as Ronnie tersely says, alluding to increased casualties in the Spring offensive, 'You can't have the sun's warmth on your face without breeding maggots in your back garden.'

There's an enormous chatter in the street outside. What is it? A dispute over some charcoal which two fat women both think they bought. The policeman is roaring with laughter; a small girl is filching something out of one of the women's baskets; two boys are bullying the other woman's child.

My love—David

14 April 1942 Lisbon

My darling love—MEW are still mad, perhaps viciously mad. A week ago the French Legation spoke to me about the competition there was going to be for Portuguese sardines this season. They were buyers and we were even bigger buyers, would we agree to eliminate competition, and they would be content to let us buy for them? I reported this astonishing offer to London and received today a raspberry to the effect that 'it would be more appropriate if the French asked the Germans to buy for them'. Have they taken leave of their wits at home? Have we not enough enemies already but they must force forty million French to join the Axis? This is one of the most disgraceful and unchristian episodes in our history—our post-Armistice relations with France—and the time will come when the world's judgement will brand these men for ever and for ever. And what I loathe about the whole business is the stream of insinuation that my 'pro-Vichy' attitude is unpopular, bad for the career, etc. The worms!

My sweet Syb, I love you very much and pine to be with you; someday we shall really be together again, till then I live 'careful and comfortless', as Spenser wrote.

Love to the children—David

16 April 1942 Lisbon

My darling love—Ronnie Tree[1] and Cyril Radcliffe[2] were quite unexpectedly on the Embassy doorstep after lunch yesterday. They came to dinner and we talked home front. Cyril returned again and again to the phrase, 'The people in England want to get the war over and are wild keen to do anything—however tough and violent—to achieve this quickly.' This sounded bad to me if the emphasis were on the 'quickly' and not on 'tough' or 'violent'. He admitted the justice of my fear, but went on to give his opinion that the Germans would collapse this year, and we be left a neglected middleman between America and Russia who would manage the world. Nothing but a Russian peace could come. At the time of the German surrender only Russia would have first-class influence *and* know what she wanted. The USA would have the influence but wouldn't know what she wanted, we would neither have the influence *nor* know what we wanted. 'But,' said I, 'I know what I want.' 'Then you're unique and must be mad.'

The day before yesterday I found a fattish, pleasant-looking young man sitting in my parlour before dinner. 'I am Walter Baels, I have a letter for you from Pepe Mamblas.' Mamblas[3], my very good friend, wrote that Baels was the brother of the girl who has married Leopold of Belgium and that he had something to say to me.

This Baels is a very poor creature but his messages were interesting. He had been taken prisoner in May 1940 and had lived since with the King in the castle. The Germans let him out on parole after promising that he would not accept any position under the Belgian refugee government (Pierlot and Spaak). His object was to go to the USA and there explain the King's surrender and subsequent behaviour. The Pierlot government has not got, he said, a single friend in Belgium, if ever those men return they will be strung up, and they can never be reconciled with the King who has firm hold on the loyalty of his people. Why do we support a bunch of third-rate *émigrés* who are completely out of touch with Belgium? I made the stock reply that we supported the men who had had the courage to get away and carry on the fight, if there were better men in Belgium, let them come out and replace those we now worked with.

He said that the Germans are for ever telling Leopold that they want a compromise peace or Europe could not be saved from

Communism. Nonsense, said I, you must choose sharply between our world and the German world, and if the Germans talk about compromise it shows they know they cannot win. 'That is what the King thought too, but he asked what would happen to Belgium if the Russians alone beat the Germans?'

Now there you have it straight from the King's mouth, 'What would happen if the Russians alone beat the Germans?' To which question, we do not know the answer. But isn't that a scandal, a tragedy, a colossal sin?

All my love — David

PS On thinking over the Baels interview I came to the conclusion that he is well in the German pay.

1. Conservative MP for Market Harborough 1933–45.
2. Barrister and later Viscount Radcliffe, Director-General, Ministry of Information 1941–5.
3. Vizconde de Mamblas, Spanish diplomat in MFA.

21 April 1942 Lisbon

My darling love — Last night I dined in company with Stafford Cripps,[1] his plain but well-travelled daughter, Gerald Palmer[2] (his PPS), Sir Harold McMichael (in corduroys) and some others.

Cripps is more than ordinarily handsome, his face well shaped and the carriage of his head very good. His voice admirable. He was very tired, and depressed about India (Sam Hoare with his realist cynicism had prophesied the mission would be a failure, 'The Hindus won't fight anyway so what will it matter?'). I began to ask Gerald P to take some more silk back for you, but he shied off on moral grounds, and to rouse Cripps I said to him, 'What could we plant on Gerry so that he could be arrested at Bristol?' The dialogue flew like hard-hit tennis balls.

SC A letter in a curious cypher.
DE Written in invisible ink.
SC On mauve paper.
DE Smelling of gardenias.
SC In a female hand.
DE To a man with a foreign name.
SC Living in Kensington . . .

The whole party was delighted and turned to general talk. Beforehand I had thought I must find some subject, rehearse it carefully, and try to hold Cripps's attention for five minutes. I had picked on Laval.[3] Now was the chance, so I threw down the glove: 'Why do you think that Laval, realising as he does his own unpopularity, after he has had one bullet, takes office again at a moment when his German friends are in obvious difficulties?' Then came a variety of answers most of them wide of possibility. Cripps said, 'Laval thinks he can make a German victory sure, and if there is no German victory he'll lose his head.' I replied with Macbeth's lines (carefully learned before dinner!):

> I am in blood
> Stept in so far, that, should I wade no more,
> Returning were as tedious as go o'er.

A man bound to his destiny, a view attractive in its tragic simplicity, but inconceivable with Laval's character. He was known as the trickiest man in Europe; no fixed principles or emotions there; self-interest his only obsession; a very astute and wide-awake crook. He must know that the Germans were losing (I heard reliably that he had said so about 2 April) and that his own unpopularity is so great that if he tries now to push France into a closer collaboration there will be a revolution, and his throat the first cut.

'Couldn't he,' said Cripps, 'either get the French Navy to fight us, or to lend the Germans their ships?'

All our evidence showed that the first was impossible and the second technically very difficult (to operate someone else's gadgets) even if possible in principle. Here one of our Service attachés broke in saying there wasn't a French naval officer left who would lift a finger for the Germans. In the last six months they had come over in a body to us. Cripps was impressed.

The French Legation here has been instructed officially to explain Pétain's move in taking Laval back as 'foxy'; the Germans had seen how elated the French public were at our air raids and had demanded greatly increased collaboration in defence, etc., or they would do this and that. Darlan was too weak in face of this situation. Pétain had to take Laval back as the only means of gaining time.

What of Laval himself? I didn't think he would have taken office if he had thought the Germans were sure to win, he would only have to wait to be made dictator of France. Nor could he believe that his assistance would tip the scale in favour of a German victory. He knew too much about French public opinion to give himself that illusion. Therefore, he must have taken office either with the idea of double-crossing the Germans or *against his will.*

There is still another explanation. Germany wants a revolution in France and has paid a gangster his price to bring it about. This doesn't make sense because the Germans haven't at this moment enough troops to take advantage of the revolution, i.e. to occupy the Peninsula and North Africa as well. I admit that sometimes my instinct tells me that if I were the German general staff I should dig in on the Egyptian border and face about, going through Tunis and Algiers like butter, and on and south to Dakar.

Cripps was very depressed. He spoke about the Americans doing nothing, the supplies reaching Russia being inadequate, the almost certainty that India would be lost, the loss of our ships.[4] We said that if he were in Berlin he would have far more cause to be gloomy. Physically he is tired, a little rest and he'll be different.

22 April

Now I have the real story of the Laval crisis. How I wish I had known it when Cripps was here. Pierre Baraduc[5] came back from Vichy last night and straight round to tell me the news. Pétain had no difficulty up to the end of March in resisting German pressure to take L back. Chiefly *because L did not want to take office.* Early in April, however, something took place, on the initiative of the Americans—I will tell you what later—which caused the Germans to present P with an ultimatum. P unfortunately was embarrassed by my old and farcical friend Henri du Moulin who had been plotting on his own to do away with Laval. Result, both he and L had to give way and L most unwillingly took office. His only ambition is to regain his popularity in France and obviously now is a bad moment to try, especially when he had had no time to prepare his own team or liquidate Darlan's. Since his ambition is single he will play up to the French people, concentrating on improving the food supply and distribution, and on maintaining relations with the USA. All his new staff stressed the point that he would not break with the USA. He knows quite well that if he pushes the French towards revolution he will be the first to suffer. L enjoys one considerable advantage. The whole of France knows he is a clever crook and therefore believes him capable of successfully double-crossing the Germans just as he has double-crossed his other friends. This gives him some liberty of action and a kind of negative popularity.

There you have the key to this mystery: Laval did not want to take office. I wonder if the true history of France since 1940 will ever be written?

Our Portuguese negotiations limp badly, we can do nothing with the Doctor in his present irritated, if not vindictive, mood. However, patience is the key, and with the firm co-operation of the Americans we may come out all right. When you have a man like Salazar who says, 'I would rather my people starve than give you a guarantee not to export olive oil to the Germans, not because I like the Germans but because I will not compromise my right to trade with any other country,' what is one to do? I wish I saw some prospect of getting home but as yet there is none. I want very much to talk to you and to be in the fight together; here, out on the limb, it is chilly and uncomfortable beyond description. Dearest Syb, we are too long apart. Damn the Portuguese!

All my love—David

1. Lord Privy Seal and Leader of the House. In March Cripps had been sent to Delhi to try to persuade Congress to wait until after the war for Indian independence. He was now on his way back to England after a further visit to India.
2. He and I were at Winchester together.
3. From the Armistice in 1940 to his trial, condemnation and execution at the end of the war, Pierre Laval was the most unpopular man in France: the ugly symbol of collaboration with the Nazis.

When France fell he had stage-managed the end of the Third Republic by persuading the Assembly at Vichy to vote itself out of existence. In recognition of this act and because he had approved of Laval's pre-war policy and now needed a colleague agreeable to the Germans, Pétain appointed him Vice-President in his government. The two men could not have been more different: Pétain the soldier, immaculate, precise, lucid, honourable; Laval a practised demagogue, dirty, foul-mouthed and dishonourable. Laval set about collaborating with the Germans behind Pétain's back. By December 1940 the Marshal had had enough and sacked him. Laval expected to be shot, but the Germans intervened and he was not even kept under arrest. Then, in April 1942, to the astonishment of Allied and neutral opinion, Pétain took him back as Prime Minister.

4. *Prince of Wales* and *Repulse.*

5. First Secretary at the French Legation at Lisbon.

24 April 1942 Lisbon

My darling love—Tommy Brand[1] turned up yesterday hoping to take the next clipper to the USA. Harry Hopkins has persuaded HMG to send a supply chief to Washington and Tommy is going to make his bed.

Tommy says I ought to go with Oliver as soon as possible before all the jobs are filled. But how can I get home? First I ought to have one try at Selborne to see if he would adopt the economic warfare policy which I know is right. You never know, he might.

Production in the UK is evidently very good but as our manpower is now fully engaged it cannot be shifted on to new types of weapons without some considerable loss of current output. In the USA there is as yet no manpower problem, you can build another factory on the end of an existing plant without cutting down the output of the old works. In this fluid state it is most necessary to see that old-fashioned soldiers, such as always command at the beginning of a war, do not order new machinery to make old weapons. Tommy regards this as a huge danger. I said that if the civilians succeeded in persuading the Washington soldiers—and I knew how grim and hoary they were—to plan a modern war they would be very clever, and if they did succeed, and the war lasts a year or two, we should find that only the USA was producing really useful weapons, and what then? Then, said Tommy, the Americans will turn to us and say, 'We don't care whether you antique cockroaches go on fighting or not, we have enough here to finish off the war—our war—by ourselves.' Very pleasant, I thought, and all the more reason to send the right people to Washington. I don't see any reason why the partnership should not flourish.

The wretched bag is closing, I love you very much and will think specially of you this weekend: why, I don't know, but I shall.

All my love—David

1. Afterwards Viscount Hampden.

26 April 1942 Chute

My darling dear—In the greenhouse the tomato plants grow tall and sturdy—what a bottling there will be in July and August! What a pickling in September!

Yesterday Barbie and I had our bicycle treasure hunt for fifteen local children. It was a huge success—followed by a magnificent tea when the hot and exhausted competitors struggled back to base. Followed by 'Sardines' and 'French and English' in the garden which we kept up with wild noise and wild enthusiasm until 8.15 purely because no one would go home! Finally—in the twilight—we arrived back—our hair awry—our faces shining—very stiff in the leg and broken in the wind—to be met by a flock of indignant hens whom no one had remembered to feed, then supper to get (Mrs A is on a week's holiday), then wash up—the blackout—and so to bed.

It's Sunday and if this is to catch the post I must pound up the hill.

My love to you, darling David—Sybil

29 April 1942 Chute

My darling dear—Michael Alexander arranged a glorious Tank afternoon for John. He had half an hour at speed in the turret of a cruiser tank and was taken over pot-holes and entanglements—'engaged the enemy' and made two 'jumps'. Afterwards we inspected the cunning devices for training the boys. Whole landscapes built in relief and to scale, miniature vehicles moving with clockwork precision along the tiny roads and across the pocket-handkerchief fields—while the trainee crouches in his turret and takes mock aim with a spotlight for a bullet.

I was thrilled with your presentation of '*l'affaire Laval*'. Here it is impossible to obtain anything but the most orthodox interpretation of that situation—and the orthodoxy is always inspired by a narrow and cordial detestation of Vichy and all things French.

The RAF are giving the Germans a great plastering, aren't they?

Bath has had it very badly—she is hardened to devastation but it draws a tear to think of those graceful Terraces, those Rotundas and Circuses in ugly ruins. I hope—for the sake and memory of our pleasure-loving past, that Saxton,[1] that classic old balletomane, came out of it all right.

Thank you—sweet, for some exquisite gloves. If you buy any more—choose them a trifle larger for your wife's wartime hands.

I love you and think of you and hope that wolfram goes a little better.

—Sybil

1. Sir Saxton Noble, Bt.

30 April 1942 Lisbon

My darling love—Yesterday I went and jollied the Minister of Public Works in an attempt to get a new ally. He is odd man out among the Portuguese ministers; he has the agreeable appearance and manner of a well-preserved impresario with several provincial successes to his name; he is the man who gets things done, making enemies and losses with an equal indifference; the owners of the land which he requisitions are seldom paid but the final cost of his projects still bears no relation to the estimate. He has, for me, great charm: he likes knocking down slums and poking fun at the Minister of Economy. He disposed Jock Balfour[1] and me in two armchairs and placed himself upright between us with his arms on a small oval table. He began the show with pleasantries (a bow to Jock and a wink at me) about career diplomats who cannot say yes and seldom say no. He had no faith in official negotiations, '*Ça donnera rien, ab-so-lu-ment rien*,' with a fat thumb and finger making a zero. It was all in the best burlesque manner and we enjoyed it hugely. I think he is won over.

Oliver's broadcast was scantily reported but I was tickled to see my phrase, 'more state planning and more private initiative', that is the way, advance on both hands, left and right. He might captivate the people by his gaiety; I wonder. I have written him a note asking for the full text and saying that I want to be with him.

All my love, dearest Syb—David

1. Sir John Balfour, later HM Ambassador in Madrid.

6 May 1942 Lisbon

My darling love—A rotten morning in the Embassy, one obstacle after another, bumble-bees that buzzed and sometimes settled, and I was thinking on the way to lunch, 'What hell this life is, always in trouble, never any progress, somehow or other I must get out of Lisbon.' Dragging himself up the stairs of the British Club was a middle-aged man, looking very sick, one hand bandaged and a cut on the head. 'Don't wait for me,' he said, 'my bloody pins are dying on me.' I looked at his surface wounds, 'Splinters from Jerry.' They told me he was the skipper of an English freighter, had been twice torpedoed, and last week was attacked by a Heinkel coming in to Lisbon. His arthritis is so bad that every time he goes on board they lug him up to the bridge, where he has some sort of easy-chair for a bed, and there he stays till the end of the voyage, frightened of nothing except the Admiralty should discover his infirmity (they know all about it) and give him a shore job. Negotiating with neutrals didn't seem quite so heroic.

The last news is that Walton [Butterworth] may be coming to the Peninsula to do for the US Government what I've been doing for HMG these two years. I put the idea into Winant's head when he was here and I shall be enchanted if it bears fruit. What a good thing Winant is back in London! I shall run to see him as soon as I get home, he must lend me his copy of Emily Brontë's poems,[1] which are so impossible to get hold of. I've seen Leahy. He has his wife's body with him which casts a gloom over the conversation, but he's a shrewd man and his views about France tally with mine *exactly*; this is a great reinforcement as he is better able to judge than anyone else on our side. You will find that all expert opinion will in the course of time rally to the view that we overestimated the danger from the French (fleet, bases, etc.) and underestimated the co-operation we might have got from them if we had treated them differently. When in the event the French do not attack us with their fleet or give away bases in North Africa, in spite of Madagascar,[2] most of the boys at home will pretend they never were afraid these disasters would happen, but you and I know they are horribly afraid and that this imagined cancer eats at better relations day in, day out. Laval's filthy remarks to Tuck (the US Chargé d'Affaires at Vichy) on the subject of Madagascar are only interesting because of the last sentence, in which he said that come what may the French Government would not break off relations with the USG. This is the essential point; the rest is dirty scum.

The Portuguese can never defend their empire; whoever controls the Atlantic calls that tune. Salazar used to talk to me about 'a sense of the world as a whole'—I very much liked the phrase but I little thought I should understand it so much sooner and better than he. We are going cheerfully to pool our sovereignty with America because we must create a repository of force great enough to deal with our largest possible enemies, but not by an inch will these miserable Portuguese bate their cardboard pretensions to their sacred self-determination. When I am dealing with an American official I make no difference in my conduct towards him than I would towards one of our civil servants. I admit this costs an effort, but if we are not prepared to lose our separate identity we shall never preserve what is essential—our liberty and our honour. The results of marriage—where for better or for worse at least one partner abandons a large measure of independence—has not deterred the ladies from entering these contracts. They know very well that no status is accorded to maiden aunts, and that if they marry they may in fact rule their husbands before equality is admitted as a convention, and that they can work towards equality as a convention. We need not crawl to the USA or abdicate our policy to them; no one could accuse me of this kind of calf love; but partners must trust each other or the firm goes to pieces. In the Anglo-American negotiations, which we are having with the Portuguese, I run the performance, and the Americans realise this is so, and they show appreciation—no sign of resentment. When I come to some negotiations in which the Americans take the lead and act wisely—as they are capable of doing oftener than our old gentlemen will allow—I shall remember these wolfram battles and try to behave to them as they now do to me.

A refugee just arrived from France was talking to me about the food supply. Rabbits are in great demand and a ferret fetches a thousand francs and more. He knew a poacher, in his village near Arles, who had a specially good animal which he was so afraid of losing that he carried it about inside his shirt wherever he went. 'Pretty smelly,' I said. '*Ah! mais non, il le parfumait toujours.*' Can't you see the anxious peasant pouring a little attar of roses on that cruel head? I don't know why, I thought it funny.

All my love. I'm afraid this is a letter more businesslike than personal to you, but really I can't pay you any better compliment.

Kiss that Polly—David

1. In the event Winant gave me a copy of the Columbia Press 1941 edition.
2. Madagascar, part of the French Empire, was attacked on 5 May 1942 and the main naval harbour captured on 7 May. The island surrendered on 5 November after an interval allowed for the Governor-General to amend his pro-Vichy attitude.

7 May 1942 Chute

My dearest—I am sitting in a borrowed car outside a local factory—all day I've been on tour—propaganding for the War Time Nursery—country women are not so well acquainted with Social Services as their metropolitan sisters. They look doubtful when the Nursery is suggested and one can read the thoughts revolving in their heads: 'I reckon I'll still leave Pat with Flo.' So I have to make speeches to them pointing out the good food and extra milk that Pat will have at the Nursery to build her up for the war's fourth winter—and sometimes I'm the victor and sometimes I leave defeated. It's all quite fun and as long as they provide enough petrol to keep me ambling along the roads on these heavenly days—I'm quite content.

My love to you, darling David—Sybil

10 May 1942 Under a plane tree at Ludgershall

Darling love—I seem lately to be always writing to you from strange places. At the moment—greatly impeded by an enormous gas mask attached to my chest and weighed down by a ghastly tin hat I scribble from the shelter of Ludgershall Castle walls—awaiting a messenger who will doubtless appear in his own time, aged twelve, purple in the face from excitement and importance to conduct the Ford to an incident. From all this you will know that Ludgershall is once again preparing for the Boche. I hope they give me some petrol for my part in it!

I ran into a real live cloud of gas on my arrival from Chute—round the corner spun the Ford at 40—there we were in it. What a surprise. Gently with the brakes—out with the old mask. But it was put on too quickly and not quite straight so I got a tasty whiff in at one corner.

We chatter to each other at the Aid Post. A column of soldiers has just marched past—followed by a grinning group of civilians in tin hats on bicycles. There are cheerful cries. It's all very jolly—but I wonder what we should really be feeling like? Mr James[1] has adorned his boy messengers with brilliant armlets embroidered largely with M. They are so proud and pedal on their errands wearing a look of exaltation.

With love I often think of you—your wolfram and your Doctor and your life in general of which in my heart I really know so little—in spite of the best letters in the world.

Sometimes I don't seem to be living my own life any more. Do you know that half-awake feeling? I think you do. But always somewhere profoundly there is the conviction that one day we will be on firm ground again and together.

All my love—Sybil

1. Headmaster of Ludgershall Secondary School.

12 May 1942 Lisbon

My darling love—I love to think of you as a solitary stalwart for the French: keep at it. There are forty million of them in between us and eighty million Germans; that is the fact to catch hold of. Probably there will not be enough wisdom in England to treat the French as we should after the war, and we, you and I, will raise our voices in vain, and perhaps earn considerable unpopularity; but even if we cannot turn black into white we can struggle to bring a greyish tinge into the darkness.

Madagascar was a bad blow to the Vichy representatives and even my well-trained colleagues thought the French Legation wouldn't speak to us for a while. So I went straight round and bearded the Minister and his counsellor, who had the Madagascar telegrams in their hands. I argued gently that such things must happen, a man confined to bed must sigh to hear the schoolboys in his orchard; when he was up and about again all could be put right. They took it very well and we are on the best of terms as though the incident had never happened.

At the peace conference there will be no neutrals, the victors will range everybody on one side of the table or on the other. Those who have not been obviously with us will be counted against us. Take Portugal. It is all very well for Salazar to say, 'I rely on the Anglo-Portuguese Alliance; all I ask at the peace settlement is to be left as I was before.' We shall have the Americans and the South Africans clamouring for bits of the Portuguese Empire, and probably Spain asking for something in Africa, and then how shall we defend an Ally who didn't conduct herself as an Ally? I can see the Portuguese heading for some bitter disappointments. To test out one facet of this problem I called yesterday on Dr Pienarr, the South African Minister here. He has been for some months in 'Coventry', partly because our Embassy, led by Ronnie, don't like him and his Boerish wife, and partly because his fourteen-year-old daughter's marriage has had to be lived down. Salazar had asked Pienarr to see him last week about Madagascar and Mozambique, and P had found the Doctor much more optimistic and gay than we have lately found him. After some skirmishing I came to the point: do you want Mozambique? The answer was evasive but plain enough to those used to roundabout replies. The future of Africa is worth thinking about. I suppose it would suit us to have a strong Union of African States (all red on the map of Africa except the west coast above the Equator) as a counterpoise to some other blocs; that is what Rhodes wanted and the Union of South Africa wants today. And then what about Mozambique and Beira? Two very useful ports. We shall see.

I have to go to a meeting. Let me know if there is anything you want.

All my love, dearest Syb—David

14 May 1942 — Chute

My darling David—This morning we went to Ragged Appleshaw to fetch a pig bred by a man who combines horse slaughtering with pig breeding and owns the filthiest farm. Michael McCarthy, however, had assured me that if I could overlook the dirt and smells I would find Mr B both cheerful and honest and a provider of stout healthy pigs. We waded through the muck and mire and met Mr B hot-foot from the slaughter house, smelling most odiously and with blood on his nose! I glimpsed a gory interior with heaps of entrails lying about. The pigs—oh! glory—nosing among them and bunches of manes and tails hanging from hooks in the ceiling—carefully edging the children away from this grim sight we picked our way towards the piggery.

Too late—too late. Polly—trust that female—had spotted drama in the slaughter house and only with difficulty was restrained from rushing to the ugly scene.

We picked our porker who was unsuspectingly asleep, tucked well into the cosy stomach of his mama—seized him by the ear—popped him head first in a sack—tied the top and laid him in the van—where he grunted and struggled all the way home.

Hawkins carried him like a baby to the sty and set him free. I awaited the verdict uneasily—Hawkins looked him over with the eye of an expert—presently he said, 'He's a proper sharp little pig—lively he is.' So that was all right. Thank goodness. For I'm no pig fancier. He's a large white saddleback cross which they tell me means leaner bacon.

My love to you—Sybil

Twenty minutes later

The pig is lively indeed. He jumped the sty and we have had to chase him over the fields nearly to Chantry. Huge joy of Simon and Polly. Turner says, mopping his brow, 'I've never seen a pig run like it—never.' 'More like a rabbit,' says Hawkins.

The pig is caged—Miss A[1] is making him some bread and milk and I'm handing out cider all round!

1. Miss Alexander, Polly's governess.

14 May 1942 Lisbon

My darling love—I've just met Monsieur Motte again. You must meet him. He is the Belgian Minister and his Legation is on the floor below my flat. He is reckoned the perfect drawing-room (others say 'old-school') diplomat, always a flashing smile and a pointless pleasantry. He fascinates me. We pass on the stairs two or three days a week and he makes a beautiful gesture of pleased recognition, choosing one of these two phrases, '*Ah! Ha! vous rentrez, moi je sors,*' or '*Ah! Ha! vous sortez, moi je rentre.*' Today I lurked an instant on my landing in the hope he would come in while I was on the way down, and sure enough he did: '*Ah! Ha! vous sortez, moi je rentre.*'

You can see in a man like Ronnie Campbell what really good manners can do. Among the pushing and shoving of careerists, the prickles and suspicions of foreigners, to be gracious and easy at all times is a wonderful gift. In its highest form I doubt if it could accompany a character that created things, made history, for there is something negative about refinement, the original material is shaped and loses its savage and fertile qualities. I wonder if Richelieu or Talleyrand had exquisite manners to everybody? Still, manners are a necessary weapon in the diplomat's arsenal, the pity is that so many people have thought them the only necessary accomplishment. That is not true and I stick to the rules of this game which I have worked out for myself:

(a) You must be really interested in foreigners as human beings.
(b) You must know your subject better than the man you are dealing with.
(c) You must be seen to be honest in your dealings with the government to which you are accredited. (Being honest is not enough, the conviction that you are must be carried home to the other party; that is why the Germans take such immense trouble to sow the seeds of distrust in foreigners' minds about particular English officials.)

Should you be pleased if John went into the Foreign Office? He would do well provided he learns to be interested in live as well as printed matter. I think the real conquests of diplomacy come when something very like love is established between the negotiators. We managed that in Madrid, and certainly again in Washington, and here with Salazar in 1940. Now our opposite numbers are not *à la hauteur* and Salazar is a trifle mad, so that it has been impossible to create that atmosphere of real delight in negotiation which is necessary to remove prejudices and achieve agreements.

Last night I had Couve de Murville[1] of the French Treasury and Leroy-Beaulieu to dine; they had both come straight from France. When I asked how Laval had come to take office they said it was a mystery and largely 'accidental'. There are many more accidents in history than historians will allow, because they always want their characters to seem consistent, so that they can point the motives for all the great men's actions. Is it so in real life? I don't think so. You are suddenly swept into a job or a policy because A dies or B met you in the lavatory or C has gone off with a woman. There are great trends in history which are beyond the control of individuals, the rise and fall of empires, the industrial revolution and such things, but within the trend it seems to me very accidental that one man and not another should lay his hand on the tiller. I don't see how else one can explain the sort of people who do get into prominent positions or the spate of folly which they indulge in when there.

To go back to Laval: the Frenchmen said we must remember there was no such thing as 'the Germans', in France: there were four German groups, the army; Ribbentrop and the Foreign Office; the civil administration; and the police, and what pleased one never pleased the lot. Laval was essentially the creature of Abetz and Ribbentrop and for this reason alone was disliked by the German Army, who were particularly angry at the prospect of having to be milder, in deference to Laval's diplomacy, towards subversive movements among the French public. I said that it didn't appear as though the army had had to modify its policy of repression. They replied that it was early days, and anyhow Laval was already thoroughly disliked by three out of the four German groups. They even suggested that the Marshal was a clever old fox to have Laval back in such unfavourable circumstances, since he must soon hang himself. I suspect that the Marshal just tries to keep alive, from one day to the next, both himself and France.

All my love—David

1. Afterwards Foreign Minister and Prime Minister of France.

16 May 1942 Lisbon

My darling love—Pretty good: your letter from under the Ludgershall plane tree arrived today. I know what you mean about feeling half asleep in this enduring crisis (you have a precedent for the feeling, but not for the outcome, in Desdemona); but if we are now under an anaesthetic there should be no difficulty in starting again, where we were, before the operation began.

I see no scars from the confused private life which I have led, but now have learned to dominate. At first I was amused, flattered and defeated by the number of women who said they were in love with me—I never lost my heart, as you know. You must remember that, except for a clumsy assault from Pavilion Road no one disturbed our peace for twelve years, and in this placid state what need had I to make up to man or woman?

Then suddenly I took to a trade where the art of social intercourse is an essential weapon of success, and I found, as may happen to people who adopt a hobby late in life, an aptitude for the seduction of men, and, as a by-product, of women; to keep *Latin* men on my side I had to stand well with *Latin* women, this is a rule to which I know no exception, and I admit that I played the game with the enthusiasm of a convert; and I did many disgraceful things by making women think I was ready to go to bed with them when I was not. This was wrong, and I have cured myself.

I think of you a great deal, and long to be with you, and altho' I know you would enjoy the diplomatic life and be much better at it than the ordinary run of FO wives, I still would prefer this period to be an interlude between the two acts of our joint lives, and I am glad that you aren't mixed up with it because if you were I shouldn't feel sure how either of us would be able to return to the real life, which we must make together in England.

French officials have told me that early next month negotiations will begin in Madrid for a wide commercial treaty between Spain and France, and if a satisfactory agreement is reached very obvious political consequences will follow. Under the bewildering ban of inactivity which HMG have laid upon us, I can do nothing to help or hinder these negotiations, although both parties would like us to take a benevolent interest. Do we want a Latin bloc strong enough to put thumb to nose at the Germans? Is it to our advantage that Spain and France should come together or keep apart? In these questions of two or more states drawing together one has always to distinguish between which is water and which is wine. In 1940 we all agreed to put some Portuguese water in the Spanish wine, and a great success it was—can we consider a Peninsular policy good for France, Belgium, etc.? As Nazi Europe is a house with drawn curtains, and all the light given artificially from Berlin, my instinct is to welcome any attempt to peep at the sunlight of our world. Instead we seem bent on helping the enemy to black out the Continent. Is this the way to win friends to our side? Who was the greatest capturer of men in history? Obviously Saint Paul. Did he stay at home and refuse to speak to those who disagreed with his faith? His whole life after his vision—and perhaps this is the point, we *need God* to open our naturally blind eyes—was a protest against inactivity. All things to all men. And I don't think Saint Paul's enthusiasm for his cause would have made a bad showing against Mr Elmer Davies's for his, and I know under which flag I serve.

18 May
I have read again what I've written above. I want you to know how much I love you, and I had a moment's panic that you might think I was trying to buy you off with letters—a quite horrible thought! I don't tell you often how beautiful you are and how much I would like to touch your hand in between courses at our own dining table—but I will when I see you again.

All my love—David

17 May 1942 Chute

My dear love—A long letter[1] came from you yesterday—posted by a safe hand in Happy Hampstead. Who can it have been? I loved your story of the brave sea captain. What men they are! We don't think half enough of them.

At the time of Dunkirk we told ourselves too often that we bore the French no grudge—patting ourselves on the back for a magnanimity that was not genuinely felt. Beneath the skin and in the guts, age-old resentments seethed and bubbled anew—and the wound has festered ever since.

It will take a good deal of skill and education to put things right.

Do the French feel much better about us? They may want us to win—just because they don't want the Germans to be victorious—but afterwards? Making the peace—what then? People are still hopelessly nationalist-minded. You're right about pooling sovereignties, etc., but nine out of ten times when two or three are gathered together and one so much as suggests that possibility it's to invite murder with oneself as the victim.

The pig has settled down and Polly sends her love—she is losing her front teeth—isn't it sad.

All my love—Sybil

1. 6 May.

19 May 1942 Lisbon

My darling love—There was no bag out yesterday so I shall send you two letters in one cover. We've been hearing from Count Kerchove—a huge friend of mine, more of him later—how the Hungarians whom he met last week in Berne want to get out of the war. Here is a typical story current in Budapest about an interview between Welles[1] and Roosevelt:

SW Mr President, you ought to declare war on Hungary.
FDR I can't follow all the changes in Central Europe. What's the constitution of Hungary?
SW A monarchy, Mr President.
FDR Who's the king?
SW There isn't a king, Admiral Horthy is regent.
FDR That's serious, an admiral, they must have a fleet.
SW They have no fleet, Mr President.
FDR Well, what are they doing in the war?
SW They're fighting Russia.
FDR Have they any claims against Russia?
SW No, Mr President, but they have claims against Austria, Roumania and Italy.
FDR Are they at war with Germany, Roumania and Italy?
SW No, Mr President, they're giving aid to those countries.
FDR They're crazy, Mr Welles . . .

Old Kerchove, he really should be called Boss Kerchove, is a vast sack of a man who was Belgian Ambassador in Rome when the Germans invaded his country. He immediately resigned and took on the direction of the Belgian Relief work so far as concerns the purchase of food from European neutrals to be sent for distribution in Belgium. Portugal is much the most abundant market in Europe so his headquarters are in Lisbon. We provide through the Bank of England escudos to the value of £250,000 a month for his purchases, and I negotiate all his financial arrangements with the Bank of Portugal on behalf of HMG. My heart being in the business and my relations with the Bank of Portugal first rate I have really brought off a minor coup in securing that these considerable funds are at his disposal—considerable because food is getting short here and permission to take out £3 million a year is no sneezing matter. He's grateful and I'm delighted, so we are the best of friends. He promises us—you and me—a royal welcome in Belgium after the war and I've no doubt we shall get it. (It will please me enormously to show you some of the European I have either worked in or for.)

He's against Leopold for the same reasons as ours against Edward VIII, and I remember Daddy saying that in the *Golden Bough* Frazer noted that the earliest custom common to all primitive nations was a refusal to allow the head of the tribe to marry anyone who wasn't a virgin. Mademoiselle Baels, about whose brother I wrote you, was perhaps a case in point . . . and the Belgian aristocracy won't stand it. Some of course say that the institution of monarchy is so sacred that they must put up with the King, who makes an ass of himself, but most hope he will abdicate.

All my love. I long to be with you—David

1. Sumner Welles, American Under-Secretary of State.

21 May 1942 Chute

My dear love—Our day in Kent was a huge success. We were taken round by an energetic middle-aged country spinster. Full of humour—with a face like an amiable and trustworthy horse and very efficient and likeable.

We lunched afterwards at her home, a large Georgian house—

full of light and ancient, faded chintzes—cabinets of china and mahogany gleaming against the papered walls. Upstairs the paint was well washed and peeling—drawings of favourite hounds on the landings, a fox's mask over the bathroom door and a [fox's] brush in the lavatory.

She lives there with an old mother and deaf bachelor brother and now have come to join them the other brothers' wives and their bunches of children.

We tidied our hairs and were asked if we would like to see the beagles. What answer was there but yes? We were rewarded by the evident satisfaction of our hostess who said briskly, 'Then let us go at once, shall we, and wash our hands after.' We went.

The beagles were just beagles and rather more smelly than usual on their war diet. But our reception was hearty. She told us they were the treasure of her brother's life.

After the collapse in '40, when invasion seemed to Kent inevitable and imminent—they dug the beagles' graves and her brother slept with his gun at his side to be ready to shoot his beauties at the first sniff of a German.

He even polished off a few in preparation—I suppose in case he didn't have time to do the lot at one go! And then was justifiably annoyed when the Germans failed him.

You don't save four last bullets for mother and sister when there's a beagle to be considered!

We thought he must be rather nice and wished we'd seen him.

All my love—Sybil

23 May 1942 — Lisbon

My darling love—I don't know where we are with our negotiations. Walt [Butterworth] is definitely coming to Lisbon. MEW expects him and other Americans in London in a week's time and have asked Jack Nicholls[1] to return to discuss with them what is obviously my business; but I do not complain, for my immediate job is to secure the wolfram and I will not leave Lisbon until all these months of bargaining are rounded off with an agreement. The rats, therefore, nibbling away at my cheese, leave me undisturbed. Further, I have got the famous French tankers out of the Mediterranean, Laval or no Laval, for they sailed from Oran today. They are my peculiar children, since London and Washington have been frankly sceptical of the whole affair. Always I shall regard the result as due to handling the French with honesty and understanding.

Last night a bird of passage described the political scene in London as follows: I give you his account without prejudice and without comment.

(a) The PM's stock is rising perhaps for the last time.
(b) The Beaver[2] is preparing to return to the stage and will attack the PM and back AE.[3]
(c) Oliver [Lyttelton] is relying too much on Brendan [Bracken] who will go down in the turmoil let loose by the Beaver.
(d) Cripps has a following in the public but no party machine and so cannot win an election.
(e) The future lies with the man who can tie up with Rab Butler and the Conservative party machine.

All my love, sweet Syb—David

1. First Secretary at the British Embassy, afterwards Sir John Nicholls.
2. Lord Beaverbrook.
3. Anthony Eden.

25 May 1942 Lisbon

My darling love—We are still angling for your next winter's sardines: seventy-five million boxes of quarter-club, I can talk Billingsgate with the best of them. The Portuguese fishing and canning industry would like to sign up with us but the Portuguese Government thinks it can usefully bargain a little longer with their Allies' food supply. Last week the Fish Institute gave me a banquet lunch, presumably to show their government where their sympathies lie, and you may imagine the spread. We began with twenty-one kinds of fish hors d'oeuvres, helped for me by the President, no escape, and how good they were . . . then turbot, fat as a jelly, leg of lamb, strawberry ice, and cream cheese with the port. Afterwards a tour of the Institute, remarkable for the chemist, a Frenchman of seventy years, white hair *en brosse*, tired blue eyes in a wise rabbit's face, and a charm that would distil the most refractory of elements.

His tests to prove if any metal had been absorbed from the tin by the sardines were particularly good. Fish attack metals, different fish different metals and in different degrees. No one knows why. Fish are not acid but they combine in marriage with lead easily, with iron less so, and with tin least of all.

26 May, later

Ronnie has been teaching me the trade secrets of diplomacy. 'If you call upon a colleague or a Minister of State and he does not rise to greet you—as will happen when he thinks he can set the tone by such a show of incivility—walk over to his window and ask, "What is that palace or that knot of persons that I see?" He will get up and, in moving to share your curiosity, he will learn his lesson.' I feel myself at the last hour of my diplomatic life, which is dying fast, and I cling to these vestiges of a bright day that is done.

I wonder how much you feel the *frisson mélancholique* of our unstable world. Sometimes I have thought that you are lucky enough not to. You remember I called you 'good' like a 'good pear' and I meant by that a sound and sane creature who did not forge doubts for the pleasure—the vice rather—of shivering. I don't mean that you are insensitive—oh! no—but you don't create situations for the fun of playing the artist. Isaiah's verse, 'Thou shalt fear and thy heart be enlarged,' is true of our present experiences. Your fears are perhaps more natural, less cerebral, than mine, and certainly we need each other to restrain the darker side of our imaginings.

You said that in this interval of conscripted chaos you live half asleep, yes, yes, that's right, but how much do you dream? There's the point. I dream so much and so vividly that I cannot draw a line between reality and fiction—and why is a dream, which one experiences after all, any less real than a newspaper article which one reads with such distrust? How comes it that I trust my own fancies beyond the policies and ordinances of great men? Is this 'freedom of action' or the blindness of vanity which the gods lay upon their victims? We are very lonely in this world if we are brave or foolish enough to rely upon our own understanding, and are willing, as Nelson said, by it to stand or fall. Our only comfort is someone's love, in my case, yours.

All my love, darling Syb—David

28 May 1942 Lisbon

My darling love—Last night we argued about the degree of vindictiveness we ought to show after the war towards those people in neutral countries who worked for the Axis during the war. One means of waging economic warfare is to publish lists of persons and firms in neutral countries who are known to be trading with the enemy, and to forbid any British subject to deal with them, and to warn other neutral persons that if they deal with them they will get no more of our business. By this Black List we divide the sheep from the goats, and there is little doubt that our sheep have to forgo many occasions of profit which become the monopoly of the Axis goats. What should happen to the goats after the war?

After the last war the Lists were abolished and British traders soon became indifferent with whom they dealt—ex-sheep or ex-goats. The tough young Blockaders of today would like to prolong the operation of the Lists after the war as a punishment to the goats and a reward to the sheep. They believe that the Portuguese who now trade so merrily with the Axis do so largely because they feel sure that even if Germany loses England will not punish them. Therefore, say our modern warriors, let us now tell them that we shall be vindictive for five or ten years after the war.

The advocates of revenge, when pushed, always fall into the trap of saying, 'Well, what do you think the Germans would do to *our* friends if *we* lost the war?' Then I smile inwardly, because they are caught and I can stage a counter-attack which leaves them in heaps. It is curious how many of my brightest colleagues have so little sense of the difference between the ways of life for which we and the enemy are at war. Self-preservation is enough for them. They see the enemy winning victories and impressing neutrals, and immediately they cry out that we must copy his weapons.

What motives prompt the neutral firms who remain faithful to us? Some have always been sure that we shall win and we need look no further for a reason for their support—the others, much more numerous and interesting, who have not been certain of our victory, have worked for us because they *want* us to win; they believe our victory is in the interest of the world, of Portugal, of their religion. Should we try to recruit these people by bribes and promises of rewards? I have never thought you could rely on people's goodwill if it is bought, still less if it is obtained by threats; men must believe in what they do or they are ready to change their course at the slightest puff of wind from a new quarter; and if we started a long-term system of rewards and punishments we should take away just that idealism, that sense that all we do is not done for money, which must flourish if civilisation is to be preserved. Then say the tough Blockaders, 'But we have been soft too long, now we must be hard and ruthless.' So we are only fighting the war to imitate the Nazis! I suppose it is so long ago since the British people had to fight for their freedom of thought, so long since the Americans set up by themselves for just this reason, that our newest generation doesn't know what our tradition is. We ought to be sterner than our fathers, but according to some principles of justice, not merely by an exercise of superior power: between a strong leader and a greedy bully there is a world of difference. I don't blame my friends for wanting to be tough. You see how one is always brought back to the same point: unless we know what sort of life we want to lead in England we cannot act consistently or make full use of our natural advantages in any sphere of our foreign relations. It is for this reason that I would now like to turn from the foreign to the home battlefield.

A better letter next time. I am very hurried.

—David

30 May 1942 Chute

My darling—I have your letter of 16 May and onwards—Remember of this one what you will. I just have to write it. I am to believe that you love me. This has become very difficult—Your letters have been the anaesthetic that seduced and bewitched me through the first one and a half years of war. They have lost their power and make me dream no longer.

Why should I think you love me? Because you need me—or are lonely for me—or want the comfort of my presence? It is by these things that I judge love and you desire none of them. I recognise the arguments—the reasons, the denials. Let us discard them for the truth is not there. You are one of those whose life moves by in periods, to one of these I belonged—was essential, perhaps—but the scene has shifted, the journey moved another stage and I am out of step with the Pilgrim's progress. Neither at home nor abroad am I necessary any more—your letters are the dividend of a generous heart to capital invested long ago. In your presence I often recognise them for that. We had some good years—you call them 'placid' now. It's a sad, pale little word. For me they were made brilliant by my love for you. Sometimes I was dazzled by our life and would wake at night shivering with apprehension. When at last it did pass I stored the memory as Daddy does his claret. It wasn't gone, only out of sight in some cellar of the mind. A possession of infinite rarity—not for clumsy handling.

So you dealt a harsh blow when you told me that even in love we had always been calculated and deliberate. It was like a stab. I can see your face as you said it—the dress I was wearing—how the people looked around us.

The reel snapped and the camera was still. I think it was then I saw that by my pursuit of something already beyond sight I might goad you to destroy the lost years that for me still held reality.

How much of our life together had reality for you I could, and can no longer, calculate. It would be folly to attempt it. The war brought you an opportunity to lead a life beyond your dreams. In youth we were confined within our bourgeois upbringing. We married—had children—moved house—wandered together in lands other than our own—kissed and made love. Secure in happiness I failed to recognise the waning star. A clap of war, and you were gone. To success and flattery—to women and the company of people either brilliant or beguiling. At first you made a few gestures towards me—these ceased and have been followed ever since by a trickle of reasons designed to keep me at a distance—for you required nothing of me and I should spoil the fun. You say there should be no difficulty in starting again where we were. We can never do that. Make no mistake. You would be incapable of it for you no longer need or desire me—and I am not a piece of furniture to be withdrawn from store. With patience we shall find new ground to share. If I have been slow to recognise this it is because there is always one who loves and pines the longer. Pity the poets if it were not so. I have been much at fault—rebellious and vain and have paid for it in hours of the most extreme misery and dejection.

All this is past. The proof lies in this letter, which couldn't have been written a few months ago.

When you last went away I determined in our joint cause to acquire a fresh design for living. Since then my life has taken me down new and unaccustomed ways that have comforted and cured most strangely. When one day you return I think I can promise a quiet life to both of us.

My love to you, dear sweet David—Sybil

3–4 June 1942, *midnight* Lisbon

Très chère Madame—Your letter of 30 May is true and welcome. On some small points you are wrong, but in the main you are right, and right with a grace that takes my breath away. If I am not to be in love with you, I may admire you very much.

I've known you've been very unhappy, and when I think how I am responsible I hide my head. And there's one thing that puzzles me. You know I always wanted you to have your own life and be square with me, not a follower-on, and for what perverse reason have I lately forgotten this sane principle? Explain me that.

Your letter tempts me to summon up days that would prove how happy I was, but I won't look over my shoulder. No more anaesthetics. We must get level again. The first thing is to press on with your own independence; in my sensible moments I never wanted you to be shadowy Mrs Eccles, and when you took your name again, and gave it to the children, I was glad. That was the right road and I am so very excited you are back on it. (Rab[1] writes that you are on his Social Services Committee, is that true? I hope so.)

I have had many occasions to fall in love with other women. I haven't done so, and in these last months I have begun to see why. Now it is your turn to go through that experience. I have no right to be jealous.

I wish I could make you financially independent, I will as soon as I can sell the pictures, for unless you are free in every sort of way we shall not surrender to each other again. That, you see, is what I intend. Burn up all the past. Divorce in fact if not in law, and then try to marry you again. If you don't like the idea I shall answer that you didn't much like it the first time, and if I won you once I may be able to do it twice. So make a clean sweep of your old love, put up the barricades, engage mercenaries to help in the defence, regard the children as yours only—I'll not climb in by that window—now suddenly I've thought what I could do. I care more for Chute than anything else, will you let me make it over to you? Say the word and it is yours.

We need one more telegram from Washington and I think we can settle wolfram. I had just made up my mind to come home at once, and had been thinking of sending you the 'arriving tomorrow' signal, as soon as the agreement is signed. But I will go back to an older plan, and make a tour of our mines in the north, and perhaps take a look at Madrid, and then in high summer return, very frightened, to the most important battle of my war.

My love to you—David

1. R. A. Butler, President of the Board of Education 1941–4.

3 June 1942 Chute

My darling David—Letters up to 28 May from you today and yesterday. The aeroplanes are wafted to our shores on the sudden blissful summer breezes.

I read this morning's in the walled garden—surrounded by tools of labour—sitting on the wooden seat beneath the apple tree and the wood was warm to the touch though the hour was early.

All the day the garden has lain quiet and pale beneath the sun. No sound above the hum of summer flies and the industrious rustling of the gardeners. With evening colour has flowed back into the borders. Forget-me-nots against the grass are blue as today's sky and in this slumbering light one sees no longer that the wallflowers are beyond their early beauty. Soon your irises will stand like lovely sentinels beneath the sycamores, from whose boughs the birds tonight cry out in triumph and astonishment that June is come at last.

Your letter of 29 May came with the postman this morning. I was thrilled with it, for of course you are right to fight the Blockaders who would prolong the bitterness and emnity of war into the economics of peace. How are we to build a new structure for Europe—within which we must hope may dwell confidence, faith and prosperity—and perhaps peace—though we shan't keep that for long unless we work like the devil to preserve it—if we are going to divide sheep from goats? Wagging our finger at the bad lads outside the charmed circle to whom we will not give an entrance ticket. It just doesn't make sense, does it? Surely these 'tough' chaps can't have quite forgotten the tragedy of Versailles. Wasn't one of its principal errors the failure to bring everyone in, to share in reconstruction and the revival of trade?

All my love—dear David—Sybil

10 June 1942 Lisbon

My darling Syb—How can you be quite so self-controlled? You write a letter on 30 May that turns my guts inside out, breaks and I believe re-makes the direction of my life, and here you are on 3 June hoeing and weeding and ruminating in the quiet sunshine as though nothing had happened . . . do you think your pebble made a lazy ring or two and now the surface is glassy again? Pebble indeed! The rock you hurled has quite dispersed the pond, there is nothing of it now but a craggy hump with a shivering D clinging on top. You've left me chattering with fear, not just naked, but without my skin, exposed to all the blasts of an uncommonly active fancy. Oh! my sweet dear, you imagine what it is to come back to your senses after such an absence.

Oh! dreadful is the check—intense the agony—
When the ear begins to hear, and the eye begins to see;
When the pulse begins to throb, the brain to think again;
The soul to feel the flesh, and the flesh to feel the chain.[1]

Do you remember how we used to chase round the modest drawing-room at No. 8? That's what I would do if I came on you now in the wall garden, chase you, but without much hope of catching you—so soft and sedentary is my life—still old Hercules would have a try, and you could give in if you felt like it.

We may be poorer, not much if I'm in the City, but if it's politics we'll be pinched, who cares? We've amassed another kind of capital that pays an untaxable dividend, higher each year, and if we can be ambitious without being jealous of competitors we'll make a fortune out of public service. Here's a letter showing that if wolfram hadn't nailed me to this parish pump you might have been the wife of the Member for Salisbury. How would you have liked that? I wonder if Devizes will be going next election?

Write more about yourself. I love to hear about Chute and the children and the flowers, but much more about you. Have you any new clothes or old ones re-vamped? Do you do your hair in the same way? I dreamed you had cut it off. Do you want any sunburned shade of powder? Here I can get you anything.

Later
The French Legation say that the Italian claims on Corsica and Nice, which figured in the news recently, were trumped up by Laval and Mussolini; one to have an excuse for putting troops on the French frontier and therefore not in Russia, the other to have an easy chance to become popular with his own people, knocking down the enemy's claims which were never seriously meant. In a world of double-crosses, it may be true. This is true about Laval: you remember his rude note to the US Government on Martinique? He told his staff to spread it about that this note was only for show, to please the Germans, and that the note he had really sent was much more amiable.

My love to you. I pine for your letters—David

1. From 'The Prisoner' by Emily Brontë.

13 June 1942 London

David—Your letter has come on to London where I have been this week. It was honest and I was so grateful for it that I forgot for a moment the hard laws of latitude and stretched out my hand to touch and thank you. I must have been more afraid than I knew, that you would not perfectly understand. Now we are both released and how good it feels. You've been at large for some time. I am that swimmer lately in danger from the burden of his waterlogged clothes—who by a final effort shakes himself free and gains the bank, there to pant and recover in the sun whose warmth he had thought not to feel again. It is delicious on the bank and I'm absurdly happy.

No—don't give me Chute. We made it together and I have always thought of it as belonging to both of us.

That will still do.

I don't want any more possessions.

I'm glad you are not coming home at once. I need some time before we take possession of our new house. At this moment I would find it hard to decide upon the rooms in which we mean to live—

My love to you—Sybil

12 June 1942 Lisbon

My darling Syb—There's an extra bag and I've time to write you a scrap. Who should I sit next to at lunch but Harry Hinton![1] Looking like an ancient animal from one of Beatrix Potter's books. When I declared my Dawson connection he was enraptured. Immediately, unaccountably and bewitchingly his creaking mind spun back thirty years to a spaniel called Sue, a splendid little dog, Daddy had taken her to France in the last war, and left her there, covered in boils, he'd met the man, a Major thingumibob, who'd had to destroy her. A splendid little dog. And then he fumbled his way up the stream of memory to you and your visit to Madeira. 'Remember I told her the first night at dinner to look out for bats. Hang 'emselves behind the picture frames. Sybil was ever so nervous and turned her head. I rumpled her hair, what a fright she had! Thought it was a bat. HA! HA!' And how he sent you a wedding present apologising he couldn't come to the wedding and you wrote back 'better luck next time'. Then up the stream of memory again to see you blue with cold bathing at Torridon. He is charming, but he seemed nearly angelic for he could talk about you.

My love—David

1. An Englishman who became a leading figure in Madeira.

20 June 1942 Tenbury Wells

I do indeed want to have your letters, dear David. I like the things you say and the way you say them. Now that the curtain has been rung down on the masquerade I can once more see an envelope in your hand without that constriction of the heart and mind which has made the reading so painful for so long. I try to understand the sickness of your imagination which you so beautifully describe—to me it just means—ceasing to love—but to this I know you will retort that a woman is like a good pear, hanging languidly among the leafy boughs—content to feel the sun's warmth and the wash of the rain—her life reduced to terms of the purest simplicity—few questions and few cares. Perhaps you are right and we but rarely know that turmoil and confusion of the soul that men must suffer. I wish I had realised sooner that you were out of love with me. Perhaps there have been moments of trouble and doubt for several years—but I think I knew a year ago.

Scotland[1] was the final struggle—the last *grande déception*—you were quite right to be terrified. I blinded myself into happiness for ten days. What fools we are to pursue lost things and then deceive ourselves into believing we have recaptured them. And what horror it must have meant for you—I shake with shame at the memory of that. I cannot yet see what manner of life awaits us and it isn't much use to try at the moment for I simply can't think at all in terms of our two selves. When I try to, it frightens me, so far has my heart wandered at last. I had thought it could never escape from your keeping.

With my love—Sybil

1. Where we spent a week of my last leave.

14 June 1942 Lisbon

My darling love—I'm wildly impatient for your next letters, but in the meantime will copy you and write as calm as a cucumber.

You've met Señor X . . . his sister has long been a friend to all the British Embassy in Madrid. She is, I suppose, forty-five plus, handsome and stocky, too much and too-dyed hair, wears too many jewels, and laughs like a horse. We all love her for being pro-British and gay and indiscreet. She's here for a week's shopping and after lunch yesterday we had this conversation. Why had she never married? She'd been very silly, she said, she ought to have married, *n'importe qui*, to have a status. At seventeen she had fallen in love with a married man and their affair had lasted till she was thirty-two, when he died, otherwise it would be going on now. She'd been stupid but it had been worth it. In Spain affairs before marriage were very bad, after marriage you could do what you liked. In Scandinavia it was the reverse and she thought the northern habit much better for the family; but, I said, as there is easy divorce in those countries the people there get it both ways. That, she thought, was cheating God and man.

She was sure the English did not understand how Spanish women loved. The Church declared that adultery was a sin, but every Spanish girl was brought up to believe that once and once only in her life she might find her true love, and then she could go to him and be forgiven for love's sake. She mused over her own long affair, '*era mi hombre*', he was my man. From the man of their heart Spanish women do not expect marriage, and it seems that Spanish men often pardon infidelity in their wives if it is a clear case of 'their man'. And she went on to describe the toughness of a Spaniard's love, how it never changed unless the man insulted and insulted the woman, he could have mistresses by the dozen, every Spanish woman understood the *coup de moineau*, but he would be forgiven unless he flaunted them in her face; and how the greatest passions in Spain were always accompanied by a clear recognition of the failings of the man concerned; there was an Andalucian proverb, 'My man has lost a hand, one charm less, I love him just the same.' 'One charm less' was symbolic, she said, of Spanish loyalty and Spanish fatalism.

She then put names from the bright world of Madrid to illustrate what she had been saying, and knowing many of these passionate creatures I was fascinated and occasionally disturbed. Spain is a country where you hear constantly the names of two people linked together, like Paolo and Francesca, seen to be indivisible till death separates them.

The personal relations of English men and women are very seldom as important as this either to themselves or to their neighbours. Is this really true, or is it because we hide our feelings? I think it is true because hiding, which has gone on so long that Elizabethan passions are almost as strange to us as modern Spanish, has had its effect, and what is not nourished by the light of day, the admiration, opposition or at least gossip of the world, wilts and loses both character and force. In the dim light of the English scene could there not be one torch of stouter flame?

Flames remind me that last night was Saint Antony's night when the Portuguese jump through bonfires and are lucky in love. I was dining with Marcus and Connie Cheke[1] who live on the fringe of Lisbon. The farm buildings elbow the big house and behind them on the grass were trestle tables set for the peasants' feast. The diners were to have a huge cauldron of fish soup, which we all tasted out of the wooden spoon, delicious it was, and then a roasted sheep; the cowman enchanted us because he was the very man, the Strong Man, who does his turn at the end of *The Blue Danube*;[2] there he was, with a shock of black hair, a red face, a short-sleeved cotton vest his only upper garment, baggy trousers always needing a hitch-up, and spitting on his hands before he lifted the cauldron.

After our dinner we came out armed with fireworks, rather poor little things, but they spluttered and banged, and greatly helped that battle of the sexes which is a regular feature of peasant orgies—the dozen girls huddled in a giggly bunch, taking refuge behind a farm wagon, scattering with shrieks when a boy crawled underneath with a handful of squibs, coming together again in a rush—it seemed to me impelled by some wild force of nature—to seize the first straw for the bonfire. The bonfire was made on the flagged courtyard in front of the house. Only straw is used because it gives a big flame and little heat, and the bottom doesn't accumulate hot ash, which would make the jumping dangerous. Then over and through the flames they went howling and chanting and working us all up, crying, 'Lucky in Love!', 'Lucky in Love!' louder and louder, till Marcus was rushing and I was rushing, and the next moment we had passed through the fire and were rubbing the smoke from our eyes and the sparks from our legs.

15 June

My affairs are boiling up in London. 'The Office of the Minister of Production' has written a funny letter to the Establishment Officer at MEW enquiring if I am house-trained as *I* have *asked* them for a job! This is one of those inverted jokes the Civil Service loves to play. Henry[3] is annoyed, he calls it 'surprised', another CS misrepresentation. I showed the correspondence to Ronnie, whose advice is categorical: 'Get out of MEW as soon as you can, and go to Oliver in any capacity.' I need *your* help to prepare the way and to head off trouble. See Oliver if you can. Isobel Cripps put Stafford into the War Cabinet.

All my love, I long for you—David

1. Marcus Cheke afterwards became HM Minister to the Vatican.
2. A ballet.
3. Henry Drogheda, Director-General of MEW.

23 June 1942 Lisbon

My darling Syb—Your sheet of minute paper with its long-awaited answer has come. I am very glad that you are happy. I have tried to make you happy for fourteen years, and lately failed, and now if to succeed again, it is necessary to do it in this way, it must be so. As for me, I have been slipping again into a wild turmoil of thoughts and desires and unresolvable doubts; it's so bad that it should happen just when Walt [Butterworth] arrives and I ought to be as clear as a bell, bad I mean for our cause, which looks sick. I won't tell you how miserable I am because I don't want your pity or to excuse anything . . . if I could see you I could tell you with conviction what I have to say, but I can't write it, you have taken away my belief in the honesty of what I write. Thus is my lifeline snapped. It seems to me that I was born rather unusually dishonest but that I made a real and steady effort to be honest for your sake, and that I have failed. The effort may have been worthwhile, that I don't know yet, but if it hasn't, then something horrible will come.

Damn the education of the English gent, I never succeeded in explaining to you the sensitive nature of my thoughts, and damn the cold-fishiness of the education of an English lady which prevents you from explaining to me your physical reactions. What self-control we exercised! Christ, and I thought always it would come right again!

Am I selfish? Of course I am to that devouring and dangerous extent you find in all men who have in them the seed, undeveloped, but swelling, of great power over their times and fellow men. Don't imagine you or I can control what happens inside my head and body, there is a strange power that is far stronger than my conscious will. We can influence its direction, if we act together, but if that is not possible, then I see no light. I see two courses open to me: I could deny the world and go away and read and write and pray, it would not be very hard for me to do this, I have it often as a longing; or we could together plunge into the treacherous waters of public life. But what I *will not* contemplate is any compromise between these two. If you fancy a cold partnership you must look elsewhere. I am a monopolist through and through, but for you I tried always to make the exception and to treat you thinking of your point of view. Well, as far as my present muddy feelings will let me know my thoughts, I don't think I can do that again, and I shan't try to be happy, never never, with any other woman, I might sleep with half a dozen and be none the worse, but that's nothing to do with my idea of happiness, nor could I find my idea of happiness living with you only as a friend—and I am quite ruthless over these things, as you know I cut losses like a piece of cake . . . So though you may be basking in the sunshine on your bank, and I am glad, I am adrift, and must now go to a meeting with Walt where I shall use the wrong arguments and the wrong phrases.

—David

24 June 1942 Lisbon

My darling Syb—Yesterday I wrote you two twisted pages in bed, and got up to spend the day in fruitless negotiation—all hope of success killed by the surrender of Tobruk. In the evening I had to pull hard at myself to produce the telegram surveying the ways of retreat open to us. Then, tired and wretched, I went to dine with an Englishman who has gone half native and is married (for the second time) to a dancer from Seville. He fifty, gay and lascivious; she thirty, beautiful as a peach that is just over-ripe. They had invited six people but no one turned up except me. We are having ARP practices in Lisbon and the cowardly snivellers would not risk going home in the black-out, and as this exercise had only been announced in the course of the day, there was the table spread for eight. The lady showed taste in refusing to eat in the dining-room and having a card table laid up in the library.

Across the cocktails she said, 'Eccles is unhappy; he has lost his girl.' 'True,' I answered, 'very true.' 'Then he must get drunk.' 'No, I will not, I have no wish to forget.' 'Ah! what splendid passion, I always said Eccles was Spanish at heart.' We ate, we drank, well and copiously, I was talking Spanish mysteriously better than ever before, and with a real eloquence, something that astonished all three of us, and me most. But neither wine nor iced soufflé nor the gift of tongues could hold up my slither into dejection, and that essential woman, whose lap had probably received the tears of a dozen men, noted every decline in my spirits. To her husband's annoyance she walked out when the coffee came.

Suddenly we heard a gramophone shouting a wild tango. 'Good God! Teresa's going to dance.' Pale as his napkin he led the way to the drawing-room, we approached it as if it were on fire. The carpet had been rolled up. There was nothing there except the maddening music. We sat down and waited. The biting and blood-curdling chatter of the castanets began in the passage. She came in scarlet flounces, gold shoes, mantilla comb, and a carnation in her teeth. From our sofa, she seemed some waving blood-red anemone on the sea-bed, bending and whirling in the eddies of unseen currents, and all the time the castanets pecking and drilling into our vitals—an army of death-watch beetles gnawing through the last prop that holds up the roof of the mind—as the music changed she moved in and out, a different shawl, a different flower, at last after an hour she stood in front of us and spoke quietly to her husband, slowly because her breath was exhausted, 'Eccles is still unhappy; there is only one thing more a woman can do for him; may I do it?' 'You may, but I shall kill you afterwards.'

The servant brought in the whisky tray, and I soon went home in the moonlight that mocked the black-out and made a bridge from the unreality of what had just happened to the narrow certainty of my single bed.

Later

Walt is getting a grip on his organisation. He will dominate his own legation, and when I'm gone, it is a fair bet he will dominate our Embassy too. The Americans never before took a live interest in Portuguese affairs. They have been observers and not active partners in the diplomatic game, their intervention being confined to protecting the rights of individual American citizens. Now they have to put a big finger in the pie of policy. And of course this means the end of the easy social life which their ministers have led for a century. Mr Bert Fish, the present occupant of the job, doesn't like the ups and downs which attend any active attempt to influence the course of Portuguese history. He behaves just like a child who doesn't want to go to a party, is afraid of dropping a brick or being pointed at. The nursery is so much safer. I have been, and Walt will now be much more, his mother, urging him to run along and brush his hair, for when he gets there he'll enjoy it tremendously. Experience, wisdom, is just this: you can recognise the patterns on the brocade of life quickly and surely enough to make your dispositions when only a few stitches have appeared.

I feel better today, but inside my head very wobbly.

My love—David

27 June 1942 Chute

My darling David—We've had two Social Service Committees so far and I'm determined to reserve judgement as yet. The first impressions inspire me with little hope that the committee gathered round the table at Palace Chambers will prove leaders of the world. Our Chairman—a handsome ex-Mayor of Birmingham—has charm and humour. But he doesn't stay the course particularly well and either loses patience and rushes us from one decision to another with catastrophic haste—or lights his pipe and slackens the rein—allowing any member to pop on to a hobby horse and ride off in any direction he pleases. This is lamentable for one by one we gallop off and are lost to view. But it isn't always like this. Maybe we are very raw and will settle down to it better when the hot air has cooled. The politicians among us are hopeless slaves to the party system. Terrified of an original thought or a novel recommendation lest it might be judged 'disloyal' to the machine. They never for a moment take their eyes off the next election. 'Our decisions must be in harmony with the general trend of party opinion.' All that and a lot more. The Chairman has no patience with this and shows his displeasure pretty clearly. But the gents from Westminster are not put down for long—up they pop again, with their cautions and their obedient fears whenever anyone launches the smallest squib.

I must be off to Ludgershall. We are eating our first peas and new potatoes for lunch. It's a greedy thought—I shall hurry back with longing.

With love—Sybil

3 July 1942 Chute

My darling David—Your letters bewilder me and I no longer have any certainty how to answer them. I never had any wish to hurt you—yet I seem to have made you unhappy. When we are miserable we always look inwards—this is what I have been doing for a long while now and thus perhaps have failed to recognise that which you call the 'sensitive nature of my thoughts'. I don't know. Maybe I have never understood you—have always been inadequate for the task. I shouldn't be surprised. As you very well know—for you have often laughed at me for it—I used always to wonder what you married me for! It was a genuine conundrum—and at one time, a delicious speculation as well. I have always known you for a person whose character and will bore as many facets as a well-cut diamond. I knew you were often at conflict with yourself, that you wandered down ways where I might not follow—and dwelt in regions where I had no place.

This never troubled me—nor should it have done—each one of us has a right to solitude of that kind. But you know very well that it became more than that. Until you only gave yourself to me in letters—when we were together you were impatient and eager to escape again—both of us ill at ease—I from love and you from lack of it. What a situation! There was a war on and plenty of work waiting to be done. Here was I, addled with my own troubles, no use to anyone and an intolerable bore to you. Somehow I must struggle out of bondage and begin again. So I did. And was somewhat astonished and perhaps dismayed to find how simple it could be.

When I wrote to you in May I quite honestly imagined you would be glad and grateful. But now it seems you are unhappy and write to me at first that I was right and now that I am wrong. Dear David, you have me quite bewildered. One day perhaps I shall understand. I will try to anyway.

One thing I do know—I couldn't have gone on as I was or I should have driven you mad as well as myself. Something had to be done about it. Last February I took stock and decided the moment had come, perhaps rightly, for the other day someone said to me, 'How different you look—at the beginning of the year you were a frightening sight.' 'Dear me,' I thought—'was it as bad as all that?'

Your letter about the dancer and her absent dinner party was magnificent. I have read it again and again in pride and envy. But please do not be wretched. You know that I can never love anyone as I have loved you and I cannot bear to think I have made you unhappy, when I thought to do the opposite, and lift from you the burden of that disguise we had assumed in trying to prolong the past into the present. And please—no more talk of monasteries—book and bell and mountain top. It has always pleased you to play with this fancy—but you are not true to yourself when you do so. You are for the arena if any man is—and will have the smell of sand and blood in your nose, the dust to blind and the sun to dazzle your eyes for many years ahead.

With my love—Sybil

PTO Later

I've just read this through and I don't think I've got the measure of you or your feelings at all. I suppose I never had. Perhaps I've simplified it all too much—and looked only for the reasons that were easiest to find. Selfishness again—for I have drawn the most happiness from simple emotions and suffered my sharpest pangs from their absence.

You are not acquainted with life on these elementary terms—and I cannot follow you far into the jungle—I soon begin to trip and stumble as the light dwindles to a pin prick behind me, and you must go on alone. How little we ever know of each other and upon how delicate a balance are our relationships set.

in bed
1 July 1942 Lisbon

My darling Syb—For the first time I love you because you don't understand, and how marvellous it is to feel even a fraction of that shapeless pain you have felt for my sake! If instead of these useless letters, which seem to have deceived you when God knows I thought they laid me naked at your door, I could now creep within your hearing I would, if words came at all, just ask you to forgive me for failing to trust you with a clearer explanation.

Oh! do wait for that; and in the meantime makc some distinction, some little difference, between the everyday event of a man ceasing to love A, transferring or being willing to transfer his love to B, and what has happened to us. Don't throw all that I've thought and prayed down the sink of boredom. You must know more about the relations between men and women than to confuse desire with the whole of a man's love. You are more honest than I am; partly by nature, but partly because I have had to represent truly a number of contradictory facets of my nature, like a diamond I honestly twinkled different colours ('*On peut dire de M Churchill*,' said a friend to me last week, '*qu'il mentirait sincèrement*') but now they are fused into a white light. You have been dreadfully hurt by me, but you haven't understood why, and since I was aware, or at least sufficiently aware, of what was going on, the responsibility, the guilt, is mine alone, for not giving you clearer explanations. An example: when you gave me a book like *Livingstone's Travels* and I didn't read it, I saw you saying, 'Oh! there's nothing he wants from me', and I went thro' agonies of inhibition, which completely passed you by, and I wanted you not to know because I believed I should find myself whole again without having to take the risk of your reaction to the explanation.

But there has been a great flowering of my spirit, the war has made me whole, and I am ready now to speak to you as a single personality. Don't cast yourself away until we have given each other a chance to look straight at our new selves. We owe this much to our first chapter of happiness and to the responsibilities we have assumed. I promise never to chloroform you again. Caustic soda always. I am all yours, entirely and absolutely, if you will have me. If not, then like the artist who paints an altar piece for a church that refuses to accept it, I must send myself to some museum, where the public will gape and admire but the real critic will weep for the lost setting.

I do not love any other woman. It seems absurd to have to write 'two and two make four', but I'm not sure what you will accept now. You must tell me whether you love any other man. Then there will be a fight such as you've never seen before. And it will not be pleasant for anybody, but salutary I dare say, and it won't end in any compromise peace. I am a new man, hard, whole and dangerous, and desperate to live squarely with you again.

—David

4 July 1942 Lisbon

Look here, Syb darling, we're all in too bad a patch to continue private warfare. We are landsliding down the slope of history; Norway, the Battle of France, Crete, Singapore were defeats, but neutral judgement rates this present disaster as a disaster beside which the others were accidents (e.g. the Lisbon bourse has collapsed more sharply than when the Germans reached the Pyrénées). Neutrals had thought we could win this war, and hopes are the measure of disappointment. Therefore I humbly beg a truce of you, on any terms you like, provided you will wait till I come home to settle our lives.

Do tell me, am I wrong? I believe most firmly that you and I have it in us to complement each other's usefulness and mightily to stem this landslide in our national fortunes. In our letters we often told each other that our new way was clear. Do you want any other ally in this fight? I don't. I make no appeal to the past, what we have done together will be with us always, mark us every single day of our lives, but I'm no capitalist of memories, I'd willingly throw away all such possessions rather than live a pale *rentier* on someone else's earnings. We were someone else. That is the point. Volume One has closed snap—bang. That's why an armistice is needed before we touch Volume Two.

I have avoided the children as an issue. I love them very much, and, when wandering is over, I am going to take a hand in shaping their ideas, but beside you they are unimportant. It is not with them that I can plan and execute for England, it is not to them that I look for the infinite help this will require, and above all it is not for them that I am made whole again. No, it is an independent you, a you as you are, we as we are and not as we were. Don't think I am ungrateful for what you have done for me. It is part of myself, but looking backwards takes the eye off the next step. Memory chokes, like ivy. I don't ask you to renew a subscription to a pre-war club. Before your letter of 30 May tore the veil, and I was still in my cocoon, I mumbled something of this sort; but not again, never again.

Pause and choose with the greatest care; I am not sanguine you will accept to look into the second volume, to make peace with me. But you should agree to a truce. I am a thousand miles away, not by my own will, and you would not want me to desert this mission in this trouble. I have faith in our future, but I can't express it or my love through letters—forms—which you have condemned as untrustworthy; the parallel would always be a ghost in your mind.

My love—David

Begun 10 July 1942 Lisbon

My darling Syb—What are you doing these summer days? It's a month or more since you spoke about your work. What does it mean now? Describe it to me like a prospectus, a little about what the firm has done and a great deal about what the firm is going to do. Do you run about the country? By road or rail? Do you want a small car? Buy one if you do. Do you go singly or with colleagues male or female? Do you make reports, plans, speeches? If speeches and you write them out, please send me a sample.

The same afternoon
Cecil Beaton, who left Cairo five days ago, lunched with me today. This is a curious man. The Portuguese word '*exquisita*' is half-way between our 'exquisite' and 'odd' or 'queer'. It suits CB to a T. He's a serious artist with his camera, and his desert pictures will rank high. As he left Egypt at the worst moment I discount some of his gloom—which was not too bad. We see many observant civilians on their way back from the Middle East and their pictures have some definite characteristics, which by constant recurrence must be true. The contrast between the

depravity of Cairo and the hardships of the desert; the muddle over material; the astonishing exploits of the Commandos under this figure of romance David Stirling; the ignorance of conditions in England amounting to a deliberate blindness on the part of officials who have been in the Middle East over a year.

We raged together over an article in a popular American journal on the lines 'Britain is a liability' and talking of us as in the same relation to them as Italy is to Germany, 'America's War and America's Peace', etc. There are two ways of tackling this sort of thing. One can answer back; have the offender on the mat; complain officially to the USG; or one can be without exception indifferent to particular cases and go all out for counter-propaganda on general lines. Of course, I much prefer the second. Partly it is a question of temperament, a man of value is either negative and defensive, or positive and constructive. Mixtures are usually failures. History seems to show that in order to pursue a consistent policy—I might almost say 'any policy'—any statesman or official must shut his eyes to a great many small difficulties and keep on in spite of obvious checks and disappointments, and weaknesses which time reveals in his original design. Cromwell is an outstanding example. Macaulay, writing of the Protector's dependence on his own army, says 'that he might ordinarily command, he had sometimes to obey'. This appears to be a rule of the world, and it is the very young who wonder that characters like the Viscount [Halifax] have so often to compromise with 'the multiplying villainies of nature'.

Macaulay has a wonderful phrase about English gardens: 'Nature dressed but not disguised by art, wears her most alluring form.' I wish I could walk with you in ours, that would be happiness indeed. The Portuguese Government could not be behaving worse. Walt has gone to Madrid more or less disgusted.

My love—David

12 July 1942 Chute

My darling David—Yes, please let us have a truce—I want one badly being—as I have told you—quite out of breath from the lightning thrusts and turns of your letters. You should know after all these years that I am not a quick-change artist. Decisions mature slowly in this one-track mind. The *volte-face* isn't my strong suit. Maybe a letter dated 30 May sounded the resurrection for you. Maybe you are made whole again. Maybe. How can I know? You must not expect my surrender to these arguments. Have I not learnt that your letters represent one facet of the diamond while in flesh and blood you twinkle quite another? This discovery turned me derelict and I'm not willing to run the risk again. It isn't worth it. Oh! dear David—you really must see the truth of that. If you are made whole again—so am I. Whole for myself. And as such I mean to remain until we can look at each other with the new eyes of honest dealing. Who knows what discoveries—good or bad—await us? We cannot tell. We are unknown to each other. As you know—I don't want to look back into Vol. One. But strangers should not sign a deed of partnership. It would be the height of imprudence. We will not commit that folly. Vol. Two must remain on the shelves until we meet again. Till then—a truce.

Your letter has decided me to read *The Conditions of Peace*[1] again and make the notes I always meant to. I'll take it—with the children—to the pool this afternoon. Do you approve of lending our Cézanne to Lefèvre for an exhibition? *Environs de Gardanne*? He says he might sell it.

My love to you—Sybil

1. By E. H. Carr (Macmillan 1942).

11 July 1942 Lisbon

My darling Syb—I'm so awfully sorry, sweet, that I bewilder you with so many marches and counter-marches, turns to right and left, I just want to get it out of my system, and I have, I have, I'm sure. I didn't know how jealous I was. Waking up in the night and fancying you off with a tawny moustache, or crinkly black hair. Oof! Do forgive me. I want to be with you now so much; this time when I can't be.

I felt a great release when your 30 May letter came, and reacted *tout d'un coup*. Then came those 'saucy doubts' and all the realisation that a precipice was near, questionings and a growing desire to do anything to renew our love. I make too much fuss about the bran-pie of my thoughts; it's unhealthy; what matters is you, and I know if I can have you always I shall be all right, and that your mind, although different from mine, is just as good along its own line.

This is written in the ante-room of the Minister of Public Works as the bag goes tonight.

My love—David

14 July 1942 Lisbon
(Oh! prehistoric anniversary!)

My darling Syb—Your last letter wasn't properly answered. I had only a quarter of an hour at the Ministry of Public Works in which to write. Now we're in a terrific heat wave, very bad for work and thinking. It seems to me all to the good that you should make me anxious about yourself. High time indeed. I am only sorry it didn't happen before. We don't want to be absolutely alike, or completely to understand each other. Love flourishes on overcoming differences. Identity of sensations and thoughts is nine tenths a body-born illusion, and generally weakening, since it allows the power of co-operation to remain rusty.

I've never wanted to live with anyone but you. No one could have made me happier (I know that I cannot describe this happiness in terms that would satisfy you or me: that is a failing of all romantic writers who must end their story at the words, 'They lived happily ever afterwards'); now I am changed; the 'I' that lived happily with you isn't the same 'I' that writes this, and if our future relationship is not to be that of a woman and a ghost, you too must change. This truth, for so it appeared to me in a white light from the pages of your letter of 30 May, flashed upon me and I wrote it straight down in my reply. Then I fell a prey to various imaginings, which owing to unrelieved pressure of work I could only record for you fitfully—send you half a dozen cuts from a long movie which was unwinding all the time—so that again you have had some contradictory evidence. But do not pay attention to the direction of the waves—just now I see them marching up the Tagus backed by a strong breeze from the Atlantic, but the tide is running out apace—the stream is towards a new life. Now whether you will want to live this new life with me, and how different it will be from the old life remains to be seen. We neither of us know. I have thought you were unlucky to marry someone who had to combine the Anstie (half Swiss) blood with the Eccles blood; but now I think the fusion is accomplished and that I have more or less purified the mixture.

You must have a very strong hold on me, I have often wondered at it, and been glad of it. To you it seems that you lost your hold, to me the very reverse. We can't convince each other of these mysteries, they appear to be near nonsense on paper, but have no fear, there will be a chance given to me to make you understand that I speak as one in possession of a clean mind in a whole body.

In the meantime I love your letters and to hear anything about you. My rages about the bags are an Embassy joke. I pine to send you little presents, and often gaze at shop windows, and sound out possible conveyors, but somehow I don't like to, you might think I was bribing, or dusting your eye. Friday I go north and I will try to tell you what the mountains are like.

Love—David

19 July 1942 Chute

Darling David—We have been stoning cherries and this afternoon mean to make jam—I'm beginning to fancy myself as a cook and yesterday made a few pounds of strawberry and Morello that rival Mr Tiptree, in my eyes at least. Miss A[lexander] is back from her holiday—brown and happy—wearing a look of the sea and bringing a whiff of salt with her. People returning from holidays are like strangers, their inward eye and their thoughts are still upon the distant scene, yet must they carry unspoken the burden of its mystery. We look upon them with a twinge of envy for that hidden secret which we may not share. Sometimes, when memory is at bursting point, they will break out into the description of some picnic or excursion, until our polite attention saps their courage and reduces them to silence.

My love to you and I do hope the PG aren't too intractable—it must be hellish when they are.

—Sybil

I've just been to put the hens to bed—the lime tree smells too delicious for words and is still busy with bees although it is half past nine and a cold night.

Begun Sunday,
18 July 1942

Minas de Panasquiera,
Fundaeo

My darling Syb—When we heard Roger [Makins] was coming I put off starting for the mines until Saturday. He arrived more deathlike than ever, unshaven, but robust. I couldn't meet him at the airfield, he was whisked straight off to the Ambassador's house, where I joined them after tea. They were unsmiling, both had told the other hard things about the progress of our affairs at home and in Portugal.

He had met you in the street, said you were flourishing, and was very complimentary about your looks, he likes you very much which pleases me very much. I took him off to dinner, he ate hugely of lobster mayonnaise, cold meats, salad, raspberries and cream, and drank at least a bottle. I suppose I shouldn't tell you his estimate of the members of the War Cabinet. He thinks less than nothing of that newcomer who so suddenly enchanted the British people. Says he is the greatest flat-catcher (what a Roger-ish word!) alive, selfish, unconstructive and quarrelsome. He gave pictures of the various grades of our society: Cabinet, H of C, General Staff, Civil Service, the ordinary people; only the last was satisfactory, as he worked towards the peak the shadows multiplied. What a topsy-turvy nation we have become! But the reverse, as in Portugal where Salazar is the only outstanding man, is much worse, for then there is no hope, but with our people there is every hope, only the discarding process is so long and expensive. I appreciate so much the careful way Roger sets about educating me. It is really charming and I shall be grateful all my life. He thinks I should leave MEW but he had nothing definite in mind and was rather damping about Oliver. I said that it was clear enough at this distance that O didn't do well in the House, but that he was brave and modest, and given those qualities would learn. O's real trouble is just what Sam said it would be, he hasn't got a department of state behind him, and the minister without portfolio is a tree without roots. Personally I want to leave MEW and start again in any capacity. A phase in my life is over, and to mark its end plainly is right.

I tried, as you know, to fight the economic war on modern lines. I never hesitated to tell my ministers and their henchmen how out of date and inadequate their policy was. They looked the other way. I know I was right, and they now gather the fruits of their blindness. MEW (apart from the statistical, intelligence-gathering side run by Vickers[1]) is dying. Gladwyn's failure and Henry's rise to DG put the patient beyond recovery. Whatever can be said about the way in which Gladwyn's boys went to work, and God knows it was disastrous in a country like Portugal, they had the right idea. They saw this was a civil war, a war in which total populations were engaged and not all of them willingly on one side or the other side. They realised there was a difference in technique between the static warfare of Flanders trenches and the mobile tactics of tanks and aircraft. Between barbed wire and parachutists lies a revolution in ideas as well as methods. The Blockaders set about their business like scarlet grenadiers on the Horse Guards parade. Their manoeuvres had more folly than courage and I think history will reserve them a black page. Take Madagascar: when I was in Washington I proposed to the Americans that we should capture this place by economic penetration, by guile, spilling a little money instead of much blood; as the Americans wanted the island's mica and graphite they were inclined to listen; no one on our side bothered; and now, we haven't even finished the business off with a large expeditionary force. Did the Germans take Roumania that way? The world will judge hardly. Our children will not believe the French hated us so much more than they hated the Japanese that we could not have knocked a handful of Vichy officials off their perch by fifth-column methods. Réunion just the same; all you had to do was to promise to buy the sugar crop at a fancy price, and then sell them what they wanted in the way of harmless luxuries, also at fancy prices. Lord! it was easy. But MEW wouldn't do it. *Adios* Berkeley Square! *Yo me voy.*

Later

The wolfram mine lies under the top of one of the major spurs of the Estrella, the highest mountains in Portugal. The manager's house looks over a beautiful valley to the main peaks of the range; half an hour's walk brings you to the summit of the Panasquiera spur from where there is a view that would rival any in Europe. I was very comfortable among Mr Smith's Waring & Gillow. The canteen of silver-plate and the easy-chairs with the movable bar and notches behind their square of cushion fascinated the eye. In practice I preferred a deck chair on the veranda.

Going underground, inspecting the mill, looking at houses, at plans for a hospital, how I enjoyed it! Always I was thinking of our visits to Pilgrim's Rest and to the Diceys at Nordkap.[2] After fruitless negotiations give me a production job! The little I learned in Johannesburg, added to more recent ideas about the treatment of labour, was enough to propose a sweeping change of policy for the increase of output and the improvement of the miners' conditions. I think we can double the production in six to eight months.

Before the war there was plenty of hungry labour in the surrounding villages. The mine was meanly run and made only small profits. The men walked over the hills to Panasquiera, brought a week's food on their back, slept on the bare ground, were paid 2*s*. 6*d*. per day, and deserted whenever they felt like it. Now the great rise in the value of wolfram has made a hundred other ways of working more remunerative than coming to our mine on the old conditions. Down went our labour force and our production. While HMG was paying on the black market £5,000 a ton for wolfram the Board of the Company was disputing whether wages could be raised by the equivalent of £25 per ton. I proposed a bold and striking scheme of houses for the men, a hospital, cinema, a barber's shop and a drug store, and a basic wage of 4*s*. a day—what extravagance!—with bonuses if output increases. If we can double output it will represent something really important to our war effort. Oh! why didn't I go to the mine before? In all that we have done we have been so inefficient and unimaginative. I explode with filthy language when I think how it is the same in every case.

Here's a conversation I had with the mine doctor, an admirable Portuguese:

DE Any cows on the concession?

Doc None, and no milk of any kind.

DE What about the children? (There are six hundred families on the mine.)

Doc They get what their mothers give them. The mortality rate under one year is fifty per cent.

DE What about water facilities?

Doc There isn't any for lavatories, but there's a tap for every seventy to eighty men.

DE What equipment have you for dealing with accidents?

Doc Well, very little just now. You see, the mine insures Employers' Liability with a Portuguese company which has to pay the cost of accidents. They've just written to me to say that iodine is too expensive to use any more. They don't suggest any alternative.

We shall change all this. But why so late? Forgive us for what we have left undone. We'll visit the mine after the war and see how they are getting on.

26 July

Walt has been looking on at life in the British Embassies in Lisbon and Madrid and says reflectively, 'The war has discovered sex for the English, before they thought it was only used for making babies.' We are in a new wave of quite extraordinary sex intemperance on the part of the Lisbon Embassy. Roger was 'amazed', but I told him it was ever so, and he might just as well accept it. Is it the damp warm climate which seems to irritate the ladies? For in the last three Embassy scandals it is beyond dispute which party began it.

27 July

Walt and Hugh Millard and I went bathing at our favourite Portinho de Arrabida. It can only be done now if one or other of us supply gasoline from a diplomatic reserve. The water was delicious, and shot with myriads of sardines flashing about like the blades of knives. We talked for hours about Anglo-American relations and I begin to see how best they can be shaped. We returned at midnight after watching the moon for an hour from the top of the cliff. It is curious how the water, which was ruffled by the night breeze, appears to be moving towards the moon's white path from both sides. You see the moon's attraction, her power over the tides, illustrated in actual fact. Of course what one sees is an illusion, but it is more true than what the camera would show, because it symbolises the essential quality of the moon, that she gathers up the waters and seduces the hearts of all that behold her. We were very struck by this sight.

My love to you and kiss that Polly and Simo'.

—David

1. Sir Geoffrey Vickers.
2. In South Africa.

25 July 1942 Chute

Darling David—Your last letter was written on the point of departure for the mines—I wonder how it was and whether you discovered strange and unexpected beauties among the Portuguese mountains. I'm writing in the car on my way home from a meeting and with the prospect ahead of veal (VEAL mark you) for Sunday lunch. At the bottom of the hill is the post box in the Fowles's garden wall—I shall fling this into its maw and sniffing like a Bisto Kid will make haste to the dining-room. The country is still lush and green from lack of sun and the bees find some comfort from our lime tree since few flowers are tempted into bloom by these continued grey skies.

Our Morello cherries are the only things to flourish in this chilly atmosphere. I picked 8 lbs of them and made some jam like rubies.

My love to you—Sybil

1 August 1942 Lisbon

My darling love—Once again I can only write you a snippet. I must do so to congratulate you on your letter about the '*mystique des vacances*'. You did it so well. And I like to think you would rather have a half-sheet than nothing. Perhaps this is only vanity, but it consoles like a bar of choc when the train is late.

Henry [Drogheda] writes that Oliver has definitely said he wants me but can't say in what capacity till he knows when I shall be available. So that's that. Henry writes very flatteringly about past services to MEW. We shall all part friends and in the lower ranks of MEW there will be some genuine regret.

You would be surprised—perhaps you wouldn't as you knew him well and you have an excellent flair—how careerist Walt is; there is Walt, the USA, and the war; and because he has a broad mind and a good heart the pursuit of these three interests seldom conflicts, but he never annihilates the first two in order to concentrate on the third, and if by any chance there is a conflict he puts these interests in the order I gave. He is very difficult to handle but it is a constant delight trying to do so. Having found out some of his peculiarities I like him the better.

My love—David

Begun 1–2 August 1942 Lisbon

My darling love—Oh! I'm so bored here; it eats into my vitals. If I couldn't be at home why did I ever leave Spain? Every Spaniard I see falls on my neck and says, 'How could you desert us for these ugly unmanageable clods?' I thought I was more wanted here. I built up the staff in Madrid so they could get on without me. And so they can, altho' I'm pleased enough when Spaniards say—there is a big delegation here trying without success to make a commercial treaty with Portugal—'*Despues de su salida no hay gracia en la Embajada Britannica.*' Of all the compliments the representatives of another nation might pay none could be more choice than to throw 'grace' as a bouquet, and coming from a Spaniard . . . I loved them very much and they were as willing to trust me as I was to trust them. But here all is dust and bitterness. We have lost the benefit of the doubt. If the Germans say, 'A is true about this business,' and we say, 'No B is true,' the Portuguese incline to A. That's a handicap I never imagined I should have to carry. Apart from the natural suspiciousness of the Portuguese this incredible situation is due to two special causes, one Timor, the other I can't tell you now. For Ronnie, who is the best, the straightest of ambassadors, it must be particularly horrible.

3 August 8 a.m.
Yesterday was Sunday. I had refused two weekend offers and decided to spend the day on a beach with the Tomas Pinto Bastos. Then I woke up feeling I must be alone and read, so I sent Jack Nicholls off with an excuse that I had work that must be done. I looked in at the Embassy at eleven, read some interesting telegrams, noted the cypher-girl on duty was reeling from an all-night party, at an Estoril cabaret; very bad, I thought, I didn't tick her off. A shrimp omelette at a low-class restaurant and I took a tram for the outskirts. I climbed a hill near the wireless station overlooking the mouth of the Tagus, and found a newly-made

corn-rick level on the top, a perfect resting place, I could have sun or shade as I pleased by moving round a few sheaves . . .

Later
Hooray! Hooray! When I paid my morning call on Ronnie he handed me a telegram from Henry saying that Oliver wanted me at once, and I was not to carry out the survey of the mining district round Viseu which had been contemplated. Now I know what a balloon feels like when the ropes are cast off which hold it to the earth. Unless you hear to the contrary I shall arrive at Bristol on Thursday 13 August. This is later than Oliver may have thought, but I must hand over my many strings in an orderly way, for Ronnie's sake. Do you think I could get a taxi from Salisbury to Andover? The 4.40 from Bristol did arrive about seven at Salisbury. If you think this impossible please telegraph as I will then go straight to London. Will you come up to Bryanston Court?[1] Please do. I will try to telephone Chute from the airport round 3 p.m. on Thursday. Our new adventure is beginning!

All my love—David

1. My father's flat in London.

APPENDIX A

An Afterthought on the Character of General Franco

To what conclusion will the reader of this book have come about Franco's real intentions? In the twelve months following the collapse of France, when half Europe thought we had no chance of winning, did Franco want to enter the war or stay out? The nature of the man is worth considering. Whatever he may have said in public to please the Germans and their friends his instincts and his behaviour during and after the war point to a deep preference for neutrality. Shakespeare allowed the plot to suggest the characters, but in history, especially in a country like Spain where individuals count for so much, it is often the other way round. Franco's character has had a decisive effect on Spanish history. He was, so everyone says, a brave and successful young officer in Morocco. I could never persuade a Spanish general to comment on his qualities as Commander-in-Chief in the Civil War. But in civilian affairs he quickly earned a solid reputation for caution, doing nothing in a hurry and showing great skill in selecting, limiting and craftily modifying his objectives. When I was lamenting with Marshal Pétain, the French Ambassador, the snail's pace of our joint war trade negotiations he made this comment, 'In the delays I see the hand of Franco. He reminds me of a village fête in France, at which one competes in bicycle races. There is a prize for the boy who stays longest on his machine and covers the shortest distance. Franco would win that prize.' An inclination to remain inactive, to wait and see, was in the make-up of this complacent Spaniard. In 1939 he had reached the top rung of the ladder. His interest was to stay there and he adopted the policy of neutrality as much by instinct as by calculation.

It may be said that I had to believe in the continuing neutrality of Spain or I could not have argued for the economic aid which seemed to me essential. If so, I had reason to be of this opinion for I had friends who were very close to Franco. Once or twice they said the pressures on him were so great that he might have to surrender to the war party but they never said that he wanted to join the Axis. Quite the contrary.

Trying to be objective about Franco prompts me to ask how anyone can be sure that he remembers and writes truthfully about a war in which he took part? Each day, each event, each man is either for you or against you, or at least you think they are. You put labels on them when you ought to reserve judgement. But gradually one learns that just as the struggle between good and evil never stops inside oneself, so modern wars are civil wars. Inside every country, belligerent or neutral, not everybody is on one side or the other. Some care more for their religion or for human rights than for anything else. Show them, if you can, that what they care for you are fighting for, then you make friends and allies where the politicians at home see only villains and enemies. I tried to do this in Spain and Portugal with what success others can judge.

APPENDIX B

Bibliography

The following is a short list of books which refer to the events reported in the letters. The books themselves and the passages cited are chosen to illustrate views of importance relating to the attitude of Franco's Spain to World War II.

Churchill, Winston S.
The History of the Second World War (Cassell 1948–54)
'Spain held the key to all British enterprise in the Mediterranean'
—Volume II, p. 460.

Hitler's letter to Mussolini 31 December 1940:
'Spain has refused to collaborate with the Axis Powers. I think Franco's idea of receiving from the democracies raw materials and wheat as a sort of recompense for his abstention from the conflict is extremely naïve . . . we had completed our preparations for crossing the Spanish frontier on January 10th and to attack Gibraltar at the beginning of February.
Vol III, p. 11

Eisenhower, Dwight D.
Crusade in Europe (Doubleday, New York, 1948)
'Britain's Gibraltar made possible the invasion of northwest Africa.'—p. 95

Feis, Herbert
The Spanish Story (Alfred Knopf, New York, 1948)
A well-researched book which gives the best account of the rivalry with the enemy for the wolfram produced in Spain and Portugal. Feis, a distinguished American civil servant, was an intellectual who disliked Franco and Salazar on principle. He is interesting on the bitter choice inside the United States administration between giving aid to a country strategically important to the British and punishing a detestable Fascist régime. Feis gives no credit to the part played by Portugal in keeping Spain neutral.

Hinsley, Professor F. H.
British Intelligence in the Second World War (HMSO, two vols, 1979, 1981)
Vol. I, p. 256 says that in the autumn of 1940 there was a threat that the Germans would invade Spain without Spanish connivance. All that we heard at the time proved the contrary. The Germans and their friends in Madrid were quite clear that an opposed entry was out of the question. The resistance to Napoleon's armies was remembered. It may be that in the Embassy we knew more about the anti-German views of the Spanish generals than the Intelligence Service did.

Vol. II quotes a report made on 7 August 1942 by the Joint Intelligence Sub-Committee to the British Chiefs of Staff:

'If only because of her dependence on the Allies for essential imports, Spain would resist German pressure to move against Gibraltar, unless it was backed with force.'

The JIC go on to say that since the Germans did not have adequate forces in readiness to attack through Spain, the Allied North African Expedition [Torch] could go ahead without fear of the Spanish airfields being used against us. The Americans, however, questioned this, correct, appreciation.

Hoare, Sir Samuel
Ambassador with a Special Mission (Collins, 1946)
This book is discussed in the sketch of Sir Samuel Hoare on pp. 100–4. It is worth reading provided the vanity of the author and his unjust neglect of the part played by Portugal are kept in mind.

Kay, Hugh
Salazar and Modern Portugal (Hawthorn Books, New York, 1970)
This book is an honourable exception to the long list of failures to do justice to the part played by Salazar in keeping the Peninsula neutral. Unfortunately he does not know how closely Portugal and Spain co-operated in economic and political decisions. He appears not to have been told of the help we received from Nicolas Franco, who was Spanish Ambassador in Lisbon.

Leahy, Admiral William D.
I Was There (Gollancz 1950)
An important account of the early years of Pétain's government.

Liddell Hart, B. H.
History of The Second World War (Cassell 1970)
Refers to the plan which Hitler set on foot in the autumn of 1940 to close the western end of the Mediterranean: 'This was too small an operation to satisfy his gigantic ambition.' That may be true but Hitler abandoned the plan because Franco would not invite the German Army to cross the Spanish frontier.

Medlicott, W. N.
The Economic Blockade (HMSO/Longman, two vols. 1952, 1959)
Many references to the activities of the Ministry of Economic Warfare in Spain and Portugal. He was writing the history of a Department of which, in the years covered by most of my letters, Hugh Dalton was the Minister. The book is naturally pro-Dalton, and therefore does not make a case for the flexible use of the Blockade which I advocated from the beginning. In respect of the Spanish theatre Medlicott says:

'Time had been gained by a policy of economic and financial aid for Spain, a policy which was *believed* [my italics] to have played no inconsiderable part in the maintaining of Spanish non-belligerency.'

And in a footnote he adds: 'This policy was based on the Anglo-Spanish war trade agreement . . . negotiated by Mr David Eccles.' Volume II, p. 283

Murphy, Robert
Diplomat Among Warriors (Doubleday, New York, 1964)
Murphy was the American architect of the policy of limited aid to the French in North Africa. In his Chapter Six, 'Struggle to save French Africa', he covers the same ground as Chapter Six in Vol. III of Weygand's *Mémoires, 'Relations avec l'Angleterre et les Etats-Unis'*, but the two accounts differ in respect to myself. Murphy writes as if he alone negotiated the 'Murphy-Weygand Accord'. He does this because we deliberately chose to present the draft Accord to our governments as his work with no British participation. We knew that in both London and Washington there was powerful opposition to any deal with Weygand. This opposition would, we thought, be more easily contained if the Accord was seen to be an American initiative. When we met in Washington at the end of March 1941 it became obvious that I was

a partner in the agreement, and Murphy's reference to me is very generous. Weygand knew nothing of our decision to present the Accord which he had signed as a solely American draft. Therefore he records my part in the discussions with Murphy in Lisbon and afterwards in Tangier.

Like me, Murphy was never told everything relevant to his work by his government. At the time we neither of us knew that on 19 February 1940, Halifax called on Sumner Welles, Under-Secretary of State in the State Department, and asked that all negotiations with Weygand should be suspended. This request was made following a report from Gascoigne, British Consul-General in Tangier, that the Germans had taken over the French Air Force bases in Morocco and were about to occupy all of French Africa. As Murphy says, this report was 'wildly inaccurate'. Knowing nothing about it, when on 26 February I arrived in Tangier I reported to London that there were plenty of rumours about a German invasion but absolutely no evidence. No doubt this was what made Gascoigne shut up like a clam when I asked for his ideas and help.

Both Murphy and I were exceeding our instructions in drafting so detailed an Accord with Weygand. Time was running out. The General said he must have supplies quickly or there would be trouble, especially among the Arabs, and the Germans would have the pretext they were looking for to occupy French Africa. The Tangier negotiations were the only occasion on which I did not report every detail to London. Nor did Murphy report everything to the State Department. If he by-passed his superior officers he said he could count on President Roosevelt's support.

Villard, Henry Serrano
Affairs At State (Thomas Crowell Co., New York, 1965)
Mr Villard, whom I knew as an able member of the State Department, gives an excellent description of the split in 1941 between the neutralists and the belligerents inside the Department. He makes one realise how astonished some of them were when I insisted that the USA must come into the war or we should lose it. He also says that Mr Hull, the Secretary of State, complained that the President would not tell him what he was doing with Murphy in North Africa—'Murphy's most important reports have not found their way into the Department's files.' On p. 211 he writes:

'If State Department officials leaned over backwards to avoid the hypothesis of United States involvement in the war . . . British visitors were not so reticent. David Eccles sent over by Churchill as a representative of the Ministry of Economic Warfare . . . helped change the attitude of the British Embassy to one of greater leniency towards the economic accord [with Weygand] . . . he did not hesitate to put down on paper his feelings that the exercise could be looked upon only as "a curtain-raiser for a military adventure".[1] "Unless," he bluntly told Wallace Murray[2] on 4 June 1941, "something tangible in the form of American military assistance could be expected, the British Government was not interested in permitting economic supplies to reach General Weygand from the United States." '

Weygand, General Maxime
Mémoires (Flammarion, Paris, three vols. 1950–7)
Essential reading to correct the anti-Pétain/Weygand accounts given by the supporters of de Gaulle. The key passages are quoted in the sketch of Weygand on p. 189.

Woodward, Sir Llewellyn, Editor
British Foreign Policy in the Second World War (HMSO, five vols. 1970–6; abridged edition 1962, amended 1977)
Clear on the importance of Spanish neutrality and the determination of Churchill that everything must be done to preserve it.

Yglesias, José
The Franco Years (Bobbs-Merrill Co. Inc., New York 1977)
'Franco kept Spain out of the war because he simply could not have waged it and kept the Spanish people under control.'

This is true. Germany could not have replaced the food and raw materials we were helping Spain to import.

INDEX

This index is mainly confined to personal names. Some subject headings have been included for details of interest in the letters, but the main themes of economic warfare and diplomatic relations are largely disregarded since they recur throughout the book. The offices held by public figures during the period covered by the letters are listed.

INDEX